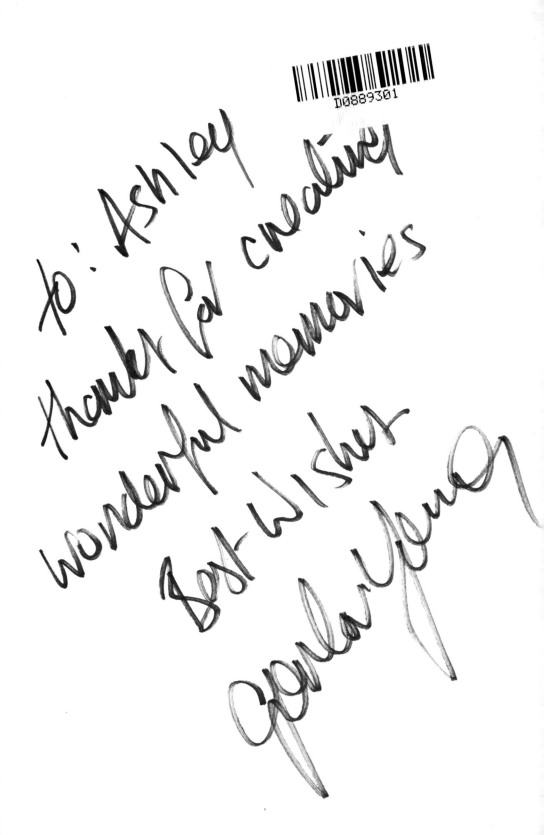

to: Ashley
thanks for creating
wonderful memories
Best-Wishes
Gordon Young

Gordon Young:
Licence to Skill

AS TOLD TO STUART HALL

Gordon Young: Licence to Skill

AS TOLD TO STUART HALL

Acknowledgements and dedications

'd like to dedicate this book to my mum Margaret and dad Wullie, for their love and guidance. They encouraged my sister Carole and I to be the best we could be, in an environment where family was the most important fabric of society.

Also to my wife, Yvonne, who has supported me throughout my whole career, with constant belief in my ability and who has never at any time stood in the way of opportunities that arose, and I know will continue to do so in the future. She more than anyone is responsible for our family being as close as it is and deserves more than a mention for her backing.

To my children Jenna and Robbie who fill me with immense pleasure and pride at how they have matured. It is a joy to see the things they have achieved already, inheriting my ambition to travel and to never be afraid of failing. They are everything to Yvonne and I.

I have been blessed to have so many friends who have helped and humoured me along the way, but I give special mention to Peter Millar without whom I wouldn't have considered a career in coaching at all. So I also dedicate this memoir to them as well.

In an industry where heroes and legends flourish annually, the aforementioned are my heroes forever, but a massive thanks to Stuart Hall for helping me with this piece of work and hopefully he enjoyed bringing this story to the page as much as he says. A truly top bloke with an incredible appetite for making the dullest conversation transcend into a colourful journey with a skill to craft and enhance an anecdote to capture the scene.

To all of you and the fantastic people I have worked with and hopefully mentioned in this book, I am eternally grateful, so raise a glass to yourselves…cheers!

Gordon Young

Thanks also to: Sally, Amy, Andrew and Emma Hall, The Taylors, Lorraine Ferguson, Colin Leslie, Craig Cowbrough, 'Wee Kev', Fraser Kelly, Scott Coull and Paul Greaves (Typesetting), David Aitken (Design), Simon Munro (Printing) and Campbell Deane.

ISBN 978-1-80068-331-0

Printed by J Thomson Colour Printers Limited, Glasgow

CONTENTS

Chapter 1: YOU ONLY RETIRE TWICE.. 13

Chapter 2: THE MAN WITH THE GOLDEN TEAM 27

Chapter 3: DOSSERS ARE FOREVER 35

Chapter 4: GOLDFINDER 51

Chapter 5: TWO OLD GUYS WHO LOVE ME 69

Chapter 6: LICENCE TO SKILL 87

Chapter 7: NEVER SAY GANNON AGAIN... 95

Chapter 8: OCTOCLASSY 103

Chapter 9: FROM INDIA WITH LOVE 121

Chapter 10: GOLDEN AYE... D'YE KEN THE SARGE...........................151

Chapter 11: BANTAM OF SOLACE 177

Chapter 12: ODD JOB IN EAST FIFE...191

Chapter 13: DR NO WAY MAN..199

Chapter 14: THUNDERBAIRNS..223

Chapter 15: ON MIXU'S INTERNATIONAL SERVICE 237

Chapter 16: LIVE AND LET LIEPAJA..249

Chapter 17: THE LIVING HIGHLIGHTS.. 267

Foreword

Craig Brown

At the side of the Fir Park pitch on 5 May, 2010, Gordon Young stood beside the Motherwell management duo of Archie Knox and myself as the game against Hibernian went from end to end. When, with only three minutes remaining, Lukas Jutkiewicz scored a Van Basten-esque equaliser to complete a most amazing comeback, the remarkable 6-6 scoreline made it the highest-scoring top division match in the history of Scottish football.

This incredible and unique event was going to take some explaining to the voracious media corps in waiting. Aware of the anticipated searching questions, I turned to my coaching colleague and said quite spontaneously: "How am I gonna explain that result, Gordon?" With typical words of wisdom, tinged with a fair modicum of humour for which he is noted, he replied: "Tell them Archie coached the defence and you worked with the strikers."

That was not the only time Gordon came to my rescue. His assistance throughout my time as manager of Motherwell FC was invaluable. No colleague could have been more diligent and respected by all players, from international first-team members to the development team of under-20 youngsters in the academy, who were his prime responsibility.

Reading Stuart Hall's fascinating account of Gordon's stellar career provides ample evidence of the successful and eventful experiences he has had in the game and the high esteem in which he is held. My good fortune has enabled me to have the undoubted privilege of playing for and managing three teams in Scotland, working for three in England as well as enjoying 15 years with the Scottish national team, eight as manager (or in modern nomenclature, head coach). This fortunate experience I have savoured has put me in contact with luminaries of our great game. This enables me to say with complete candour that few, if any, have had the impact on Archie and me that Gordon Young has had.

I was privileged, and I am old enough, to have seen Gordon as a professional player of fine standard, but having comfortably attained the highest qualification possible, the Uefa Pro-Licence, he then excelled in a coaching capacity. His undoubted competence has made him sought after, not just at home but further afield - in the USA, England and Eastern Europe, where he not only qualified club side FK Liepaja for European competition, but also assisted his former managerial colleague at Dundee United, Mixu Paatelainen, at the highest level with the Latvian national team.

When, four years ago, our former captain at Aberdeen, Paul Hartley, was manager of Falkirk he asked Archie Knox and me to identify an assistant. Our knowledge of the capability, industry and integrity of Gordon Young made it easy to recommend him without reservation. We have never regretted that advice. I'm sure neither has Paul! In this book Gordon outlines his experiences with his trademark modesty in a lucid and engaging manner. It's a great read!

Craig Brown CBE

You Only Retire Twice

*Hanging up my boots from Junior and Amateur football
and the inspiration for the start of my coaching journey*

S tanding there with the two elder statesmen of Scottish football, Craig Brown and Archie Knox (or Jack and Victor as they were referred to at Motherwell), I'm wondering whether I should tell them. Nah, I'm sure Craig will remember, after all he had embarked upon his illustrious coaching career at Motherwell FC in 1974 under then manager Willie McLean. He'll be remembering. Then again, that night Craig was just seven weeks away from his 70th birthday and he could be forgiven for a wee lapse now and again. They both could!

The main stand diehards – and those who were still left inside Fir Park on the evening of Wednesday 5 May, 2010 – were grumbling behind us, which, to be fair to them, they were arguably entitled to do given that their team were 6-2 down to Hibs with 25 minutes left to play. I was rehearsing what I would say in my mind, while also trying to encourage a response from our players, who had missed some golden chances in what was already a pulsating clash up to that point. "It's tradition Craig, they'll have to do it." I convinced myself that would be the best way to explain to the manager that win, lose or draw Motherwell players always parade themselves round the pitch at the end of the last home game of the season in a lap of honour… or would it be dishonour? With such a poor result at that time on the cards, as both sides vied for the final Uefa Cup spot on offer in a spectacle that was being broadcast live on TV, the prospect of taking a lap of honour inside the big cat enclosure at Blair Drummond Safari Park with barbeque sauce smeared on our legs seemed like a better prospect than strolling round Fir Park at the end of that game.

Several times the cameras panned round to see Craig and Archie gibbering away to each other and then me pitching in with my tuppence worth, about how we could get back into the game. But there are a couple of occasions where I'm seen considering whether this is the moment to tell them both about that 'tradition', at the same time glancing around to make sure the paramedic with the defibrillator was close by. Then, before I step up to give them the bad news, Giles Coke chalks one back to make it 6-3. That gives us a sniff, I think, and five minutes later the sniff turns into a full nasal twitch as Tom Hateley makes it 6-4. I'm still eyeing the paramedic to make sure he is close to both Craig and Archie, because they might need a wee bit of treatment for over excitement if we grab another. By this time many of the home supporters who had left prematurely in disgust seem to have returned and they are getting right behind the team as we know they can.

Remarkably, we pull another one back with 14 minutes to go through John Sutton and it's game-on for a grandstand finish at Fir Park. Hibs – who were in complete command of the game at 4-1 at half-time and again at 6-2 shortly after the restart – are shell-shocked and at sixes and sevens. The pressure is relentless on the visitors' box and Lukas Jutkiewicz latches onto a nice wee ball played into the area, nips it past onrushing former Motherwell keeper Graeme Smith and is clattered to the ground. Penalty! Fuck's sake, I can hardly take this myself as a dyed-in-the-wool Well fan. I glance at the fans celebrating in the Davie Cooper stand and memories and fears flood my mind of Davie scoring a dramatic penalty against Wales to help Scotland qualify for the 1986 World Cup and how it was just too much for Big Jock Stein's heart. I'm seriously considering calling the club doctor and the back-up ambulance crew over as cover for the nearest paramedic, in case Jack and Victor have a couple of senior moments!

Substitute Ross Forbes confidently steps up to claim the ball in a bid to write his name in history, as it would make this match the highest scoring Scottish Premier League game of all time. As it stood at 6-5, it was equalling the previous best tally in an SPL game, which was also set at Fir Park, on 20 October, 1999, when Aberdeen edged it. The goalies that day were Andy Goram for the Well and Jim Leighton for the Dons – two of Scotland's best ever keepers! The keepers in the game that was unfolding be-fore me were also top quality. Graeme Smith had started his career at Rangers, played with Motherwell for four seasons, made a full Scotland squad and secured the No 1 jersey at Hibs…our goalie was John Ruddy, a future England cap and current Wolves shot-stopper! But none of them it seems could 'keep hens oot a close' when the excite-ment was building at Fir Park!

My chest is puffed out as I'm proudly admiring the way Ross – one of my Academy protégés – has stepped up to the plate. What stature, what bravery for a young lad who has done well this season… what a numpty! He's fucking had it saved by 'Buzz' Smith. Rosco is a smashing lad and had as nice a left foot as I've seen in the game, but his wand couldn't make the ball disappear into the back of the net that night from the spot. Craig and Archie are under no illusions what's at stake and are gripping each other's arms for dear life. Thank goodness Wishaw General Hospital is just up the road, I think… though it might also be that Rosco will need a visit there, too, if the score stays like this, after I see the look in Archie Knox's eyes once the lad's kick is saved.

Now deep into injury time, watches are being watched and the Hibs fans are whistling for the ref to blow for time up. A hopeful ball is lifted forward into the left-hand side of the box and big Lukas is after it. He holds off the challenge of a worried defender as the ball bounces up perfectly on a poor surface, and from a tight angle, he volleys it high into the top right-hand corner for the equaliser. The home crowd, which seems to be more than when the game started, goes crazy and so do we. As the full-time whistle blows and we have all witnessed the best ever Scottish Premier League match in history, I think this might now be the optimum time to tell the elderly management team about the lap of honour tradition. Funnily enough, they take this news very well and are actually looking forward to it. Aye, nae doubt! I had just spent 40 minutes of the second half worrying how to break it to them and in the end it turns oot to be one of their most enjoyable laps of honour ever.

What an experience! But even though they were only at Fir Park for a year, every day with Craig and Archie was a valuable experience and like a school day for me. It's impossible to overestimate the respect I have for them as people and for what they know about the game. Even to this day I am honoured that I can call them to ask their advice at any time. And all joking aside about their ages, these two legends of the game were calm, measured and knew exactly what they were doing during that 6-6 draw. Craig was quoted as saying afterwards: "I was quite calm throughout. I was very pleased with the response from the players when they went behind. I said to them that the worst thing in any sport is a losing lead. We were behind at half-time, and I said if we pull Hibs back they would have a fit of the jitters, and that's how it transpired."

During this match the three of us had a conflab and made a tactical masterstroke of making a triple substitution at 6-2 down – boy did that work! Four days later in the last game of the season we were 3-0 down at Ibrox against Rangers and came back to draw 3-3. We scored nine goals in two games and came back from a combined deficit of seven goals down. From that incredible week I realised that you should never ever think you are beaten until the final whistle sounds. I know that is a cliché, but I have seen first hand how things can be turned round very quickly on a football pitch and Craig and Archie made me believe it. To this day whenever I'm in a dressing room at half-time and my team is losing, I recall this game as a battle cry to my players, demanding that it's never impossible to turn around a deficit, and more importantly I absolutely believe it, because, as they say "I was that soldier."

But what was the basic training I had to go through to get to this point, I hear you ask? Well, we start at the end in Carluke, South Lanarkshire. The end of a 19-year professional footballing career where, in my view, the goals only counted if the nutmegs were even. Everyone knows that the best thing that ever started in Carluke was the 41 bus to Motherwell, and that the residents take the pavements in at night, but that's where I decided to bring to an end the privilege I had of being paid to play fitba and where my journey into coaching began to take shape. It's also a privilege to hail from Lanarkshire myself and I know that most folk from that neck of the woods can take a joke and some gentle ribbing. Fingers crossed that those from further afield referenced in the pages ahead of this memoir, can too!

At this point I'm player/manager of Scottish Junior side Cambuslang Rangers and we're up against Carluke Rovers at the Lanarkshire village's Loch Park Stadium. We're mid-way through the second half and I'm taking up position on my favoured right wing against a worried full-back. Is there any other kind? Lots of things are going through my mind. What to do next? What to do? That garage door needs fixed for a start. I could ditch my marketing role with Nestle and form my own business. This time next year, Gordon, you could be a millionaire! Right, concentrate. Billy Holmes is scampering down the left wing. He's been brilliant for me this season and was one of the best players I'd ever played with. I'll need to start signing talks with him for next year… but that's not my job any more. Will I miss this life? Coaching's not for me anyway, is it? You can bet yer dinner money his delivery will be good but if he doesn't beat the first man with this cross, he's on doggies (sprints) on Monday. I'll make sure my trusty partner in the dugout, Andy Cunningham, tears him a new arsehole. All my 'tanner baw' playing experience tells me to wait… don't go too soon. Don't go too soon… that's a thought… should I continue in the game? No, maybe a break from it is what I need. How to end it? How to end it? I'm 35 years old and still got the take-off speed to get past a fit, younger opponent (at least that's what I'm trying to convince myself). Decent flight on that from Homer as per usual, my striker's making the run to the front post taking two defenders with him, and I'm on the move towards the edge of the box. Always nippy, good balance, standing 5ft 7ins in my socks, I'm eyeing this ball like Pele did before he smashed his bicycle kick into the top corner in Escape to Victory. I heard he did that in the very first take. That's what I've got now, one take. I've caught it flush with my right and smashed it into the net. How to end it? A right-footed volley into the net as my last touch would be a great way to finish… "Ref, substitution!"

My last poignant touch in Junior football. As I walked off, everyone was staring incredulously at me, especially Andy, my managerial partner. I think I can still catch the No 41 bus, but my car's parked outside so that's a bloody stupid thought. I stride right past my mate Andy, give him a high five, straight up the tunnel, into the changing room, quick shower, changed and away. They're still playing when I leave the stadium. That's the way to end a playing career. Any regrets? Only that it was still only two subs

'He tortured me for the whole 90 minutes'

For your eyes only

Former Rangers, Hearts and Larkhall Thistle full-back Hugh Burns knows Gordon well. Gordon has also appeared as a guest pundit along with Hugh on Bill Young's Talking Football radio show.

Hugh said: "The banter is always great with Youngy and he is funny. Gordon is current because he is still in the game and they tell me the job he is doing up at Cove with Paul Hartely is different class.

"As a player, I remember meeting him latterly in my career after I had gone back to play Juniors with Larkhall Thistle. The wee man was at Cambuslang Rangers and I had heard he was a wee bit of a cheeky chappy, so I thought I had better get tight to him.

"In the early stages I was getting the usual stuff out of the wee cheeky winger and he was saying to me: 'How are you doing Burnsy? How's yer wife these days? That's a nice house you've got.'...and I'm thinking how does he know that's a nice wee house I've got and how does he know my wife, has he been giving her one?

"So, I am trying to get nearer to him and get tight on him, when he's produced one of the best nutmegs I have ever had done to me in all my career as a professional footballer!

"I think they had to screw me out of the pitch at the end of it as he tortured me for the whole 90 minutes!

"Chirpy, cheeky, great skill and he'll not like me for saying, but he should have played at a real top level as he had great ability.

"A funny, funny guy and I wish him all the best."

back then and we had used them both at that point, so it was a wee bit like the Alamo for my team-mates to hang on with ten men for the win in the last 15 minutes! No wonder they were staring.

"Gordon, phone! And before you agree to anything, get that garage door fixed." Yvonne, my wife, has been a brilliant support and to show how much she means to me, she makes an appearance at the start of this book. I would like to tell you in true, dramatic fashion that I drove away into the sunset and became a football coaching guru straight away. Moving from club to club, association to association spreading supreme zen-like karma fitba philosophy in some bizarre version of Keepie-uppie Kung Fu starring David Carradine, from the long-running TV series of the 70s. But, of course, that's not how it happened and this is where the hard work began. The phone call was from Cambuslang wanting me to come back. An offer was on the table to continue as player/manager with Andy. Even more than that, the big dramatic career-ending finish I had fashioned was tempered a wee bit as we still had one more game to go at home – Somervell Park. Sometimes that old West of Scotland work ethic can pop-up out of nowhere and tug at your emotions and pride. I agreed to go back and take the team for that final game, but I kept the suit on and stayed in the dugout.

Season 1999/2000 had been a strange one indeed. At the end of the previous season manager Peter Millar – former Motherwell legend and a great mentor to me – had been sacked by the "Wee Gers". Big Gas Meter (Peter), who had bought yours truly twice in the Junior ranks, organised a guard of honour for me against Arthurlie FC to mark my 300th game (in two spells) for the "Wee" Rangers and I'd go on to make another 33 appearances, totalling 333 in all, notching 72 goals in the process. I can state categorically he was the catalyst for my move into coaching, something I will be eternally grateful for. I visited him on his death-bed in 2013 and, smiling, he hugged me, telling me how proud he was of me. The strange thing was that I had originally phoned his wife, Jean, to tell him that I'd be in to see him when I got back from a foreign coaching trip a week later, but changed my mind at the last minute and went to see him that afternoon. I'm so grateful I did as he passed away just days after. This was one of the hardest players to play in Scottish football, yet as he was lying in the downstairs lounge of his home he looked every inch the gentle and loving father and grandfather that he was. When I left the house Jean grabbed me by the arm and told me: "He was waiting for you." I never saw him again but he is one of the people - along with my children and my parents - that I dedicate this book to. Big Gas Meter, I owe you a drink.

As a senior Cambuslang player and one of the higher earners, I was asked – at the recommendation of Peter as he left – to become one half of a management team along with my team-mate Andy Cunningham, who was also on the verge of hanging up his boots. I must admit, being a boss had never entered my mind. I had always been the joker in the dressing room and the last thing I wanted was to take on the responsibility of managing players, many of whom were also good mates. However, I took on the role with Andy for the rest of the season, but I was finding it difficult to concentrate on my own form while trying to give instruction on the pitch during games. Every Friday night I would go up to see my parents, Margaret and Wullie, and have a cup of tea and chat with my old-man about Saturday's game. I'd always have two teams in my mind, one with me in it and one without. After a few months of this, he said to me: "This isnae working for you, son." And he was right. You need to either play and enjoy it - something I've passed on to lots of players that I've worked with, along with the advice to play as long as you can - or coach and enjoy it. Whatever you do, you have to enjoy it. But at that point I was not enjoying this coaching lark, and to keep up the bird metaphors I ducked out with my Carluke swansong... well, apart from the final cameo in the dugout.

A Motherwell boy born and bred, I still live in the town and am a Well fan through and through, a supporter of the Lobey Dossers and a worshipper of the 'Grew - legendary club striker Willie Pettigrew, all hair, teeth, snotters and pace, in the 70s at least. That's the thing, we all support a club growing up and whether you're a player, coach, referee or running the line, if you love the game you can support a team and still work for another and it doesn't affect your performance, your desire to win or your impartiality (if a match official), as you get paid to work in an industry everyone would love to be in. I'm a Motherwell fan and it makes me laugh when some bell-end who has had a good game against one side of the Old Firm, gets signed by them and then promptly grabs a scarf and pronounces his undying love for the green or the blue. I'd also get pissed off when you tell someone who your favourite team is and they follow up with: "Yes, but who's your 'Big Team'… who do you support between Celtic and Rangers?" "Eh, none of them, are you asking me if am I a Proddy or a Tim?" Believe me, I've had this question all over the world. To put my theory into perspective, I remember my good mate Peter Ritchie telling me that one time he met my dad soon after I had just been transferred to a new club. Peter said to him: "That'll be another scarf you'll have to buy, Wullie!" and my dad replied: "No son, I'm a Gordon Young fan!"

Like the 'Grew, though several years after him, I attended Dalziel High School as a youngster and played for the school team. When I was 15 I also turned out for the Former Pupils amateur team – poached to play while still at school by Economics and Accounts teacher Ian Duncan and Maths teacher Ian 'Saucy' Brown. At one tasty snowball fight in the school playground, I was under an ambush along with my aforementioned friend and minder Peter Ritchie. Peter played in a couple of the same teams as me too. During some games, after I had received some rough treatment from a left back, he would wander out of his own accord from the middle of the park to put in some similar tackles on the defender and give him a good look at the studs on his size nine Stevie Highway Stylos, whilst I fannied about in midfield. I would then happily move back out wide to terrorise the wary defender for the rest of the game. My kids would say later in life that: "Peter would do anything for you dad." How right they were. Anyway, I emptied Mr Duncan out with an overarm snowball fling. The place then fell silent as he marched me up the stairs with a big red coupon, thanks to my well placed ice ball, to tell me the kick-off time on the Saturday was 1.00pm and he'd drop me off at Fir Park after the game finished, so I could catch the second half of the Well match.

Before moonlighting with the FPs, I started with Fir Park Boys Club, Netherdale Boys Club, then on to Fairholm Boys Club, who were the hottest team in the area and from 'across the water (River Clyde) in Larkhall'. Motherwell reserves would follow and then down to Stockport County for a short time. But I found my love, and probably my level, back in the Scottish Junior game with Larkhall Thistle, Shotts Bon Accord and most successfully with Cambuslang Rangers, where I ended my professional career. I was lucky to play more than 600 games and score 128 goals in a 19-year career (17 as a professional), which saw me also pull on a shirt for Wishaw Juniors as a 16-year-old (loaned out from Fairholm Boys Club), and met some wonderful people along the way. If this book is a success I promise to write a prequel about 'The Junior years', as I still keep in contact with many of the colourful characters I played with - and boy could they play. In those halcyon days the top junior players were better paid and played in front of bigger crowds than the lower senior professional leagues, due to the anomalies associated with historical player and club ownership. That's where the introduction of the pyramid system a few years ago has brought a degree of synergy with the most 'progressive' Junior clubs as well as both Lowland and Highland league clubs, changing the dynamics of the game. This has seen the emergence of Annan Athletic, Elgin City, Edinburgh City and a certain Cove Rangers (more on them later), entering the leagues via the play-off system. But the trailblazers to this were Ross County and Inverness Caledonian Thistle, who despite a short SPFL history, have both won a major trophy in recent seasons.

By way of a wee Junior story taster, John Clark, the famous Celtic Lisbon Lion, bought me for Shotts Bon Accord when he was boss there. A wonderful man and a true legend who must have known his stuff as the forward line was Colin Walker (former Airdrieonians and Stenhousemuir), Frank McGarvey (former Celtic and Liverpool and Scotland international) and yours truly. McGarvey was just as enthusiastic then as he was in his pomp and, if you put the ball in the box, he'd find some part of his body to put it in the net. The Celtic fans said he was made of rubber and could bend his body to connect with the ball. That was evident when one night after a match, I took him to my local - the Electric Bar in Motherwell (more on this place later, too) - along with a few other players and from there we ventured over the water to Hamilton and The Palace nightclub. We're at the bar and I get the drinks in, hand Frank his and as he turns around he takes a couple of strides and promptly falls down a 30-step staircase, spinning and tumbling until he reaches the bottom, where he immediately springs up onto his feet uninjured and not a drop of his drink spilled. That's uncoachable.

One particular match springs to mind, a Scottish Cup tie at Shotts' Hannah Park home, the biggest playing surface in Scotland. This was brilliant for a winger as the ball seldom went out of play, allowing those out wide to be very much key players. With 30 minutes to go, we were winning 2-0, when the opposition centre-half cleared a ball out onto the running track which surrounded the pitch – whit a fucking blooter that must have been! As the ball headed for the dug out, I sprinted to retrieve it to take the shy and get the game restarted, but before I could, I felt a tap on my shoulder and John Clark saying "that'll do for today, son" as I looked up to see our sub taking my place.

'Fuck, I should have let it run out,' I thought… and let some other mug go running after it. But there was certainly something about his quiet, authoritative and specific tone that made it sound perfectly plausible. Exactly how big was this pitch I thought to myself, that in the act of retrieving a ball, the sub had whipped his tracksuit off and the boards were being smashed together to attract the referee's attention and he was on the park before I had got the ball ready to shy? Aaahhh, the wisdom of a Lisbon Lion.

When I was in talks to sign for Shotts from Cambuslang, John called me and said that the two clubs had agreed a fee and I had to "look after myself" when my future new club's board came to my house with the signing-on fee and wage offer. I knew the amount Shotts had agreed with Cambuslang and they also threw in a player, which possibly meant there was more in the pot for me. The four-man delegation from the committee then rocked up to my wee flat next to Strathclyde Park and Yvonne offers them a tea or coffee. At the same time, Jenna, my ten-month-old baby daughter, is crawling around the living room floor. "Yes please hen, three teas and a coffee for the president." By the time Yvonne had come back with the tray of refreshments, I had managed to undersell myself by a few quid and the officials were up and away to complete the next signing on John's list, without even taking a sip of Yvonne's refreshments. Looking back it was brilliant tag-team work by them, and a wee bit of retribution for me, as I was a sales manager at the time. You couldn't outfox the old junior committees. But despite that it was a very good offer that I received and like any successful negotiation, if both parties are happy then it's a good deal.

Also, just to elaborate on the gap between the Junior and lower level senior professional clubs at the time, when John named the team at Shotts, he'd often send an unused player 'down' to play for Albion Rovers as a trialist, as a favour to his old Celtic team-mate Tommy Gemmell who was their manager at that time. Picture the scene, the Shotts squad would be sitting at our pre-match meal and as the team is announced one or two of our players would get a tap on the shoulder to inform them that they were dropped to go and play 'up a professional football level'. Funnily, I never got that tap. John was a lovely man with a humble manner given his success in the game. I'd meet up with him later in my journey when he was kit director at Celtic, and anytime they came to Fir Park I'd search him out to offer him my hospitality, given my respect for him.

But, after saying goodbye to Junior fitba that day at Carluke in such dramatic fashion, it was an intriguing offer from one of my good friends – Brian Sheldon – which enticed me to pull the boots back on and go and join him for a new challenge at amateur level. Dalziel FP – my old team – had through the 90s and early 2000s, become one of Scottish amateur football's powerhouses, claiming a Scottish Amateur Cup, three West of Scotland Cups and dominating the Caledonian League and it's cup competitions, along with the likes of Bannockburn, Milton and Drumchapel amateurs.

But they were looking to mount another assault on the Scottish Cup in season 2000/01. As a player/coach himself, Brian coaxed me to join their squad. Church elder and pillar of the business community by day, Brian would kick the head off a giraffe if it was on a football pitch on a Saturday. The thing was he was a great passer of the ball and a great reader of the game. But he'd knock the ball a wee bit in front of him intentionally to entice a player into thinking he'd be able to nip the ball away, then – BOOM – what an assassin he was.

The FPs were eager to embark on another successful campaign to secure the top cup and had assembled a talented group of former pros and ex-junior players. It was tempting and it would also mean I could concentrate on playing. The pressure was off and I loved that full season, which culminated in us winning the Scottish Cup at Hampden. After a good night out in Phileas Foggs – at that time one of Motherwell's most salubrious night spots – I awoke to a phone call on the Sunday morning and an invitation to play for the Scottish Amateur team against Ireland and Wales. More happy playing memories at the tender age of 36.

Prior to our Scottish Cup win, which is a tremendous achievement for any amateur club given there were about 900 teams who entered the competition, we had won the League Cup at Lesser Hampden. This was a pre-curser to us winning the big one and the team was full of gifted and experienced players. Playing that season gave me a chance to play with guys who were my friends and Alan Percy was one. In that League Cup final we won 2-1 and 'Pepsi', as he was known, scored the winner, a thunderous strike from 25 yards worthy to win any final. As we were standing waiting for the trophy to be presented, the PA system announced the 'Man of the Match' award and Pepsi, who had played very well, started his walk towards the officials at the podium to collect his gong, only for the announcer to say…"Dalziel number 7, Gordon Young!". "Sorry about that", I nonchalantly quipped to Pepsi, the same cheeky aside I used to say to any full-back I had nutmegged during my career. Pepsi – who played for Dalziel all his career – was slaughtered for this over confidence by our circle of friends, but he'd continue to argue his case at any given opportunity that he should have been the recipient. So that Christmas, I wrapped the man of the match trophy up and gave it to him as a present. Upon unwrapping the trophy he duly scored my name out and replaced it with his! You see players in the professional ranks getting testimonial games to reward their loyalty, but a case can be made that they were well-paid, doing a job they loved. It is in the amateur and Junior ranks where there are clubs full of tremendously loyal servants to their clubs and the game. Pepsi was one of them and a great servant to Dalziel FP.

During this season 2000/2001 Peter Millar had by this time taken on a coaching role with Motherwell's Under-15s at a time when the club – and many others around Scotland – were looking to restructure and create their youth academies. He asked me if I wanted to come to the small Astro-turf area behind Motherwell's East Stand and impart some of my experience to the young lads, as he really felt they could benefit from my thoughts on the game and the advice I could give. I always had great respect for Peter and was close friends with him and his family – as mentioned previously – and to be mentioned so prominently in his eulogy at his funeral in 2013 was very humbling. That tearful day at the crematorium, I sat beside two of his former team-mates and true Motherwell living legends, Bobby Graham and Willie Pettigrew. This strong bond I had with him was in my mind when I mulled over his request, and as I was only training twice a week with Dalziel, and Fir Park wasn't far from my home, I took him up on his offer. After a short while I was starting to enjoy these coaching sessions and began to look forward to them. For the first time, committing myself to coaching badges became a possibility, then an obsession, as my thirst to learn more about the game grew.

Football in Scotland at this time – late 90s, early 2000s – was changing. Junior football, inclusive of the East of Scotland and Highland League semi-pro set-ups, which is the equivalent of England's non-league game, was moving slowly but surely towards a pyramid set-up. The theory was to promote advancement of clubs towards the professional game, with play-offs for promotion and relegation being incorporated into most leagues, from the Scottish Premiership down to the lower Junior leagues, as highlighted earlier. Also around this time the top professional clubs were transforming their youth set-ups to become academies and this reorganisation was having a much-needed positive trickle-down effect, to the whole of the nation's youth football.

The Scottish FA grassroots coaching badge scheme is key to opportunities to coach professionally in the game, with the SFA brand respected globally. It takes great commitment and dedication to navigate your way along the pathway from early entry level through to the Uefa Pro Licence. However, it is something that you have to plough through to be able to mine the real valuable coaching gold that awaits you after the 1.1 Early Touches, 1.2 and 1.3 courses. Even though they are basic, these courses – like being PVG checked - are essential and important for any registered coach involved with youth football in Scotland and they can take between six to 12 hours to complete. They are usually organised over a full weekend or several evening three-hour sessions, to take account of those attending having to work for a living.

Despite attending courses for coaching adults during my stint as player-manager of Cambuslang, I was still obligated to complete these SFA Pathway courses for grass roots coaches. It was while I was in the process of working my way through one of these early badges, that I once again questioned whether I would be able to cope with ticking these boxes and progress in a career to teach the game the way I think it should be taught. It was a rainy winter's night. My full-time marketing job had taken me to

Edinburgh on a Friday afternoon and once I had finished for the day, I had to zip back along the M8 to the indoor football facility at Toryglen, near Hampden, for the next instalment of this particular badge. Grumpiness is not something I succumb to very often, but I hadn't had the best day at work, the traffic was terrible, I was hungry and I wasn't looking forward to listening to the uninspiring and patronising SFA coach – who shall remain nameless – who would be leading the session that night.

I made it by the skin of my teeth. I parked and rushed to the changing room muttering and cursing under my breath. Out on the astro-turf, I gathered my thoughts and resigned myself to getting through the simple drills and theory. My fellow learners that night – to their great credit, volunteer boys and girls team coaches every one of them – were every shape and size and almost entirely without much personal football-ing experience, above low level amateur or five-a-sides with their mates. But without the commitment and dedication of these volunteers, youth football would not be able to function in Scotland. The respect I had for those there that night notwithstanding, it did not help my mood that several of the basic technical drills were breaking down quickly as the trainee coaches themselves were taking part in them and the session was not flowing well. In addition, I was still playing at that time and I was thinking ahead to the game the next day, so as they say in my best Motherwell vocabulary, 'my heid was up my arse'.

My partner in the group was a lovely middle-aged woman, a teacher from West Lothian, whose only reason to gain her badge was to be able to take her wee school team. Hats off to her, she must have had to inch her way along the M8 earlier on that night to get there, too. We were doing our best and encouraging each other to carry out the instructions of our erstwhile head coach, when he turned his unenlightened attention to us.

"Helen, do you think if I throw the ball to you, you could control it and pass it to Gordon? Gordon, do you think if I throw this ball to you in the air, you could control it well enough to pass it to Helen and continue the exercise?"

Something didn't exactly snap inside me, it was more that it clicked assuredly into place. I know from a coaching point of view I wasn't yet qualified and I was in no way trying to show I was 'Johnnie Big Baws' who was too good to be there. But the mitigating circumstances of my day prior to me showing up, meant I couldn't take this patronising tone from a wannabe Mourinho.

"Listen you cunto! You can boot that ball right up into the rafters of this fucking indoor stadium as high as it will go and I'll bring it down with any part of my body you want, killing it dead like a bag of cement and then I'll pass it politely and accurately to Helen. She'll then take eight touches to control it and then toe it back to me… landing at the feet of Angus from Auchenshoogle United Boys Club, who will fumble his own pass to Wullie from Bonkle Athletic AFC and so on and we'll all be chasing round looking for our own balls for the next half an hour. Can you please just get fucking on with this? Sorry about the 'cunto' and the 'fucking' there Helen."

I questioned my coaching path after that night. As far as I was concerned, Early Touches 1, 2 and 3 ticked the boxes for me, Motherwell and the Scottish FA to allow me to continue training the under-15s. But all it really gave me from a coaching point of view was the ability to blow the balls up, put up the nets and iron the bibs. Truthfully, for someone who has played football seriously it was piss easy and I wasn't inspired one bit. With a mouthful of crisps and a chocolate bar from the Toryglen centre snack machine – ironic as I was muttering under my breath at the same time how I'd bet that Angus fae Auchenshoogle United hadn't missed a single meal since 1978 judging by the size of him – I trudged back to the car that night saying: "Fuck it, I'm not going back." But something told me to stick with it... could a Keepie-uppie Kung Fu philosophy really be guiding me? Nah I was just hungry. Little did I know on that frustrating evening in the south-side of Glasgow, that I would end up with a Uefa Pro Licence and go on to coach all over the world. It's days like these that challenge you as a coach, but which you can look back on and laugh... and feel a little bit smug that a wannabe Mourinho is still coaching early Touches 1, 2 and 3! The coach delivering the education course that night has crossed my path many times since, and every time I see him I smile smugly as I realise what I have achieved in the game... and that I could keep a beach ball off him in a phone box (copyright Davie Cooper), while setting out cones for a passing drill!

Hunger to keep on playing, when I should have retired after winning the Scottish Amateur Cup with Dalziel FP and then winning three Scottish caps at that level, made me make the wrong decision to sign on for another season at Dalziel. I was also upping the coaching sessions with Motherwell – and enjoying it more and more. By the October of the 2001/2002 season I had decided I had had enough and called time on my playing career for good. I would now be concentrating all my efforts in football on coaching and seeing where it would take me.

However, there would be one final twist on the playing front, which might even trump completing my Junior playing career with a final-touch volley to win the game. Shortly after saying my goodbyes to Dalziel, the Scottish Amateur International select manager Hughie Carswell called me to ask if I would play for Scotland against the Republic of Ireland in the decider for the Home Nations Championships in Dublin – which had to be held over due to the foot and mouth disease outbreak, which crippled the agriculture and farming industry the previous year. I told him I had retired, but he said that didn't matter. If I was fit and ready to play, I'd be on the plane. The matchday programme read 'No.7 Gordon Young... Club – unattached'.

On the Friday night at a meeting between Hughie and the two most senior players in the squad, Mick McCabe (who had also played at a similarly high level) and myself,

Hughie suggested that the players could go out and have one pint of lager to help them relax before the game the next day. "What the fuck, Hughie?" I said. "We're in a hotel in the middle of the Temple Bar district in Dublin and you want to send them out for a pint the night before a game! Get them into bed early and post a sentry on the door, win the match and let them go out tomorrow night after a great result, persuade the Committee to stick a few quid in the kitty and then it's OK if they end up upside down in a wheelie bin, singing Molly Malone!" Thankfully, he agreed. However, this must have been an early indicator to me that I was reaching a coaching style maturity, and realised that tough management decisions had to be made.

So, we finally come to my very, very last match and with the game tied after extra-time, we went to penalty kicks to decide the outcome. Yes, you've guessed it, I scored the winning penalty to win the Championship! Now, I hear that Raul scored with his last ever touch for Real Madrid, Didier Drogba scored a penalty with his last touch for Chelsea to win the Champions League and Patrick Vieira's last touch for Arsenal was an FA Cup final penalty to beat Manchester United, but they all still had several seasons left to play. I haven't heard of anyone retiring from two codes of football with their last touches both being goals… Surely that's worthy of being a quiz question.

CHAPTER 2

The Man With The Golden Team

*Family, friends and formative years reveal what
influences made an impact on this fun-loving Well fan*

I think the brilliant people involved in my early life laid the foundations for my coaching journey. Without them it would not have been possible and I will be eternally grateful to them all. My parents, Margaret and Wullie Young, are the only remaining original occupants in a row of maisonettes in Glen Court, Motherwell. They've lived there for more than 50 years and I remember my dad taking me to see my new home being built and telling me we'd be moving there from Range Road some 100 yards away. "No big deal," I thought until he announced that the old tenement buildings we were living in at that time would be pulled down and a football pitch would be laid in place of them... "Fucking yaldy! Why did you not say that earlier, I'll start packing and start demolishing them myself right now." And so my love affair with the beautiful game began with the destruction of my own home!

Fifty years ago these new houses were the local council's flagship dwellings, complete with underfloor heating and piping that wasn't made of lead. There were 42 apartments split into blocks of six and crammed with sports-mad boys and girls of mixed ability and religious affiliation. I can't ever remember seeing any fights over religion between my mates who lived nearby growing up in the 70s and early 80s. There was a three-way split of predominantly Motherwell fans along with the customary Celtic and Rangers fans. All were mates regardless of whether you were wearing claret and amber, green or blue. It wasn't a problem, just get on with life and get a ball out for a game. Anyone who had a ball would get a game and get first pick and everyone would then pray that the ball owner wouldn't be the one who got shouted in for their dinner or we'd have no game.

Believe it or not, the Rangers and Celtic fans in our area would leave together to go to Old Firm matches. They would split up in Glasgow and then return together later that day and play football in the communal grass area – if they could get a game, as it was so competitive! Being a Motherwell fan also put you in a great position of being able to take the piss out of Old Firm fans equally. I remember standing on the Fir Park terracing and singing Celtic songs when the Gers came to town and Rangers songs when the Celts visited. We made it a point to do anything to get a rise out of the visiting Old Firm fans and wind up them up and the players on the pitch. Traditional Well songs also back this up, with references to beating both sides. And, as BBC Off the Ball presenter, journalist and Well fan, Tam Cowan, also mentions from time to time, it was great to see legendary early 80s Motherwell goalie Hugh Sproat wear a green top when Rangers visited Fir Park and a blue one when Celtic came calling.

It was a joy to be brought up there with the focal point being the year-long sporting calendar. Obviously, we'd play football all year round, but would stop for major sporting events, which were covered extensively on the TV. Remember we only had BBC 1, BBC 2 and STV at that time. Even Channel 4 was only a blink in the TV repair man's eye.

When Wimbledon was on, we'd make courts using the play-pens and chalk lines as reference markers. When the British Open was on, we'd make a course 'down the Glen', chipping over bushes, playing from elevated tees, putting into tin can holes dug into the ground and marked by flags nicked from the Motherwell Cricket Club some two miles away. We'd replicate the Olympic Games and as many events as we could, including athletics – from sprints to middle-distance runs and even the marathon. But I must admit trying to replicate equestrian dressage using Raleigh Choppers, wasn't our finest hour. This even stretched to 'The Grand National' and we'd go over the road to the more salubrious Annan Grove (where I'd buy a house later in life, coincidentally from ex-Motherwell coach Billy Campbell, who coached me in the reserves) where they had rows of privet hedges, which we straddled before the residents held a stewards' enquiry. To squeeze in some extra sporting time, we'd play a 25-a-side game of rounders, where everyone would try and hit the ball over the three-storey apartment building for a home run. Everyone seemed to have superb hand to eye coordination back then. Fuck knows how we would have been able to cope, if Channel 4 had been on at that time with it's alternative sports such as American Football, Kabbadi (an Indian sport which must have inspired British Bulldogs) and Countdown!

Growing up our family was sport and football orientated and every holiday we went on, the first stop would be to a shop that sold footballs. My sister, Carole, was a year younger than me, but was also very sporty. She played county-level volleyball and also ended up playing for an early Hamilton Accies women's team. There were no exotic vacations abroad back then, but we'd regularly venture to the south east coast of England, which itself was an epic journey in a wee Triumph Toledo, registration WVD 24H.

My dad and sister played football with me everywhere we went, and my mum was in charge of first aid and catering… namely a rub down with her hand if we took a knock and a drink of Tizer. Happy days indeed. We'd drive down south each summer and once I had procured a ball, I'd get Carole to come with me to the first beach or nearby park to have a kick about. On one occasion we went to Scarborough and, after we had booked into the B&B, off we went with a new size 5 to what we thought was a great big park, with benches around it and immaculate turf. Cue the jumpers down, Carole in goal and the ensuing shots, slide tackles and overhead kicks. This was followed by the appearance of an irate, odd-looking geezer wearing a white coat and several jerseys tied around his waist, with a floppy hat on his head. I thought it was Worzel Gummidge – a popular kids' programme of the day – but soon found out it was the umpire of the county cricket match, which I can only assume had stopped for tea. "Aaahhh," I thought, "that'll explain all the people sleeping on the surrounding benches." You can imagine my dad's face when he entered the ground to see us being chased off the grass. I always thought it was a daft game, but I think this episode stamped a subconscious dislike of it onto my psyche.

The first big football game I can remember being taken to was Motherwell v Tottenham Hotspur in the Texaco Cup at Fir Park on Wednesday, 3 November, 1970. This competition was sponsored by the huge oil company and was a defacto British Isles and Ireland tournament for teams who had not qualified for Europe. The previous week the Well had travelled to London and were defeated 3-2, but 22,000 fans – including yours truly – converged on the Fir Park terraces to see if we could spring an upset against Spurs, who had the likes of Jennings, Mullery, Peters, Chivers and Gilzean in their ranks. It was more than 50 years ago and I still remember the swell and sway of the crowd and the smell of the liniment wafting up from the dugouts, as we were in the enclosure next to the tunnel. What a memory for a six-year-old, seeing your heroes such as Joe Wark, Bobby Watson, Dixie Deans and Brian Heron, take the game to the English giants and beat them 3-1 for a 5-4 aggregate win. We ended up beaten by Hearts in the semis of the tournament, and they themselves were beaten by Wolves in the final. But that game lit a football fire under me. Thereafter every second Saturday my dad would take me to the home games. He stood in the same spot beside the floodlight stanchion behind the goal, along with his friends from the MFC Wishaw supporters club. In those days, everybody had their own patch where they stood with their mates and I think it was mandatory to have a hip flask.

As I got older, he'd lift me over the turnstiles and I'd run off to meet my own mates in the covered terracing and so the journey began to get serious. But it didn't stop there, every second Saturday as was the norm back then, we would be away from home and that was the cue for the Young family to head to towns and cities across Scotland. My dad and I would go to see Motherwell play and Carole and my mum would go shopping in salubrious places such as Falkirk, Dumfries, Dundee and Aberdeen. Why did I not see a football obsessive pattern developing here? After the game we'd get a fish supper and head back home, via Motherwell Cross, where we'd pick up a copy of the Saturday evening papers to catch up with the scores and reports of the other games. No Final Score, teletext, mobile phone apps or social media then, which can tell you where and when a player has farted. My dad would come out and play 'cuppy' and 'combine' with me and my mates. He was referred to as Wullie by everyone except me, quite unlike most parents who were referred to as Mr and Mrs such and such. My parents were so supportive of my sister and I and they sacrificed so much for the sake of their family. My mum, Margaret, was the only one in our house not sporty, but was a brilliant mother, housewife, chef, kit woman, first aider and water-girl all rolled into one, always ready with a sticking plaster, a supportive cuddle and an encouraging word.

My dad was a Time Study Engineer who worked at Anderson Boyes (ABs) Coal Cutting Engineers and also at the world-famous Motherwell Bridge engineering firm. It was here the equally famous Motherwell, Liverpool and Scotland striker, and ITV Sports presenter, Ian St John, was his apprentice, in his pre-professional football days. It was sad to hear of 'The Saint's' passing at the age of 82, just as we completed this book.

Wullie left school when he was 15 and was forced into early retirement at the age of 59 when ABs closed down. The creative adventurer in him took over when he turned 60 and he decided to go back to college and study art, as he had always had a love of painting and drawing. But can you imagine him trying to sell that as his intended career to his own parents, living in deepest, darkest Lanarkshire some 45 years previously? I'm glad he managed to pursue it in later life and it is something he still enjoys to this very day. In many ways his return to his favoured vocation mirrors the way I eventually managed to make football my full-time professional career. This is something I am eternally grateful and thankful for and all the while inspired and encouraged to do so by my mum and dad.

Wullie watched all of my games at every level I played when growing up and could always give me an honest opinion of my performance. He did this by assessing from a distance and not being a raving parent on the sidelines, living out their own dreams through their kid. This excellent attitude must have transferred to me, as later on when I was taking my son, Robbie, home from an under-9/10s match, he was sitting in the car and obviously had something on his mind. So I asked him the usual: "How did you enjoy that? What did you do well?" Etc. When he says: "Dad, why do you not stand with the other dads and shout?"

When I explained to him that if everyone shouted their opinions at the side of the pitch, then he wouldn't hear the coaches' instructions, and, anyway, on the way home was the best time to discuss the game.

"Oh, OK then, fair enough."

It's the best back-handed compliment he has ever paid me and I can say the same about his grandad!

I think the sporting genes are strong throughout the Young family. Robbie himself is still playing at a high level coming through the Motherwell FC Academy before heading to the States to complete a soccer scholarship and a degree in sports science. He also became an 'All American' – the best in his associated football position – at Lander University in South Carolina. He now plays semi-professional for East Stirlingshire in the Lowland League, the fifth tier of Scottish football. My daughter, Jenna, is also very athletic and as well as playing football for Hamilton Accies, like her aunt, Carole, has played netball and badminton to county level. You'll not be surprised to hear she's a PE and Guidance teacher. I'm as proud of them both, as my parents are of my sister and I.

The glue that has kept our family together has been Yvonne, my wife, who perhaps unknowingly throughout my kids' childhoods has adopted the role my mother and so many more mums in Scotland took on, that of kitman, chef, first aider, etc. How cyclical life seems to be at times and Yvonne tells me that her biggest problem on a Saturday now is what game she will go to watch. Will it be Cove Rangers where I am assistant manager or East Stirlingshire where Robbie is playing.

I had wanted to be a footballer and this was evident early on when I won a national keepie-uppie competition for my age group. To give you some indication of the quality taking part, former Motherwell and Liverpool hero and Scotland captain Gary McAllister won the age level below me! At the end of the competition, only Gary and me were left juggling the ball…Uri Geller is never there when you really need him! However, without going too deep into the whys and why nots of how I never made it to the top level, I could always see myself involved in the game. Although as you read earlier, I couldn't see myself going down the coaching route, and certainly never saw the journey ahead, which I have been fortunate to enjoy.

I suppose when I look back, I had good people in my corner right from the start. People like Wilson Humphries, my English teacher at Dalziel High School and a 1952 Motherwell Cup final hero as well as a Scotland cap. He was also a coach at Fir Park and I remember walking into the Motherwell dressing room for a reserve match and he announced to all and sundry: "Do you know Youngy has an English O grade?" To which an older experienced player remarked: "Hope it helps him with his new fucking career!" That's the banter that anyone who hasn't played fitba will never have experienced. The changing room can be a ruthless place and there is a 'survival of the fittest' environment at times. Many people will say: "Oh this guy was a good player and that one was a good player." But certainly back in my era, it was mainly the players with the toughest mentally and the ones with the most desire that made it. Wilson also had a party piece which he hooked me in with. He'd toss a 10p coin in the air, trap it on his crinkled old soft leather brogue and then flick it up into his tweed suit top pocket. I did my pocket money in gambling against him before I mastered it.

Ironically, Mr Humphries was still teaching at Dalziel High School a couple of years after I had left, and my writing partner who started the school at that time, also cites him as an inspiration. Although he did not have him as a class teacher he proudly says Wilson,who was also a football coach at Dalziel, picked him as the only first year in the Juvenile football team (for 1st and 2nd years) in 1982 and claims the legendary Well striker thought he was a "great wee player, with a smashing left foot." But having also played with my erstwhile ghost-writer at the tail end of my career, I think Wilson must have been teaching his English class Shakespeare's 'Much Ado About Nothing' that year.

Another inspiration was Marjorie Nimmo, my guidance teacher, who wanted to explore the opportunities of a soccer scholarship in the USA for me. That was never heard of back then, and how spooky it would be that Robbie would choose this pathway.Marjorie ended up as Ernie Walker's assistant at the Scottish FA. One Friday afternoon I was there at the old SFA Park Gardens offices with a club secretary looking to rush through my 11th-hour transfer from Shotts back to Cambuslang, and, as we were sitting in the foyer waiting to be called, a stern female voice said: "Bring Gordon Young in. The deadline has passed as he has homework due for me from 20 odd years ago!" Brilliant, that would get you a peg in a dressing room, Miss Nimmo, no problem at all.

I have met some wonderful people, been to some incredible places and had an absolute ball along the way. Family, friends and life guides have been so important and are too many to name, and for fear of missing people out, I am not going down that road too much. But I really do have to mention two of my best mates, for no other reason than the fact that I played football with them, they protected me and I know what they were capable of on the pitch. Both were hard as nails and at least one of them was a good player.

This evolved from my younger days when hairy-arsed defenders would try and kick me up in the air at the instruction from their brutal coaches, who would encourage tumshies to "Smash Young early and see what he's made of." Defenders in those days were people who, in my opinion, were only capable of heading and kicking the way they were looking…and I mean ball or man. Therefore I adopted a philosophy, which continued throughout my career to the despair of my managers. I'd default from the game plan to making an arse of the full-backs by nutmegging them and quipping:

"Sorry about that!" As I passed them by and left them bamboozled, I would sometimes mimic throwing them some spare change for them to buy me a pie and a Bovril on their way back into the ground… "Brown sauce please and some pepper in the Bovril!" Before adopting the proactive humiliation of full-backs approach, I'd often complain to the referee. But after the 15th time in a season that some Bangkok kick-boxer with a fitba jersey on, had put me in the terracing in the first minute, and the ref had replied: "Awe wee man, it's his first tackle."

I'd bite back with: "Fuck off arsehole, your leg gets broken with the first or 25th tackle and anyway what do you know? You've never played the game and were bullied at school."

Yes, Gordon, that's how to win friends and endear yourself to authority.

But, to combat the lack of protection from referees, I did have a protective shield, in the name of best pals and enforcers such as Peter Ritchie and Brian Sheldon. Peter even showed his undying loyalty to me during one drunken trip to Blackpool when I encouraged him to prove our friendship with a tattoo. He was bowled over when I ripped open my shirt to show him my new tattoo of a British Bulldog on my chest with his and his girlfriend's name written in ink below it. Close to tears and a little emotional from a good few beers, Peter disappeared and came back a couple of hours later with a Tasmanian Devil and my name neatly tattooed below it on his back.

As much as he would have done anything for me, I think he would have gladly done me in then and there by throwing me off Blackpool Tower when, in full view of all our mates, I took a damp cloth and wiped off the impermanent Henna drawing on my chest and Peter was left with the real deal and my name on his back.

Still he regularly tries to get some semblance of revenge on me by exposing his tat to the great and the good of Scottish football whenever I introduce them to him. "Look what that wee bastard done to me!" he'd say before telling them the whole story, chapter and verse. Trust me, I could write another book about all my mates, what they mean to me and what a big part they have played in my life…maybe I will.

But let's just say, without them all I would not have been able to become who I am today. You know who you are and I salute you and I'll see you soon for 'one for the ditch' in my local, the Electric Bar.

Dossers Are Forever

*Coaching my boyhood heroes with help from wonderful mentors
and the beginning of the Motherwell Academy transformation*

I t could not have been any more surreal if Santa Claus had knocked on my door and invited himself in for a port and brandy and plonked his sack on my living-room chair by the fire. "Naw you've got to play Murphy through the middle to start with. His pace will scare the shit out of Davie Weir. If you play Sutton, he'll be in Weir's back pocket-picking fluff oot his crack for 90 minutes!" My dad, Wullie, has a great way with words.

"Fair point, but maybe Nick Blackman, who's even quicker, could be the man for the job and Murphy could play off him, cutting in from the wings in a 4-5-1 formation. Two players, fast as whippets, could cause problems for the Rangers back-line. Saša Papac is as slow as shite in the neck of a bottle!" My nephew, David, wasn't too shabby with the old vernacular either.

Christmas dinner 2010 was in the process of being cleared from the table at the Young household. The full family was there. Eighteen of them, Motherwell fans to a man, woman, boy, girl and dog… and all eager to get their views out on how the Dossers should play against the Gers on Boxing Day. A unique moment for them all, as they had the man who was to take charge of the team – me – as a captive audience to their views on how Motherwell should play the beautiful game. The successful Well management team of Craig Brown and Archie Knox, who I worked closely with as their first-team coach in the dugout, had been unable to resist the call of Aberdeen and had moved north in mid-December. They would later go on record to say that not insisting I went with them was a mistake. A huge compliment from Craig, the man who took Scotland to the 1998 World Cup. But instead I was installed as caretaker manager while we looked to bring in a new boss. Plenty were interested in the post, but given the immediate fixture list – Hearts at home, top of the league at that time, Rangers also at Fir Park on Boxing Day and Celtic away on 30 December – no one was putting their cock on the block until those games were navigated. A rearranged game against Hearts at Fir Park on 14 December was my first game in charge as boss (in my second stint as caretaker manager, more on my first spell later). To get a wee break before the games, I went up to a holiday time-share in Kilconquhar, Fife, with my close friends, Fraser and Meg Dunn, Peter and Karen Paterson, Graham and Tracy Dodd, Peter and Yvonne Ritchie and were hosted by the kindest communal friends we share, Alan and Charlotte Murray.

As we sat down to dinner, the estate manager, knowing our Motherwell background, asked the company: "As a Jambo, I'm thinking about going to the game on Wednesday night, could you get me a ticket?" This was mainly aimed at Karen Paterson (who was also MFC's football administrator, who I'll later mention is the glue that keeps Motherwell Football Club together). Her husband, Peter, replied the quickest. Pointing to me, he said: "He's the manager, come early and you can get a game!"

The game finished in a 2-1 defeat and was not without incident. Midfielder Steven Jennings had an agreement with Craig Brown that, once he had gone over the disciplinary threshold (of which he was one booking away from), he could have an operation to remove a wisdom tooth which was giving him excruciating pain. This duly happened in the Hearts match when Steve got a yellow card for smashing Jambos' big forward Kevin Kyle in their own half. In a crazy grandstand finish, in which we were battering Hearts with 15 minutes to go, Jamie Murphy went down in the box for what seemed a stonewall penalty. But not to referee Stevie O'Reilly. A bit too officious if you ask me, as he sent off Jenno for grabbing his shorts in protest at the challenge.

After the game, I spoke to the press and went through the usual post mortem about decisions etc, and then went back to the changing room and de-briefed the players on how well they played and, in my opinion, how they were unlucky not to take something from the game. The plan for the following day was to recover the players who played and work with the remainder who didn't. That's not unusual, as Tom Jones says, but what was unusual is that I got a call from MFC chief executive Leeann Dempster, who was in a panic as there had been an alleged betting scandal regarding the previous night's match, virtually unheard of in our country.

Apparently, investigations were underway to determine why unusual betting patterns, featuring cautions in the game, occurred and whether there was any involvement from our player(s). I cannot believe it myself and totally refuted the allegations to the press after speaking with the players. But Sky TV are outside along with the BBC and STV looking for a story and the inevitable interview with the manager. Only in the job as a caretaker, and I'm having to field off questions from the national press on an alleged betting scandal. I'd been doing lots of media work, but wasn't really ready to be grilled live on Sky TV and also by the BBC's John 'Digger' Barnes and Raman Bhardwaj from STV. But give them their due, and my gratitude, as they gave me a wee heads-up by telling me that they would ask me the important questions twice, as their producer would be prompting them and looking for me to either flap or inadvertently 'cock up' and give everyone a scoop. I appreciated that and haven't forgotten that assistance. Who says the media are wolves? Most are really good guys with a job to do, but some can twist a little in order for audience or reader exposure. One that shines out a mile is Andy Devlin from the Scottish Sun who has been a mate for 30 years and always kept me right despite me sending him on a few wild goose chases. But, to be fair, he can more than hold his own and gets his own back at my expense in front of the Electric Bar gallery. In the end, after a two-year investigation involving the Association of British Bookmakers and the police, the case against Steve Jennings was dropped and he was totally vindicated. I think I am a pretty good judge of character and I can say, hand on heart, that I never doubted Steve was involved in anything illegal on the pitch that night. Motherwell chairman and owner John Boyle was also in the dressing room after the match had ended and is quoted as saying that the lad was totally "distraught" and that, if he was faking it, he was a better actor than Sir Laurence Olivier.

Right, game No1 navigated with a defeat and having to deal with a shit storm in the press. Now I was looking to even up my first-team managerial record by giving the blue half of the famous Old Firm a doing at Fir Park on the 26 December. Not to worry, however, if that failed to materialise, I would have another chance to notch a win, against the green half of the rivals on the 30 December! Talk about a managerial baptism of fire.

Now, on Christmas Day, my family were really giving me the once-over using condiments, half-eaten Brussels sprouts, unwanted cracker toys and left-over pigs in blankets as players on my dining-room table, now a substitute for the Fir Park pitch.

"Right, Gordon, keep it tight for the first 20 minutes and then the Bears will be getting right pissed off and moaning at their players every time they lose the ball. That's when you want to let Tom Hateley (son of Rangers and England star Mark) – symbolised here as a yellow plastic jack-in-the-box – off the leash and allow him to bomb forward. That'll piss the bluenoses off seeing their hero's son take them on." Jings, my sister, Carole, must have been hammering the Babycham during the main course!

She'd not long finished that sentence when my phone rang. It's my stalwart centre -half, Shaun Hutchinson. "Wee problem, gaffer. We went to Tom's (Hateley) for Christmas lunch and eh… em, I think he's got food poisoning."

"Fuckin' great!" I said, and motioned to go back to the drawing board (or rather the dinner table, as it looks like it could be the next revolution in football tactics!), but realised I had to ask a dreaded question.

"Eh, Hutchy…" trepidation in my voice… "how are you?"

"I'm fine, gaffer." He answers and, with relief, I remember he has the constitution of a horse. Turns out he had seconds of the contaminated turkey, but managed to shit it out and shrug it off. This is the guy who earlier in the season ran into a cast-iron rugby post at our Dalziel Park training ground, swallowed his tongue in the process, only for our physio, John Porteous, to retrieve it.

Club captain Stephen Craigan was physically sick as the paramedics were treating him. But afterwards Hutchy walks out of the ambulance and asks: "Wonder what's for lunch today, boys!" At this point in the proceedings, my nephew, David, and my son, Robbie, are arguing about who should come in at right-back and the merits on suitable replacements are being scrutinised with me, an innocent bystander. I'm just the manager, what do I know!

What I do know is how great those players were for me in that three-week spell, with their commitment and support. Randolph, Saunders, Reynolds, Hateley, Hammell, Hutchinson, Craigan, Humphrey, Lasley, Sutton, Jennings, Murphy, Gow, Blackman, Fitzpatrick, Forbes, McHugh and Hollis, were all excellent for me.

"These are all decent observations, but who'll play in midfield with Lasley, as Jennings is suspended?" Fuck it, maybe they'll come up with an insight that will surprise me, I think.

"Jennings is that the boy who was accused of…" My mum Margaret asks, "YES", they all shout in unison.

Assembled round the dining table – moving various pieces into position like RAF Battle of Britain Command and Control HQ – my dad picks up a sprout and a piece of what everyone thinks might be sage and onion stuffing and manoeuvres them into position.

A pepper pot is offered up.

"Reynolds…"

Our best china gravy boat is put in place.

"…and Craigan…in the heart of defence, Saunders at right-back (a player I thought and wished would go to the very top) and Hammy at left back are the engine room and key to your game-plan tomorrow.

"They can inspire the whole team and with Randolph in goals – and I'm using my new binoculars as Darren – just what I wanted by the way… then you could well nip a draw!" Thanks for that insight, Nicola, my favourite niece (only one I have).

Did any of you do an Early Touches 1.1 course by any chance, I wonder?

"Fuck it… whit yeh want to dae is get on the phone tonight and re-sign former Motherwell hard man Gregor Stevens. Disnae matter that he's in his mid 60s noo, he wis a quality centre-half. He'd half his granny and take oot the referee as well, leaving the match abandoned, and by the time a rearranged game has been organised a new boss will be in place." Fuck sake, that was my own internal monologue speaking and I was eyeing the cheese wire guillotine on the table as big Gregor! Pull yourself together, Gordon, It's going to be fine and another fantastic moment in my career. I'd like to say we won and had an open-top bus parade. Instead Rangers – who would go on to win the league – were outstanding and beat us 4-1.

Gers boss Walter Smith was first class with me and called me during my spell as caretaker to offer his support and comment on how well I was coping with the situation. Like the whole of Scottish football, I was shocked and saddened by the passing of Walter Smith on 26 October, 2021. He was a lovely man and will be greatly missed.

Ally McCoist, Ian Durrant and Kenny MacDowell were all great with me as well, as was Jim Jefferies, manager of Hearts. Steve Wright, then head of security at Celtic, was also very helpful to me in my last match at Parkhead against the Hoops on 30 December. Why do I mention Stevie? Well he came to the dressing room and said he had watched me in the two previous games, which were live on TV, and said: "I can't believe you're doing all of this on your own." He offered assistance on things like complimentary tickets and other similar time-consuming hassles. He arranged for my family and friends to be looked after with logistical assistance for them pre and post match. I really appreciated that. Incidentally, the hospitality and welcome I have had at Celtic any time I've gone as a scout or visitor coach has always been outstanding.

This was the final game of my stewardship. Former Rangers, Everton and Scotland midfielder Stuart McCall had agreed to come in and would start the next day, on Hogmanay, 2010. Stuart was a top bloke and we actually had a mutual friend in the game, so we became good friends and developed a great working relationship, which extended to his assistant, Kenny Black, Stewart Kerr, our goalkeeping coach, John Porteous, the physio, and his assistant, Anthony Stewart.

We had some great times together and he managed Motherwell to second in the league at the end of 2011/12 (Rangers had finished runners up to Celtic, but were demoted to the third division due to their financial problems) – and secured Champions League qualifying status for the club, which was a truly great achievement.

Throughout my caretaker role, club chief executive Leeann Dempster briefed me every day on the managerial situation. She also arranged for the club to pay me a bonus and for the board to write me a letter thanking me for my efforts, something I really appreciated.

The game at Parkhead to finish my stint, was the most disappointing for me as I felt we should have taken something from the game. We played really well, bossed the game for long spells and lost a soft goal right before half-time against the run of play. Keith Lasley hit the bar in the closing stages, with the home crowd whistling for full-time some 15 minutes from the end. I look back and laugh at the duties I had to perform that day, especially when I watch the multitude of match-day staff employed by the bigger clubs. I coordinated with club administrator Karen Paterson on the pre-match meal and travel arrangements and fielded requests from agents about our players who were going out of contract next day. Heartless bastards... the agents, not the players.

If you've ever flown by popular low-cost airlines and landed at various airports about 50 miles from the city destination, it always seems to me like there's only one guy that runs the full place, complete with a bag of hats like an old Tommy Cooper sketch. As soon as your plane taxis to a halt, a driver wearing a set of ear-muffs manoeuvres the mobile stairs up to your plane. As you get into the terminal off the plane, it looks like the same guy is now a border guard stamping your passport. Two minutes later, what appears to be his triplet is offering you some aftershave in the terminal kludgie. Then, as you head out the main entrance, the very same guy is sitting in the driver's seat of the coach waiting to transport you the 50-minute drive to the centre of the city.

Well, I was the equivalent of this fictitious guy as Motherwell caretaker manager. I did the press duties in my suit, changed into my track-suit and took the warm-up and delivered the tactical presentation and team talk. Then I changed back to my club suit for further press duties and managed the team from the sidelines!

As my time as Motherwell boss came to an end, I had a zero for three return/record and was feeling a wee bit sorry for myself. But always trust your friends to lift you at times like these. My mate, Billy Scott, was quick to point out, "Statistically, you're the worst manager in Motherwell's history!" Your mates really know how to put a smile on your face and put you back on a level pegging. Perversely, later in my career when I had three games – two wins and a draw – as caretaker manager of Dundee United... the same logic was used, "Statistically, he's one of Dundee United's best managers ever!" Another of my great friends, Fraser Dunn, would take pride in telling Billy. How I wish these stats were reversed.

I also balanced all of these extra-curricular first-team duties, whilst being academy director. Looking back, I think this could not have been possible without great family and friends. But how did I come to become the defacto manager of my childhood heroes?

With my boots well and truly hung up after playing against Republic of Ireland amateurs in October 2001, I put my shoulder to the grindstone and threw everything into coaching. By this time, my son, Robbie, aged 13, was a signed Motherwell player within the pro-youth system. My daughter, Jenna, then a 17-year-old, was embarking on a career in education, studying to be a PE teacher at Edinburgh University. So I felt I could commit more to trying to make my coaching work, with the full backing of my wife, Yvonne.

I have to admit I was getting a rush about Motherwell FC and what the club was trying to accomplish. Growth of its football academy was the goal and it was in need of a new structure and process from a football point of view and a new outlook on commercial thinking. This is where my HNC in Business Studies and years of working in sales and marketing jobs would come in handy, too. Now, I played with Motherwell as a teenager at what was then Fir Park Boys Club and also played in the reserves, but I never managed to play for the first team. I was a small, tricky winger in the mould of Celtic legend Jimmy Johnstone who hailed from a similar neck of the Lanarkshire woods – ie. give me a ball to myself and the other 21 players on the park another one. But, in the late 70s early 80s, the game was changing away from giving the ball to a wing wizard, for him to lead the full-back a merry dance and deliver a decent cross into the middle for the big striker to stick it into the net. In my heart, I knew this style of football that I loved, also had to change.

It was with this realisation in mind that I was right behind the push by former Motherwell captain Chris McCart – Motherwell 1991 Cup-winning hero who was at that stage in charge of Motherwell's youth development – when he dragged the club's youth set-up from a glorified boys club towards an academy fit for the 21st century.

Chris was a serious operator and had the vision to lay the early foundations for where it has grown to now and he and I got on extremely well. He, along with the management team at that time of Terry Butcher and Maurice Malpas, were the catalysts for the evolution of Motherwell as the club we know today despite the fact they had just entered into administration in April, 2002.

These were dark days for the Well. Manager Eric Black had resigned, they were £2million in debt and the club reluctantly had to make 19 players redundant, including current Belgium manager Roberto Martinez. We finished rock bottom of the Premier League and were only spared relegation as First Division winners Falkirk FC were denied promotion, as they did not have a stadium that met SPL standards. The Dossers did not have a pot to piss in as the pot had been sold for scrap and the piss was being bottled and sold as a remedy for jellyfish stings, anything to try and raise a wee bit of cash. Things had to change for the better and one of the main imperatives would be transforming the youth set-up to help develop quality players for the first team and eventually turning them into assets, which could bring in much-needed funds for the club. The coaching revolution was beginning across the country and conditions and standards had to improve at Motherwell.

We were very big on making our kids technically better and this would transform the academy, and propel Chris on to greater things at Celtic FC, where he reshaped their own academy. But, when he was still at the Well, he encouraged me to push on and take the badges I needed and to get involved with as much as I could at the club. This I did with great gusto. From helping with the under-15s, I moved on to the under-17s and then the reserves. Yes, seasoned professionals were gaining the benefit of my expertise as well as the newbies. I also welcomed getting involved with the junior academy, from nine to 10-year-olds, as my love for the club propelled me into helping them anyway I could.

When I look back I am immensely proud that not only did I play with my hometown professional team from teenager to the reserves, but that I managed and coached them from their under-10s to their first team. I doubt there are many in the game who could say that! To be able to do that, you need to carry qualifications from the children's licence pathway, via the youth version and culminating with the adult certificates.

Some people will focus on one of the pathways as it was set out as a three-tier model designed for coaches to hone a particular skill set. But I felt if I was going to head an academy, I would like to be equipped with all of the qualifications and pass the exams giving me knowledge of all departments in the academy structure. A similar analogy would be getting a McDonald's franchise, where despite having the money to invest in a unit, you have to work in all the areas of the process chain in order to seal the deal.

So I learned the football equivalent of sweeping the floor, flipping the burgers, ordering the baps and blowing up the Big Mac balloons, to give me a position of reality when dealing with coaches at all levels. I would also doubt that there were many coaches who could say that they ran into a hotel via the back stairway that was being evacuated by the fire brigade, just to keep up the pretence that they were snuggled up in their bed.

Of the many memories I have with Peter Millar, one that puts a great big smile on my face, is when we were away with two under-17s teams at a tournament in Newcastle. We were on our night off (honestly) and two fellow coaches were on night watch duty in the Caledonian Hotel, where our players were staying. Peter and I ventured out across the road to a nice hostelry for a wee chat and a beer. We had a window seat and a view of our digs and were just enjoying the first sips of our lager when the Geordie fire engine blues and twos came screaming round the corner. An evacuation of the hotel was underway and guests in various states of undress were starting to appear on the pavement outside. Peter and I looked at each other nervously even though we had nothing to feel guilty about as we were legitimately on a little time off. However, on some subliminal level, we both just understood that our charges would be less than amused if they were to be left standing in central Newcastle in their jammies or less, while their erstwhile coaches were sipping the amber nectar in a wine bar across the road.

Peter and I took one more sip and legged it out across the street and up the fire-escape at the side of the hotel, the only fools to run into a potentially burning building, shedding our clothes as we went. By the time we got to our room we were in our boxer shorts. We dumped our clothes, grabbed a T-shirt and headed down the stairs, managing to join our fellow coaches and our players at the muster point, with them being none the wiser. Standing on the pavement waiting for the all-clear to go back in after the false alarm, we eyed our two pints of lager on the table by the window of the bar, with only two sips taken out of them, being cleared away by the barmaid! Peter laughed as it was my round.

When Chris McCart left to join Celtic as head of youth development in June, 2008, he suggested to the Motherwell board that I take over his mantle. Chris himself was recommended to the great Scottish club by the legendary Tommy Burns, who played for and managed the Hoops with dignity, style and humility. This is another moment to cherish and I'll be eternally grateful to Chris for his belief and courage to champion me to take his place.

I have always been an avid reader of sporting biographies and memoirs – though not sure yet if I will ever pick up the one you are reading right at this very moment - just who does this Gordon Young prick think he is? – and, having read about the New Zealand All Black rugby team, I am struck by how apt one particular ethos of theirs is … 'Always leave the jersey in a better state than you found it'. I would like to think that when I left Motherwell in 2013 as academy director, I left the youth set-up in a better place than when I took it on from Chris. And I know for a fact that Chris certainly left Motherwell in a much better place when he went to Celtic. What he had crafted at Fir Park gave me the springboard to develop and enhance the club with new ideas and determination. When I took over, I was given carte blanche to raise the bar and raise the standards even further, to change the way we operated.

I brought in Willie Falconer – who had a fantastic career with Aberdeen, Watford, Middlesbrough, Sheffield United, Celtic and Motherwell, among others – to become my assistant as we had worked together with our under-17s. Someone who on the pitch could play anywhere, but mostly striker, Willie, like me, had a wee glint in his eye. He liked a laugh and was similar in character to me. Sometimes people say that you are better with opposites on your team as they attract, but we were the same and it worked a treat.

By this time I am academy director and I'm on yet another Scottish FA course, but I am now getting real enjoyment from these courses and lapping up the knowledge I am being exposed to. The interaction with qualified and experienced coaches was inspiring me, and I'm developing skills and networks that will serve me well for the future.

It was aslo getting to the stage that, even though Willie was my assistant, because of our excellent relationship, both personally as friends and professionally as a respected coaches, I was more than happy to give him responsibility to take teams on match days.

One such match against Dunfermline under-17/19s sticks in the mind. Now, my philosophy in coaching is, and always has been, to focus on the development of players. This doesn't mean to say I am not interested in the score during games my teams play, but I will say it is secondary to what I am really interested in, as it is not definitive for me. So when I call up Willie after the Dunfermline game for an update on how things went, my questioning went something along the lines of: How did we play? Who played well? Who needs more work? How was the preparation for the game? What was the attitude of the lads like before and during the match?

All fine according to Willie. Such and such was particularly strong and thingymyjig needs a bit of confidence. Oh, and we won 3-1. It was then, with great surprise, a couple of days later, I noticed in my in-tray a letter from the Scottish FA, ordering me to a disciplinary panel to answer for my red card during the match against Dunfermline!

I'm going to play this cool with my big mucker, I think and keep things calm when we meet up for a debrief and a cup of tea later in the week.

"So Willie, Dunfermline was a good game… now you've had time to reflect, anything more to report?"

"Well, Youngy, it was a decent performance, they kept their shape well and scored some good goals. A few could be doing with some refreshers on their role, but nothing major." Willie has a slurp of his tea. The conversation continues in this vein for 15 minutes until I drop the bombshell.

"Any reason why I would get a letter from the Scottish FA summoning me to a disciplinary meeting to answer my red card against Dunfermline FC and to discuss my suspension?" I enquire.

"Oh, Aye, I meant to tell you about that."

Willie went on to explain how the referee on the day was a "bell-end" and how he was not giving Motherwell anything at all in the way of fair decisions. Upon request to calm his remonstrations in the direction of the official, Willie then instructed the said referee to "go away" and enhance his officiating skills, whilst letting him concentrate on his own - in not as many polite words.

This infuriated the official even more and he produced the red card. On enquiring of his name, quick-thinking Willie had blurted out Gordon Young.

"Right, Mr Young, you need to leave the pitch side and you'll be reported to the SFA!"

Thanks, yah big numpty. So off I go to Hampden to face the beaks for something I didn't do. But I had a stroke of luck as embarrassment on behalf of the presiding disciplinary committee ensued and the complaint was back-heeled into the bin.

It turns out that a referee mistaking a famous Scottish professional player who is 6ft 2in tall, with a full head of hair, swarthy complexion and pretty good looking, who is clearly wearing the initials WF on his tracksuit top, for a 5ft 7in baldy with the initials GY is something they do not wish to be placed on record. Case dismissed, but I'll get you back later, Falconer!

The evolution of our academy was coming along, slowly but surely. According to the Club Academy Scotland criteria, I had to fill positions and roles, some of whom turned out to be well suited and others less so. There was one who I promoted to a full-time post as recruitment manager, who left one training night and I'm still waiting to hear from him that he has resigned, some 10 years later.

Some could step up to the demands, others wilted under the strain of creating excellence. This didn't apply to people like Paul Burns, my trusted shadow, Brian Reynolds, Graeme McArthur, Willie Burns, Stephen Hanley, Willie Pettigrew (yes the Grew himself), Steven Cadden, Willie Devine, Ricky Wadell, Raymond Murphy, Laura Wedlock and Chris 'Hilly' Hillcoat.

Hilly was outstanding on and off the pitch and went above and beyond so many times, including enlisting any member of his family who could contribute. He'd get his daughter to film games, his wife to make sandwiches and his brother-in-law to use his carpentry skills to make anything that came into my mind and, believe me, this was daily! And all this was on the back of being a first-class coach.

Of course, there were others who contributed and I know they benefitted reciprocally with the new structure. I even established links with the University of the West of Scotland to bring interns in to help medically, carrying out video analysis and helping on the IT side of things. Again all this was on volunteer basis, but we were able to offer free tickets to matches and access to the club as reciprocal trade. However, I can't stress enough how the entire staff at the club pulled together to totally transform the whole organisation, very often without any money and always begging, borrowing and doing everything short of stealing to make it work.

Ever seen 'Field of Dreams'? I loved that film. Kevin Costner's performance apart, it was a good movie and Burt Lancaster, James Earl Jones and Ray Liotta, really raised the bar. But the sentiment promoted in the story - "If you build it they will come" - always resonated with me.

In 2008 the training of our youth academy players was operating out of a 80x40 yard astro-turf area behind the East Stand next to Knowetop Primary School. Murray Park (Rangers' training ground now called the Hummel Training Ground) and Lennoxtown (Celtic's training complex), eat yer heart out! Leeann Dempster – the chief executive brought in by owner John Boyle from his Zoom travel firm – did a hard job well at that time and was spinning plates and robbing Peter to pay Paul, in order to keep cash in the business. She had to make a lot of difficult decisions given that the club had just come out of administration, and did a fantastic job.

At the Well, all the first-team managers 'got it', as I created a succession plan with a picture of every player from under-10s through to the first team by age and position. When you entered my office from left to right, you would see every squad on the wall from the youngest through to the first team, incrementally, highlighting the journey required from 'wee boy to man'. "You come in the front door and leave by the front door". This mantra meant that at any time we could see where the overload or deficiency by playing position was evident. That would trigger the recruitment process to fill any voids and trim away any surpluses we had, in order to be fair to each player brought in.

However, Leeann, in my opinion, was listening to the wrong people who were advising her that 'community financing' was the way to go, as it produced income on a daily basis and prioritised income streams and funding pots from the local and national bodies, who had money to be pitched for. Unfortunately these are one hit bids and not repeat revenue, so ultimately the well ran dry... if you pardon the pun. The academy was the pipeline to not only fuel the first team, but provide saleable assets which can be the difference between survival or closure for a club, particularly if you don't have a wealthy owner prepared to bankroll the organisation.

For me at that time the most important thing I was involved in was to find a home for the Motherwell Youth Academy and a self-financing package to keep it going. This would be the holy grail for the completion of a player pathway, that would end up yielding players for the club's first team, who could then do well and attract big-money transfers to benefit the club's operating coffers. So, like some bizarre version of 'Location, Location, Location', I would drive around the greater Motherwell area, scouting potential pitches that could be turned into an academy facility at a peppercorn rent. It was time consuming, but what a trip down memory lane it was for me, visiting all those old grass and ash pitches I had played on when I was a lad.

Names to conjure with: Netherdale Community pitches where I started playing the game, The Calder, The Dallies, Pather, King George V, The Ashy, The Great Soprendo... just kiddin' about the last one, but the fitba magic we produced on these parks would have been something a 70/80s TV illusionist would have been proud of, even though I do say so myself.

Little did I realise that the answer to our prayers was hiding in plain sight right under our noses, in the form of another of my best mates, Ian 'Stan' Murdoch, the education manager of North Lanarkshire Council. Stan and I had played together and through that friendship our families had been very close all our lives. He'd be my go-to guy, he was also my best talent scout and would leave Motherwell when I left to join Sheffield United. He moved to Rangers, where he currently works as one of their top youth scouts. "It's a no-brainer, wee man," he said to me as he made a professional approach to North Lanarkshire Council to see how they could possibly assist their premier professional club.

North Lanarkshire Council covers a large area and hosts several respected professional clubs such as Airdrie, Albion Rovers (Coatbridge) and Clyde (Cumbernauld), but Motherwell is by far and away the biggest of these in terms of history, support and stature in the game.

The impact a football club can have on a town is immeasurable especially, as in Motherwell FC's case, when its fans are inexorably and historically linked to steelmaking and, in particular, the Ravenscraig Works. Boasting 'The Steelmen' as one of its nicknames, it is not hard to imagine how the running down and subsequent closure of the massive steelworks in 1992, affected the community and the town.

Winning the Scottish Cup on 18 May, 1991, galvanised the area and brought everyone closer together, despite every man and their dug knowing that the writing was on the wall for the town's major job provider. It was a depressing time, but the pride in the victory, bringing tens of thousands out onto the streets of Motherwell for an open-top bus parade the day after the 4-3 win over Dundee United at Hampden Park, left an indelible mark on everyone, especially the powers that be.

Quite simply, the club means a great deal to the whole town and the local council know that more than most. So when I outlined to Stan – who is not even a Motherwell fan – what we needed and what we were looking for, he realised that this was something that North Lanarkshire Council would try their best to help with.

You know when you see statues of John Greig at Ibrox, Jock Stein at Parkhead, Billy Bremner at Leeds and you think: "Aye, they deserve to be immortalised in brass outside their spiritual fitba home," – you instantly recognise how synonymous with that team, how much success they helped to bring and that they totally deserve the accolade. I believe, if you used that analogy, then a statue should be installed of Stan outside Fir Park because of his immense input at that time on behalf of Motherwell FC, and you get the gist of how much respect I have for this man. I personally owe him a great debt of gratitude. It was he who, in 2010, introduced us to Braidhurst High School in the Forgewood area of North Motherwell. As a former Dalzielian (pupil of the town's Dalziel High School) I had played against them several times at school.

They always had a great team and I remember playing against Gary McAllister, who, as mentioned previously, once he had tired of keepie-uppie, would go on to play for Motherwell, Leicester City, Leeds Utd, Coventry, Liverpool and who lists Scotland captain amongst his achievements. He was until recently assistant manager to Steven Gerrard at Rangers. When I met the head teacher, Derrick Hannan – at that time an Airdrie season-ticket holder, one of our derby rivals – I wasn't sure if he was going to be the person to make our fairytale come true. That dream was creating a Fifa-registered, two star, Astro-turf pitch that would give us the basis of operating a youth set-up, which would deliver the standards required by the Club Academy Scotland regulations, categorising where clubs sat in the new football academy revolution. If I didn't get Motherwell to the top table, I ran the risk of recruiting a lesser standard of player, or other decent ones who would invariably choose the Old Firm or worse Hamilton, St Mirren, Hibs and Hearts over us, given we would have been playing lower-standard opposition and training in mediocre facilities.

It was a difficult enough job attracting potential young players in the Lanarkshire area, given the competition where, as well as traditional local rivals, the Old Firm and the Edinburgh clubs, you also have to counter the lure of Dundee United and Aberdeen who had satellite centres based in the area as well.

At a later Club Academy Scotland Heads of Youth meeting, I remember a proposal being discussed about the creation of regional academies. This was creating a 'shit storm' amongst the provincial clubs, who were deemed small enough to merge leaving the chosen few to remain autonomous. Some ended up going down this road and history will tell you that Falkirk suffered most, given that their academy, which was initially very successful, has only recently remerged after a period of inaction.

Anyway, I indicated at the meeting that Motherwell would be interested in exploring this proposal, which raised a few eyebrows to say the least. Yes, we could merge with Hamilton (unthinkable and unmanageable), Airdrie (maybe even more so) and Albion Rovers, I suggest.

"Gordon have you lost the fucking plot?" Read the message that is passed under the table to me from my colleagues at the meeting.

"Yes this is workable." I announced, "But we get first option on all players with a Lanarkshire postcode!" And you could hear SFA and big-club pin badges drop, as I delivered my coup de grace. Needless to say they moved on to the next item on the agenda very quickly.

Turns out Derrick Hannan too could have joined Stan on the plinth as he bought into my vision for world domination. He was outstanding and immediately recognised the benefits that could be brought to the school and to Forgewood – a historically deprived area of the town – with sports cash investment and backing from the council and Motherwell FC.

Soon a £1million facility – including changing-room block and a state-of-the-art Astro-turf pitch, full access to gym halls, sports barn, library for our after school programme and biscuits from the heidy's barrel - was in place. We transformed the dilapidated grass area into a match-approved facility for training and playing, "ya dancer", we were off and running.

North Lanarkshire Council offered us a ten-year rental agreement, but at that time all the club could offer back was reciprocal trade agreements... 500 free tickets for home games at Fir Park, helping to set up Braidhurst High School as one of the first 'Football Schools' in Scotland with the teenage players we signed – all within a 35-mile radius – attending the school for their academic and football education and giving something back to the local community.

The partnership between Braidhurst and Motherwell FC gave the school a new status in the area. And I used my sales and marketing background to rebrand the link within Scottish football as the 'Motherwell School', much to the consternation of other clubs outwith the Old Firm - who had their own initiatives. Alan Burrows, who was then head of media at the club, but is now current chief executive officer, and a self-confessed Well fan, must have been fed up with my requests for signage, banners, artwork and anything else I knew would make it "our school". He saw the benefit of the Academy and, in his then role, supported me and showcased us any way he could. My only regret is that we never had today's social media and TV platforms, which everyone uses, as we could have taken it to an even bigger level. Wow, steady down there wee fella.

Our model was envied across the country and ended up being copied by many other Scottish provincial teams, to support their own academies. In return for using the school campus, which we maxed out to the limit, I was more than happy to allow our academy players who attended Braidhurst, to play for their school team – many clubs still to this day do not allow this to happen. Every year Braidhurst prides itself on fielding some of the best school teams in Scotland and, as a result of our cooperation, they have won the Scottish Cup every other year. This should not to be confused with 'pot hunting' but rather as a benchmark for the school standard at all times.

Derrick and Stan were quite simply fantastic, and for them to buy into my vision was brave and insightful and has certainly paid dividends for the club, the school, the council, the town and Forgewood itself. Without being over dramatic, the Motherwell Academy would not be in existence without the tri-party alliance of North Lanarkshire Council, Braidhurst High School and, of course, Motherwell FC. Ian (Stan), Derrick and myself ensured this would not only happen, but succeed.

As we developed the academy through the Scottish FA's Club Academy Scotland (CAS) initiative we had to embrace change throughout the club. Roles, responsibilities, pay grades and governance procedures all had to come into line with the recommendations of Mark Wotte – who was the Scottish FA's Performance Director and Technical Director of National Teams from 2011-2014. And all clubs in Scotland with an academy had to comply.

Making academies accountable allowed clubs to claim compensation if bigger clubs came in and lured away our best players. So it was important that we had all our ducks in a row and paradoxically – even though we were not in a great place financially – we were in a good position to revamp our whole youth set-up to meet requirements.

We quickly moved away from the 'fans-with-tracksuits' stereotype that was associated with youth set-ups at professional clubs. A workforce was assembled and even if they were not Motherwell oriented, they soon became so.

A strategy document was created, making us accountable to the governing body and professionalism was oozing from the club's pores. Not only did it satisfy the governing body's requirement for funding assistance, it was a blue print for a generation of young players who would grace the Motherwell first team and/or be sold to give the club a financial safety net for the future. A Motherwell philosophy was emerging – it was a gruelling period to go through administratively creating the strategic plan as a document – but I was more proud of how it was implemented. I can look back now and applaud a dedicated coaching staff who can hold their heads high and see the fruits of their labour sitting in the club's bank account. It was ultimately worth it when you look at the talent that has come through the Motherwell Academy and contributed to helping the club to become debt free in early 2020, after becoming the first UK top-flight club to become entirely fan owned in 2016 thanks to the innovative Well Society, which was established in 2011.

It has been these fans, more than most, who have been the beneficiaries of the academy and its philosophy, as they welcomed a conveyor belt of ready-made, golden-boy homegrown heroes, whom they could worship from the terraces.

CHAPTER

Goldfinder

Discovering stars of the future worth millions - and then holding on to them - took hard work and a brilliant team of staff

The Academy and the link with Braidhurst High School had now become part of the heartbeat of the club, and had even been studied closely by other teams. I know for a fact we were discussed in premier club circles in Scotland and England, as I used this successful model as a blueprint when Sheffield United poached me in 2013 as their International Academy Manager (more on this later). In 2008, Braidhurst became one of only seven Scottish FA designated School of Football facilities in the country, where young players from Lanarkshire could apply for a place to study. The school would also be awarded the SFA Quality Mark Award for outstanding educational provision and National Sports Comprehensive Status and become a Scottish FA Elite Performance School of Football. As for Derrick, who retired in 2015 after 23 years as headteacher at the school, he has gone from being an Airdrie season ticket holder when I arrived, to never missing a Motherwell home game at Fir Park! And I would always make sure that he would join us at the annual photo-shoot with all the Motherwell Academy players… That's enough to make the old 'Section B' Airdrie stalwarts choke on their Bovrils. But what a champion of North Lanarkshire he has become. Derrick was old school, a respected BB officer and a real disciplinarian at the school and I loved him as he backed me all the way.

I also made sure incumbent managers, senior players and any contacts I worked with in the game, all came in and visited the school. That was the norm not the exception and staff, pupils and parents loved it. When then manager Mark McGhee left for Aberdeen in June 2009, club captain Stephen Craigan and I led the first two early weeks of first-team pre-season on the Braidhurst grass pitch, in preparation for early preliminary Europa League matches, as Dalziel Park wasn't ready. The Braidhurst High School facility quickly became synonymous with Motherwell FC and was referred to regularly as the 'Motherwell School'. It very quickly became a place where professional clubs dreaded to visit, as they knew they would be up against some of the best teams in Scotland.

It also had an added dread, which led it to becoming known by another name. Willie Burns, a native of Forgewood, was one of my best coaches and a bank manager to trade… hey, that's two or three things you don't read very often in a sentence about someone from Forgewood. After a few months of resounding victories and impressive displays – which attracted the locals out to support us – Willie turned to me and said: "Youngy, you've created the 'Colosseum' down here." He was of course referring to the growling young gladiatorial locals who would gather to watch us play and try with great success to intimidate our opposition. Granted – and let's give them their due – they gathered to watch us train as well and successfully managed to intimidate the hell out of us too! "You should get majestic lion statues and monuments and pillars placed around the pitch to capture that feel of ancient Rome," Willie continued. But we couldn't get the planning permission! However, I'm sure the hedonistic orgies, gratuitous violence and free-flowing wine Forgewood was famous for, more than made up for it. OK, joking there, well maybe about the hedonistic orgies… that was more the Greenacres area of the town!

What we did manage to get permission for was to create a special football area to get the Forgewood young team onside. Our groundsman and his staff helped to transform a wee grass area into a usable surface and we gave them portable goals, balls and even strips for them to use to their hearts' content. They were delighted and the abuse fell to just the one "Fuck off yah Dobber!" per training night.

As with everything in Scottish football, the Old Firm are never far away in anything that you do. But the great thing about Motherwell as a club and its long history, is that we like nothing better than seeing the big two brought down a peg or two. I remember Willie McStay – brother of Celtic legend Paul and a top player and coach in his own right – brought a team of his best down to play us at the Colosseum. As usual the big club had their demands… how many periods of play there would be (two, three, or four), how long they would be, how many subs we could use etc… and Willie was also very insistent: "Oh and our lads will be doing the Huddle before the game." Without missing a beat, I informed him: "No problem, our lads will be doing the hokey cokey!" I was buzzing and to be fair to Willie, he had a giggle to himself. Sure enough, the Forgewood locals also made sure they put their left legs in and their left legs out, and shook it all about pretty comprehensively, as they watched their favourites in claret and amber take on the Hoops that day. Likewise, a Rangers Under-17s squad led by top youth coach Billy Kirkwood ventured down to Forgewood to play a Well side taken by two outstanding coaches, Chris Hillcoat and Ricky Waddell, both part of my inner sanctum war council. The Motherwell team boasted up and coming youngsters such as Chris and Nicky Cadden, David Ferguson, Jack McMillan, Robbie Young, Ross McLean and Dylan Mackin. Davie Kirkwood said to me later over a cup of tea in my office, that playing at the Colosseum was more hostile than playing in an Old Firm match! I think the locals were out in force that night, too, and let the visitors know exactly what they thought of them. I took what Davie had said as a big compliment, as it showed the passion our fans had for our club. I did have to draw the line, though, at the offer from a local who wanted to take his mates up to the top of a neighbouring block of flats adjacent to the pitch, and use the opportunity as target practice for their air rifles.

The belief right the way through the Motherwell Academy was growing and with the right people in place, everyone was buying in to what we were trying to do. Within in a short space of time there was a vibrancy and energised environment at the club that was tangible, exciting and helping to move Motherwell in the right direction. Every single coach and member of staff in my team played their part and at the weekly meetings you could see the pride that was being taken in their work, as they excitedly gave their player reports and news.

As well as rolling out the coaching curriculum, I was using my marketing experience to create income streams and came up with many ways to add a few quid to the kitty. I was using topical merchandise to customise our brand and the 'live the dream' wrist-band, based on Lance Armstrong's version, raised a whopping £25,000 from our fan base. This effort was particularly poignant for me as the club gave me a weekend break at Stobo Castle Hotel and Spa as a thank you, and I took great pleasure in passing it on to Yvonne and her wonderful mother Jean, who was sadly at that time, fighting her losing battle with cancer. Dog tags, thunder clappers and annual calendars, were other money makers for us and the families were terrific at supporting me as the funds were primarily ring fenced for tournaments, where I thought the players would gain additional learning in their football development.

We were living and dying together by two key sayings. No 1: if you come in the front door, you go out the front door... in other words, you treat everyone with respect, regardless of how long they have been with the club. No 2: Is he good enough to play for our first team? We would make that decision collectively as my five-member inner circle (lead coaches in the Junior, Intermediate and Senior Academies, the Head of Recruitment and myself) would have to agree.

We were using a system similar to 'Moneyball' – where smaller teams compete by using statistical analysis, buying assets that are undervalued by other teams and selling ones that are overvalued. In this we were making strides with strategies and operating systems which would yield some impressive returns later, given it takes a cycle of about ten years to harvest the stock, if you are able to plan and prepare well, akin to the

Olympic 10,000 hours practice theory. Succession planning was very important to us at Motherwell. If we sold or lost a player, we knew exactly who was above and below them on the grid and who was in the pecking order to move up. As we all sang from the same hymn sheet on our style of play and how we wanted our players to play on the pitch, in theory a player could step up and fill the role vacated in the team above.

I created a curriculum bespoke to Motherwell and targeted specific traits in young players with emphasis on technical ability, laced with the ingredients I thought were necessary to create a professional player. I insisted in all players being able to "handle, deal with and control the ball" regardless of their physical prowess and we were "building from the back", even before Manchester City! I would instruct the coaches to create players comfortable on the ball as well as demanding things like taking all dead-ball situations short, to encourage ball mastery and confidence. The curriculum would be topical in terms of themed sessions, but I wanted each coach to take our 'signature drills' and put their stamp on it depending on their age-specific teams, and create the pathway for our 'best' players.

Money was still extremely tight, but because we were all true believers in our goal of producing a conveyor belt of talent for the first team, if we needed something done or built, we would find a way, call in a favour from a tradesmen mate, twist an arm, or do it ourselves.

'Field of Dreams' was once again nagging away in the back of my mind, when I wondered what we could do with the void empty space situated in the bowels of the South Stand at Fir Park. It may house 4,000 away fans but, especially after Rangers and Celtic had rocked up, there were a few dozen fewer seats after they left the stadium, due to the fact that a small section of their crowd would insist on ripping out some to take home with them every time they visited. I have a vision of some Glasgow dwellings boasting an away section of their very own with a seat from every SPL ground. "Aye come in mate, take a seat, I know I did...Guffaw, Guffaw... Aye anywhere in the second row there between McDiarmid Park No 74 HH and, Fir Park 42 P. Now what did you say you wanted officer?" And yes I do realise all clubs have their own troublesome 'small' section but the Old Firm, worryingly, tend to have several more than anyone else with extreme plastic seat fetishes!

Anyway, the space wasn't massive, but it wasn't insignificant either. I had been mulling it over when we took on a lad who was out on a probation scheme from prison. Motherwell had become very good at outreach projects such as this, trying to give something back to help the community. He was a painter and decorator by trade – when not getting banged up – and we had a few jobs ready to go for him. A few days earlier, I had taken my son Robbie in to run the rule over the benefits of Kevin Keegan's Soccer Centre, which had pitched up at Braehead at the time. Robbie loved the concept of what was really disguised practice, except you got your arse felt for the

'I can't thank him enough for all he has done for me'

David Turnbull, Celtic and Scotland star and former Motherwell Youth Academy graduate, said: "Youngy had a huge impact on me at the start of my career. I was asked to come into Motherwell's Academy when I was about nine, for a six-to-eight-week trial period, and, after one or two weeks, he wanted to sign me. He was regularly speaking to me and my mum and dad and that support was really helpful. He was a top coach, and, as head of the youth academy, he would take our training some nights and I always really enjoyed it. In fact, we all really enjoyed it, especially the tactical side of things, despite us only being young boys at that time. He was serious about his coaching, but he could be funny, too. One pre-season we were doing a keepie-uppie drill and one of my team-mates – a good player – was struggling a bit with keeping the ball up and Youngy got it off him and punted it over the fence as far as he could and told him to fetch. That gave us all a good laugh. I remember he would give me freedom to do what I wanted to influence games as much as I could, and knowing that he had that kind of faith in me, was a real confidence boost. He was also very encouraging when it came to selection for Scotland squads and I wasn't getting picked, and I remember one night at training at Braidhurst he pulled me out of the session. I was a wee bit scared to be honest that the head of the academy was wanting to see me like this, and I wondered what I had done. But he just wanted to explain to me that he had just had words with Mark Wotte at the Scottish FA and he had told him what he thought about me not being picked for a specific squad! He is a top man as a person, too. Even after he left Motherwell, he has kept in touch with me and my dad and he will still text me with encouragement and support and I'll text him back. After my first medical at Celtic picked up on the issue with my knee, Youngy texted me and we met up for a coffee and he helped me make sure my mindset was OK and said he would be there if I needed anything. He is one of my favourite ever coaches and I can't thank him enough for all he has done for me."

privilege to the tune of £15 a pop. It was all lights and lasers in a football box and was billed as the latest thing to develop technical ability in young players. Well, for all the hundreds of thousands of pounds old Kevin spent on his idea – no doubt earned from falling off his bike and scraping his back on BBC's Superstars – I created something just as effective with four cans of paint and 60 metres of duck tape. "Oh, he'd have just luuvvveedd that!", recalling his meltdown at good old Sir Alex. Mind games in football are something I've always loved and no doubt more than a few of you will relate to how Fergie hooked Keegan in, back when he was challenging Manchester United for the league title with his Newcastle side.

I hope my very own Dossers' Da Vinci is reading this book so he can get in touch with me and let me know how he is getting on. I'll bet he runs his own successful business now, because he was truly brilliant with what he came up with, armed only with my A4 piece of paper and a few dimensions. He created possession boxes, passing zones, dribbling tracks, keepie-uppie areas and head tennis courts, all colour coordinated. It proved to be somewhere our young players would and could practice, pre and post training, on all their technique to perfect their skills. It was something I would replicate everywhere I went after Motherwell, with great success. And all I paid for it was £40 for paint and essentials and a homemade lasagne, which my pro-bono painter managed to smuggle into Shotts Prison. I still meet players now who remembered the 'Skill Centre' and my obsession for them to 'check' their shoulder with a look, before performing each technique. Campbell Money, former St Mirren goalie and now respected coach, paid me one of the best back-handed compliments ever, when he said: "Youngy, if you put all the teams in different kits, you'd still know who the Motherwell players were by how they checked their shoulders to encourage spatial awareness." Cheers Campbell, but if they didn't check their shoulder I'd volley their ball away, so that they had to run after it.

The thing we were really looking for was a major sponsor to cover the seven teams that made up the academy. Again, a very good mate of mine was to help us with an introduction that would prove fruitful. I mentioned Billy 'The Buff' Scott earlier. Well, at that time he was (and still is) the Scottish Manager of MITTON, a large Bradford-based shop outfitter, and I floated the idea to him of his firm becoming the one exclusive major sponsor of our Academy, instead of the seven individual ones we had at that time, ranging from local garages to well-heeled fans. I set up a meeting with the owners of the firm, who were big football people and keen to evolve their footprint in the West of Scotland region. "Your timing is good wee man," said Buff, "they're keen to get involved and are down to earth guys. Keep it sensible and we'll get it over the line." Jackpot, I thought. Before they flew up to meet me and have a tour round the facilities and the club, Billy and I had a wee catch-up so that I could run past him what we might be looking for in a three-year sponsorship deal. I was itching to put my negotiating skills to good use and I was also looking for a steer from Billy on what MITTON might be able to stretch to. To sponsor all our teams for three seasons – which would include name on strips, trackside advertising at Fir Park, programme advertising and regular hospitality packages – we would be looking at £5,000 a year. I told Billy. He thought that might be possible, but only just. After a good meeting, an even better lunch and some agreeable refreshments, I was asked by the MITTON owner's son Steven Taylor – as Billy intimated, a top guy – "Well Gordon, How much?" "£20,000 a year, should cover it!" I thought, as well in for a sheep as in for a lamb and watched as Billy Scott's jaw hit the Fir Park boardroom carpet, like Wylie Coyote's does in those Roadrunner cartoons when the bird takes off at 1000mph! Billy's face was a picture and I wish the boys from the Electric Bar had seen him, as this is the guy who will tell us he's never wrong. In fact, I'm told he once auditioned for Mastermind and Magnus Magnusson asked him what his specialised subject was and he said, "Oh just you pick one." Once the smelling salts had revived Billy and we had put his jaw back in place, another couple of drinks were ordered and we agreed a three-year deal for £50,000. What a great result for the academy and for MITTON, who were delighted. Ironically, later that year a Motherwell live Sky TV game had to be halted due to high winds. A sponsorship hoarding had come loose from the top of the East Stand and the aluminium banner was waving in the wind. Yip, you've guessed it, there was MITTON'S branding wafting around for all to see and what a great bit of free national exposure. Granted the tradesman who fixed up the hoarding probably had a few questions to answer!

At this point I also need to mention Sandy Kilpatrick, owner of Maxim Power Tools, who was then and still is another unbelievable supporter and sponsor of the Motherwell Academy. He is a shrewd businessman and in order to access his extremely generous contributions, he would insist on the rationale behind each donation. We struck up a great rapport and he backed my ideas every time.

It's guys like Sandy and the many others too numerous to mention, that every club needs to back them.

While all this was happening players had to be scouted and games had to be played and Motherwell was building a formidable reputation for developing young players, who were regularly being poached by both sides of the Old Firm. I used to tell any player and his family if I had received an enquiry for them from the big two, long before this was mandatory. My rationale to them was for our player to wait, work hard and make it at Motherwell and then make the move to Glasgow when they came back in with another offer down the line. If they did this they would go as credible first-team players and they'll be even more keen to buy them… ahem, step forward David Turnbull and Jake Hastie, two players I signed. Rather than go as a young potential players and run the risk of being swallowed up by the machine, they waited and developed at Motherwell before signing for Celtic and Rangers respectively. I can put my hand on heart and say that not many, if any, who chose the early switch option to the Old Firm, made the breakthrough. However, you could never compete against young players who were dyed in the wool Rangers and Celtic fans. They just wanted to play for their heroes, no matter how much you tried to explain to them they would have a better chance of making it and playing first-team football by staying with the Well.

My objective was to create players who could play for Motherwell's first team and if not, to develop players to be the best they could be and stay in the game at preferably a professional level, or in the other strands of our game. This is something I think has been achieved when you see the numbers who can quote Motherwell as their formative development club. Still we managed to nurture youngsters who were regularly being picked for international representation at under-15, 17, 19 and 21 level. No mean feat for a provincial Scottish club, who would only seriously consider signing players who lived within a 35-mile radius of Motherwell, as we were aware of the taxing commitment it is for parents and siblings to get their starlet to training and games up to five times a week.

I also worried that young players were being over-hyped by their parents, and also worried that a bi-product was the potential detriment to a sibling's personal development, as all energy went into 'the blue eyed boy', who they were sure was going to earn £100,000 a week. The reality is that only two per cent of youngsters 'make it' and therefore you should have a strong exit strategy to support 98 per cent disillusioned wannabe millionaires. These worries made me make sure that when young players signed for the club as an academy prospect, I insisted that there were nights off for Halloween, Bonfire Night, as well as Christmas parties, to allow kids to be kids. I'd also recommend that during their downtime from the Academy they should increase their social inclusion by participating in other sports and recreational activities, especially with their respective schools. When you play with your mates, your family and school friends, you'll do things that you won't necessarily do within a structured practice session, so you're learning in a different environment. I also wanted them to go away in the summer and 'park the ball' to give them a hunger when they returned, as well as enjoying 'being a kid'.

This was all much to the consternation one day of a blinkered parent who would tell me that wee Johnny would be out the back practising every day during his six-week summer recess. What a misguided fool! Stop living your dream out through your son and stop his performances being your sole offering in the pub gossip with your mates. If he's not one of the two per cent, you'll have nothing to talk about in the boozer in a few years' time and then let's see if you can devote the same amount of time to him, when he'll really need your support in redirecting his career at the same time his dreams have been crushed.

In my early days, as well as creating a strategic plan, which opened the door for a 'periodisation' and full coaching curriculum, I developed a log book for each player acting as a personal planner for their development. Within the log book - which encompassed: diet, nutrition, recording of sessions, sports science results, as well as advice on how preparation and recovery would aid the desire to be the best they could be - there was a section devoted to their attributes, which was assessed by their coaches every six weeks. This included basic principles which served as a barometer for their development and a simple tool to highlight any progression or regression, meaning we could build a profile on each player and if anyone was needing extra attention, it would never be any more than six weeks before it was provided, with every log book being signed off by coach, player and parent. For example, if someone went three cycles (18 weeks) without improvement, alarm bells would ring and we would enter dialogue with all, to ascertain any reason for regression. This may have been anything from growth spurts, exams at school, domestic changes in their life or some other non-football issue, as opposed to an 18-week loss of form, which isn't possible.

Furthermore, as I watched most of the games at the weekend and delivered signature drill sessions to all age groups, as well as being there every night when all groups trained, you needed the back up to your mind's eye and the coach's opinion, which I got in the form of the log book. In addition, I wanted everyone to record their personal information and build up a record year-on-year of their vital characteristics, which could be used as part of the exit strategy I referred to earlier. If they didn't make it as a footballer, I was confident that if they were in an interview process in any given industry and they produced the log book highlighting commitment, team playing ethics, lifestyle and organisation, then any employer would see that as important to any qualifications required for any particular position.

One day, I was going over the log books with a coach from the under-13s and one particular player is flagging the 18-week regression, which prompted a parents meeting. I'm assured everything outside the Academy was fine and not to worry. But I was still worrying as this kid had been a prolific scorer the year before and always cut about with a smile and a swagger. This went on for 24 weeks and in academy time that is half a year of the programme, triggering another assessment. At this point I suggest a break from the Academy for the lad and we'd look at his situation with a six-month sabbatical to regain confidence with less pressure, at a designated boys club which we had links with for this particular purpose. Well, the dad went mental and accused me of all sorts, from favouritism towards other players to well, just being a prick… aahh the banter. If you're stuck for words in Scotland, call someone a prick, male or female it doesn't matter. A month later I get a call from Karen Paterson, our admin guru, who says the dad wants another meeting with me and I suggest a time outwith the Academy hours. I put in my gum-shield, but get a shock when both dad and son come in at the designated time. The dad hands me a bottle of whisky, reaches out to shake my hand warmly and announces that his son has something to say to me. "I've not been enjoying playing football for a year and I want to play guitar in a band," says the new Eric Clapton. Turns out his father had been pushing him to feed his own ego and the kid had been wanting to pursue another route. There were no hard feelings from either party and this is why you need to have a particular skill set to manage an academy. They came in the front door and left by the front door.

There are many stories I could tell about the players who I watched develop during my time as Motherwell FC Academy Director, but one or two contrasting tales stick in my mind. One is regarding a serious hot Scottish talent at that time – Paul Slane – who came through the Academy and into the first-team squad. I had realised his potential as a kid and pestered Chris McCart to take him in full-time. He was my type of player, a pacey winger with a trick and not short of personality. Chris wasn't convinced he did enough in games, but I felt what he did was more than some players could achieve in terms of end product. Ironically, he would sign for Celtic once he had broken through at Motherwell.

I fostered a strong relationship with his family and championed him for the under-age Scotland squads constantly. I'm sad he never realised his true potential as he had exceptional talent. At this time he had broken into the first team and was in the fans' opinion 'the next Faddy' (James McFadden) and I wanted him to stay with Motherwell and sign a new contract. So when I took charge of the first team when Craig Brown and Archie Knox left, I was adamant I could get him to sign a new contract. My Academy pathway conveyor-belt eyes – which judged Paul to be a kid who had kicked on and would be a top Motherwell player – must have misted over as I gave him the nod against Hearts at the expense of flying Jamaican winger Chris Humphrey. I had misjudged the situation, thinking Paul would sign the new Well contract on the table, and put him in the team. In the end he reneged on the deal and ended up signing a four-year contract with Celtic. Very soon after I went to see Chris Humphrey and apologised to him for a poor man-management decision. Chris would go on to become an excellent player for Motherwell, terrorising defences with his pace and delivery and claiming international honours in two or three great seasons at Fir Park. I would later coin an adage to sum up situations like this: "We rave too much, we judge too early and we risk too little." Such is the subjective nature of Scottish football.

I can also state for the record that every decision I ever made regarding team selection and player recruitment, was done with the clear purpose of good intentions for the player and for Motherwell FC, and never for personal reward or recognition.

Great wee players too numerous to mention stick in my mind, but it is impossible not to have favourites. As mentioned previously, staving off the Old Firm vultures was always the hardest task when players were doing well. They would come in, make offers and turn the heads of players and their parents. However, some would really believe in our philosophy and the pathway and Bob McHugh stood out for me in this respect. In my opinion he was the best centre forward of his age-group in the country. Capped for Scotland at every age-group apart from senior level, Bob was a colossus emerging from the colosseum, even though he was only 5ft 10 inches tall. Still currently playing, at the age of 30 with Queens Park, Bob made 70 first-team appearances for the Steelmen between 2008 and 2015, though I always fancied him to make a bigger impact in the game at the top level. Bob was similar to Wayne Rooney and could score goals anywhere, from a yard out to the half-way line. He was also an early bloomer in terms of his growth spurt and physical development. He was also similar to John Fleck, who was playing with the maturity of a man in the academy leagues for Rangers.

Also, like Rooney, he was a real character in the dressing room. For a full season I did not realise he was wearing a Celtic top underneath his Motherwell strip and underneath that, he once also proudly sported a cock and balls on his torso, drawn with a 'Sharpie' pen before a match, by one of his team-mates. Not sure Ronaldo, Giggs or Scholes ever did this to Rooney for a laugh at Man United though! Regardless of who he supported, Bob's commitment to Motherwell was unwavering. One day I had just named the team for a game against Kilmarnock with McHugh as No 9, when the bold Bob sidles up to me pretty sheepishly and says, "Boss my mum's forgotten to pack my boots in my bag!". "Your mum does not play for us Bob, so you are not playing for us today," I replied. Such was the strength of our squad, Ryan Martin came in and scored a hat-trick as we won the match. But Bob would knuckle down at training during the week and would start up front in the next game, and he never forgot his boots again.

Steven Lawless – who in January, 2021, re-signed with Motherwell from Burton Albion, before leaving once again in October of the same year – was another kid with a story. I had taken over from Chris and was doing a walk round of the teams one training night and found out that due to an anomaly, he had been released after breaking his ankle. I spoke with his dad and offered him a stay of execution, which he grabbed with both hands. He earned a full-time contract, international caps at age-group level and is still making a great career from the game, all this despite the humorous intervention that night of his good pal Peter Innes, who himself was a product of the system and a very funny lad.

I always made a point of scouting clubs beneath us in the food chain and had success in bringing in Steven Saunders and Gary Smith from Queen's Park, who at that time were amateurs. Scotland's oldest club would refuse our compensatory offers due to their status. Another was Nicky Devlin. He would definitely have gone on to play for the first team and become a long-serving player or have been sold like some others, but for a bad knee injury which I'm delighted only stalled a sterling career. I liked him at Dumbarton and they gratefully accepted the compensation, which I had calculated and got approval for from the board. However, I hadn't expected the phone call I received after we had signed Nicky which came from his 'agent' demanding his cut. Jings, who would have thought 17-year-old Dumbarton players at that time would have had an agent? I explained the club wouldn't pay agents for youth players and we could look at inserting a sell-on fee if he was sold, but he wasn't having this and was even threatening to take legal action. I couldn't go back to the club, so I paid him £500 out of my own money. I hope the agent concerned reads this and hangs his head in shame.

That was a great squad, with the likes of Coutts, Gallacher, Saunders, Hutchinson, Quinn, Halsman, Devlin, Innes and Meechan supplying a forward line consisting of Martin, Lawless, McHugh, Smith and Slane. Eight of that squad were under-19 internationals and I even got a call from the SFA to announce Hutchy was to be another, before I had to remind them that he was in fact English. I also secured the services of Jonathan Page from Portsmouth, Adam Cummins from Everton and Zaine Francis- Angol from Tottenham Hotspur, who would all go on to play for the first team at home and in Europe. They'd soon be followed into the first team by Ross McKinnon, Keiran MacDonald, Lee Erwin and Jamie Pollock – I'm still surprised Jamie never went to the top and can see similarities in him with how my own career turned out. There was more to come and Stuart Carswell, Luke Watt, Darren Brownlie, Jack Leitch and Keiran McGachie began to lay down their top-team credentials. Then we brought in Brett Long, Ben Hall, David Ferguson, Adam Livingstone, Craig Moore, Steven Hetherington and the Cadden brothers Nicky and Chris. Soon it would be time for David Turnbull, Allan Campbell, James Scott and Jake Hastie. Chuck in the support acts of Kyle Connell, David Devine, Stuart McKinstry (who has just made his debut with Leeds United), Reece McAlear (who joined Norwich City in 2019) and Murray Miller… are you starting to get the picture of how all this hard work off the field was beginning to pay off on it?

I loved that initial group of players and also the ones who would follow them. They all had personalities and character in abundance and it was important for us to develop a viable exit strategy for players who did not make the grade as a professional footballer, but wanted to stay in the game. One of the ways I did this was by forming close relationships with the Lanarkshire Junior clubs. After four nights of training in and around the Well 'training centre', I was determined that a match day should be different for the 13-19 age groups and felt that the experience of them playing in a stadium environment on a Sunday and getting changed in traditional dressing rooms would be beneficial for their development. I'd seen so many games over the years played at training venues, and although practical in terms of logistics, they morphed into glorified 'bounce games'. Having extensive playing experience in the Junior ranks myself and as well as knowing that these clubs sometimes struggled during the week to find floodlit training pitches – and personally knowing the managers who I had played with or against in my career – I offered them our floodlit Astro-turf area behind the East Stand at Fir Park. In return they allowed our lads to play their home games at the Junior grounds on a Sunday. This allowed our players to develop a matchday experience to differentiate from practice sessions and gave them a flavour of professional football organisation set-ups. This subsequently strengthened our relationships with teams such as Thorniewood, Blantyre Victoria, Bellshill Athletic, Shotts Bon Accord and Bathgate Thistle. Playing our homes games at these clubs' grounds also showcased our up and coming youngsters and as a result many were farmed out to Junior clubs as they developed. It also meant that the Motherwell Academy players who did not make the professional grade, were able to easily transfer over to the Junior game and continue with a worthwhile and profitable playing career.

As mentioned previously, I was open to player recommendations from far and wide, with agents providing me with talent which supplemented our pathway programme. One such addition was a young Polish goalkeeper called Sebastian Korasowski or 'Fucksake' Seb as he became better known at his age-group. This was a result of the striking firepower we had at that time and the quality of finishing at training, where frustrated defenders would end up saying "Fucksake Seb" every time a ball flew past him. He was a smashing lad and made a vow to learn to speak English, which he did at a rate of knots as quick as the speed of the shots going past him. When he told me his dad was coming over to visit him, I invited them both to dinner at my home. Yvonne mentioned this to her dad who joined us all one Sunday along with Jenna and Robbie. This then descended into a two-hour situation comedy style performance with Seb in tears of laughter, as his own dad didn't speak English and both him and Yvonne's dad developed a mutual sign language with each other, demonstrating the usual flapping of arms to denote chicken and horns to denote beef in the steak pie. The best was when Yvonne asked her own father if he wanted peas and he automatically replied in pigeon English: "No, I... PAUSE... do... PAUSE... not .... PAUSE... want... PAUSE... peas." To be fair, my Polish visitors both seemed to understand my hospitality when I asked: "Do you want another drink?" Yet another comedy gold scene in the Young household as my inspirational dining room table moved from Motherwell FC Christmas tactics board to encouraging cordial diplomatic relations with European visitors to our shores.

One of the things I covertly offered the under-19s who were professional apprentices looking to make a career, was win bonuses. This was a small gesture, say £10 a win, and I'd get people to sponsor the outlay, although a lot of the times I'd bite off more than I could chew and end up paying them myself. I felt that if and when they transited to the first team, they'd be in a dressing room with pros who might be depending on that win bonus to support their families and hoped it would bring home the reality of what winning means in the professional game.

I was never one for sugar coating things. I probably learned that from when my dad took me to the dentist to have a tooth removed and I asked if it would be sore. "Yes!" Wullie replied without blinking. Fuck me he was right, but at least I was prepared.

Anyway, we're up at the Highland Academy in Dingwall one day to play Inverness and with only a few games to go in the league, we are neck and neck with Celtic in the race for the title. However, the home team Inverness are sitting third with what was their best crop of youngsters to date. I tell our lads before the match that they're on a tenner to win. At half-time we're 1-0 up, so I tell them that a clean sheet takes us top of the league and promptly double the £10 to £20 if they do so. We go 5-0 up and with five minutes to go, Inverness counter attack on us from our corner and their big striker breaks through from the half-way line in a one on one with our goalkeeper, Steven Coutts. But then out of nowhere appears Peter Innes, not the quietest boy you'll ever meet, but as mentioned earlier a funny gem of a lad. He finds a turbo blast from somewhere and cements the attacker just outside the box. A straight red awaits him and every Motherwell player rushes to embrace the East Kilbride kick boxer and almost carry him off the park. That's what £20 means to young kids and reinforces my decision to incentivise them. As Peter is walking to the dressing room, I see my old mates, Terry Butcher and Maurice Malpas – the incumbent management team at Inverness – signal to me in amazement asking, "What the fuck just happened there?" Important player development I think to myself.

If I was hyper-critical about Leeann Dempster, it would be that she did not see just how important it would be to not only back the Academy, but invest in it. From time to time she asked me if we had any £1million players in the Academy, which I explained was not measurable and that these would come in good time, as well as stating that it was market forces that would determine a player's worth. It fills me with immense pride that the club has enjoyed the honey-pot of player sales because they stuck with the process and names such as Jamie Murphy, Mark Reynolds, Shaun Hutchinson, Fraser Kerr, Chris Cadden, Tom Leighton, Lee Erwin, Stuart McKinstry, Murray Miller, Reece McAlear, Jake Hastie, James Scott, David Turnbull and Allan Campbell have all been sold for good money after coming through the youth system I was involved with.

If I am being honest, the only area I didn't find great success with was goalkeepers. But in PJ Morrison, I think he might be the exception and be a stalwart for the club and/or a saleable asset like his peers above. In addition, there were scores of kids who came through the system from my tenure, broke through and then found their level, and are now still enjoying a living from the game. Nicky Cadden, Jack McMillan, Steven Hetherington, Dylan Mackin, Dom Thomas, Euan Murray, Robert McHugh, Steven Lawless, Zaine Francis-Angol, David Ferguson, Ross Forbes, Jonathan Page, Adam Cummins, Luke and Josh Watt, Steven Saunders, Stuart Carswell, Morgyn Neill, Darren Brownlie, Craig Moore, Ross Meechan, Ben Hall, Adam Livingstone, Ross MacLean, Ross Stewart, Willie Muir, Kyle Connell, Kyle MacDonald, Jack and Robbie Leitch, Brett Long, Keiran MacDonald, Ryan Watters, Robbie Young, Jordan

Armstrong… the list goes on and apologies to any I've missed. I take great pride, and never miss an opportunity, to greet all of these guys when I find the club I'm working for is playing against them and I'd take any and all of them now. And I'd be confident of putting a side together more than capable of competing in the SPFL. Just as important, I ask how their parents are getting on as well, as I never forget the commitment they made in the early years

I know David Turnbull is the club's record sale after moving to Celtic for over £3 million in August 2020, but he was the standout talent and it was a case of nurturing rather than taking credit for transforming him into a player. I'm on record as saying that he'd captain Scotland one day and I was very proud to see him gain his first Scotland cap against Holland in June, 2021, in a friendly, and deservedly taking his place in the Scotland Euro 2020 squad for the delayed championships in the summer of 2021. I truly believe he will lead out the national team one day as he is so rounded and grounded as a person, given his family background of decent hard working people, who trusted me in his formative years.

We always had good relationships with local boys' clubs and they would notify us of any boys who were doing well. That would trigger a scout to monitor the situation and invite them into the academy for evaluation. So from the moment we saw David, it was a no-brainer. It was easy to see his potential. He was different to anything we were producing and he always reminded me of Gary McAllister, who loved getting on the ball and dictating play. I've no doubt about the heights David can reach. I can see him playing at the top level in England or abroad. He's such a down-to-earth boy and a joy to deal with. His family will be so proud of him.

Believe me, if he wants to go to the very top, Celtic will receive a huge return on their investment and if Motherwell have a sell-on clause (possibly up to 20 per cent), which is a certainty, then their bonus could be twice the initial transfer fee. Using Kieran Tierney – who I nearly got to Motherwell as a result of a wee lull in his love affair with Celtic and the fact I grew up with his father – as a transfer fee benchmark, then Motherwell could expect to more than double their record transfer fee through a sell-on clause, in what will be seen as a bargain.

Going back to Kieran Tierney – who was born on the Isle of Man and brought up in Wishaw, not far from Muirhouse where I live – you have no idea how close we were to signing him and having him rampage up and down the left wing of Fir Park in the claret and amber. There was a wee period around the age of 14 when the current Arsenal star wasn't settling at St Ninian's High School in Kirkintilloch, where Celtic send their academy players. I had told his father, Michael, who I knew well, that if there was any time his son was unsettled, I'd happily call Chris McCart and set the ball in motion, quite literally, for Kieran to move to Motherwell. One day I got that call and immediately said that if his mind was made up, then so was mine. Our youth team was due to play Rangers that coming weekend and we were trying to make the move quickly to get him in to face the Gers. The fact that he'd been with Celtic since he was ten, however, forced the powers that be at Parkhead to make sure Kieran's unrest was temporary, and therefore my excitement fell flat once the prospect of Mick's boy coming to Motherwell evaporated. Mick, a diehard Celtic fan, would have had no hesitation about his son's switch of allegiance if it was in his best interests and was never one of those parents living out a dream through their boy. Turnbull and Tierney will be Scotland legends and both grew up a bye-kick from me.

Celtic fended off the attention of a host of English clubs to land Turnbull, Scotland's Young Player of the Year for 2018/19. But I couldn't understand how some senior people at the Scottish FA – namely performance director Mark Wotte - could not see the advantages of picking David for national squads. Two instances stick out for me. First, his father, Eddie, asked if David not going to the performance school programme at Braidhurst High School would hinder his chances, as he wanted to stay at Coltness High with his pals and peers. I explained his attitude and ability would more than make up for him not attending that particular programme. A-plus to Mr. Young. Secondly, I used to argue with Mark Wotte, who wouldn't pick him for Scotland, and he tried to palm me off with a line about him not being a certain style of midfielder aligned to the Dutch numbering system! What the fuck does that even mean? "Is he a 6, 8 or 10?" he'd ask me.

My argument was simple. David was the best midfielder in the country at his age and a country our size should be accommodating him. That's how much I believed in him.

We had good scouts and good coaches who all played their part in David's journey. But I'll always be grateful to his mum, grandad and especially Eddie, who stood by me year upon year when I would tell them of interest from other clubs. They trusted my vision and, although we had good players like Allan Campbell, Jake Hastie, James Scott and many others, I always instructed the coaches at David's age group to shape the team around him. Jake had the pace, Allan had the steely determination and James had a knack for scoring, so you can see where David was the creator in chief.

When I came back from America and went to Falkirk in early 2018 (later chapters to come), I said to Bairns' boss Paul Hartley to get David out on loan and even consider buying him, because at that time he wasn't an automatic pick for Motherwell. But David was always destined to make it in the top flight and there were certainly a lot of other clubs desperate to get him into their programmes. After speaking to his family, though, I was always confident that we'd take him to Motherwell. They were so easy to deal with and believed in what our player development pathway could offer. It's no coincidence that Chris Cadden, Allan Campbell, Jake Hastie and James Scott to name a few, are where they are today, as their parents were the same - supportive of their kids and supportive of myself and the programme. Even when I left the club they would continually update me on the landmarks they hit. David's dad would ask for advice anytime he was at a crossroads or a decision had to be made on his future and I would happily advise as best I could. I'm delighted for David and I have no doubts whatsoever that he has a massive future in the game.

At the time of publication of this book Motherwell will have received in the region of £6/7 million in total for the following players: Lee Erwin (Leeds United), David Turnbull (Celtic), James Scott (Hull City), Jake Hastie (Rangers), Reece McAlear (Norwich City), Stuart McKinstry (Leeds Utd), Murray Miller (Rangers) and Allan Campbell (Luton Town). All those players – who were either sold or left for a development fee - were all recruited, coached and nurtured along the pathway under the guidance of my excellent staff. That's not a bad return on investment and only possible by the transition of the academy down at Braidhurst. This has been a massive contribution to the survival of the club at a time when there was no credit limit available due to administration, and through Covid which was/is a blight on humanity, never mind a football club's ability to remain solvent. There's no doubt selling David for £3 million and James for £1 million in the middle of the pandemic has given Motherwell FC the breathing space it needs to work its way through the current situation and beyond. Other clubs will not be so lucky.

I don't expect any remuneration, but I would like some acknowledgement, not for my personal gratification though. I know in my heart I've contributed something substantial, in some way, to the club I was brought up to support and love. However, I do want the acknowledgement so that I can give recognition to the coaches, scouts, support staff, invaluable contacts, as well as sponsors who backed me to lead their Academy. My relationship with North Lanarkshire Council, Braidhurst High School, Dalziel High School and their respective head teachers Derrick Hannon and Brian Miller, Ian Watson from Dalziel High School Trust, countless businessmen and the various groundsmen at Dalziel Park, were ultimately borne from my local standing in a wonderful community.

I look back and smile when I think about how and where the Motherwell Academy was placed in the pecking order at the club and the vague questions being constantly posed, about where the next million pound player was coming from. Why not just trust the people you have hired and give them time to implement a strategy based on accountability, flexibility and hard work. When Motherwell won the Scottish Youth Cup in 2015/16 – just a couple of seasons after I had left – I watched the incumbent staff dine out on the work of the previous six years, where the maturity of the assembly line was in full display on the Hampden pitch, as the young Well stars demolished Hearts 5-2 in the final to win the accolade for the first time in the club's history. I sent a good luck message on the day of the game and was offered a ticket, very much, I felt, as an afterthought. I went to the game with my son, Robbie, as a very satisfied fan, knowing the work that had gone on to produce these players through the system. Sitting beside me that night in the south stand were Stan, Brian Reynolds and Paul Burns, all stalwarts of the dark times, and in the 'prawn sandwich' seats were the current owners of the feast. Immediately the phrase which I stand by in football came to mind: "success has many fathers… failure is an orphan."

The game is full of glory hunters, hangers on and wannabes, but beneath the surface is a hard core of dedicated professional people with a work ethic and credibility, that the real football people know. Sadly these are not the people who make a fortune from the game, but then the world is full of unsung heroes. Stand up and take a bow you guys, you know who you are. We judge too early, We rave too much, We risk too little!

Anyway, I'm sitting at the Christmas dinner table – remember that? – and all of this is flashing before my eyes as I wait to hear what my fanatical Well fan family come up with next to help me put out a team to beat Rangers. As much as part of me is relishing this challenge of leading my boyhood heroes, part of me for inspiration is also recalling Jim Gannon, the manager prior to Craig Brown, with a rueful chuckle and thinking… if he can be manager of Motherwell FC, then I sure as fuck can! What a six months in charge he had after taking over from Mark McGhee, who had left for Aberdeen in June 2009. He was without a doubt in my opinion, as weird as a box of frogs in a Weird Al Yankovich music video. I remember the time he… no, maybe later. As highlighted earlier, this book is primarily about funny experiences I have encountered and not an excuse to humiliate people – they can do that themselves, and some did when I was around. The good guys know the events and I know where the bodies are buried.

True to form, as results and confidence in the manager dwindled, Gannon was out after the 2009 Boxing Day defeat at home to St Johnstone. I took over for my first outing as caretaker boss for the next game at Hearts and then in came Craig Brown and Archie Knox… both of whom would mentor me and reshape my future coaching journey.

CHAPTER

Two Old Guys Who Love Me

Craig Brown and Archie Knox were still game despite being in the twighlight of their careers and were great mentors to me

As far as football was concerned, Craig Brown and Archie Knox had already been there, done it, seen it, bought the T-shirt, washed the T-shirt, seen the T-shirt turn pink in a white wash with a red sock hidden in it, thrown the T-shirt in the bin, bought a new T-shirt and then forgotten about the T-shirt, to instead focus on a polo shirt. But I'll bet the shirt off my own back that they'd never seen anything like the events that took place at Fir Park on Wednesday, 5 May, 2010, which ended with a scoreline Motherwell 6, Hibs 6! It was wisdom that they both displayed on that evening – and described at the start of this memoir – that drew me in as soon as the former Scotland manager and his illustrious assistant arrived at Motherwell.

I had prepared the team for a game against Hearts on 29 December, 2009 (my first stint as caretaker boss) following Jim Gannon's departure the day before. Craig and Archie came in on the day of the game, a Tuesday night at Tynecastle. "Right, Gordon, brilliant work you've done," said the bold Broon, "pick the team, do the team talk and, if we win, it's my team, if we lose, it's yours!" Brilliant, I thought this is a guy I can work with, his sense of humour was exactly on my wavelength.

Even today after a Cove Rangers match, Paul and I will invariably get a text from him after we've won, which during 2019/20 season was most of the time, saying: "I see Olivia (Paul's three-year-old daughter) picked the team today." We were beaten 1-0 at Tynecastle by a goal from Michael Stewart – now a popular, and sometimes controversial, pundit on BBC Scotland – that night, so it was 'my team'. But we had played well and the first thing Craig did was make me first-team coach and add me to the bonus system. I now had even more of an incentive to help build a winning team. At the end of the season 2009/10, without me even asking, I received a letter from Craig thanking me for my efforts and contribution in the first six months since his arrival and full reimbursement of any bonuses due. A real touch of class.

I was lapping them both up and the things I learned from Craig and Archie have stayed with me and influenced the way I have operated throughout my career. How could you not be influenced by the last man to take Scotland to a World Cup in 1998? Or how could you not learn from Archie, Alex Ferguson's right-hand man at Aberdeen and Man United, who also formed a formidable partnership with Walter Smith at Rangers and Everton? As first-team coach, each day was like a football Open University course for me. Their man-management was exceptional, Archie told me he had mellowed – and he definitely had… a little.

But Craig's team talks were masterful and they were both tactically exceptional. It was this duo who – strange as it may seem – encouraged me not to watch the player on the ball too much when at the side of the pitch, but to cast my eyes around to what the other players were doing. Are the ball player's team-mates making the correct runs, taking up the best positions, defending properly? As much as we were coaching peripheral vision for our players, Craig and Archie were teaching me about my own coaching peripheral vision and helping me to see an even bigger footballing picture than I had previously. Craig and Archie were to become a very big influence on my career.

If anyone has ever seen Still Game about the hilarious adventures of two 'Craiglang' widowers on TV, you'll see why they were known around Fir Park as Jack and Victor, the main characters of the show. They were apt to finish each other's sentences and worked so well together, that they instinctively knew what the other was thinking and shared everything in relation to what they thought about players, the style of play, tactical changes, formations and training. They even shared a pair of glasses!

I remember we all came back from training one day and we're all in the manager's office – which they shared – and Craig (70) and Archie (63) at that time, were hunting for the specs. The two of them were underneath tables, emptying out bins, searching through drawers and desks and throwing papers all over the room hunting for the only pair of glasses they had between them. I just sat there with my cup of tea taking it all in and wondering when they would both realise the specs were perched on top of Craig's head. When they found them, the recriminations started about who was the biggest arsehole for not realising where they were - Craig for having them on his napper, or Archie for not being able to see them when looking straight at his big mate. It was like this all the time. They were meticulous, professional, thorough, very knowledgeable, but escapades such as this one with the specs were regular occurrences, which made them all the more endearing to me and made my learning journey all the more enjoyable during my time with them.

Another notable moment arose when we arrived back from training a bit later than expected. We were sitting having our debrief and cup of tea in the manager's office discussing the earlier training session when chief administrator Karen Paterson popped her head round the door.

"Craig, you do know that you are running late for that 2pm meeting?" Karen reminded her boss.

"What 2pm meeting?"

"The 2pm meeting with the Motherwell Dementia Café group."

Archie Knox nearly pissed himself, as Craig, a little sheepishly, tried to talk his way out of how he had managed to forget to go to give a presentation to a group, which specialised in supporting people who were losing their memory!

As amusing and ironic as this was, groups such as the Dementia Café were another example of how Motherwell FC lead the way in helping and supporting their local community, and this award-winning group continues to do excellent work meeting regularly in the club's Centenary Suite at least once a month.

I am very proud of the good work the club does in the town and my chest swelled even more recently when before season 2021/22 started the fans raised £70,000, which was matched by the club, to provide 1,000 free season tickets to local under-privileged families and unemployed people.

The double act kicked in big style during a team talk at Easter Road. Craig was giving a masterclass at man-management - as he always tried to lessen the blow for players who would not even be making it to the six-man subs' bench that day and would have to watch the game from the stands. Craig knew he couldn't afford to alienate our players, as a couple of injuries would leave our 22-man squad stretched. He wisely wanted to keep them all on board and feel part of what we were trying to achieve, so his first words in the team talk were for the players who were not stripped. Young defender Jonathan Page was first to get encouraging words. "First of all Jonathan, you're just coming back from a wee niggling injury and it's just too soon for you to feature, son, but keep your head up as you are close." Esteban Casagolda – a Belgian-born striker with a Spanish mum and Uruguayan dad, we'd just recently taken a wee chance on – was next: "Dag meneer Esteban or should I say 'hola'," the educated schoolteacher background of Craig made a wee appearance from time to time. "It's great to have you with us, but today is a day for you to watch how we play and get yourself ready for your chance." Our big Cypriot Under-21 fringe player Angelis Charalambous, was next for the treatment and Craig was scanning the Easter Road away dressing room for the big swarthy defender, who was soon to leave us to complete his Cypriot National Service duty back in his homeland. Craig spotted him and paused for a second, thinking how he could break the news to him gently and positively that he's not playing when Archie chips in… "And you big Angelis, just you stand outside that door with your rifle and make sure nae fucker gets in!"

The circumstances around signing Angelis – who had a lot of promise and was eventually capped for his country – were a wee bit surreal in themselves. Just two weeks after Craig and Archie had arrived, I took the under-20 team to Cyprus for two weeks of warm-weather training and friendlies, taking advantage of the Leonardo Da Vinci sport initiative funding to help promote physical activity and national and international cooperation. We struck up a cordial relationship with Anorthosis Famagusta FC and the programme operates a reciprocal agreement for participating clubs and organisations to information share and for them to work in partnership. This would entail me taking training sessions for them and their coaching staff putting our squad of very talented young players through their paces. It was great for our lads to have perfect training conditions for a fortnight in the middle of January and Craig and Archie were delighted that they could get this experience. Incidentally, that was the year that Flyglobespan Airlines went bust just a few days before we were due to travel. Luckily, we were able to reschedule our direct flight from Glasgow to Larnaca, to another flight from Luton to Cyprus.

We drove from Motherwell on a bus which 'iced over' at Lesmahagow on the M74 in sub-zero conditions. This left Willie Falconer and myself taking turns to scrape the window from the inside, to allow the driver to see going down the snowbound motorway all the way to Luton. And so I added human window wiper to my roles at MFC! From there we flew to Limassol on the other side of the island, followed by another bus journey – minus the snow, thank goodness – to our training camp. You'll do anything for a two-week camp in the sun. I struck up a good relationship with Anorthosis youth coach Michael Hayes. He was the son of a former Scottish soldier based on the island, who had met and married a local lass, when he was stationed in Akrotiri. Turned out his dad was born in Stonehouse, only a bye kick from Motherwell, and thankfully he acted as my interpreter before we struck up a friendship which is still strong today.

Whilst there, I was asked by the hosting club if I would like to take the first team for a training session. "Why not?" I thought to myself, it's nice to be nice and it's another wee bit of experience under the belt. So I'm out there in the middle of the Antonis Papadopoulos Stadium with their first-team squad, most of whom had played in the Champions League group stages before Christmas. This was the first time any Cypriot club had reached that far in the competition and they were up against Werder Bremen, Panathinaikos and Inter Milan. So I was training players with a good pedigree and a wealth of experience, as their veteran chain-smoking 'and bald' Serbian coach Slavoljub Muslin (a legendary coach in Eastern Europe) sat watching what I was doing from the stand. When from nowhere, the new president of the club (I understand there had been some unpleasant publicity surrounding the previous president, and he had left his post before the last game of group stages) triumphantly strolls onto the pitch with a gaggle of local press and broadcast media and what would turn out to be their new signing. He's waving for us all to stop what we're doing and he's beckoning me over for a chat. It's plain he is not that familiar with his own management team as he's gabbing away as if I'm his best friend and calling me his coach. Obviously it's all Greek to me and I'm searching for Michael to swoop in and explain to the new club president that I'm not his team's boss. I also hoped he would clarify to new signing and former Liverpool £5 million man Bruno Cheyrou – Gerard Houllier once hailed as the 'New Zidane' – whom he had brought with him onto the pitch, that 'Wee Youngy' from Muirhouse in Motherwell would not be telling him and the Cypriot Press how to optimise his play in the Christmas tree formation for the rest of the season. Though for just a fleeting minute I thought, if I could lay my hands on ten Regal King Size, I might just give it a go!

Anyway, Michael managed to explain away the reasons why I was leading the session and it was back to fitba coaching in the sun, and casting my eye over a 6ft 4ins right-back recommended to me by my half-Scottish interpreter. Angelis Charalambous is his name and I like what I see and call Craig and Archie, who, by chance, were looking to bolster that position in our squad. Soon after, our fortnight came to an end and I returned with the under-20s to Scotland.

When I got back, Craig, Archie and I scanned the videos we have of Angelis and they decided to go for him as the added incentive is, we can get him on loan for 'free' as he was the only Cypriot in their first-team squad and the club wanted to get him experience. Maybe I was too slow and should have taken Bruno Cheyrou, given him a false passport and blamed it on too much sun on my wee baldy head. Now that would have been a story, not that the then club president would have known any different.

Craig instructed me to take Yvonne and head back to the island in the middle of the Mediterranean, get the signing done and have a wee holiday for a couple of days as a reward for my diligence. What a thoughtful gesture and an easy sell when I got home that night. "Eh, Yvonne, do you want to stick the heating up a bit, or head out to Larnaca for a few days?" The funny thing was that while we were at the club finalising the paperwork on the signing, the new president, who thought I was a 57-year-old Serb the week before, had now done his homework and offered me the job of head of their academy complete with a villa, car, private schooling for my kids and £100,000 a year in the hippy. It was a tempting offer, but one I graciously turned down – not least due to their questionable job security record and regular turnover of managers, presidents and ball boys. When I explained to the president that I couldn't take up the offer due to the insecurity, whilst thanking him for the offer, he tossed me out of the office, muttering that I had disrespected him, according to Michael who was translating. We burst out laughing now that I was out in the street with a bone china cup in my hand half full of coffee, the other half spilled down my shirt. Now that's diplomacy. Apparently the man in charge lasted only another few months and the club appointed two more presidents that year. Probably one of my better decisions.

Over a period of time in the game you build up a network of scouts, contacts and people who will help your recruitment process and, as the years have gone by, this has grown globally for me. But back in the day I'd get calls from people I'd played with and against and from friends as well as agents, who would give me a recommendation on a budding superstar, who had come across their radar. With my holistic model in place, I never turned anyone away from a trial who was recommended outwith our normal recruitment process as, you never know, you might turn up a diamond that has so far been unpolished. As always they would be scrutinised under the "could he play for our first team" methodology structure. If it didn't cost the club anything other than my time, players could come and they did - from all corners of the world. They came under their own steam and sometimes with proof of accommodation normally put up by a distant relative, friend of a friend or more often than not, paid for by an agent, hoping a wee contract would repay the B&B overnight stay somewhere in Lanarkshire.

One day I got a call from a 'so-called' agent Jonathan Hope, who had previously hooked us up with Esteban Casagolda, a nice lad but who had a touch like a blind rabbit in a minefield with divers' boots on. He was touting this new top prospect, but said he had to meet with me to explain his circumstances. It turned out that the player in question, another really nice boy, was the son of a London-based diplomat from a country in southwestern Asia, and was enrolled in David Beckham's academy.

Bingo, I thought, I know Gordon Strachan's son, Gavin, who works there and called him for a wee bit of background information. "He's a good kid, big and strong, but maybe not for you," he replied, but, as he's on his way up, I park the information and trust my eye and that of my staff. Gav was spot on with the assessment and it mirrored our evaluation. I relayed this to the agent and expected that to be that, but what happened next was a first (but unfortunately not the last) for me and took me aback.

I am told that if we sign him, I'll be given £10,000, someone else will pay the player's wages and accommodation and they'll also look at some sponsorship for the club, if he progresses to the first team. "Woaahhh, hawd yer horses and steady on there!" I'm not about to tarnish my own reputation, but, as mentioned previously, every penny was a prisoner for the club and I'm weighing up contacting the board to ascertain their thoughts on this unusual proposal. Then I thought, I'm put in this role to make the decisions that are best for the Academy and that of the club. So I made an executive, and morally correct decision, to chase this agent out the door. By 2017, Hope had been discredited, disgraced and was deceased. Once I dug a little deeper, after he made that approach, I discovered he wasn't someone I nor the club wanted to be associated with. Bullet dodged and lesson learned.

Domestic Premier League football would throw up some great learning experiences for me like when we were up at Pittodrie, losing 1-0 to Aberdeen and playing terribly. Midway through the second half Archie turned round to Craig and said: "Right. Get that cunt aff the park." To which Broon replied "Which one?" and quick as a flash Archie retorted: "Any 'fucking' wan… they'll all get us the fucking sack!"

And how could I forget during the Lanarkshire derby at home in early February against Hamilton Accies and, as the half-time whistle goes, we were drawing 0-0 and had been pretty poor. Craig held Archie and I back in the tunnel and waited until our full team have disappeared into the dressing room.

He said: "Let's just give them a few minutes to compose themselves before we go in there and talk to them."

So we stand there, the three of us composing our own selves, when Archie decided that he was composed enough and burst away from us to run into the dressing room like a one-man SWAT team. Craig just looked at me calmly.

Ready to make an impression and express how he felt about the insipid first-half performance, he immediately spied an empty plastic box, laid out specifically by Alan 'Aldo' MacDonald, our excellently efficient kitman. Archie aimed a kick at it and put his foot right through it. As Craig and I walked through the door, Archie was continuing with his constructive criticism in full rant mode, never missing a beat while he parades around the dressing room trying at the same time to extricate his foot from the plastic container. Craig's looking at me and we're both thinking that we're glad Archie took a minute to compose himself with us in the tunnel, before he went in, or who knows what he would have done! Using the advantage of his years Craig described it as like seeing an old vaudeville music hall spoof tap-dancing act on Sunday Night at the London Palladium. It did, however, break the ice as well as the box and the players all had a good laugh at Archie's expense. It must have worked a treat as they seemed to relax in the second half and put in a good display to win 1-0. Archie had that ability to blow his top and still look in control, with Broon commenting that "half the guys he's killed are still alive." Comedy gold from two top professionals.

Similarly, Craig was happy to delegate the touchline and dugout duties to Archie and I on certain occasions. One of those was a League Cup match against Brechin City in September 2010. Craig chose to sit in the Glebe Park main stand as he took a look at how his squad was shaping up for the new season and the tests that were to come. To say that this historic old ground is compact and tight is a bit of an understatement, and it's fair to say that a booming Archie Knox could quite easily be heard clearly, even if he had been sitting in the fridge at the furthest away pie stall. But he was in the dugout just in front of the main stand and within the first half an hour he had watched our talented right-back – and future Scotland cap – Steven Saunders slice three up-field passes in a row out of the park. Archie – on the touchline – turned round and glared up at Craig in the stand and shouted, nearly deafening me and half the crowd in the process: "Haw Broon, if Saunders is playing on Saturday, I'll no be there!" Craig just mildly laughed it off, much to the amusement of the Brechin faithful in the stand. It was Archie's memory that was lacking the following Friday when we were all sitting discussing the Saturday game and Steven Saunders was named in the starting line-up. Craig turned to Archie and said: "So are you going anywhere nice with Maggie (his partner) tomorrow Archie?" A speechless Archie just grabbed the communal pair of glasses from Craig, looked at the team on the list that had been drawn up and mumbled something unintelligible under his breath, about how Maggie could do a better job than Steven Saunders, based on the display he had dished up at Glebe Park. But it has to be said that they've seen so many players and managed so many games, that the players respected them and loved their anecdotes and opinions.

Turns out he also needed the glasses to look up his number for Stephen Kean at Blackburn Rovers FC to get the gem of a player we had been looking at… but only just. Craig and Archie were so well connected and knew so many people in football, that we were in a great position to perhaps land one or two rough diamonds from top English sides, who were looking for them to gain some first-team experience on loan. Kean, the Scottish manager of Blackburn, had already alerted us to a young striker by the name of Nick Blackman. Archie, who had worked with the boy when he was assistant manager to Paul Ince, decided to send our scout, Bobby Jenks, to go down and watch him play for the Rovers' reserves against Bolton Wanderers for a current update on his capabilities. Now Bobby was a real character, serving the club with great distinction in various roles and typified the sort of people around clubs across the country then.

I asked our goalkeeping coach, Stewart Kerr, to go along and keep Bobby company and the pair drove down to Lancashire. That afternoon my phone rings and it's Kerrso, who has made his excuses to Bobby that he's off to the kludgie, so he could literally pish himself laughing and call me to let me know we might not be getting a scouting dossier on the player we want.

Bobby, in his infinite wisdom, has mixed up the teams. He thinks the team playing in blue and white is Blackburn when it is, in fact, Bolton and the team in yellow is Blackburn playing in their away kit. "I clocked it straight away, Youngy," says Kerrso, "and I thought Bobby would too. But it just got funnier and funnier listening to him sitting there moaning to me about the 5ft 10ins white Romanian striker he was composing a report on, rather than the 6ft 3ins black striker Nick Blackman." It turns out our naughty goalkeeping coach had been listening to Bobby wondering why we were even considering signing 'this dud' in the first place. "Youngy I've been biting my tongue for an hour. He's been writing up a report on this guy and the irony is, he's been saying we should have gone for 'Bolton's striker' (Blackman) instead, who he thinks is a great player!" I had a wee laugh myself at that, but I told Stewart to go and put Bobby out of his misery and get some form of scouting report back up to Craig and Archie.

At the management meeting the next day at Fir Park, Bobby presented a short but glowing report on Nick Blackman. "Is that all you have, Bobby?" says Craig, "It's pretty positive, but there's not much of it." It didn't help matters that, when Kerrso got back to his seat and broke the bad news to Bobby the day before, Nick only lasted another 10 minutes before being subbed after an excellent performance for Rovers. In the meeting, Stewart Kerr – who is still giggling away to himself – cannae let it lie and digs up Bobby about his confusion, who seems pretty pleased with himself that Craig and Archie are impressed.

As Craig passes the report and their glasses to Archie and hears about how they were nearly reading about a Romanian journeyman midfielder rather than the player they wanted, he looks at Bobby, throws the report up in the air, digs out his phone, calls Stephen Kean and gets a personal run down of the lad's attributes. Archie then gets the phone number for Nick and honestly barks at him down the line: "Just you get your arse up here and stop fucking about."

Nick arrives on loan the following week and goes on to have a great six months with the Well, scoring ten goals in 18 games. Craig and Archie must have been impressed as they also took him to Aberdeen with them on loan when they left Fir Park.

This was another impressive aspect I observed while working with Craig Brown and Archie Knox - they knew absolutely everyone who was anyone in the game of football. That's why they had the gravitas to be able to call up the manager of an English Premiership club and ask him to give a full rundown of one of their fringe players, so they could make a decision to sign him or not. Sitting in their office for our meetings, always with Sky Sports news on silent in the background, was like a game of Footballing Who's Who. Whoever came up being interviewed on the screen was known to at least one of them, and, more often than not, both of them.

They would then look up at the screen and Craig or Archie would say: "Remember the time when we did that or I did this with them...?" It was unbelievable. A day would not go by without one of them taking a call from Roy Hodgson, Gerard Houllier, Brian Kidd, Glen Hoddle or Alex Ferguson. I remember them taking me out for a meal in Glasgow one day and we ended up in Sir Alex Ferguson's company, all old pals together reminiscing. I was dumbfounded and speechless and didn't know what to say when Fergie turned to me and said: "So Youngy what aboot this team of yours and the big fella Erwin (referring to a top prospect I had at the time, Lee Erwin)?"

It was my turn for the memory to go, as I forgot for a second how to string two words together. I think it's the first time in my life I couldn't speak and once I stopped stammering, I rambled on about something which was inaudible. The man has an aura which is hard to explain, but when you are talking about fitba, a subject loved by everyone round that table - Craig Brown, Archie Knox, Sir Alex Ferguson and Gordon Young – you very quickly find your feet and settle into a pattern of play.

What an afternoon! Another member of the company that day, a great guy and friend of the exalted company, was the veteran broadcast journalist Chick Young (no relation). He turned to me at one point after my interaction with Sir Alex and said: "Aye you were stumped for words there, wee man." No kidding. It was like being in a wet dream being had by famous Scottish impressionist and actor Jonathan Watson. "Heh, Heh, Heh!"

It was the same in Europe. Motherwell qualified for the 2010/11 Europa League competition and we had a run of three fixtures in Iceland, Norway and Denmark respectively and everywhere we went they were revered and their reputations preceded them. There was always someone who knew them or was passing on regards from high-profile mutual friends and acquaintances. Our first game of this campaign was against Breidablik from Iceland. We played the first leg at home on Thursday, 15 July, and I was tasked with being the MFC representative to meet with the Uefa delegate, in the police control room at Fir Park before the match.

The Uefa delegate for each European match basically has to tick all the boxes the governing body deem necessary for the tie to go ahead. Everything needs to be checked and ticked off the list: from the colour of bibs to be worn, the size of the numbers on the back of the shirts and the regulation size of any sponsors' logo, or branding on the front of the strip, to some important questions on crowd control… or which would be important questions if the team you were playing were bringing a big away support or had a history of trouble.

So, I'm in the Fir Park police control box at the back of the main stand with the Uefa delegate, the police match commander and the Breidablik representative, who turns out to be their president.

The Uefa delegate asks me a battery of questions:

Question: What is your segregation policy? Answer: Away fans are normally situated in the South Stand, but if there aren't that many, we can accommodate them in a segregated section of the Main Stand.

Q: Do you have any known Motherwell Ultras? A: Similar to most clubs, police have in the past identified a minority of troublesome fans through their own intelligence gathering methods over the years. But there is no reason to expect any issues at tonight's game.

Q: Is there any risk of trouble – missile throwing or flares being set off? A: Motherwell fans are very rarely involved in any violent behaviour, especially at home European matches and we are very confident there will be no behavioural issues involving our fans this evening.

Q: Where will your Ultras be situated? A: We have an animated and exuberant group of fans who sing songs and bang drums called the Bois. They create a vibrant atmosphere in the East Stand close to the South Stand.

"Thank you Mr Young," says the Uefa delegate and he turns to my Breidablik counterpart, who has arrived with his party of 48 from Iceland on a commercial flight – including the full squad, all officials and a total of 19 fans.

Question: Do you have any known Breidablik Ultras attending the game tonight? A: I fucking hope not, 27 in total have travelled and they are all related to me!

That box was well and truly ticked and Ross Forbes gave us a first-leg lead going into the next tie. We then chartered a plane for the second leg a week later. One third of the seats are for players and officials, one third for the press and one third for the fans. There were people I had grown up with on the plane with us and it was very humbling to see them search me out, shake my hand and take so much pride in seeing me as first-team coach at their beloved club, helping lead them into Europe.

One elder gentleman who grew up with my dad in Craigneuk, near Wishaw, was on every trip and he beamed with pleasure on each occasion as he told his own son about his relationship with my dad, and would bear hug me to stamp the approval. I wanted to win for these guys and never forgot that it was a privilege for me to be there knowing I was paid to go on board, while these Motherwell diehards spent their hard-earned cash to follow their team.

For European matches you have to be in the country where you are playing at least 36 hours before kick-off, and you need to be given the opportunity to train on your opponents' pitch. The only thing was, like so many teams in Iceland, they have communal facilities that also serve as leisure facilities for local people. Breidablik's pitch and surrounding facilities were more like Wishaw Sports Centre during gala day! As we emerged to train, we had old folks doing their aerobic exercises, several locals walking their dogs on the athletics track around the pitch and families having picnics, watching us train. Archie had them all pegged as fitba spies, hoping to take notes on how we were going to play and how to combat our set-pieces. He was raging and wanted the Uefa delegate to have them all vacate the area, or we were going to walk away. It took his better half, namely Broon, to convince him that these were local punters who had never even heard of Motherwell and they couldn't give a rusty fuck whether Jamie Murphy would work up a dummy and darting run into the penalty area when we get our first free-kick just outside the box. In the end, Jamie scored to give us a 1-0 away victory which would help to secure our spot in the next round, and, as soon as we left the pitch, the attendants came out to put up the badminton nets. As those qualifying rounds come quick and fast, you knew your next opponents immediately (Aalesund in Norway) and the initial plan offered up by the chairman was to leave after the forthcoming league match against Kilmarnock two days after our return, and travel by coach to Aberdeen, then fly to Denmark where we would get a ferry to Aalesund. "Really, said Craig! Why don't we just fly direct to Aalesund?" Which we did, recording a good 1-1 draw, before scudding them 3-0 at home in the return leg.

The afternoon of the away match, our club doctor, Mark Bonnes, and I walked around the city to have a coffee and, as we sat gazing down the fjord, along came the newly refurbished QEII and docked a short corner-kick from us. When we were sitting there enjoying the spectacle, Mark casually remarked, as if he was asking me to pass the sugar, that his elderly parents were both enjoying a cruise on that very liner!

Coincidentally, the day before we travelled I'd put Jenna and Robbie on the 'wave bobs' down at Strathclyde Park, only because my mate worked there and got us on for free. He doubled up that role with another one in M&Ds on the shores of the loch. He would end up being sacked, but took them to court for funfair dismissal! The Doc loved that line.

This led us into the draw with bigger named clubs and we snared Odense from Denmark in the Europa League play-off round for a place in the group stages. The first game was away and, as injury time approached, we were 2-0 down, but we were still attacking, looking for the vital away goal. Our efforts delivered us a free-kick just outside their box. All three of us, Craig, Archie and I are screaming at Tom Hateley to shoot, but he either ignores us or can't hear the instruction and he crosses the ball into the box. However, the ref calls for a retake and this time, we make sure he gets the message. Tom sets himself and then rifles a drive into the top corner, just seconds before the whistle goes for full-time. What a fighting chance this gave us of an upset and showed how Craig and Archie's experience of European and international football was paying off for the club.

After the game we were all in the dressing room and Craig was trying to calm everyone down. "Remember, lads, we are only halfway through this game and there's a long way to go. Let's keep calm and focus on what we have to do in our next league game first, before we focus on Odense at Fir Park," says the boss. Just at that moment the owner of the club, John Boyle, and his lovely chairman, Bill Dickie, have totally lost their own focus and come waltzing in through the door. They were holding each other up, having enjoyed the hospitality a bit too much, looking like they were wearing the same coat and singing like we've won the Europa League!

However, it was Odense who were smiling and singing a week later in the return leg. Honestly, watching Motherwell is like watching the Scottish national team in microcosm at times, as it was another European hard-luck story for long-suffering Well fans.

Odense, despite having two players sent off and us missing our customary penalty, turned in a professional performance to win 1-0 and knock us out of the competition.

After the match finishes, as is also customary, players want to exchange shirts, but another Uefa protocol is not to do it on the pitch. Aaahh, remember the good old days when everybody would run straight to Pele, Maradona or Willie Pettigrew and do the back and forth finger thing to signal that they swap shirts? But no more.

So, one of my duties was to ask our players if they wanted to exchange their jerseys and I met my opposition club counterpart in the tunnel to organise the requests. Easy job, hell no! Odense had a few notable names in 2010, Traore, Djemba-Djemba, Halland, Roy Carroll in goal and the matchwinner, Peter Utaka, and most players' tops are all claimed and sorted. But I have two jerseys from a big lump of a sub – former Swedish international Andreas Johannson – who is past his best and unknown to our lads, maybe because he played wearing a protective mask…protecting who we wondered?

He came on early in the second half and couldn't kick doors at Halloween in terms of the ball, but was a scary sight for our lads as he was built like a brick shit-house and kicked everything above the grass wearing a claret-and-amber sock. After the game, truth be told I'm feeling a wee bit sorry for the guy and I can't pluck up the courage to tell him: "Look mate no fucker in our dressing room wants your strip…oh and can I have the Motherwell one back as our player disnae want yours?" What a red-neck for the guy. Luckily, ex-Man Utd keeper Roy Carroll, who it turned out was a top bloke, told the big Swede to stop the strop and hand back the Well top. All it cost me was a case of beer from the Centenary Suite at Fir Park to settle up with Roy.

Craig, too, was playing the peacemaker post-match after an incident where I witnessed a whole new side of Mr Brown. After the Danes had a player sent off for the challenge in the 85th minute that led to a penalty for us, Odense sporting director Kim Brink – 52 at the time – inexplicably ended up in our technical area and barged into Craig. But the 70-year-old swiftly responded with a right hook. Brown said at the time: "I think it was their sporting director that got a bit carried away. I don't know why but he came to our dugout. We had a wee bit of a disagreement, putting it euphemistically.

"I got a shove and I had a retaliatory punch. I'm a calm guy, but, if anyone is old enough to remember when I played the game, I was accused of being quite aggressive. I don't want to get messed about and I wasn't going to be messed about."

The visiting assailant was whisked away by our chief steward, we missed the penalty and they finished the game with nine men. The police made some inquiries, Mr Brink apologised and it was not taken any further. Craig added: "They (the police) asked me if I wanted to take the thing any further and I said no. You want to keep these things in football and, anyway, it could have been the other way around." No shit Sherlock… for all his pleasant demeanour and calm character, Craig Brown was certainly not a pensioner to be messed with.

I was like a sponge soaking up every drop of knowledge and nous they were showering on a Motherwell side, who were playing some good football and maintaining their top-six credentials in the Scottish Premier League. They may have only been at Fir Park for just under a full calendar year (29 December, 2009, to 9 December, 2010), but what I learned would change my outlook on coaching and man-management forever. One particular Saturday sticks in my mind. I was taking the under-19s on a Saturday morning, a rescheduled fixture due to our break in Cyprus and we were away at Kilmarnock with an 11am kick-off. Three hours later in my role as first-team coach I would also be up at Fir Park, preparing the team and delivering the warm-up for a home league match.

My under-19 striker, Bob McHugh, would be there too, as he was in the first-team squad that afternoon as well. The brief was to give him 60 minutes in the morning and have him up and ready to make an impact as a sub if needed, in the afternoon. As usual Bob – a prolific scorer – scored his usual brace of goals against the Killie under-19s and he was subbed off after an hour. I also remember Lee Erwin – who would go on to sign for Leeds United – bagged the other that morning in a 3-0 win. After the game Bob jumps in my car and we head back to Fir Park. We've been up since about 8am and the bigger game is to come, so we are both trying to get mentally prepared. I call Craig to let him know we are on our way and give him a wee rundown of the game. We eventually get into the dressing room and the entire first-team squad minus Bob, are there and Craig, who is just about to start building everyone up for the game, clocks us sneaking in.

He immediately recognises the efforts we have both made that morning and puts Bob at his ease and gives me a boost simultaneously, by announcing to the whole room: "Here you go lads, Bob McHugh, one of the top young strikers in Scotland, has netted two fantastic goals at Rugby Park this morning and will be on the bench for us today to give us a real threat if needed later on. And your first-team coach Gordon Young, one of the best youth coaches operating in the country, is here to get you all ready for today's game. If that doesn't help get you up for the match, I don't know what will."

It was moments of sheer class like this that he and Archie dished out regularly. Sure they both had a steely edge to them, which could be deployed at a moment's notice, but they could make you feel ten feet tall, just when you needed it. I have remembered and employed this well in my career and recognise how much this psychological wisdom can positively affect a player's performance on the pitch.

Another small, but important, thing that Craig did was that he always referred to me, the office staff, the groundsmen, the game-day stewards or anyone he worked with, as "my colleagues". He had a way of making you feel equal, on a par with him as an employee of the club and it made you want to raise your game and do the best you could for Motherwell FC.

From time to time, throughout this book there will come reference to a place and a clientele that have a special place in my heart as it was and still is, my local pub. The Electric Bar, not far from Fir Park, is where many of my closest friends congregate and this support network has been right behind me every step of the way as I embarked on my coaching career. It would also be a place where I would also introduce more than a few Motherwell managers to during their tenures. It was probably one or two of the regulars' sons housed in the East Stand who would have started the chant at Fir Park a couple of times during matches, which has brought a tear to my eye… "Gordon Young, he's one of our own!" So it was a no-brainer, with a couple of hours to kill before stalwart Motherwell captain Stephen Craigan's testimonial dinner at the Bellshill Hilton – now there's another two words you would never think of linking together – that I would invite Craig and Archie down to the Electric for some aperitifs.

We entered the bar on Saturday 27 February, 2010, around 5.30pm, just after the Dossers had defeated Kilmarnock 1-0 at home and tucked away another three points in the race to secure a top-six place. The Electric – a traditional sanctuary for Mother-well fans – was bouncing and in good spirits even before the Well's management trio, led by yours truly, walked through the doors. Craig and Archie were literally mobbed by well-wishers, fans shaking their hands, patting them on the back and buying them drinks. At one point tea-totaller Craig, had about ten drinks waiting for him, such was the adoration he was held in by the regulars many of whom had watched their favour-ites, managed by the man of the moment, land a victory that very afternoon.

Everyone wanted a piece of Craig and Archie – who was not a tea-totaller or a big drinker, but was happy to knock back one or two of the gratis libations on offer. For once I was quite happy not to be the one being quizzed about how we were playing and where we were going to finish in the league, and I was delighted to watch two legends of the game relish the company of all my mates.

The EB is where I'd regularly drop in and meet my pals, who with sincerity would want to know the ins and outs, of what is our staple diet in Scotland, 'the fitba'. The attention would be constant and, on more than one occasion, one of my closest friends, Peter Ritchie, would have to step in to save the day. It was probably due to the clam-our and Peter having not spoken to me since I had arrived in the bar that night that prompted him to shout: "Right, shut the fuck up the lot of you. He disnae ask you all how to make steel, deliver the mail or make dodgy porn, so leave him alone for five minutes!" That's the type of place and people you love. I'd like to say that was a conversation stopper, but that would be met with a retort to Peter of: "Shut up baldy, gie's mare grass!" A reference to bowls and not an illegal recreational pastime.

Spending time in the Electric with Craig and Archie was an excellent way to wind down after a tough match and wind-up to a great night, celebrating an excellent professional's well-deserved testimonial. On another occasion at the end of the season, Craig, Archie and I decided to go into Glasgow for some lunch, and a couple of stories spring to mind, just like a normal day in their company. Firstly, we go to Archie's house and drop the cars off. We head down to the closest train station near his home, just outside Glasgow and get the two-carriage train into the city centre.

Archie and I are cheekily drinking a bottle of beer each on the train – still cannae believe I'm swallowing a 'kerry oot' on a train intae Glasgae with two Scottish fitba legends – when the ticket inspector comes on. Obviously he recognises the two 'famous' passengers and before he strikes up a rapport, Craig pulls out his OAP travel card and says: "Two concessions and a half for the boy." I was 45 at the time. The second story arose later in the day when we were at lunch. Craig's phone rings and it's Christian Dailly – former Dundee United, Derby, Blackburn Rovers, West Ham and Rangers player capped 67 times for Scotland – who at that time was under contract at Charlton Athletic.

He says to the man who picked him in his 1998 Scotland World Cup Squad: "Are you looking for a goalkeeper Broon?" And as a matter of fact we were, as our No 1 John Ruddy – who had been brilliant for us – was going back to Everton after his successful loan spell. Dailly's recommendation was a young lad called Darren Randolph who was looking for a new challenge away from Charlton, and what a replacement he became for us.

In his three years at Motherwell, I honestly don't remember a 'howler' from Darren, which is uncommon given the position he played. He also broke John Ruddy's club record of 15 clean sheets in February, 2011, in a 2–0 win over Celtic and became a fans' favourite in his 111 games for the Well. He was so calm and collected and I'm so happy for him on what he's achieved in the game since he left the club in 2013. He moved to Birmingham City, West Ham United in the English Premier League, Middlesbrough and back to West Ham where he is currently starring. He has also become an important international player for his country notching 42 Republic of Ireland caps.

And this all started with Christian Dailly calling Craig Brown during an end of season Motherwell management lunch. Another example of the Craig Brown contact network planting seeds and watching them grow.

I was also honoured that Craig would attend my daughter Jenna's 18th birthday party. He was at a loose end one Saturday night after a home game, and I mentioned to him what my plans were and whether he would like to come along. Let me say how unusual this was, as this is a man who is constantly requested to speak and host dinners most weekends, mostly accepted and delivered free of charge. He was thrilled to be invited and said he would be delighted. And for three hours that night he was the centre of attention for a bevy of very attractive 18-year-olds! He even asked me at one point: "Haw Youngy, how would you like me as a son-in-law?" Just before Jenna grabbed him up onto the dance floor for the Slosh… yes Craig Brown was giving it large on the dance floor to the Slosh at my daughter's birthday and I have photographic proof! But that summed the man up, his warmth, sense of humour, and friendly nature saw him becoming best of friends with my whole family, with an age range from teenagers to octogenarians. What a personality he is and what an influence he has been on me and continues to be!

When Craig and Archie departed Fir Park for the lure of Pittodrie, just under a year after taking up the reins, Craig admitted later that their biggest mistake was not trying to take me with them as their first-team coach. That is huge praise indeed from two men with the stature and reputation they have earned in the game.

As we have covered previously, I was left in charge as caretaker boss until Stuart McCall took over at the end of 2010, but their move did leave a certain bad taste in the mouth of some people at the club. This came to a head when Aberdeen next visited Fir Park on league duty on April 2, 2011, where that steely side of Craig Brown emerged once again.

The home crowd certainly made their feelings known to Craig and Archie, mainly because they were sad to see such a successful management team leave the club. But to summarise a series of surreal hysterical events in a few words is hard, when you see two people you respect nearly come to blows. However, what I remember is being told that Motherwell owner John Boyle was in a taxi that drew up outside the front entrance to the Main Stand shortly before the match ended. He allegedly asked the taxi driver to wait. Before anyone knew it, John was in the tunnel at the end of the match, a handshake was offered, it looked like the club owner had a word in Broon's ear, then Craig and Archie – who were in dispute with the club over bonus payments – and a melee of others were scuffling and ruffling a few ties and suit jacket lapels.

I did catch a glimpse of Craig's face though and, in typical Broon style, he, and Archie too, were laughing whilst we watched John swinging his arms like an octopus falling out of a tree. The old boys had seen it all before here, there and everywhere. The new management team of Stuart McCall, Kenny Black and myself were also pishing ourselves laughing.

History shows that statements were taken by the police and investigations carried out, and the SFA eventually censured both Craig and John. But I suspect that calm, measured, professional and experienced Craig Brown – who had sorted out a younger

Odense official just months before with a right hook – would have been more than able to handle himself when push came to shove in a tight situation, and I'm not just talking about making room for himself to show off his Slosh moves!

CHAPTER

Licence To Skill

My pride at attaining the Uefa Pro-Licence, the most sought-after football qualification in the world

I realised I must have been destined to complete my Scottish FA Uefa Pro-Licence when I sat at the reception of the headquarters of European football in Nyon, Switzerland – there as part of a site visit involving the course – and saw that my father's and grandfather's faces were already there adorning the wall. Granted they were adorning the wall along with 127,619 other European Cup final attendance record-breakers, in a photograph of a packed Hampden Park at the 1960 European Cup final between Real Madrid and Eintracht Frankfurt, which both attended - so they were in the throng, somewhere. I think they were the only two without bunnets on! I would trump them later on when I recorded a hit single in October, 2007. Well, I was one of 47,000 at Hampden for Scotland v Ukraine when Runrig recorded the iconic version of Loch Lomond.

I started this course in December, 2012, as Academy Director at Motherwell FC and finished it in October 2014 as International Academy Manager with Sheffield United. I've no doubt that my participation on this Pro Licence course helped me in this job transition. Without hesitation, I would strongly recommend anyone fortunate enough to be invited to participate on the licence, to definitely do so, as the learning experiences are second to none. At the end of my course I produced a 246-page, 50,000 word, A4 binded book, complete with relevant photographs, graphics, tables, charts and quotes and submitted this as my final assessment to be marked. I am really proud of the work I put into this and, taken overall, sums up my footballing philosophy and how I go about my work, incorporating knowledge from guest speakers, challenging workshops, group working, site visits and trips, analysis of games, teams, coaching styles, tactics, negotiation, motivation and psychology, and moulding it all into a progressive and innovative style that suits me and has worked for me in my football coaching career. Only those possessing the Uefa A and B coaching licences are invited to attempt successful completion of the Uefa Pro-Licence qualification. It has opened many doors for me and it is greatly respected across the world as the highest football coaching badge that it is possible to achieve.

It was held in such awe, that during my time working in the USA over the years, I was commissioned to provide 500 copies of my coaching manifesto to all attendees at the NorCal Premier League International coaching symposium.

Accompanying me in my class on my journey through the course were Brian Deane, Douglas Freedman, Andrew Gould, Lee Johnson, Russell Latapy, Craig MacPherson, Lee McCulloch, Darren Murray, Ricky Sbragia, Lee Carsley, Duncan Ferguson, Stephen Glass, Ann Helen Graham, John Kennedy, David Longwell, David McCallum, John McLaughlan, Brian Reid, Barry Smith, Gavin Strachan, Paul Williams and Edward Wolecki Black…some big names from Scottish football and beyond in there, eh? And Edward Wolecki Black was literally the biggest.

I got close to Eddie and appreciated the success he achieved with Glasgow City, transforming them into a Champions League club still dominating the women's game today. We would keep in touch – something I'd do with most of the guys on the course as it's a network of reciprocal benefit – in a game where I've learned that, if certain people say good morning, you go out and check the sun is out. So you can imagine my sadness when I found out he had suffered a stroke at half-time in a game against Cowdenbeath, whilst he was manager of Airdrie. I was assistant manager at Dundee United at that time and we had beaten Airdrie in the previous round of the Scottish Cup and were in Dingwall to play Ross County in the quarter-final, when I checked my phone after the game to see a missed call from Eddie that morning.

As we were preparing for the game, I had my phone switched off, so I tried to call him on our way home, at the same time catching up with good wishes messages due to our success that afternoon. His phone was off and I only heard the bad news of him taking unwell after receiving a message from Iain King, then director of football at Airdrie. He told me Eddie's life was saved due to the proximity of Central Park to Edinburgh Royal Infirmary, as well as the excellent medical staff in attendance at the game.

I went to see him and it's a credit to his strength as well as support from his wife, Emma, that has seen him recover to continue his career, which has seen him move to Motherwell, then Celtic and return to Motherwell Ladies in 2020. He left again in March 2021 and is now director of football at Gartcairn Juniors.

Scottish football nobility Jim Fleeting and Donald Park were the double act who delivered a fantastic learning experience for us all, which I continue to draw upon today and which will provide a great deal of my strategy forming in the future. I also can't forget Ann Quinn, who was terrific in her support role and provided tireless help and answers to every query.

Reading biographies of the great and the good of world sport – not just football – was suggested required reading while we were taking the course and, as I was already an avid reader of these sorts of books, I lapped up the opportunity to gorge myself on some I had my eye on, but never got round to.

These included: Muhammad Ali: King of the Ring, Chris Anderson & David Sally: The Numbers Game, Dennis Bergkamp: Stillness & Speed, Marco Ceccomori, Luca Prestigiacomo, Andrea Riva & Mauro Viviani: Soccer's 4-4-2 System, Sir Alex Ferguson: University of Harvard Presentation, Graham Henry: Lions Tour of Australia, Arthur Hopcroft: The Football Man, Zlatan Ibrahimović: I Am Zlatan, Shiv Khera: You Can Win, Massimo Luchessi: Coaching the 4-3-3, Ellen McArthur: Single Handed, John McEnroe: Are You Serious?, Donald McNaughton: 12 Hidden Laws of Performance, Barney Ronay: The Manager, Arsene Wenger: The Professor, Jonny Wilkinson: My Story of Dedication, Jonathan Wilson: Inverting the Pyramid, John Wooden: A Lifetime of Observations, Sir Clive Woodward: Winning! The Autobiography… I was going to read Lee McCulloch's autobiography, but it was all pictures! I found them fascinating and it's amazing the small things you pick up on from a sporting legend, that you would never think really mattered. But it is the small margins and the detail collectively, that can make the difference for talented professionals to progress to become global superstars and for all teams, coaches and players to markedly improve their performance. Summarising the course section by section – or chapter by chapter as referred to in my end of course book – is probably the best way of giving you a flavour of the intensity and comprehensive elite coaching learning that was involved in the Uefa Pro-Licence. But the guest speakers and workshops were spread out throughout the course and not lumped together in one go as each section suggests. Even I might have been getting slightly irritated while listening to eight international managers in a row, no matter how influential they have been in their careers.

In the first section I give a report on all the international managers who came to talk to us, and what my thoughts were on each. Not sure if I've mentioned it before, but I worked with Craig Brown at Motherwell and he was a big, big influence on my coaching career. He encouraged me to go for this course and despite the fact that he didn't speak or present any practical sessions during it, it was a privilege to be at a dinner held in honour of his contribution towards Scottish football. The dinner was well attended by colleagues, friends and family who have supported, benefitted and contributed to his achievements over the years and I was pleased to see such a large turnout, and so was he, as he managed to steal the glasses away from Archie Knox to read his speech, before he took his seat!

Despite the large number of the great and the good of Scottish football being present, Craig had the humility to work the room and what an ego boost for me to be mentioned in his speech, whilst sitting with my fellow peers from the course making up one of the tables. Again it shows the class and humility of the man, which is world renowned.

One of the first speakers on the course was Gordon Strachan – then Scotland manager. Right from the start he had me interested in his methods of studying how other teams play and, in particular, his take on his favoured system adopted by the German national team. His explanation of how the front three should be upwardly mobile was particularly insightful. He argued that they should not be stereotypical or inflexible in their play, like perhaps the Dutch, who would have a main central forward and two wide attackers – making a strike force of three – and resulting in five defending, with a pivotal number six.

Players and their intellectual ability was another topic widely discussed by Gordon. He contrasted between players whom he had worked with previously and those he was working with then, and this led to interesting comparisons on what information they could absorb. It was suggested that, ultimately, a time would come when a decision would have to be made based on a player's ability or inability, to carry out desired instructions. I remember him telling me in conversation, where I was present alongside his good friend, Mark McGhee, about young players who had to hear the same message four or five times in order to carry it out correctly. At this frustrating point, it is difficult to see how the penny will eventually drop for some players, though you do always hope for the best. The discussion on staff and whether you hand-pick them based on previous relationships, or work with people you inherit at a club was a very topical one, with preferences expressed for and against.

Some years ago I remember talking with former Aberdeen and St Mirren manager Alex Smith – a highly regarded and reputable football man in my eyes – when he came into Motherwell with Maurice Malpas. He explained to me that when you go into a new club, there will be good people there who are depending on you to keep them in work and to provide for their families. This is a great principle to adopt and Gordon was a firm believer in this ethos. However, he differed slightly as he would also take certain preferred individuals, who he had a sound working relationship with and could also integrate with any staff he would inherit at a new club.

It is also the case that there might be talented people at the club who had been underutilised by a previous management team and who might thrive under a new leadership given the chance. Again I have experienced this situation personally at a club, and have seen how a departing manager gave certain staff members a new freedom and confidence, where previously they felt undermined. A lot depends on the size of the club you are moving to, but I like the idea of evaluating the staff in place and, if they can buy into your philosophy or strategic plan, then everyone can benefit.

Also, there will be a need for local knowledge – on local culture, internal club politics, etc. – where it can be useful to have a heads-up from incumbent staff.

In summarising Gordon's refreshing and dynamic football philosophy he has said himself that if he "left a training session where either an individual or team did not benefit from my knowledge, then I would be disappointed." Paul Hartley and myself currently use this analogy when we debrief a session at Cove Rangers and ask ourselves: "Would we have liked to have been a player in that session?"

This highlights someone who plans for development and strives for improvement of not only their team, but themselves. Gordon's vibrant character and personality meant that he was always very good company to be around. From a Scotland staff perspective, it was evident there was a great deal of chemistry between Gordon and his assistants, Mark McGhee and Stuart McCall, a combination which oozes a tremendous amount of personality and character as well as undoubted knowledge of football at the highest level. Having worked with both Mark and Stuart, I appreciated exactly how they would like their teams to play, and both fitted into Gordon's mind-set of entertaining football, whilst maintaining a practical outlook to achieving this.

Although they all complemented each other, they were strong enough characters to provide an opinion and not be 'yes men' to Gordon, who undoubtedly took on board ideas and suggestions to ultimately achieve a positive outcome. Gordon also encouraged his entire Scotland national team staff at that time, to present to us and give us an understanding of their preparation for an international match covering the opposition, video analysis, sports science and physiotherapy and all of it was extremely useful and illuminating.

Also on the speaking bill were international managers Mixu Paatelainen (Finland) – who I would go on to form a great friendship and professional working relationship with – Lars Lagerbäck (Iceland), Michael O'Neill (Northern Ireland), Roy Hodgson (England) and Peter Taylor (England under- 20), all of whom would reveal some outstanding wisdom, advice, knowledge and tales. Club managers who gave us the benefit of their experience included: Malky MacKay, Brian Deane, Walter Smith, John McGlynn, Eric Black, Alex Miller and Archie Knox. And from the world of sport, business, media, management and administration, the experts kept on coming, including: Alastair Campbell, Darryl Broadfoot, Dick Bate, Donald MacNaughton, Frank Dick OBE, Gregor Townsend OBE, Jacques Crevoisier, Jim Fleeting, Mark Wotte, Ray Kelvin, Stephen Maguire, Stewart Regan and Vincent Lunny.

In my pro-licence book I have summarised all their guest-speaking gigs – just as I did with Gordon Strachan. But there was much more than just taking notes on what eminent people had to say. We were taken on site visits to places such as Everton FC, FC Luzern and the Uefa headquarters in Nyon Switzerland. Throw in the club visits to Stade de Reims and Tottenham Hotspur, as well as an eight-day match analysis stint at the Under-20 World Cup in Turkey in 2013, and you start to get an idea of the course content and commitment required to navigate through the assignments and assessments.

If you also include the business management assignment delivered by the University of Stirling, as well as a mandatory French language speaking course - "où est le fitba" - then you start to see the content of such a highly acclaimed qualification.

Suffice to say it takes some people two or three attempts on the bi-annual process, to obtain the full qualification due to the time required for course completion. I like the social aspect of football and the release needed at times with a glass of wine or a bottle of beer, helps with the relaxation and camaraderie building. But I can honestly say that the group I studied with, among whom are great friends, never had time for a social night out, let alone a drinking session – and that's as high a testimony I can offer due to the intensity of the course and the dedication from the chosen candidates.

This fact is a wee bit in contrast to my Uefa group study visit to FC Luzern, a beautifully situated Swiss club where I participated in a four-party information-sharing week with representatives and delegations from Bulgaria, England and the host country Switzerland. The Swiss were terrific hosts and my counterpart was Gareth Southgate, who was, at that time, representing England and would go on to become their national team manager. I can't remember the name of the Bulgarian representative who joined our trio, probably because his contribution was next to nothing and he was more interested in dipping the shoulder from the sessions to go out and have a cigarette.

Here's where I have a confession and apology to make to Gareth. After a particularly long day of pitch and classroom work, we all retreated to the bar after a late dinner and I took up his offer of a "half lager" as a nightcap.

Gareth duly drained the mouthful – who drinks a half pint? – and sauntered up to his room. Just then the waitress asked if we wanted another round. "Absolutely mademoiselle same again!" was the cry, at which point the sultry Bulgarian came to life for the first time, especially when I suggested we should order bigger glasses of the local brew.

To be fair another reason he perked up was the fact that he didn't have to do any work, which was the norm for his week's effort. I think he was the rogue party gate-crasher as his fellow countrymen from the Bulgarian delegation all seemed to be a great bunch of lads.

The priority of the guy we got landed with appeared to be pocketing anything that wasn't nailed down. It was just our luck he wasn't as committed or enthusiastic about what was happening on the coaching side of things. Thank fuck he was a size 11 and not my size 7, or all my gear could be on Sofia's answer to Gumtree right now! Anyway, little did I know that the tab was based on the first person's order and therefore being charged to their room, at least I don't think I did!

Friday morning arrives and I can hear the lovely sound of the birds singing on Lake

Lucerne. This was interrupted by Mr Southgate, who I imagine is standing with a reel of paper resembling a small toilet roll, and arguing that it wasn't his bill…

"But monsieur… I don't even drink pints!" I could have sworn I heard from the direction of the reception desk.

Ah well, you can take the boy out of Motherwell.

Back to the serious stuff, and after discussions with various contacts regarding my club visit, I decided to take the advice of my agent, Scott Fisher, and use his contact in Stade de Reims, and focus on the provincial French club as my special project.

They kindly allowed me to come over to visit them for seven days to find out about their set-up, shadow their management team, watch their training sessions, examine their styles of play, assess how the their club operated as a business, look at their academy structure and progression routes and find out exactly what they were looking for in a player.

These visits are self-funded and highlight the student's commitment in terms of fitting around a busy work schedule and financial outlay, in order to complete an important part of the qualification.

Reims gave me complete access to all of their departments and answered all my questions, before presenting me with a first-team jersey complete with YOUNG printed on the back. And to cap it all, when I went to check out of the hotel I stayed in for the week, the bill had been settled, that's a touch of class.

Another example of a flourishing club friendship came when I wrote a letter of thanks. They replied saying it was they who were honoured that I had chosen their club to do my dissertation on. What do you make of that? They must have seen that last goal I scored for Cambuslang at Carluke. Their manager at the time – Hubert Fournier – was exceptionally helpful and friendly towards me, offering me full co-operation each day, giving me insight into their training practices and preparation towards games. He would help me understand the 'head coach' role, which at the time differed to the 'manager' version used in the UK. But now it is a rarity, with departmental heads being preferred to a 'manager' in control of everything.

I think that this European model is a more sensible approach, as long as there is strong dialogue between the head coach and both director of football and head of recruitment. Herbert was particularly clear about this and we would discuss this and many other topics after training sessions over lunch, which would be accompanied by a nice bottle of the region's finest grape. This was a guy who played in Germany with Borussia Monchengladbach and would leave Reims to go to Lyon, although he told me his favourite team was his local one, namely Guincamp.

The reason I chose Stade de Reims as opposed to somewhere like Real Madrid, Barcelona or Bayern Munich, was that it was important for me to see how mid-sized clubs in Europe operated. I had to consider my own football background and future potential working environment, as well as the fact that the club had been through administration similar to Motherwell, and I was very interested in their transition. The fact that Stade de Reims operates in the heart of the French Champagne region was a welcome added bonus. They explained that their own footballing "philosophy" – which was unique to anywhere else I'd experienced – had an emphasis on 'champagne' players who were fast, explosive and had the energy to engage with the fans in the region who were used to that lifestyle. They based that development around wide players who could be full-backs or wingers capable of playing in different shapes, but with the focus on pace. They also recruited in the shadows of Paris and would send scouts to monitor the big Parisian clubs and the stock of players they had who would fit their model.

Topics, workshops, analysis and assessments that were set for us on the Uefa Pro Licence, provided us an opportunity to work individually and in groups to develop our own tactics, and footballing philosophies. Topics included: The Under-20 World Cup in 2013, Manchester United FC - Strengths & Weaknesses, The Boardroom: Ross County FC, mock interviews for the new Motherwell FC Manager – I was totally over qualified for that one – What Makes a Good Assistant Manager?, and the World Cup 2014.

Final assessments to be handed in, along with everyone's written overview of the course (book), included: Negotiation & Management, the French Language and John Wooden on Leadership.

Uefa Pro-Licence…what a privilege, what an experience and – as a coach – what an important thing to have on your CV along with Achievements: North Lanarkshire hide and seek champion 1971 to 1974 and Likes: Laughing, fixing garage doors and playing fitba!

Never Say Gannon Again

Working under Jim Gannon taught me one thing…never to coach or manage like Jim Gannon

There's no doubt that becoming the manager of Motherwell FC is one of the most attractive jobs in Scottish football outside of taking charge of one of the Old Firm clubs… or being the official Killie Pie taster! I say that with complete and utter conviction as I look back at the plethora of fitba legends I worked under during my time there. When I first started helping out in a coaching capacity, Billy Davies was the boss. I also served under – in order – Eric Black, Terry Butcher, Maurice Malpas, Mark McGhee, Jim Gannon, Craig Brown, Archie Knox and Stuart McCall and I learned something from each of them, some more than others.

The thing I learned from Jim Gannon, however, was not to be like fucking Jim Gannon! His tenure at Fir Park became an unmitigated disaster and it wasn't just the results on the pitch that caused a problem. The way he conducted himself left a sour taste in the mouth and I would go as far as to say that in the weeks before he finally left, it was starting to affect the reputation of the club I love. And to think that before he was confirmed as Well manager, we nearly had Aidy Boothroyd – former Watford manager and current England Under-21 boss – in the hot seat. After Mark McGhee had left to join Aberdeen in the summer of 2009, Motherwell interviewed Aidy. He must have been keen on the post as he asked the board if he could take a wee walk around the stadium and the facilities. He came up and introduced himself to me and after a short time I felt right at ease in his company. He was a really nice man and I thought he would be an excellent appointment. Unfortunately, history tells us Aidy had a sniff of something closer to home and his interest cooled and he ended up succeeding Paul Lambert at Colchester United in early September.

Jim Gannon – a Stockport County icon – was the result. And not one we wanted as it turned out. This is the guy who allegedly refused to give an interview to Sky Sports because he was raging that an engineer hadn't been out to fix his broken modem. I honestly have difficulty describing where to begin with Jim Gannon and the backroom team he brought with him, Peter Ward and Alan Lord. He did not endear himself to the Motherwell players and staff virtually right from the start. Very quickly, after a decent start to the 2009/10 campaign, we were becoming too predictable on the pitch and were getting picked off by other teams and the fans were getting restless. Added to that, because of his antics, he was becoming a laughing stock amongst everyone else in Scottish football. It was as if he came in with the mindset that he was going to show the Scottish Premier League and the country as a whole how football should be played. Scottish football, according to Jimbo, was shite and he would teach us all about how it should be played.

He was just so impersonable and the offhand way he treated people really got on everyone's tits. He would blank people totally, including me. It seemed he had made up his mind about the players before even looking at them properly and was intent on a total rebuilding job. To be fair – did I just say that out loud? – he had to replace an entire squad who were out of contract and I will give him enormous credit for his recruitment of players, who would go on to serve the club well under more personable managers.

Motherwell has always been a close-knit club – through the good and bad times – and there was always a 'we're all in it together' family feel around the place, that would see everyone help each other with honesty, humour, concern and genuine decency. The smiles seemed to disappear when Jim arrived and I even changed my mobile phone ringtone to Pink's track Funhouse - "This used to be a funhouse, but now it's full of evil clowns, It's time to start the countdown, I'm gonna burn it down, down, down" - to reflect how I was feeling and to be able to have a secret dig at the new regime every time it went off in their company. The players knew this and would phone me when I was in their company or walking past them just to rub it in.

One day I observed him organising a 'Shape Exercise' on the training pitch where he proceeded to get everyone and their dog – yes I truly believe he would have included a real dog at left-back if he could have found one handy – on the pitch to show players, who were incidentally, standing and watching where they should be. He had a 17-stone fitness coach filling in at right midfield, as he left previously trusted first-team players at the side of the pitch, who he didn't fancy. Jim had announced that he would teach the rest how to play football properly and had already decided that most of the squad he had inherited were not for him.

One player he had it in for was Steven McGarry, who I thought was a decent midfielder who did a good job for the club. One day after training Jimbo and his assistant jogged back to Fir Park from the Dalziel Park training ground in Carfin. Coaches often did this as it gave them a chance to dissect the pluses and minuses from the day's training as well as keeping them fit. The players would head back in the mini-bus. He set off on his run and after a couple of minutes the Motherwell mini-bus drives past and the contents of a water bottle hit Jim flush in the face. Looking up, all the drenched gaffer can see is the 16 members of the first-team squad trying to hide underneath the seats on the bus, as it speeds on to the ground. On arriving back at Fir Park, the first team begin tucking into their lunch. About 15 minutes later a raging, knackered and stinking Gannon arrives and immediately begins an investigation. He orders his assistant to bring what he thought were four or five of the culprits – insisting one was Steven McGarry, who was totally innocent – up to his office for questioning. The irony was that the real culprit – Giles Coke – who was one of Gannon's favourites, wasn't even among the group of suspects. I think Gannon was hoping to move a few players on and it might well have suited him perfectly if any of them were in some way implicated. In the end Giles – who was a top bloke – would go and own up to the manager that it was him, to prevent innocent parties being fined or worse for 'water-bottlegate'.

On another occasion the joke was on me. I had to get suited and booted for an official meeting at Hampden and strolled through the Players' Lounge at Fir Park on my way to the front door. As players are never ones to miss an opportunity for wisecracks, questions were loudly raised about my smart brown suit, and several asked: "Youngy, a brown suit, what's the Hampden Roar (score)?". To save face I announced to the entire throng that "Brown was in this year." Surprisingly, it was Jim Gannon who pinged back to me with the funniest thing that I ever heard him say during his short spell at the club - "Tell Brown that McGarry's out this year!". Touche Jimbo, I'll give you that one, I thought, while at the same time seeing Steven at the back of the room delivering a hand gesture as the boys all buckled. If managers could pull off some more light-heart-ed stuff like that at appropriate moments and treat people with a bit more respect at the right time, they would have more friends than enemies.

McGarry was Gannon's pet-hate and everyone who knows Steven will tell you, apart from being a very good footballer, he had a terrific personality and that pissed the boss off even more. I think this period influenced Steven's decision to emigrate to Australia. After Jim left, I was so pleased I could put Steven on as a sub in his last game. It was during in my second stint as caretaker manager, against Hearts at Tynecastle, before he left for a new and successful career Down Under.

Jim was the guy that called the SPL (Scottish Premier League) the Scottish Pub League and blanked all the visiting managers after the games at Fir Park, where it's customary to host the opposition coaching staff after the matches. There were some players – mainly Scottish ones – who he took an instant dislike to. He hammered them on a Monday at training and that meant they knew they would not be playing on the Saturday. Real stalwarts – who had all been sensational under previous manager Mark McGhee - were jettisoned and McGarry especially took the brunt of his displeasure. They ended up training with the senior Academy players at times, as the new boss and his 'yes men' assistants tried to show the remaining first-team squad how he wanted them to play. He used everyone but the players in his practice shape drills; he had assistants, and even the strength and conditioning coach he brought in, taking part in the 'shaping sessions' as a makeshift left-back or winger.

Thankfully, Jimbo more or less left me to my own devices as head of the Academy and his attitude did not impinge upon me too much. But I saw how it affected everyone else, from the players to the kitman and all the support staff at the club, who were more like my friends than my colleagues. I remember the only times he showed me any due, was on a Friday afternoon. I would be getting showered and changed after playing my weekly five-a-sides with my mates and he'd call me into his office to chat about some idea he had come up with. And the only reason he did that was because we were the only two people left in the whole of Fir Park.

"Eh Gordon, can you come in here for a moment?"

"Yes Jim?"

"What do you think of…

'This used to be a funhouse, but now it's full of evil clow…'

"Sorry Jim, I'll turn that off. That's just my mates… what are they like?"

He just looked at me, and I wondered if he ever clicked that the ringtone was a dig at him. But he wouldn't have had the nous to realise he was the brunt of the joke every time it went off. I swear my mates also upped their calls to me to make sure it was heard around Fir Park at every opportunity. Once I turned the phone off, he'd then run through a scenario about the forthcoming match and looked for my reaction. I could say at least he was trying to communicate, albeit only on a brief one-to-one situation. However, I am sure Peter and Alan would have been able to give him the reassurance he was looking for the next day.

It was as if he had more faces than the Motherwell town hall clock and it seemed to me that there was a queue of people who wouldn't have minded punching every one of them. I've since listened to a podcast by former West Brom striker Geoff Horsfield, who worked briefly with Jim at Port Vale after he left Motherwell. Horsfield described how he thought Gannon was one of the worst people he had ever met in football. It seems they ended up in an altercation on the team coach one day, so I feel comfortable with my assessment about Mr Gannon.

As mentioned earlier, the one good thing he was able to do was identify a few good players for Motherwell… I'll certainly give him that. I saw the presentation he did to secure the job and it was impressive, as were some of his ideas. The problem was his ability to manage people whilst showing humility. I've seen the top coaches do this up close and he was nothing like them. He used to live off his Stockport County promotion achievement, which granted, was an admirable one. He'd tell me "I won the second division play-off." Yip, you did mention that Jimbo. I'll see you that and raise you "Did I tell you John Clark, a Lisbon Lion, bought me for Shotts?". Boom! He did have a liking for Celtic.

Tom Hateley, John Ruddy, Steve Jennings, Giles Coke, Chris Humphrey and Lukas Jutkiewicz all came in and served us very well… mainly after he left. You add Craigan, Hammell, Lasley, Murphy, O'Brien, Reynolds, Sutton and you've got a very good squad at that point. Sprinkle in the young talented boys coming through and, bingo, job's a good 'un.

I still to this day have the reports from the SPL delegates who attend matches and give feedback on the conduct at games, and all of them point to how arrogant Jim was. One even states that he is "the most arrogant man in Scottish football". It was an unbelievable period of my career and I take no great pleasure in revealing the negative aspects of a Motherwell manager's reign, but I feel I need to use the coming pages to describe why his time at Fir Park ended after just six months.

It is always customary – across the whole world – for a home team manager to invite their opposite number to their office for a cup of tea or a glass of wine after the game. Win, lose or draw, Jim rarely did this, but the day we played Celtic he perhaps showed where his true colours lay, by inviting what seemed to be every member of his family and friends along with the Celtic coaching staff into his office for a party, after they had beaten us 3-2. It was like the cast of Ben Hur and I remember his assistant, Peter Ward, asking me: "Gordon, can you go and get more wine and beer for the Gaffer?" Really? "Why don't you go and fuck yourself with a ragman's trumpet?" I think was my response.

Now, in my time at Fir Park, I have seen some visiting managers vary the time they spent chewing the fat after a match with the Well boss. Some have stayed for five minutes, some have stayed much longer. Portuguese Hearts boss Paulo Sergio spent an hour and a half in with Stuart McCall during a visit in 2011/12 where he demolished two bottles of wine toasting his birthday, while the team waited outside in the bus and we had just beaten them! A top man and every minute was a pleasure for all involved. But until the arrival of Jim Gannon, all visiting coaches and managers had at least been extended the courtesy and tradition of an invitation to the office.

I respect any manager's desire to do things their way, but to thumb your nose at decades of convention and decency, was playing a game that was causing the club some problems. Jim would just go and sit in his locked office himself after a match and I was having to field some awkward questions from the great and good of Scottish football.

Usually this would consist of: "Where is he Youngy?". I was caught in a bind of having to take a stance as a Motherwell FC employee. I would have to be careful not to grass my boss up to representatives of another club, that he was in his office but didn't want to see anybody, which could land me in a bit of trouble. But I also didn't want to lie to some well-respected people who I had become quite friendly with in the game. Everyone knew he was in his office, as the lights were on, he was just dingying them. After playing Rangers at home one day, Ally McCoist came into my office (which was next door to Jim's) with Walter Smith, Kenny McDowell and Ian Durrant to say a quick hello and, knowing the score, knocked his door on the way out and said "Cheerio Jim, that's us away now!".

Another memorable example of this came when Hibs ventured to Fir Park and humped us 3-1 at the end of September. Gannon's difficult reputation with his peers and with the media had been spreading, and the Hibees' no-nonsense manager John 'Yogi' Hughes, was quite rightly determined to take a stand and make a point that Jim's behaviour was laughable and unacceptable. I remember Yogi marched right into a crowded Players' Lounge after the match, and with a big grin on his face shouted across to me: "Right Youngy is it hide and seek tonight? Are we going to have to go and find him?". Word was spreading about his attitude and that he was not interested in having any kind of relationship with anyone in Scottish football.

At the new St Mirren Park in Paisley on Tuesday, 27 October, we were up against the Buddies in the quarter-finals of the League Cup. Three days earlier we had earned a 3-3 draw with them on league duty and it seems Jim was intent on using some mind games to try to get the cup victory, but it back-fired big time. As the match was about to kick-off, Jim was taking his seat in the dugout with assistant Peter Ward. I was close to the technical area, when a voice loud enough to be overheard by St Mirren management team Gus McPherson and Andy Millen, boomed out words to the effect of "SPL, that must stand for Scottish Pub League!"

Gus and Andy were rightly raging at that. But they had a great night as with ten minutes to go they were 3-0 up and playing keep ball. Near the end voices were again raised again from our dugout and another comment was fired the way of the home management team to the effect of: "You wouldn't be doing that if it was nil-nil, would you?" Who would say that when we were getting our arses handed to us? But from the direction of the home dug-out came the reply: "Aye no bad for a pub team eh?".

By the start of December, it was incredulous that we were sitting on a half-decent points total of 20 (four wins and eight draws), but cracks were widening and four defeats in a row put the tin lid on things for Jim. Hibs beat us 2-0 at Easter Road, Celtic had won 3-2 at Fir Park – the day of the party in the manager's office – and next up was Rangers at Ibrox on Saturday, 19 December. Gers sub Kyle Lafferty had just scored his second goal on the 88th minute to make it 6-1, going on 16-1, and everyone was urging the referee to blow the final whistle. By the 93rd minute Rangers have the ball near the corner flag in our half and are keeping it. Embarrassingly, Jim then runs out of the dugout and appears to be loudly questioning why the champions would be wasting time like this. Once again a retort comes from the home dug-out area with words to the effect of: "It's for your team's own benefit, yah clown."

When football managers are under pressure – and after three defeats in a row, including a pummelling at Ibrox, Jim was under pressure with a capital P – they tend to desperately throw out the life rings to those around them to try and reel in some support in the hope things will change. But Jim had burned his bridges with most people outside his inner ring weeks before, and the baw was totally and utterly burst for him at Motherwell.

As you can imagine, he was clinging on by his fingernails as the coaching staff had their Christmas night out in 2009 at the Mandarin Chinese Restaurant in the centre of the town. After a muted meal, we all went back to Fir Park's Players' Lounge for a few drinks. Jim, Peter, Alan and their fitness coach are on a charm offensive and were trying to get me onside over a few drinks at the bar. "You're a good guy, Youngy. This is what we're trying to do, Youngy. There's an important role for you here, Youngy." But I knew they weren't to be trusted and I wasn't having any of it.

Regarding Jim, by this time the dressing room had gone as they say, and in the next game on Boxing Day, St Johnstone took advantage and smacked us 3-1 at home. He was sacked soon after and it shows the extent to which he had rubbed people up the wrong way during his tenure, that we were still sitting in a healthy sixth place at the time, not even in a relegation position. It was also reported that another reason for the breakdown in Jim's relationship with the club was that he was not 'fully committed' to his role as he had not signed a long-term contract. But the situation as a whole, in my opinion, had become irretrievable. Working under Jim Gannon did teach me of the importance of being a good man-manager and that one of the most essential things a new boss should do when taking on a new job, is to try to win hearts and minds first.

After Jim gets the sack, the call from above comes for me to step in as caretaker manager. No problem, I think, the Academy is down for winter break and I would be working with top guys, who are top players - never a chore, always a pleasure. But hold on, in come Hoddit and Doddit, or Gannon's assistants, Ward and Lord, who declare their undying love for me. "What do you need? What can we do to help?" they ask. Eh, thanks, but no thanks. I am quite capable of masterminding a defeat away to Hearts at Tynecastle on my own, without the help of you pair. As bad as Jim was in my opinion, however, others prove that the good guys in the game far outnumber the numpties.

Octoclassy

In my time at Fir Park, eight class managers encouraged me to strive for more… and the stories get funnier

A s I mentioned, I served under eight other classy football managers in my time at Fir Park - Billy Davies, Eric Black, Terry Butcher, Maurice Malpas, Mark McGhee, Craig Brown, Archie Knox and Stuart McCall. I think I might well have already mentioned, once or twice, how Craig and Archie influenced me, but the others also made a big impact on me in some way or other.

Billy Davies was in place when I first started coaching on the invitation of Peter Millar in 2001. Billy was exceptionally good to me and I got to know him quite well before he left, as Motherwell entered administration in 2002. He was a very clever player during his career, which included stints at Rangers, St Mirren, Dunfermline and Motherwell, and this intelligence transferred to his managerial style. He was very diligent and was a stickler for thorough preparation. Billy was also very interested in how the Academy players were developing and wanted to know what type they were and how they were progressing. The late, great Davie McParland – who played more than 400 times for Partick Thistle, who named their training ground after him, was head of youth at Motherwell at that time and was also coincidentally Billy's agent.

I was starting to discover that coincidences and spider-web associations like this crop up all the time in Scottish football. However, their relationship became strained around this time and I found myself becoming a sort of intermediary between the two, to pass on and relay information and instruction. To be honest I felt like I was going back and forth like a ball in a bizarre game of 'heidy tennis'. But this gives you some idea of the rift that had appeared between the two at that time. Billy saw something in me even in the early stages of my coaching career and recognised that I had a bit of football nous and accompanying business acumen. He recruited me as part of his comprehensive scouting network taking in various matches up and down the country. As well as helping to unearth potential signing targets, this set-up would compile reports on the strengths and weaknesses of our next opponents in the league and potential opponents for cup games in the lower divisions.

Many of the youth coaches and other staff were drafted in to do this, but you could tell who was in favour or who might have blotted their copy book that week, by the games they were allocated. I must have been doing something right as I would regularly get an SPL match such as Dundee United v Hearts, or an overnight trip with the wife to the north of England for a weekend lower league game to check out a player, rather than a jaunt to Stranraer on a cold and wet Tuesday night to see them battle with Stenhousemuir!

Another coincidence related to this particular time of my career, resurfaced recently in my role as assistant manager at Cove Rangers, when we were playing Connah's Quay Nomads in the Scottish Challenge Cup. Rocking up as manager of the Welsh outfit, who would eventually beat us, was former rugged centre half Andy Morrison. He was a cult-hero for Manchester City and Blackpool back in the day, and a player I was once sent to do a scouting mission on for Billy Davies, towards the end of his career. Billy came from a full-on footballing family. He signed his brother, John, for the club and his brother-in-law, John Spencer, who became the Well's most expensive purchase ever at £500,000 from Everton. Through no fault of his own, Billy was given money to spend at that time as Motherwell went down an ill-fated path of trying to buy success and paying high wages in trying to become the third force in Scottish football, also bringing in the likes of Andy Goram and Don Goodman. But it was unsustainable and no doubt it was one of a multitude of reasons which led to a much-publicised financial meltdown in April 2002.

His wife, Martha, was also very knowledgeable about the game and one day at Fir Park I remember Billy receiving pelters from a fan in the Main Stand and this upset his other half more than a wee bit. After the game finished, as he looked up to catch the eye of his wife, she gave him the nod towards the fan who was doing the moaning, heading towards the exit. Billy then ran along the length of the stand to remonstrate with the guy and give him a mouthful in return. Perhaps a wee bit of justified frustration letting for the coach, and maybe a sheepish reminder to the many 'experts' in the crowd, who feel they can abuse people because they have paid to get in, that most coaches try to do the best they can at all times and don't deserve to be constantly berated.

Our relationship at the club grew in the months before he resigned, due to a run of poor results in September, 2001. I was quite a bit taken aback when I learned that before he left, Billy had proposed to the club that I should become the fledgling Academy Manager! But I realised it was way too early in my development – six or seven years in actual fact – for me to take on such a role. However, it was an honour to be thought of in such a high regard by a great Scottish manager and someone I am glad to remain in touch with to this day. Again, coincidentally, Billy would go on to become Craig Brown's assistant manager at Preston North End and then when Billy took over as manager of Derby County, Craig would follow to take up a consultancy role with him at Pride Park.

When former Aberdeen and Metz striker Eric Black came in, it was noticeable immediately he would have a different way of working. You could guess straight away that he had played in Europe and his ideas reflected that. After his success winning the League and several other trophies including the Cup Winners' Cup with Aberdeen, Eric moved to Metz in France to continue his career. Sadly, he retired early in his playing career with a chronic back injury at the age of only 28, but the knowledge he acquired stood him in great stead as a coach.

You could see he had been rounded and cultured from a young age and, like Billy, he was a very good coach. But things didn't pan out too well in the seven months or so that he was in charge and, as the club entered administration in April, 2002, he decided to relinquish his contract, in an effort to save money and help save the club. He was another highly skilled orator with the humility attached, which he displayed in abundance, although I never got the chance to work with him as in depth as the others.

England's 'Captain Courageous' and former Rangers hero Terry Butcher, then came in and brought Maurice Malpas with him. It was at this point (as explained previously) that the roles of Chris McCart and myself became much more important as the club had no money. Producing quality homegrown players from the Academy became imperative, if the club was to survive. By the start of the 2002/3 season, only 11 of the 35 registered players were above the age of 21. James McFadden and Stephen Pearson were two who immediately came to prominence. They would go on to serve Motherwell extremely well and secure big-money transfers (McFadden £1.25 million to Everton and Pearson £350,000 to Celtic), which helped the club stay afloat and attain financial stability.

These two were quickly followed by David Clarkson and Paul Quinn, who were drafted into the first-team squad under Big Terry. In fact, so many Academy players were being blooded in the first team, that I heard Terry make a comment during one match when he looked round to the dugout and said that all his substitutes were "still being breastfed."

Terry had relative success at Motherwell and kept us in the league against all the odds for four seasons before accepting a new challenge to go to Australia and manage Sydney in the A-League in 2006. His assistant stayed, however, and Maurice Malpas took over the reins at Fir Park. First, he brought in the knowledgeable Alex Smith as a consultant before his old Dundee United defensive sparring partner, Paul Hegarty, joined as his No 2. Another one of those coincidences arose later in my career as I ended up working with Alex again at Falkirk when I assisted Paul Hartley there for a spell. Heggy left a great piece of advice etched in my mind: "Youngy, try not to get too high when you win, or too low when you lose." It's a solid mantra to follow but extremely difficult at times to manage, given the emotional rollercoaster ride that the game serves up.

I built up a good working relationship with Maurice, another who was a wonderful coach – but Terry was the man-manager/motivator extraordinaire of the partnership. I enjoyed Mo's company as well as his sense of humour and he was great to bounce ideas off, with a terrific football brain and sound coaching credentials.

One day I received a subjectively poor result report to a coach education course I had been on and, as is the norm based on the numbers, they were very sparse with their comments. I know what I had submitted, was happy with it and was suitably pissed off. I took the documentation into Maurice and told him I was angry and suggested there was no point in re-submitting, as I was not one of the 'exalted' favourites.

"Here, give it to me so that I can file it" and he promptly ripped up the report, before throwing it in the bin. You need people to believe in you and then have the ability to man manage the situation to give the desired effects. "Cheers Mo, I'll away and set up my training drills as normal."

Maurice lasted only a season before resigning and in strode Mark McGhee in June 2007.

To say that Mark McGhee – former Aberdeen, Celtic, Newcastle and Hamburg star – was laid back, is a bit of an understatement. I do realise, though, that the image I have of him is at odds with what happened at the end of his second stint at the Well – I was long gone by that time – when he was filmed having the opposite of 'laid-back' words with an Aberdeen fan after being sent up to the Pittodrie stands during a 7-2 defeat. Let's just say, he could certainly stand up for himself.

He may have come of age, cut his teeth and made his name in Scotland under Alex Ferguson in that great Dons team of the 80s, and gained some valuable experience with Newcastle United (twice), but it was a season in Hamburg where he finessed his football education. He really used his time playing in Germany (1984-85) to the fullest, working under Austrian manager Ernst Happel and making friends with team-mate and future high-profile coach Felix Magath. He would regularly go and visit his friends in Germany, see what was new in their training methods and try to implement what he learned with the club he was managing back in the UK. Under the influence of Mark, Motherwell adopted a more European influence and focussed a lot more on fitness, diet – especially managing body fats – and application. Small margins made a big difference and began to pay dividends on the pitch.

Several players who really excelled under 'Dingus' – a nickname that had followed

Mark since his time at Aberdeen – were the aforementioned Steven McGarry, Jim Paterson, Ross McCormack and Jim O'Brien. These guys effectively became a ruthlessly quick counter-attacking foursome within a team that conjured up an exciting style of play. They all enjoyed purple patches in the two years McGhee was at the club in his first spell.

Indeed the club would go on to receive £250,000 from Plymouth Argyle for the services of Jim and Ross moved to Cardiff City with the Well receiving £120,000 in compensation due to their impressive form under Mark. Up until Kieran Tierney's £25 million transfer to Arsenal from Celtic, Ross would go on to become, cumulatively, the most expensive Scottish player in history, racking up moves to Leeds, Fulham and Aston Villa, totalling nearly £23.5 million.

For the first pre-season training camp I, and several senior Academy players, joined the first-team squad on a trip to Overtron in Austria. Here they would be put through their paces, going for 6am runs through the forest and lying in freezing cold mountain streams in place of ice baths, to help ease the recovery of muscles after the exertion. It was gruelling, but the benefits were there for all to see. From Motherwell nearly being relegated the year before, McGhee took us to third place in his first season and qualification for Europe for the first time in 13 years.

As much as he was laid-back himself, when he gave an instruction everyone else jumped at an alarming pace. As nominated under-19s head coach at that time, I was always up at our Dalziel Park training HQ every morning with the youth players and one of our roles was to set up the equipment for the first team. I'd badger him as soon as I saw him arrive on what he needed for that day and he would say, "Relax wee man" and go and consider his options for the day. But when he did decide, all hell would break loose and the under-19s and I would burst a gut to get out the equipment, set up the drills, move the goals and mark out the areas for the first team to work in.

Nothing fazed Mark, but he certainly kept me and my players on our toes, which I understood then and now, was no bad thing. It was also good to see that he had no hesitation in using young players if they were ready and could do a job for his first-team squad. Shaun Hutchinson was a case in point. The sturdy young Englishman arrived at the Motherwell Academy in 2007 from the respected North Tyneside-based Wallsend Boys Club – which had produced the likes of Alan Shearer, Michael Carrick, Alan Thompson and Steve Bruce – as a 16-year-old left-sided midfielder.

Initially, before I took over, we were trying to utilise his stature and hit long diagonals to him during matches so we could play off his knock-downs and lay-offs. But I felt it did not quite suit him and decided to have a look at how he would perform at centre-half. The opportunity came during a midweek reserve-team game against Hearts where he would be up against the man-mountain centre forward that was

Christian Nade. It turned out to be a good move. Shaun did so well against an experienced first-team Hearts player in that game, that he quickly established himself in our own first-team squad. He would go on to have a great career in the English Championship, signing with Fulham and then on to Millwall, where he is currently captain.

The Academy was working well and Mark and Scott Leitch, his assistant – and a player who came through the Fir Park Club youth ranks in the late 80s – used it to its fullest and got the best out of graduates Mark Reynolds, Marc Fitzpatrick and Jamie Murphy who had recently emerged into the first team, albeit just before McGhee had arrived.

Mark was another expert in man-management and recognised how to get the best out of his staff. He would liaise closely with Chris McCart and myself in the Academy and would always include us in staff nights out. The Christmas night out in 2008 sticks in my mind. The gaffer was an intelligent, refined and cultured man and fancied himself as a bit of a master tactician in the kitchen as well. So he invited all 15 of his backroom staff to his west end flat in Glasgow after one home match in December and grub was up at 8pm.

We had played particularly well that day and secured another victory, which always helps if you are off on a night out afterwards. But the added spice for the evening was that Mark had told us he had a big announcement to make. Speculation was rife as we piled into the club's mini-bus for the trip into the city. We even stopped off at the Cricklewood in Bothwell for a couple of liveners on the way there, whilst Mark undertook his post-match media duties at Fir Park.

What could it be, we wondered? Has he got the Scotland job. Rumours were rife in the papers that he was among the favourites to take over from Alex McLeish in the hot seat? Had he been headhunted for a role at a tasty bigger club? Rumour also had it that he was replacing his friend, Gordon Strachan, at Celtic. Was it that he could only reveal to us over a tasty pasta dish made by his own two hands, to lessen the blow? Was he sacking the lot of us and bringing in a crack unit of German coaches, fitness experts, dieticians and body-fat boffins?

As we pondered the scenarios, we poured ourselves back onto the mini-bus for the 20-minute ride into Glasgow. But 20 minutes is a long time in football, especially with a couple of beers inside of you and three or four of us were bursting for a pish by the time we reached Barlinnie Prison on the M8.

By the time we had left the motorway and made our way into the leafy west end suburbs of the city near Byres Road, my back teeth were floating. As we parked up I was first off the bus and hairing it towards Mark's sandstone apartment block. I pressed the buzzer at the communal entrance, said hello to Mark who opened the door and ran up the stairs. I patiently waited at his flat door after knocking and greeted Dingus with a "Hi boss where's the pisser?" But, in the act of pointing to his toilet, Chris McCart, showing pace that he never showed while he played the game, nipped in ahead of me and locked the door.

Mark was killing himself laughing as I was nearly pishing his carpet and gave me directions to find the en suite in his bedroom. As I rushed in to the room I was confronted with a middle-aged man, who I had never seen before, in his boxers ironing his shirt. We both nodded to each other as I disappeared into the bog to relieve myself. But then it struck me in midflow and as I caught a glimpse of myself in a large mirror…I saw it dawning on me in my own face.

He's going to announce to us all that he's gay!

That's the longest pee I have ever had. I washed my hands and gave myself a good talking-to in the mirror. I came to the conclusion that this was going to be massive for everyone, but that Mark 'coming out' as the first openly gay football manager would be another great first for Motherwell FC as an inclusive community club.

"I'm right behind you mate!" I would say, "well done you… does your wife know?"

I composed myself and walked out of the en suite and bumped into Mark in the hallway on his way back to the kitchen after making sure the rest of the backroom staff, who by this time had made their way up to the flat, were settled in living room.

"Did you meet Mike? He asked.

"Yes, briefly." I said. Before I could pass on my encouragement and congratulations on the big announcement, he explained how he was his best mate who regularly came to visit and stay with him and the reason why I wouldn't have met him before, was that he wasn't that interested in football.

"Still in denial." I thought.

Mark proceeded to tell us all that his wife was pregnant and he was going to be a dad again at the age of 50/51. That's a lesson for gossip-mongers and conspiracy theorists alike, to wait and see rather than guess and pee!

What a night we had toasting the new dad to be and getting to know Mike as well and we had a wee laugh at how I had put two and two together and made 69!

I've often wondered what professional footballers and managers do with all the alcoholic awards they receive. Champagne for man-of-the-match performances, whisky for manager-of-the month prizes, especially if a particular person is not a big drinker, which Mark certainly wasn't. The question should be asked whether hard liquor is an appropriate gift at all to an elite sportsman or woman. I remember hearing that when George Best left Hibs – in the middle of his battle against the booze – he was presented on the Easter Road pitch with an Edinburgh Crystal whisky decanter (full of the stuff) and six glasses, by the chairman of the Hibs Supporters Club! Well, we found out what Mark McGhee did with all of his awards and I think we drank them all that night, including his recent November manager-of-the-month prize whisky.

It was only six months into Mark's first tenure at Fir Park as manager that the club lost one of its favourite-ever heroes during a match against Dundee United at Fir Park on Saturday, 29th December, 2007. Club captain Phil O'Donnell – who was a great player, a lovely man, a father of four and only 35 years of age – had collapsed with a cardiac arrest on the pitch just as he was being substituted and never regained consciousness. He was pronounced dead at Wishaw General Hospital at 5.18pm.

I knew Phil well and the club had plans for him to embark on a coaching role, which he would have been brilliant at. Above all, he was the iconic role model for a Mother-well Academy player. The way that Mark handled the tragedy as manager of the team was exemplary and endeared him to the Motherwell faithful and to his players, coaches, fans and the community as a whole.

Stuart McCall – Bradford, Everton, Rangers and Scotland midfield terrier – was another guy who I hit it off with straight away when he arrived at Fir Park, after my three-game stint as caretaker at the end of 2010. I quickly realised I could work with him and assistant manager Kenny Black. The three of us worked together in a similar way to how I developed a relationship with Craig and Archie and I spent four good years with them.

We reached the Scottish Cup final in 2011 and ended up sixth in the league, despite my pointless three games in charge. The following 2011/12 season we finished third and qualified for the Champions League third qualifying round, due to Rangers' much-publicised fall from grace and demotion to the Third Division.

We drew Greek giants Panathinaikos and I took great pleasure and pride in seeing seven starters – and another two if you count Lasley and Hammell over the two games – who had come through the Motherwell Academy. In addition there were another three on the bench, which was a testimony to the quality that was coming through. They proved too strong for us both on our patch (0-2) and in Athens (3-0), but we put up a good account of ourselves especially in the away leg, despite the scoreline.

Dropping out of the Champions League meant another crack at foreign opposition in the Europa League qualifiers, but we succumbed to Spanish La Liga side Levante.

The following season (2012/13), minus one half of the Old Firm, Motherwell cemented their place as Scotland's second-best team by finishing runners-up in the Premier League to Celtic – the highest position the Dossers had attained in the league since 1994/95. It also raised the promise of another European adventure in the Europa League qualifiers against the Russians Kuban Krasnador, but again we missed out.

I left the club I supported all my life in October, 2013, for a new challenge, but, again, by the end of the 2013/14 season, we had finished in second place – as always with former Academy players to the fore – with a dramatic 1-0 away win at Pittodrie to deny the home team the runners-up spot. That earned us a Europa League tie against

Iceland's Stjarnan, but suffered yet another failure in Europe in a tie we should have won. A point to note here is the fans of Stjarnan were so inspired by the Motherwell Bois supporters and their regular 'Thunder Clap' salute during this tie, that they wanted to use it for themselves. They decided to get in touch with the Well fans and asked if it would be OK if they could take this with them to support their national team's excellent run in the 2016 European Championships where they reached the quarter-finals, defeating England in the last-16 game. The Thunder Clap epitomizes the innovation, creativity and resourcefulness surrounding Motherwell FC, its fans and the community as a whole and has developed into a vibrant and exhilarating crowd participation activity that now rivals the 'Mexican Wave' or 'Poznan Celebration' during games. I'm proud of things like this associated with the club and also how in October, 2016, Motherwell became the first fully fan owned club in the UK's top leagues.

This period was arguably the most consistently successful period Motherwell have ever had in the top division and it was a joy to be a part of the management teams that helped lead them there. I learned a lot from Stuart and Kenny. They were, and still are, so helpful to me and I am grateful that they valued my skills and input during the time we spent together. They have also become great friends and we had some great fun to boot. Stuart was a player's manager and by that I mean that he connected with them on their level very quickly. He got them playing straight away when he came in at the end of 2010 and led them to the Scottish Cup Final against Celtic in May 2011. Unfortunately we got gubbed 3-0 at Hampden on a soaking wet day, and if I'm totally honest, I felt it was the best chance we had of winning the cup since that glorious family final of 1991. Celtic were not a great side at that time and were in a transitional period and, with hindsight, I believe another starting formation would have beaten them. But it did not put a dampener on what we had achieved under the new management team since the start of that year, where we also sneaked into the top six.

The camaraderie among the players under Stuart was first class. One memory that springs quickly to mind was when they booked themselves a long weekend away in Magaluf at the end of the 2011/12 season. Flying out to Majorca en-masse was quite the norm with squads who have battled together all season and they unwind for a few days before their own family holidays, prior to beginning another pre-season training schedule. Little did they know that the management team had coincidently booked up for the same resort, leaving on the same day and on the same flight out. It definitely wasn't planned and as the 'kids' said "we booked up first". It's also commonplace for staff to book an end-of-season jaunt and, believe me, you definitely don't want to hit the same resort as the players you've spent more time with than your family for the previous 10 months. So we felt just as awkward as them.

After the final game of the season – beaten 0-2 at home to Dundee United – the players had gone for a few drinks. More than a few of them were feeling the worse for wear when they arrived first thing at Prestwick Airport the next morning – many of them still wearing the gear they had on from the night before – for the 7am flight to the Spanish island. God knows how they felt when they saw Stuart, Kenny and I and the full backroom staff, including Adam Stokes, Bobby Jenks and goalkeeping coach Gordon Marshall, queuing up with them to check in, with cheeky grins on our faces and wearing 'Kiss Me Quick' hats. You could see them all thinking that they'll now need to be on their best behaviour, rather than their George Best behaviour. But any awkwardness soon disappeared. It was a great flight and the banter was knocking about big style. I think this would have suited Stuart right down to the ground as it may well have emulated the closeness of the squad during his successful time at Rangers in the 90s with McCoist, Durrant, Gascoigne et al, under manager Walter Smith. Years later team captain Richard Gough declared the culture was certainly "the team that drinks together wins together."

As much as things have evolved in the fitness, dietary and conditioning side of the game since then, there should still be an importance placed on building team spirit, especially at the end of a hard season. We were all big fans of this approach. When we landed, we all dropped the bags at our digs and went straight out and headed for the legendary Veronica's Bar on the beach. It was only around lunchtime and the high jinks were just beginning. The drinks were flowing and everyone was having a great time when by late afternoon Stuart, for a laugh…I think!… decides he wants to conduct informal signing talks with the players and find out what terms they are thinking of. So one by one – and with their tacit approval, but without their agents' – they all come up to the top table where the management team were sitting enjoying the ambience and a tipple or two. I act as master of ceremonies and go through a song and dance of introducing each player – every one of whom are all by now, well on – to Stuart and Kenny. Several have had a go and there are howls of laughter as both the players and management set out their stalls for what they want, what they can expect and why, all done in a fun and playful way without anyone taking the hump.

Then up steps club captain and Motherwell stalwart Keith Lasley, who does have a proper wee grievance to make known to his boss, despite having a sly smile on his face. Artistic licence at play here, but he used words to the effect of: "Well it's like this gaffer," starts Las, "I want to make sure my family and I are really looked after this year. I am the longest-serving player at the club and I've seen them come and I've seen them go, but every season it seems that someone is signed at the club on more money than I'm on and I really want to know I'm valued and to be really looked after." Stuart, responds by saying: "At Rangers Las, I was behind the likes of Gazza and Laudrup…" But before he could finish what he was going to say the half-cut captain of the club bellows back at the top of his voice, with more than a hint of dismissive disdain for two of the world's best players, "I don't give a fuck about Gazza or Laudrup… I want to be looked after!" Cue uproarious laughter from the full squad and incredulous stares from the rest of the partying holiday-makers. Meanwhile, at that exact moment things took a surreal turn, as a lifeguard comes in to report that our goalkeeping coach Gordon Marshall is nearly washed out to sea after the tide came in as he was having a wee snooze on a lilo! It's fine to rib and bubble your mates in a nice way and everyone took this carry on in the light-hearted way it was meant. But later on that evening or rather the early hours of the morning, it was me who was the butt of the jokes as Marsh and Kenny Black would rescue me from a local park bench where I'd fallen asleep after having too much seaside air! As you can imagine the rest of the four days we were there were conducted in the same vein, thankfully without any serious injuries, mishaps, bad behaviour or stories making the papers back home. As a result we all returned stronger as a group and ready for the challenges to come during pre-season training and the season ahead.

I'm a person who needs to be early for things. Be it work, family dos, getting together with friends or the opening of an envelope, I need to be there in plenty of time. Stuart McCall is the exact opposite, he hated being early for anything. This came into sharp focus for us all – especially myself as it turned out – one midweek game at Pittodrie on a cold and wet Tuesday in February, 2011. We had set off in good time and, as usual with fixtures in Aberdeen, we had arranged to have a pre-match meal at the Doubletree Hotel in Dundee. We needed to leave the hotel for Aberdeen no later than 4.15pm, but Stuart is enjoying the relaxation so much, he is looking to find how long it takes us to get to Aberdeen on his old Nokia phone, which had a Scotland the Brave ringtone. Fuck knows what he was ever able to find on that…apart from Alexander Graham Bell's MySpace and Bebo pages. Anyway he works out it's only 50 miles from Dundee to the Granite City and it'll be OK if we leave a little later. We finally depart at around 5.15pm and get to the Kingsway dual carriageway, slap bang in the middle of the evening rush hour. After we get through Dundee we are struggling to get there on time as technically we should be at Pittodrie one and a quarter hours before the 7.45pm kick-off.

The bus is at its limit, nearly hitting 90mph, as we try to claw back the time we lost at Dundee, but try as the driver might, we rock up at Aberdeen's main entrance at 7.10pm. One of my tasks as No 3 on the management team was to make sure the referee gets the teamlines in his hand in good time before the match. So I'm ready and primed at the bottom step of the bus waiting for the doors to slide open. As they do, I jump off and sprint through the Pittodrie front door, only to find Craig Brown and Archie Knox – the previous Motherwell management team now in charge of the Dons – standing waiting on us.

"Good of you to turn up," quips Archie and I greeted my old mentors with a sly grin and rush to present my paperwork to the officials. Everyone follows in behind and into the visiting dressing room to get changed and I proceed to set up and take the fastest warm-up in fitba history. The ironic thing was that we headed back down the road that night with three points after a 2-1 victory. Maybe, there was something in Stuart's tardy preparation after all.

It turns out there wasn't, as a similar episode of making a game by the skin of our teeth was to prove. This time it was the Co-operative Insurance League Cup semi-final against Rangers at Hampden on Sunday, 30 January, 2011. We had all stayed at the Dakota Hotel, near Bellshill, on the M8 on the Saturday night and had awoken bright eyed and bushy tailed on the Sunday. We all presented shipshape for breakfast and began getting the mindset right for the game to come. As usual, it was my job to fill out the teamlines and make sure they were correct, but we had a questionmark over the fitness of Chris Humphrey, so would wait until he had a fitness test from John Porteous, our outstanding physio, then make a decision on whether he should start. We also had a player on standby just in case he was unable to make it, but, luckily, Chris passed the fitness test and was pencilled in to start. We had to be at Hampden for 1.30pm for a 3pm kick-off, but, as usual, Stuart had lost all track of time and was too busy concentrating on a communal game of Football Player Hang-the-Man, which was a favourite to help relax the lads before a big game.

Bearing in mind we were heading to Hampden via the roadwork-laden Raith Interchange at Bothwell and then along the M74 at the same time as thousands of Motherwell and Rangers fans heading to the same venue, you would have thought it would have clicked with Stuart that leaving early would have been the ideal thing to do. Instead it was his turn at Hang-the-Man and he would be fucked if he was leaving the Dakota without him guessing the answer to his go. Blacky had set the questions and even gave Stuart a cheeky clue that the player in question was a midfielder for PSV Eindhoven. He was sitting for ages with 'Her_ _ van Ren_al' and still wouldn't budge from the game. Not even, when shortly before 1pm, the police motorbike outrider who would lead the bus to Hampden, came in to see where the fuck we were and to let us know we would have to leave right then, if we were to have any hope of getting there by 1.30pm, would Stuart give up on his answer. Finally, he gave in for the sake of me being able to hand in the teamsheets on time and I had to break the news to him gently that 'Hertz van Rental' did not in fact play for PSV or any other Dutch club. I made a hasty retreat to the bus, with everyone in tears of laughter at the manager's expense. By the time he trooped onto the coach himself he had thankfully seen the funny side. Lampooning the gaffer did not bring us any luck that day, though, and despite a really good performance and great goal from Keith Lasley, we went down 2-1 and missed out on the opportunity to play Celtic in the cup final.

Social nights out with Stuart and Kenny were great and we had some tremendous nights out in Glasgow. Kenny Black and I would regularly stay the night at a hotel in the city, but Stuart was always adamant that he had to get a taxi home to his house just outside of Strathaven, a rural town in South Lanarkshire. Stuart was the happiest man when drunk you could ever hope to have a beer with, but the problem was that once he had reached the limit you just couldn't get him to move. On one occasion I remember Kenny and I standing in Glasgow's Royal Exchange Square trying to hail a taxi, while Stuart was in a doorway or sliding down a window behind us. The tricky thing for an ex-high profile Old Firm player such as Stuart McCall, was that you knew that it would be best to make sure you hailed a Bluenose taxi-driver to take him home. I'm not for one moment casting aspersions on the professionalism of all the Celtic-supporting cabbies in the town, but it might be tempting for one or two to get their phones out and take a few snaps of a "tired" Gers hero lying on the back seat of a car and post them out on social media or send them directly to the tabloids. I dare say the same could be said about Rangers-supporting taxi drivers, if the fitba boot was on the other foot and he had played the best part of a decade with Celtic. Stuart was, however, also one of those ex-Old Firm players who was liked by both sets of fans and he really would have time for everybody, no matter who they supported. The trouble was Kenny Black, as a former Rangers player, was also eminently recognisable to eagle-eyed fitba supporters, and that meant that hailing duties mainly rested with yours truly.

Jings, I am so glad I'm a Well fan and don't need to put up with shit like this. Though maybe it might be different if I strolled into the Accademical Vaults at Hamilton's Peacock Cross on a Saturday afternoon singing "Joe Wark Knew My Father" or marched down Airdrie main street waving a Motherwell flag singing fans' favourite "Since I was young".

There were always one or two near misses…

"Taxi!"

"Yes sir where are you off to?"

"Are you a Celtic fan?"

"Yes I am."

"No offence mate, but we'll wait for another cab."

Honestly, it must have seemed odd at the very least and downright insanity in the extreme, as at that time in the morning after a night out, you would take a ride home from someone wearing a Scream mask and eyeing a claw hammer and a chainsaw in their front passenger seat. But it wouldn't be long until a driver of the required persuasion would be flagged, briefed and paid the fare to take Mr McCall home.

Blacky, on the other hand, brought into focus his own evening oot skill-set at a brilliant night to pay tribute to the late, great Phil O'Donnell. The club had bought two tables at the dinner/dance event in the Ballroom of the Thistle Hotel in Glasgow on the evening of Sunday, 13 March. Earlier on in the day we had played Dundee United at Tannadice in the quarter-final of the Scottish Cup and forced a replay with a good 2-2 draw, so everyone was in high spirits. The proceeds of the event to honour our legendary club captain would go towards the £100,000 target set by 12 men – friends and former playing colleagues of Phil's – who would spend 10 days trekking Mount Cotopaxi in Ecuador in aid of the British Heart Foundation. Simon Donnelly, Jackie McNamara, Darren Jackson, Kenny Crichton, Alan Archibald, Willie Kinniburgh, Greg Anderson, Ross Anderson, Craig Hinchcliffe, David Rowson, Jim Paterson and Bill Leckie were the 12 good men and true.

The Sun's Bill Leckie was compere for the evening and John Gahagan, former Motherwell favourite and renowned after-dinner speaker, was set to entertain us all, along with music from the Second Hand Elastic Band. A second-hand elastic band is a great way to describe the state that Blacky ended up in that evening. There were some mitigating circumstances, but for all intents and purposes this tale reads like a script from a Fawlty Towers-style farce. As mentioned, the game in Dundee was a lunchtime kick-off, so by late afternoon we were all back in Motherwell. I had decided to go home to get showered and changed, but Kenny and Stewart Kerr had opted to go back to Fir Park for a couple of drinks. Kerrso, our goalkeeping coach, was a man who liked a shandy, in fact I'd go on record to say he's consumed the most drink I've ever seen anyone swallow on a night out, which is quite something considering that I know a few chief keggers. Bear in mind they have also had nothing to eat and are matching each other on the white wines. But the big difference is that Kerrso is a monster on the drink, not seeming to make him up nor doon, and Kenny is fighting a losing battle to keep up. As a result, Blacky is a drunk man by the time he takes a seat at our table in the Thistle Hotel Ballroom and I'm catching up fast. Fortunately for us and the other assembled guests we are right at the back and to the side of the venue near the kitchens and the serving entrance. Kenny is enjoying himself and tucks the table cloth into his trousers mistaking it for his napkin. Of course soon after he needs to go for a piss and he stands up walking away and emptying the table of its contents, cutlery, plates, glasses and all. We're all laughing like weans, but then we realise we could be struggling for another desert anytime soon.

Oblivious to the carnage he has wrought on the table, Kenny wanders off trailing the tablecloth and boldly takes a wrong turn into the kitchens looking for the pisher. Two minutes later we see two comis chefs oxstering Blacky – who is waving at us with a big grin on his face – back through the swing doors and out of the Ballroom altogether. Luckily for everyone this slapstick routine was played out mainly for our incredulous and hilarious benefit, due to the position our table was in. So virtually everyone else in the room is none the wiser.

I remember that earlier in the afternoon Derek Weir, Motherwell FC vice chairman and director, had let it be known that the club had booked two rooms in the Thistle Hotel as a contingency and I made my excuses to go and see if I could get Blacky up to bed. As I leave the ballroom I nearly bump into the two comis chefs coming back in. I pass them and realise they have just dumped the Motherwell assistant manager – whose legs have totally gone by this point – in a lift and I can just see his feet stick out of it and the doors banging back and forth off his ankles. I'm beginning to regret my decision as 13 stone Kenny's a sturdy guy and I doubt I'll be able to manhandle him myself, when Kenny Crichton, the Partick Thistle physio and one of the 12 good men and true who are aiming to trek up an Ecuadorian mountain in memory of Phil for the BHF, appears at my side and asks me if I need a hand.

"Yes, please, Kenny… hope this helps with your training?" I say and we go and attend to Blacky. We get him out of the lift and I casually approach the reception with "fuck all" clue of what the MFC rooms are booked under. I take a wild unadventurous guess and ask the receptionist for a room booked under the name Derek Weir from Motherwell FC. Result, she presents me with the key card to one of the rooms and we are off and running. Kenny and I take an arm each and shuffle back into the lift with Blacky, who swears he's seen this toilet cubicle somewhere before! We press for the fifth floor and miraculously, barring Kenny Crichton, no one else attending the event has witnessed any of this unfolding. As we edge out of the elevator and blunder our way along to the room, I think to myself that we might just get away with this. We reach the allocated room and I insert the key card and we enter. Three steps we get and haven't even turned on the light, before a startled kerfuffle erupts and someone sleeping in the bed shouts out "what the fuck's going on here?" I'd recognise Derek Weir's voice anywhere and realise he must have decided to have an early night after his main course.

Thank goodness I didn't manage to turn the lights on when I came in I thought, as we about turned with a half-grinning Blacky and marched back out the room. We head for the stairwell and back down to the reception. Fuck knows what Kenny Crichton is making of all of this, but fair play to him he went along with it and I am so grateful that he did. Just as I make sure the coast is clear at reception, I see Derek Weir storming up to the reception with his slippers and housecoat on to complain that someone has burst into his room while he was sleeping. The receptionist is bamboozled and we have to wait 15 minutes before we explain how the mix-up occurred and make sure Blacky is sorted. I must have been off the day they covered "Carrying your hammered assistant manager up to a hotel room without being seen" workshop when I was doing my Uefa Pro Licence! But after what I went through that night, I think I would have passed the test.

Talking of getting hammered, in the 2011 Scottish Cup quarter-final midweek replay at Fir Park, we crushed Dundee United 3-0 and set up a semi-final against St

Johnstone at Hampden on Saturday 16th April and cruised through to the final with another 3-0 win. This was the first time we had reached the Scottish Cup final for the first time since 1991. After beating the Saints, it was a fantastic moment being on the team bus driving up Airbles Road in Motherwell and just outside the Electric Bar (remember that?) being mobbed by more than 500 Well fans bedecked in claret and amber. They had blocked the road and were singing happily, but it was clear they would not move until we disembarked and went into the pub for a wee celebration. The tailback of tooting cars and the police were certainly happy about this, as the full squad and backroom staff decamped from the coach and filed into my local. I have never seen it so busy and it was like a scene from 'Zulu' with everyone packed in line sardines and surging towards the bar to hear Stuart McCall standing on the worktop to promise we would deliver the trophy back here in May after beating Celtic. Sadly, it was not to be. But it was good to introduce Stuart and Kenny to the Electric and my mates, it would not be the last time they would be visiting.

At the end of another successful season in 2013, Stuart, Kenny and I and the backroom team are in Benidorm for another end-of-season break. This time it's without the company of the players, when Stuart reveals he has an important interview. We arrive on the Thursday, have a good couple of days and on the Saturday, the gaffer receives a phone call and it's Sheffield United wanting to speak to him about their vacant manager's post. Ironically, and totally independently, I had already agreed to take up a head of international academy role there and was working out when would be the best time to tell him, probably during this very trip. Anyway, Stuart decides to go home early on the Sunday for an interview with the Blades and we go out on the Saturday afternoon and enjoy the sunshine with a few shandies. I also take the opportunity while everyone is in good spirits to tell them that I have decided to leave the club I love for a new challenge with Sheffield United. There's that coincidence thing creeping in again.

Now anyone, and by that I probably mean any football fan in the UK, who has seen the Sky News footage of Stuart celebrating winning promotion to the English Premier League as a player with Bradford City in May, 1999, holding a can of lager and taking a heider off a car he is trying to climb over, then miraculously appearing back into shot still holding his un-spilled amber nectar, will know that his dress sense leaves a lot to be desired. He always used to carry a Sturridge Sports Bag everywhere he bloody went, for some reason, but he just didnae care about things like fashion or the latest style. So the vision we have before us is in our Benidorm apartment that Sunday morning, is of a wee ginger Scotsman, having spent three days in the scorching Costa Blanca summer sun, turning scarlet, wearing a pair of denim jeans, a pair of Reebok trainers and asking Kenny Black and I what one of two manky and previously worn polo shirts, he should wear for the biggest interview of his career.

"How do I look?" he says. "How do you look?" says both Kenny and I, "You look like someone about to empty the bins at Bramall Lane, rather than be interviewed as manager. Go and buy a suit!" That just shows the affable, unassuming side to a lovely man that treats people how he finds them.

However, Stuart decided in the end that it was not the right move for him at that time and he stayed another year at Fir Park to guide the Well to another second-place finish in the SPL.

I, on the other hand, was off on an adventure at a club from another steel town.

From India With Love

A new role at Sheffield United beckons and a base of operations in Jamshedpur, another steel town

Irony is a funny thing, particularly if it is used in a humorous anecdote about switching from one steel town to another. It wasn't as if I was getting rusty either in my position as Motherwell Youth Academy manager/director. I wasn't chasing a new job, especially not in Scotland as I was happy and content. But a new 'international academy manager' role had been created with me in mind at Sheffield United and I felt that, after 13 years coaching with the team I grew up supporting, a new challenge would be good for me and the club.

The Blades came calling towards the end of season 2012/13 and by October 2013 I had been announced as their new member of staff, with a remit to develop the academies of a group of clubs around the world that Sheffield owner Kevin McCabe had a vested interest in. These included Central Coast Mariners in Australia, Chengdu Blades in China, Racing White in Belgium, Ferencváros in Hungary and Jamshedpur FC in India. Jamshedpur were owned by the Tata Steel Group which bought Corus (formerly British Steel), including everything still operating in Motherwell such as the Dalzell plant. See the irony building?

It would be Jamshedpur FC in the Indian Football League (IFL) – coincidentally nicknamed The Men of Steel – and the Tata Football Academy where I would focus my attention initially as my three-year contract kicked in. But first of all I had to be unveiled to the board at a Sheffield United home game at Bramall Lane. The club had fallen to the third tier of English football at that time but, 'cliché alert', they were a sleeping giant… as can be seen from their subsequent rise to ninth place in the Premiership in 2020. In 2013 they were still getting 28,000-plus attendances at home, and it would be the afternoon of Saturday, 16 November – a match versus Gillingham in the First Division - that would be the stage for me to be officially introduced to the club.

The night before, Yvonne had conjured up her homemade curry that I was so fond of. We had a great night in anticipating my new football job based in India – with its wonderful cuisine and culture – and a pleasant four-hour drive down the M74 and M6 along with our son, Robbie, the next morning. The next day, with Yvonne and Robbie already in the car, I emerge from my Motherwell home at 7am bedecked in my new bright red Sheffield United tracksuit. I lock the door and get in behind the wheel, with the realisation that for the first time in my professional coaching career, I will not be heading to Fir Park. I feel a pang – and a couple of gurgles – in the bottom of my stomach and put it down to a combination of excitement, mixed with a tinge of regret and uncertainty that I might not be doing the right thing.

Before we get to Lesmahagow on the motorway south to Englandshire, the pang-gurgles have increased a tad, the windows front and back are rolled down more than a smidgeon and I'm beginning to think that curry the previous night might have been a mistake. We're making good time and I decide that with weeks, literally, on the trot in India on the horizon, it might be good practice for me to train my stomach to hold off on evacuation till we get to the Southwaite Services just south of Carlisle – which is my usual pit-stop for a stretch of the legs and a cappuccino when driving south. So with spirits high, we joyfully zoom past Gretna and the facilities on offer there, and head for our target destination…but shit a brick…a lorry has shed its load, lucky thing, shortly after we cross the border and we are forced onto a diversion through Hexham and deepest darkest Northumberland. Now this was driving territory I was unfamiliar with, and mile upon mile of busy Northumberland National Park country road whizzed by without a service station in sight. My belly was just about to enter spin cycle mode, and I'm seriously wondering whether the Emperor Hadrian had ever considered that his wall might be subject to an onslaught from a raging Scotsman bearing his arse, from a southerly direction.

With no end of the detour in sight, and by this time in desperation, I decide to pull over at the next available farm track and get on with the deed in hand. I manage to get to what I consider a secluded area with a hedgerow, whip down the tracksuit breeks and get on with it. When suddenly from nowhere, a 12-strong group of nature ramblers with several young children pitch up to have a discussion about the hawthorn hedge behind me and the wildlife within, cameras at the ready to record their findings. Sticking out like a Royal Mail post box in the arctic in my new red Sheffield United tracksuit, complete with the distinctive white Yorkshire rose and crossed swords badge, I'm thinking my first duty at the club might be to help the press officer work up a statement to explain how the new International Academy Manager had mentally scarred a group of nursery kids and skittered all over the home of Henry the

Hedgehog. "Morning!", was all I could muster as nature took its course. Whilst at the same time I tried to protect my modesty from prying young eyes, and the pristine red tracksuit bottoms from being splattered... jings how was it going to look if I trailed my own shit through the plush hospitality boxes of my new employers?

Luckily, the adult nature ramblers who, without exception, have no doubt made like a bear and taken a shit in the woods, recognised what was what. They clicked straight away that I was a fellow traveller who had been caught short and not some brightly dressed hedge defecating pervert, so they took their own course of action, shielding their youngsters and quickly moving on to show them something less traumatic... like the site of a battle where Romans and Picts murdered each other in their thousands. As you would expect, Yvonne and Robbie saw the funny side and I was literally the butt of the jokes as we got back on the road and made our way to Sheffield.

It's only when we get to the ground and into The Copthorne Hotel – forming part of Bramall Lane and built by Kevin McCabe and what would be my intermittent home for the next two years – that Robbie reveals he has forgotten to pack his dress shirt. Club general manager Dave McCarthy – standing at six foot three inches and with a 19-inch collar - very kindly offers him one of his, despite my boy measuring only 16 inches around the neck. This time the joke is on my son, who has pished himself laughing at me on the drive down, as I look at him sitting in the directors' box at Bramall Lane looking like Harry Hill. But it is short lived as Robbie in his own new role impersonating a comedian, points out to me the further irony from a thoroughly ironic day. Sitting just two seats away from me is legendary Blades player Tony Currie and we were enjoying the game sitting in the Tony Currie Stand. It wasn't long before my new employers and the press officer are themselves having a good laugh at my expense, as my face turns a similar shade as my new tracksuit.

I had been headhunted as a candidate for this new role at Sheffield United who were blazing a trail at that time. They wanted me to try to set up a pipeline of new talent through emulating their own academy structures at clubs where Blades-supporting owner Kevin McCabe had shares around the world. It was all cloak and dagger stuff to begin with. I got a call from an agent and had to meet him in the Westerwood Hotel in Cumbernauld for talks. Once again irony and coincidence rear their heads here, as the Westerwood would also feature prominently when my move to Dundee United hoved into view a couple of years later.

As I've mentioned earlier in this chapter, I was not actively looking for a move from Motherwell, but I knew there was a big world of football out there and I wanted to find out more about this intriguing offer from England. The talks with the agent led to another covert meeting at a halfway point with representatives of the club, and Carlisle was chosen as the venue. It was there that I learned from John Stephenson, head of football operations at United, that he had been eyeing me as the ideal man for this new job. He needed someone with a track record of ingenuity, flexibility and the ability to 'work with the cock you've got', to take on this innovative new role. John had been involved in the transformation of the Celtic FC youth academy set-up along with Tommy Burns and was instrumental in attracting Chris McCart to the Hoops. So he would have been aware of my capabilities. He was a very astute character in Academy development at that time and was part of the influential 'Watford Boys' group who included the likes of Hornets managers Brendan Rodgers, Aidy Boothroyd and Malky Mackay, who have become well known Premier League bosses, and also Nick Cox who would go on to become technical director and head of academy at Manchester United, and Ross Wilson, who became director of football at Rangers. They all adopted a progressive and innovative philosophy on youth development and were all touched by, and contributed to, the development of Watford's academy, which is held in high esteem in the UK.

At the Carlisle meeting I was informed that the Blades, under the direction of millionaire property developer Kevin McCabe, who at that time owned the club and ran Sheffield United PLC (their business arm), would be embarking on a unique mission to outsource their academy personnel and strategy to partnership clubs across the world. Apparently I was the international man of mystery for the job.

Mr McCabe – a proud Yorkshireman whose numbers include a property deal in Glasgow's Princes Square development – had a share in several clubs. It had already been agreed they would pay a fee to the Blades for their international academy manager to assess their current set-ups and to customise them to make them efficient and effective. This would facilitate a pipeline scenario where a good young player – work permits and visas dependant – could eventually progress to the first team at Bramall Lane or alternatively to one or other of the clubs in the stable across the world. In return these satellite clubs would be able to tap into Sheffield's well developed academy system expertise, with access to coaches, physios, sports psychologists, and strength and conditioning experts.

It was certainly ahead of its time and it was a model that no other club had in place. The only thing that sort of hamstrung the project, was that the club was languishing in the English Division 1 at the time and would not be competing in the Premiership until 2019-21. However, not only was it innovative, it was a solid model with various layers of value taking 'root to fruit' on a global scale. I was sold on it and was excited by the challenge ahead at such a big club, which was like an English version of Motherwell FC: based in a steel town, good strong academy, good people in and around the club and a loyal fanbase.

Still keeping it on the hush hush, I was invited down to have a tour of United's excellent Shirecliffe Academy and training facilities in the heart of the city. Reciprocal tours of facilities by coaches of other clubs is normal practice in the world of football. Representatives from Manchester City and Wigan Athletic had previously been up to see how we did things at Motherwell, so if there were any awkward questions asked of me, I could say it was a fact-finding mission of sorts, but still it was best to keep it under my hat. It was all going along swimmingly until I spied Jamie Murphy, who had been signed from Motherwell for Sheffield United by then manager Danny Wilson in January 2013. Luckily the Well Academy graduate, who had played 215 first-team games and scored 50 goals for the Dossers, didn't see me and I used my old wing skills to drop the shoulder, throw a jinky wee side-step and shimmy away in the opposite direction, before he clasped eyes on me. If he had, the jungle drums might have ended up beating in North Lanarkshire before I was ready to announce I was leaving.

However, I had already made up my mind that I was, as I felt it was a great opportunity for me to develop. True to my philosophy that you should always leave a place better than when you arrived, I presented a 28-page handover document on how to improve and help progress the Motherwell set-up and I recommended who should take over my role. I felt this was important given the work that had been undertaken and the importance of the academy to the club, which would enjoy tremendous return in the years to follow.

It takes years to bed in an academy and there is no early return, which is why recruitment and personnel are key to creating the infrastructure and best working practices at a club. Unfortunately, in my time I've seen the wrong people – many ex-players – employed mainly because, in my opinion, they wouldn't be able hold down a job in the real world. It seems to me that they see it as an 'in' to get the manager's position or a first-team coaching gig. Youth development is a specialised niche and needs to be treated as such by professional people holding the correct skill set to implement a strategy fitting the club's philosophy. DNA is important, but too many clubs employ the 'wrong' people, and more worrying is the fact that some managers surround themselves with people who aren't able to take on his job.

A lot of players are taken out of school too early, without any qualifications, and some parents seem to think this is acceptable. They believe they will make it in the game and earn a fortune, allowing them to retire at 35 and live happily ever after. Sorry to piss on your parade and burst the fantasy bubble you have created, but sadly 2 per cent is the success rate for academy graduates to gain full-time contracts. More worryingly, I discovered that only 35 per cent of scholar contracts – where players also combine football with academic study – in England are actually still playing the game at 23. Therefore you need to base the academy, in my opinion, on your exit strategy as the gems you harvest will make it if your succession plans and strategies are in place. I outlined the numbers to each and every young player and their parents who came into Motherwell under my stewardship. I also spent a lot of time reiterating the importance of education and at no times did I ever compromise a young man's academic capability regardless of his football ability, despite the delusion of blinkered parents.

Motherwell chief executive Leeann Dempster said on my departure: "We would like to put on record our acknowledgement and thanks to Gordon for all his hard work, particularly his two stints as interim manager of the first team. [I call it three stints as I took on a pre-season training schedule with Stephen Craigan one year.] We are obviously sad to see Gordon go, however this is a new chapter in his career and also an exciting opportunity for the club to appoint a successor."

I was very grateful for her kind words, despite times when I feared for the future of the Well academy and sometimes the club in general, due to the harsh financial climate Scottish football was in, and still is in. A new chapter had begun for me – chapter No 9 in this book as it happens – and my eyes were to be well and truly opened to football around the world.

I was officially confirmed in my post, shit-stained tracksuit and all, in November, 2013, but had been in and around the club in the weeks before that to get the feel of the place. Fellow Scot and former Rangers, Hearts and Scotland centre-half Davie Weir, who had arrived at the Blades in June, had just been sacked as manager after only 12 games in charge and Nigel Clough had taken over. I only saw briefly what Davie was trying to do at the club, but silky football in the English third tier was not what the fans, or the board, wanted at that time and results went against him. You could see from his philosophy and intelligence, that his ideology would work in a situation different to the "get out the league at any cost regardless of style" that was imperative. Davie had seen how rhythmically Everton operated and his experience at other top clubs was the correct approach to his first venture into management. But United need- ed to kick and bite their way out of the league, where ball possession was not a priority. He was another top bloke I met and the dignity he showed on his exit was a credit to his beliefs.

Unfortunately, John Stephenson would also depart as I felt he took it personally about big Davie, given the fact he had championed him and believed in, as I did, what he was trying to implement. In Davie's first game, United played Notts County at home and they recorded the most possession they'd had in ten years! This was pleasing on the eye and, given time, it could have evolved the playing style of the club. However, as I've learned over the years and certainly with clubs who have slid unceremoniously down the leagues, their fans still retain high expectations. So it's not how you get out, it's the getting out at all costs that matters - shedding blood, snotters and tears if that's what it requires. Oh, and a bit more blood just to make sure.

John's departure would shift the management of the international operation squarely onto my shoulders. Even though I was not a Michael Palin in terms of my passport stamps, I was able to roll out the 'United Way' with a helpful measure of the 'Mother-well strategy', a marriage made in heaven. And along with tremendous internal admin-istrative support and accompanied by my loyal colleague Lee Walshaw, we smashed it.

Jamie Murphy, who was one of my favourite players to come through the Motherwell Academy, was also struggling a wee bit at that time with form and niggling injuries and he was in and out of the team under both Davie and Nigel. I took it upon myself to see if I could help him through this period of his career, after the great success he had at Fir Park. He was a real home bird and was also feeling pretty homesick, so it was good that he had a familiar face to see around the place and have a chat with. I hadn't yet started my globe-trotting escapades and when Yvonne came to visit me we would go for a meal with Murph, his then partner, now wife Nadine, and his dad Jim, who would also visit his son regularly. Jim was a great lad and was so proud of his son's achievements and after games he and I would go out for a few drinks and shoot the breeze about the Sheffield stage of our lives.

At one meal, Murph was adamant he was going to move back up the road to Scot-land. I knew for a fact that Stuart McCall at Motherwell, Terry Butcher at Hibs, Ally McCoist at Rangers (at that time in Scottish League One – the third tier – after their enforced demotion) and Derek McInnes at Aberdeen, were all keen to bring the flying winger back up north. I knew this as they had all contacted me enquiring about Jamie's availability – off the record of course! I was a great admirer of the lad as a person and a player and wanted him to stick it out at Sheffield United and push through the hard time he was having at that point. I had seen too many young Scottish players head to the bright lights and big bucks in England, and was fed up seeing them scurry back across the border too early six months later, when their dream move had not worked out the way they had planned. I decided against making Murph aware of the interest from the Scottish clubs – especially from his boyhood heroes Rangers – and with the backing of his dad, I helped convince Jamie to stay on in Sheffield and try to establish himself as a first-team player at Bramall Lane.

Later that night in the hotel room, I remember Yvonne was raging at me and gave me pelters for heaping more misery on the lad, who just wanted to come back and play football closer to his home. Nadine was so supportive and got a job to help him stay there, before they embarked on starting a beautiful family. But Yvonne was adamant I should tell him of the enquiries and let him go home. History proves, however, that I was vindicated for encouraging Murph to stay and he became an icon at the Blades for two more seasons. He then played in the Premiership with Brighton and Hove Albion and achieved international recognition with Scotland.

Eventually he did sign with the club he supported as a boy in January, 2018. However, he struggled with injuries at Ibrox and moved on loan to Hibs, which be-came a permanent move in 2021. Shortly after he arrived at Rangers he sent me a smashing text message, thanking me for the advice and support in those dark times, although I did feel a tad uncomfortable at his wedding as I was sitting at the dinner next to his agent. It was only after that text, that I told him of all the interest from Scottish clubs – including the Gers – that he had while struggling at Sheffield United. The reason I did so, was because he had too much talent not to give it a real go in England and I knew he could do it.

As I began to settle into my role, my initial brief was to roll out the Tata Football Academy (TFA) at Jamshedpur where the Tata Group – one of the world's largest companies – is based, and manage and coach their football club. My assistant would be Lee Walshaw, an ex-Sheffield United player. Lee has become one of the most loyal, helpful and important colleagues I have had in the game and is a great friend to me and my family. We are still regularly in touch with each other today and have worked together on football projects since parting from Sheffield United. Lee is a Blade through and through and the perfect ambassador for such a proud club.

Once we had made our first assessment of the Indian club – who had ambitions of promotion to the Indian Super League and becoming an Asian football super power – we agreed on a plan of action. I would leave Lee to get on with implementing the plan, as I moved on to assess other future projects and returned to Sheffield with a progress report. This would be the norm and Lee would carry out the plan to the letter. I bonded with him straight away and it's not an understatement to say that I trusted him with my life. And let me tell you, there was more than one occasion in our wonderful two-year partnership in India, when this level of trust came in handy as we sailed close to risky waters.

I knew travelling would be long haul. Glasgow to Dubai, Dubai to Kolkata (formerly Calcutta) and then four hours on a train from Kolkata's Howrah Junction station to Jamshedpur, was pretty taxing. It was also nerve wracking for me standing only at 5ft 7 inches tall and trying to find the correct train among 23 platforms in a sea of more than 700,000 people who use one of the world's busiest choo choo stations every day. To be fair though, I was relatively tall in India! I feel very fortunate that, from time to time, we were able to take advantage of Tata's vast resources and when possible they would provide Lee and I access to one of their private jets, which would fly us to Jamshedpur from Kolkata Airport. Our favoured route would take the Sheffield lads from Manchester Airport, me from Glasgow, via Dubai and on to Kolkata. As we were frequent flyers more often than not we'd get the call which we loved "will Mr Young please come to the Emirates desk" - that meant we would be upgraded and boy was that enjoyable.

But, in saying that, what an adventure and an eye-opener it was to travel by train in India. The first time I managed to somehow find my platform and board my train,

↑ *Happy days with my wife, Yvonne, and kids Robbie and Jenna*

↑ *Family photo, from left, father-in-law John,
son Robbie, yours truly, wife Yvonne, daughter
Jenna, mum Margaret and dad Wullie*

←In the bath after winning the Scottish Amateur Cup with Dalziel along with Biscuit, our keeper

↑Here I am, bottom left, with my mate, Peter Ritchie, back right, at Netherdale

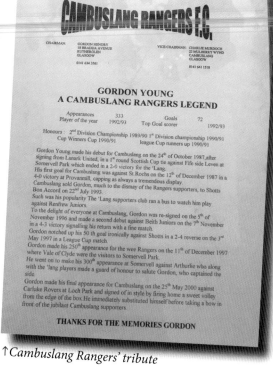

CAMBUSLANG RANGERS F.C.

CHAIRMAN: GORDON HENDRY
18 BRADDA AVENUE
RUTHERGLEN
GLASGOW

0141 634 3561

VICE CHAIRMAN: CHARLIE MURDOCH
23 MULBERRY WYND
CAMBUSLANG
GLASGOW

0141 641 1518

GORDON YOUNG
A CAMBUSLANG RANGERS LEGEND

| Appearances | 333 | Goals | 72 |
| Player of the year | 1992/93 | Top Goal scorer | 1992/93 |

Honours : 2nd Division Championship 1989/90 1st Division championship 1990/91
Cup Winners Cup 1990/91   league Cup runners up 1990/91

Gordon Young made his debut for Cambuslang on the 24th of October 1987,after signing from Lanark United, in a 1st round Scottish Cup tie against Fife side Leven at Somervell Park which ended in a 2-0 victory for the 'Lang.
His first goal for Cambuslang was against St Rochs on the 12th of December 1987 in a 4-0 victory at Provanmill, capping as always a tremendous display.
Cambuslang sold Gordon, much to the dismay of the Rangers supporters, to Shotts Bon Accord on 22nd July 1993.
Such was his popularity The 'Lang supporters club ran a bus to watch him play against Renfrew Juniors.
To the delight of everyone at Cambuslang, Gordon was re-signed on the 5th of November 1996 and made a second debut against Beith Juniors on the 7th November in a 4-3 victory signalling his return with a fine match.
Gordon notched up his 50 th goal ironically against Shotts in a 2-4 reverse on the 3rd May 1997 in a League Cup match.
Gordon made his 250th appearance for the wee Rangers on the 11th of December 1997 where Vale of Clyde were the visitors to Somervell Park.
He went on to make his 300th appearance at Somervell against Arthurlie who along with the 'lang players made a guard of honour to salute Gordon, who captained the side.
Gordon made his final appearance for Cambuslang on the 25th May 2000 against Carluke Rovers at Loch Park and signed of in style by firing home a sweet volley from the edge of the box He immediately substituted himself before taking a bow in front of the jubilant Cambuslang supporters.

THANKS FOR THE MEMORIES GORDON

↑Cambuslang Rangers' tribute

↑ *Showing off the Colosseum from the top of Braidhurst High School*

← *Signing a young David Turnbull for Motherwell*

← *My close friend, Ian 'Stan' Murdoch, supported the transformation of the Academy*

↑*Stuart McCall was another big influence at the Well (courtesy of SNS Group)*

←*Sharing some good times with Craig and my dad, Wullie*

↓Tactics with the Motherwell Under-19s (courtesy of Motherwell FC)

← Craig and Archie with me and the backroom staff at Fir Park (courtesy of Motherwell FC).

←With Braidhurst head teacher, Derrick Hannan

↑*Cheers to Stade de Reims and then manager , Hubert Fournier, who welcomed me on a Uefa Pro Licence visit*

THE ULTIMATE FINAL
1960
18.05.1960
A Record 127,621 Fans

↑*Hampden photo at Uefa HQ included my dad and grandad somewhere among the 127,621 crowd*

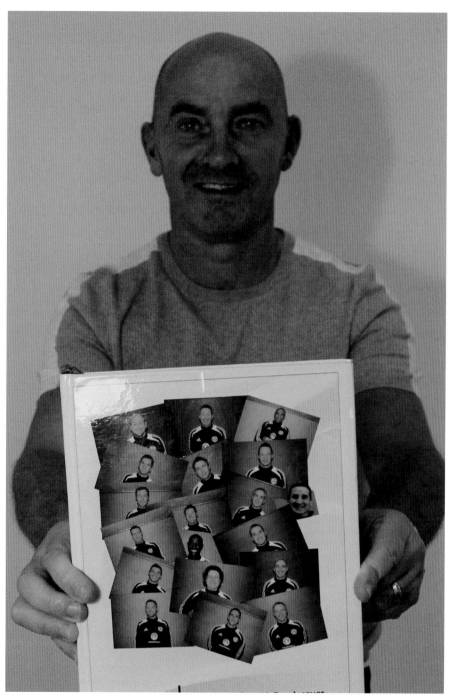

↑ *I'm proud to have gained my Uefa Pro-Licence and to have produced a 250-page report on my work*

↑*At Tata training with Sheffield United*
(courtesy of Sheffield United)

← *Waterlogged pitch in India - playable just three hours after this photo was taken, below*

↑*The players had to wash their own strips during one tournament and hang them outside their digs to dry*

↑Lee has some
words of advice
for Robbie when
he played for us
on the UK tour

←A Tuk Tuk ride
took us home after
nights out in
Jamshedpur

↑*Close shave with Lee on the streets of Jamshedpur*

←*Training at the 'wonder wall' at the Skill Centre in India*

↑*On the touchline with Mixu while at Dundee United (courtesy of Dundee United)*

↑*My last game as caretaker manager of United against Kilmarnock (courtesy of Dundee United)*

↑ Boxing training with 'The Sheriff' helped me fight depression

← Putting youngsters through their paces at Motherwell Academy Skill Centre

↑ *Supporting the Well in San Francisco*

↑*Gordon and Gavin Glinton at Impact Soccer*

←*Mikey, Jim and me at the Pride Celebrations*

←*Mixu and Gordon walking up Tannadice St on the last Dundee derby day of season 2015/16*

↑*Swapping California and Silicon Valley for California in Forth Valley*

↑Golf was great in the States. This is me playing with David Robertson, right, from Davis Legacy and his dad, Len, at Chardonnay Golf Course in the Nappa Valley

↑*Winning the Baltic Cup with Mixu at Latvia*

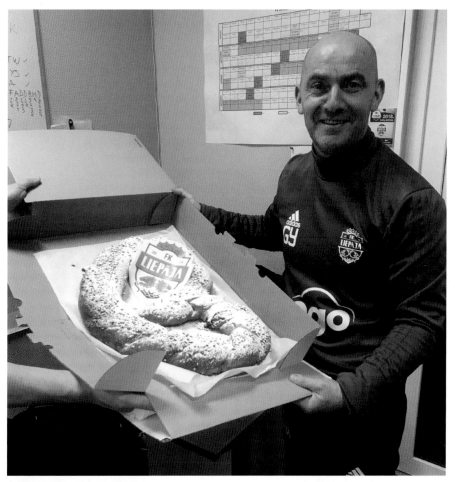

↑*Having my cake in Liepaja*

←*With fitness coach Ricky at Liepaja*

←*Checking in at Cove Rangers with Paul Hartley*

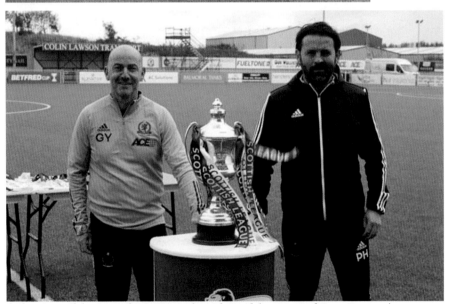

↑*Showing off the Second Division title with Paul (courtesy of Cove Rangers)*

↑*Loving life at Cove (courtesy of Cove Rangers)*

↑ *Keepie-uppie kings meet again*

resplendent in the bright red Sheffield United tracksuit. I always asked any coaches or United staff members to travel to Jamshedpur in their tracksuit as they were representing the club, on their way home it was optional. Of course I had seen on the telly images of train travel in India, with people packed in every space, on the roof and hanging out the windows… and that was first class! I just sat there incredulous in rolling stock that had seen better days, trundling quickly along at 70mph with a sword swallower entertaining me in the aisle passageway, a guy sitting next to me with a box of chickens and a shoe shiner trying to polish my suede Adidas Gazelle trainers.

Though if I wrack my brains, I do seem to remember a return train journey from a day out at the Edinburgh Fringe Festival coming a close second to what it was like in India. There were vendors of every type selling tea, poultry, books… swords. The extreme entertainer must have seen the crossed blades on my tracksuit and thought I was a British practitioner of the fine art and offered me a go. "Thanks my friend, not for me," I said, "I'm fae Muirhouse in Motherwell, not the scheme in Edinburgh." Funnily enough he seemed to understand fully what I meant.

I do believe however, that my dress code policy might well have saved a young coach's life. Ashley Foyle had successfully negotiated Howrah Junction station on the way to Jamshedpur and had spent two weeks assisting Lee. On the day of his return home he made a decision that would rescue him from being claimed by Kolkata. Howrah Junction is an incredible place with hundreds of thousands of people scurrying about like ants and if you don't keep moving you'll end up bustled and jostled into the nearby Hooghly River, such is the pace of the place. But if you stand back with a wall behind you, you can take a wee pause and admire the noise, colours and smells of an extraordinary, incredible way of life, where anything and anyone is transported to all areas of India in the longest conga line of trains you'll ever see.

When arriving at any airport or train station, a system had been put in place by the Tata Steel Group to meet any Sheffield United staff and drive them to a guest house to freshen up and take them from there on to the station or airport to continue on their journey… either during arrival or departure from India. Coincidentally, but unbeknownst by me, I was on my way back to Jamshedpur at the same time as my young colleague was making his way home. Lee had taken Ashley under his wing and when 'newbies' were travelling, we would accompany them at least on the outbound journey. But sometimes due to crossover or workload, they would travel back independently, retracing the route they came in. Quite simple really, but add in the heat, noise and intensity of Howrah Station and you can easily lose your bearings.

I had arrived at Kolkata Airport, had been picked up by a driver and taken to the guest house. I made my ablutions and hooked up with the driver again to take me back to Howrah. No private jet on this occasion. Even though I had used the station several times, it was still a daunting prospect to navigate the hundreds of thousands of people going about their daily commute, as you try to find your train. I'm only in the station a few minutes, my driver has helped me with my bags and I'm scanning the massive timetable noticeboard, when my eyes are drawn to a fleeting glimpse of someone with red hair, wearing a red top and looking as if he'd fallen off the waltzers at the village fair. As soon as I see it, the vision disappears and I bob and weave to see if I can catch a glimpse of this unusual sight again. Sure enough, the red hair and the red top pop up again as if gasping for air in an ocean of humanity. I ask the driver to watch the bags as I take a closer look and come across Ashley, who is wide-eyed and a little terrified. He embraces me as if I have just guided the Blades to Champions League glory.

Turns out he had made it to Howrah from Jamshedpur without a hitch, but then the problems arose when he couldn't find his driver liaison after getting off the train, panicked and had gone on a walkabout to locate him. I still think that if he had not chosen to wear his Sheffield United tracksuit on the journey home and instead worn his civvies, he could still be wandering around the station to this very day, trying to earn a crust as a sword swallower... though mind you, he also wouldn't have had the Blades on his tracksuit attesting to his credentials.

Ash had no money on him and was struggling to make his flight, which was due to take off in less than two hours. After calming him down, I arranged for my driver to take him to the airport so he could try to catch his plane. Luckily he managed it with just minutes to spare. It must have traumatised him quite a bit, as he never returned to help us out at Jamshedpur, but he did say the six beers he had in the airport were the quickest he had ever drank and the best he'd ever tasted.

Jamshedpur is in the north east of India in the State of Jharkhand. It borders the states of West Bengal to the east, Bihar to the north, Uttar Pradesh to the northwest, Chhattisgarh to the west, Odisha to the south and, in places, is not far from the border with Bangladesh. It has a population of around 33 million people and Jamshedpur is the largest city in the region with an urban population of around 1.3 million people. That's more than the populations of Motherwell and Sheffield combined... with about 800,000 to spare... and it is still only the 71st biggest city, population wise, in the country!

Jamshedpur, formerly Sakchi, was named after Jamsetji Tata in 1919 – a trailblazer of the Tata Steel Group – who had a vision to build India's first steelworks and create a town for its workers. Having lived in Motherwell all my life in the shadow of the massive Ravenscraig steelworks, I was prepared for it being a bit grubby, dirty and smokey, with red and black dust clouds releasing their payload all over 'yer maw's washing that she'd just hung oot to dry'. I thought I would be right at home meeting people who sounded like human bagpipes when they breathed and wheezed, because they'd had a lifetime of living and working in a steel town. I also thought that, due to the hot climate, it wouldn't be subjected to the bogging grey snow that sometimes fell in the winter, blanketing my home town. By contrast, in the summer I was expecting, as well as a heat shimmer, the air sparkling with minute particles of steel or 'scale', which would glint in the sun, and make you worth a few bob to the scrappy if you breathed them in. I remember speaking to my mates who worked in the 'Craig telling me that as they walked in through the gates and up the long avenues that bisected the huge works in the summer, it was like passing through a shower of glitter as the stour dust, kicked up from the road by the trucks, and the 'scale' combined in a plume... a sort of industrial Disneyland. Which is ironic as Naked Radio – a popular Scottish comedy show airing in the late 80s and early 90s just as the country's steel industry was dying – satirised the then 'powers that be' as thinking of Scotland as Disneyland, as "It Disnae work, Disnae vote Tory and it Disnae matter!".

On the upside, maybe the youth of Jamshedpur benefited like us, from the ten minutes of extra light we used to get at night when playing fitba out in the street as the Kress Carriers in the 'Craig poured the molten slag waste into the vast cooling pits, which lit up the black night sky in Motherwell like an evening sunrise. I would sit on the rooftop terrace of my hotel in Jamshedpur and watch the skyline turn golden, as the start of the night shift unloaded the smelting wagons, unleashing the Indian equivalent of the northern lights and a reminder of home on a humongous scale.

But thankfully Mr Tata's vision – revolutionary for India at that time – incorporated an innovative plan to design a city with wide streets, shady trees, large gardens, vast parks and excellent provision for all kinds of sports (especially football, hockey and cricket) and Hindu temples, mosques and churches. As a result, and even though the steelworks are still at full production, Jamshedpur has won awards for its cleanliness. It became the cleanest city in India in 2020 according to Swach Survekshan 2020, the world's largest urban sanitation and cleanliness survey, climbing from seventh cleanest city of India in 2010. It has also been ranked as the second best city in India in terms of 'quality of life'.

Ever since 1912, there had existed excellent conditions for workers in the steel plants of Jamshedpur, such as eight-hour days, medical leave, bonus payments and schemes to develop the skills of employees. This and the innovative town planning, even impressed Mahatma Gandhi who visited in 1925 to try to resolve a labour dispute. This Tata guy had a progressive plan for his workforce that was similar to the ideas of social reformers and philanthropists David Dale and his son-in-law, Robert Owen, who founded the New Lanark cotton mills and associated housing and school for workers' children way back in 1786. Tata also recognised the importance of recreation and sport in peoples' lives and it became part of the company's corporate philosophy. That is why Tata today have pumped millions into developing sport at their JRD Tata

Sports Complex and Academy in Jamshedpur. For all the successes of Jamshedpur and more recently India as a whole, it still has to be said, especially when you are travelling in the country, that the poverty and squalor is evident all around and life is still cheap. Many people find it hard to imagine how a country like India can have a space programme and an expensive nuclear deterrent, yet 1.8 million people are thought to be homeless, 73 million lack access to decent housing, and industrial accidents and scandals happen regularly. Tata themselves, like most multi-national corporations over the years, have had their fair share of awkward questions to answer too.

It is, however, a case of putting things in perspective in a country of more than a billion people. It's difficult to argue with India's buoyant economic position in the world and things are changing for the better each year among the less fortunate members of their society. I'm also sure we in the UK like to think this is the case for our struggling citizens, even though we have our own embarrassing homeless problem and thousands of children living below the poverty line, yet we still pump millions into our own nuclear weapons programme.

Jings, thank goodness I don't play with political footballs – there's always more than one who say it's 'ma baw and you're no playing'. I wish we could all just play more real fitba!

Dismounting from my high horse for a moment, I had a vision too, and the first thing I wanted to do at Jamshedpur FC's Tata Football Academy was win hearts and minds and try to encourage a mind-set that we were all in it together, in everything we did. Across the world there are class systems. I'm from proud working-class Scottish stock and am well aware of the elite middle and upper class which exists in the UK. It has become less pronounced since the end of the Second World War, but still rears its ugly head from time to time. Similarly in India, which it could be argued, is still dealing with a form of PTSD from its days of British rule, the caste system has become less important as their society progresses. But, as in the UK, old ingrained habits and negative social mores do still present issues and viewpoints that can be hard to change.

Taking this into account, there is good and bad in everything. Everywhere I have been, I found good and bad coaches and officials, thankfully more good than bad. No one has a monopoly on the best coaches as Vincente Del Bosque, the legendary Spanish manager, has been keen to intimate whenever people wax lyrical about "The Spanish Way". In every country there are good and bad coaches.

One of the first things I tried to alter was the culture of fear that existed between the players and the coaches, which literally saw players having to kiss the boots of coaches… they effectively encouraged that kind of deference, and here's me thinking it was the British upper class rule which had the monopoly on that kind of treatment. In the academy squad there were Hindus, Muslims, Sikhs and Christians. Lee and I had to make strategic changes without disrespecting any of these religions and the culture as a whole. But I was determined that everyone would be treated equally and with respect at all times. I made sure I would be referred to as Gordon and all other coaches would be called by their first name and not in any other deferential terms. So it was that I ended up being called 'Mr Gordon' for the remainder of my time there… all you can do is try.

What I witnessed on that first fact-finding mission curled my toes quite a bit. The coaches seemed to be convinced that flogging the players for three-and-a-half hours in 40 degree heat was the way to produce a winning team. It also became apparent very quickly, that many of the players had chronic niggling injuries that were just not getting any better. Lee and I tailored a training programme which included changes to the players' diets, giving them an awareness of food and nutrition, encouraging ice baths, recovery and days off. A day off!? Fuck me, you'd think I was announcing that cricket was cancelled in India. They don't need days off, I was told. "OK," I countered, "here's the deal… you pay me to come, I make the decisions." Thankfully they accepted. "Right," I told Wal (Lee Walshaw), "here's the deal I've struck, no pressure son, but we can't lose now." And we very rarely did after that.

Conformed dress code is, I feel, very important when part of a sports team and I asked all the coaches to wear their branded Sheffield United tracksuits to training and games. Branding is also important to me, a legacy from my Nestle days. Get the badge out there and people know who we are, was my mantra. Lee loved this and fired the Blades crest on anything that was stationary, but thankfully drew the line at the sacred cows.

Most of our new colleagues were very open to our ideas and we quickly built up a good, friendly relationship with the staff. But there's always one rogue element who rocks the boat a wee bit and becomes a pain in the arse. This guy, an experienced coach (in his own head), would rock up like 'Rag Arse Rab' wearing his own kit and white plastic football boots with the laces tied round his ankles and up around his calves like a highland dancer. He also tried to con me into believing that he had an A-Licence coaching certificate apparently from the English FA. Hmmm I thought, that's pretty unusual as that kind of thing would carry a good story, as well as a network from your time studying with your peers. "Who was on your course," I asked. "Eh, I can't remember" was the reply. I smell a rat here, I tell Wal, and bingo it turned out that he had been on a FA tour and visited a few football grounds in England and managed to get a certificate from the Old Trafford football museum. What a right Bengal Lancer.

It turned out he'd always wanted to visit Old Trafford (probably the cricket venue and not the field of dreams created by my pal, Sir Alex!) and as far as a licence was concerned, he didn't even have a driving licence. To compound all of this, he had an unwilling desire to change – he would wear Arsenal shorts and socks while we were all in Sheffield United gear and he would speak in Hindi and totally disregard the curriculum. This pissed me off somewhat and despite my attempts at a softly, softly approach, I took it personally that he wouldn't conform. I still took no pleasure in terminating his contract – I always hated that – but in the coaching trenches it was a case of him or us. I didn't want him to become a negative influence and organise a 'tunnelling committee' and eventually drive a wedge between Lee and I and our local team, who we were quickly building up a great relationship with. Just before he left he was already using the 'Johnny Foreigner' argument that no one should be coming over here to Jamshedpur to teach us how to play football… or tie our boot laces.

The hospitality that was shown to Lee and myself was fantastic, sometimes to the point of unfairness. As much as we were able to make positive changes to certain aspects of the day-to-day running of the academy, there were certain procedures we had to adhere to. This meant we would regularly fly to away matches – up to three hours away – and stay in five star hotels, while the players would travel 19 hours by train or bus and stay in two star hotels. This was a major inconvenience for us as you can imagine, but we grudgingly accepted the hardship.

The time I spent in India corresponded with the rise to power of Narendra Modi from the Bharatiya Janata Party (BJP), who became the Prime Minister of the country in May, 2014. Now, how someone votes, is, I believe, a private matter and something I have been wise to not get involved in speaking about, and I was very keen to continue in this vein while in India. But, to my eternal embarrassment, I seem to have helped with the election of the strongman nationalist leader. I was caught up in the moment and it seemed like a good idea at the time.

Modi - perhaps because of his connections and support from the Tata Steel group - was using the TFA facilities at Jamshedpur as his election campaign base and safe house during the election, and I shook his hand as I was introduced to him. I think I was carrying a bag of bibs, a stirrup pump and a few marker cones at the time when I met one of the most powerful men in Asia, and if my memory serves me well, I think he asked me if I was still drinking in the Electric Bar, though I could be mistaken.

India is the biggest democracy in the world and it boasts more than 814 million eligible voters and as such their general elections last for weeks. In 2014, it started on 7 April and ran until 12 May, with the victor being announced four days later. The state of Jharkhand alone had around 13 million people eligible to vote and let's just say, the scope for irregularities is rife and the people staffing the polling booths weren't at all fussy about who they corralled in to cast their ballot… even foreign visitors. With voting underway in Jamshedpur, Lee and I ventured out for our customary daily coffee and were walking back to the sports complex in our tracksuits when we got caught up in the celebratory fervour that was gripping the city. Everybody was in such a good mood and as we passed by a polling station – well I say polling station, it was more like two decorator's wallpaper pasting tables under a makeshift gazebo at the side of the road accompanied by reams of paper with everyone eligible to vote's name on it – we were gathered up in the euphoric crowds and beckoned in to support one of the local candidates, who as it turned out was a member of Modi's BJP Party. So with thumb and forefinger doused in purple dye we were heavily encouraged to caste our votes in the Indian general election and happily made our way back to the stadium.

When we returned we continued with our training day and wondered why a member of my local staff, a lovely guy by the name of Krishna Kumar, who was our administration manager, had still not turned up for work five hours after his shift was due to begin. He was a fantastic guy for which nothing was too much trouble and his work ethic was outstanding. He assisted Lee and I with our IT requirements. I used to call him the cleverest man in Jamshedpur, which then migrated to cleverest in India and by the time I left he was the cleverest man in the whole world. On arrival back to the training ground, Krishna said he had queued up at his own local polling station for five hours, which must have been a lot more organised than the one we used, only to be told that someone had already used his vote. What seemed like a great laugh for Lee and I and a story to tell when we got back home, had been quickly put into perspective by someone we knew, who had missed out on their hard-fought right to cast their vote. We apologised to Krishna unreservedly and after we told him Gordon Singh and Lee Singh had been press ganged into voting, a rye smile broke out across his face. But knowing him and loving him, he probably muttered under his breath: "I thought the Raj was over, British infidels!".

Apparently they are still calling Krishna 'the cleverest man in the world' as I recently met up with Adrian Dias the Jamshedpur FC strength and conditioning coach, who was completing his B licence in Scotland in 2020, and he filled me in on how everyone was getting on. This was pre-Covid-19 and due to the respect and friendship I had for Adrian I invited him to stay with me whilst he was completing his licence at the SFA headquarters at Hampden Park. He was another highly intelligent guy who travelled to the USA to further his education before settling in to his role at Tata.

Our goalkeeping coach was another terrific guy called Gumpe Rime, who had a very distinguished football career in India. He has since gone on to be a successful coach educator with the Indian FA and was a beautiful man from the North East of the country, which was christened 'Scotland' as it was the rainiest place in the whole country. He was so proud of his birthplace and had a real thirst to learn, so much so that when the Tata Academy visited Sheffield he crammed every spare minute with visiting as many football clubs as possible.

Making up the staff was Shakti Chaughan, a very keen young coach who had a great nature and a willingness to improve his football knowledge and he would go on to coach at Delhi Dynamos and ultimately win a place as a staff coach with the Indian FA. Tata was widely acknowledged as the top academy in the whole of India, attracting the best players and coaches through processes of selection, so it was important to make sure they had the character to fit into our ethos. All of these guys were outstanding converts to 'the United Way' and were all great football people with lots to offer and contribute in their own right. I am truly grateful for their support and without their 'buy in', it would have been impossible to implement our strategy and obtain the success which we achieved.

When Modi was announced as the winner of the election, he made his way to the centre of Jamshedpur to give an address to 700,000 people. The only other gathering of humanity I saw on such an enormous scale as this, was in Kolkata travelling to the airport for my first flight back home in early November, 2013. Then, more than three million people surrounded the Eden Gardens Cricket Stadium, not counting the supporters inside, to celebrate Sachin Tendulkar play his second last Test for India against the West Indies. The worrying thing for me was I was caught up in the throng whilst heading to the airport, which seemed to take forever. It was so busy that I was panicking I would miss my flight home. I remember sitting in the car thinking: "Could he not have been a shit cricketer and be partial to being bowled out for a duck." I used to tease Lee about cricket as, like so many proud Yorkshiremen, he loved both sports. Well I say sports plural, but everyone knows, as I would tell Lee, "it's just a big game of rounders", making reference to a Scottish girls' pastime popular when I was growing up. It is absolutely bizarre to see that many people gathered in the one place at the same time and find yourself a part of it. It will also not surprise you to know that while in India I attended a game of football watched by the largest attendance I have ever been a part of – the Kolkata derby or 'Boro Match' between Mohun Bagan and East Bengal, which attracted a crowd that day of 137,000. That's the sort of crowds we used to get at Hampden in the first half of the 20th century to watch the groundsman spiking the turf or spreading the grass seed!

The calibre of people that were employed by Tata, especially in relation to their football academy, was exceptional. My direct contact was one Charles Borromeo, who represented India at middle distance running in the mid 80s, rubbing shoulders with the likes of Seb Coe, Steve Ovett and Steve Cram at the Los Angeles Olympics in 1984. He was the head of sports at Tata, a terrific personality and had great contacts within the group and across the world of sport. He arranged for me to go to play my other favourite sport – golf – in a four-ball, which included himself and then Tata vice president Farzan Heerjee at his exclusive course. They both looked after me impeccably. To say it was a four-ball, though, was a bit of an understatement. First of all I had to choose a caddy from around 50 hopefuls. Then there was someone supplying me with fresh, cool bottled water and someone to carry the brolly to keep the sun off, and I dare say, if I had asked, there would have been someone to pick my nose or even hold my wee man if I went for a pish.

But every one of our four-ball had the same retinue, so by the time we teed off our group had about 30 people in it. That's not counting the helpful club employees who would line the fairways to look for your ball if it strayed, or the bunker rakers by the bucket load, or those who would pop up at various intervals to offer you a tasty snack of some description or the flag tenders on the greens. There was a job for everybody in the surrounding area. It certainly took a wee while to get used to it, but I settled down and played quite well. I felt like I was playing in a PGA tour event it was that busy, and we were the only players I could see. Lee wasn't a golfer, but had great hand-to-eye coordination so I took him along once for a game, but chose the wrong day as it was tipping 51 degrees heat on the thermometer. It was the most exhausted I have ever felt, where even swinging the club was a chore. We staggered round drinking twice our bodyweight in water. On one ten-day visit to the city, I drank 57 litres of water.

Farzan and I played a few more rounds together while in Jamshedpur, just the two of us, and I came to the conclusion that he is a great guy. I also got to know a couple of the greenkeepers at the course pretty well. They have now gone on to become good touring golf professionals. We were always keen to keep ourselves busy, so in the early days we would work constantly as there was always plenty to do at the academy. Relaxation and recreation was limited to what we were used to back home. Farzan found out I liked to play squash, so he made Lee and I members of the exclusive country club available to vice presidents of the Tata organisation. I'd play with the house pro and it gave me the chance to exercise and switch off from the job, whilst I could beat any challenges from members with a frying pan and an orange never mind a squash racquet and ball.

We made some great friends in Jamshedpur and social nights out that we did have were always great fun. I have always loved the poems and songs of Robert Burns. I have some of his words tattooed on my back. "Catch the moments as they fly; And use them as you ought man; Believe me happiness is shy; And comes not aye when sought man." My interpretation of this is that you can't control when the good times come, enjoy life and embrace it now. I would always get invited to Burns suppers at home and I really enjoy the works of Scotland's greatest ever son and the traditions associated with him. So this prompted me to organise a Burns supper one January evening in India, when I had flown out for a three-week secondment and landed along with a haggis and a bottle of single malt whisky.

I only declared the single malt at customs, as goodness knows what they would have made of the haggis, and the thought of even explaining what it was brings me out in goosebumps. Me and the haggis made it safely to Jamshedpur and I was able to coach

Nabi, the chef at the JRD Sports Complex, on what I needed him to rustle up later on that night. He was a lovely guy who'd sing Indian tribal chants to us when bringing us chai (tea). He managed to source some tatties easily enough, but I was sceptical that he would get his hands on the neeps. Much to my amazement, our resourceful cook got his hands on some excellent turnips and it was game on for Burns' Night in Tata City. Lee, Adrian, a visiting fitness coach called Luke Jenkinson, and another coach from Sheffield United called Lee Rickards and I settled down for the impromptu meal and were the source of some great entertainment for our local colleagues. We used a mobile phone internet search for Scottish music to allow Lee to pipe in the Haggis, Adrian addressed it and we took turns to toast the lassies, the laddies and everyone else we knew in Jamshedpur.

Out of all the coaches and specialists who visited from United, Lee and Luke were the most receptive and best contributors to the programme, and they both embraced the challenge with vigour. Another funny occasion occurred when Lee and I took Luke to the city zoo. I must admit it was the worst and most sorry collection of animals I've ever seen… not taking into account the 16th Motherwell BB football team. The highlight was a 'safari' which consisted of four hyenas, two dogs and a couple of wild pigs - not bad for 10 rupees with a 99 cone thrown in. Luke himself, however, became the star attraction. Standing at six feet two inches tall and with a shock of curly blond hair, the punters were queuing up to get a picture with him and the laziest rhino in the world. The proud beast was not bothered in the least that the local people only had the horn for Luke.

Our local was a nice hotel bar where we could watch English Premier League football. After our own Saturday or Sunday home matches, we would ultimately make our way there, bearing in mind we were five hours ahead of the UK, to watch the featured game. The company and the grub was good and more often than not we would have a couple of beers and end up there until late on. This led to us barrelling out of the hotel to begin the haggling session with a regular rank of Tuk Tuk drivers to take us back to our own hotel. As mentioned previously, I have always been a wee bit of a joker in the pack, and as much as I had matured and become much more responsible as my playing career came to an end and my coaching career developed, I am not shy in admitting that high jinks are never far away when I am having a good night out. Thus, on more than one occasion, I'd take a wee notion and was happy to pay the equivalent of £1 to a willing driver – for what would normally be a 4p fare – to allow me to drive us all home in the Tuk Tuk.

So, with Lee and the driver in the back, along with any guests from our hotel who we roped into going out with us, we'd race off in the Tuk Tuk into the Jamshedpur night, trying to avoid sacred cows in the process in the search of our digs. I say raced, but as I was focussed on being ultra careful and with a full load in the back, it was more like about 8mph! I expected to see Sid James and Benny Hill overtaking me as Carry on Jamshedpur played out for real. But actually people walking on the side of the road were moving faster than us. This performance would become a common occurrence at the end of a night out and, while Lee was up for it, most of our visiting guests would shit themselves at my new party piece. Now I would never condone drink driving, but if you have ever driven on a road in India, it's the sober drivers you need to watch out for. I was probably one of the safest road users ever to have graced the streets of Jamshedpur, even if I had had a couple of pints.

The other extravagance that Wal and I enjoyed was a wet shave with an open razor on the kerbside outside the Bistapur bazaar, which set us back about 10p. You'd sit on the kerbside and 'The Indian Sweeney Todd' would give you the best close shave ever, whilst cows were waltzing past and motor bike riders were weaving in and out of the throngs going about their business. Thankfully, I never plucked up the courage to pick up the cut-throat blade myself after a few beers.

In the cut-throat top level of the English and Scottish game you regularly hear about how the poor players have to deal with early kick-offs at 11.30am and having to play too many games. Well, spare a thought for our lads who one day, due to the forecast heat, had to kick-off a National Cup match – live on TV – at 7 in the morning! We had to get them up at 4am and they had their pre-match meal at 4.30am. This was a game during which I had another unfortunate skitter-related incident. In India, everyone at one time or other will suffer from a bit of 'Delhi Belly' and the evening before the match my stomach was playing the bongos and I hadn't even been within 5,000 miles of one of Yvonne's curries. The club doctor had given me some Imodium, which had just lured me into a false sense of security, as when I ran out of the dugout at half-time to go to the changing rooms, I tripped over a TV cable, stumbled and followed right through in my shorts. Thank fuck it wasn't when I was emerging for the second half or I would have been walking around in the technical area like Charlie Chaplin.

Moving on from slapstick comedy, one of the most surreal moments I have ever experienced in football – playing or coaching – occurred in India. We were playing in a semi-final against Odisha FC in Bhubaneshwar in the Kalinga Stadium and winning 1-0 in front of 30,000 fans. I am implementing what I have learned from Craig Brown and I'm scanning the runs and movement of my players and using my peripheral vision to vaguely follow the ball, when I do a double take as I notice something unusual. Now, I know that it is sometimes good to have a big bull of a centre-half in your team, but I don't remember naming a beast of burden in our line-up for that day's game. Sure enough, I rub my eyes and a cow has wandered onto the pitch and is lying in our penalty area. We've just lost possession and the ball is crossed into the middle. I have to shout to the ref, who inexplicably hasn't seen the 'Bovine in the Box' and is playing on. Half our players don't know whether they should shoo the beast or kiss it in deference. But my goalkeeper, who is Hindu, feels the right thing to do is put the lips onto the goalpost in spiritual thanks for a new addition to the defence. Thankfully, the sacred cow didn't hoof the ball into the net and with great cultural diplomacy – as it is a real big no no to mess with cows when they decide to sit down over there – Buttercup is gently enticed from the pitch and we win 1-0.

The subsequent final was scheduled bang in the middle of monsoon season and the storm clouds were beginning to match my mood, due to a tradition that occurs before every game in India. The first time I witnessed the pre-match pageant, it was a colourful, quaint celebration of culture and was a joy to behold. By the 18th time you've seen a marching band in full regalia, a parade of ceremonial elephants churning up the pitch and a troupe of dancers accompanying a speech from a local politician making hay with the crowd, by showing how much he loves his team, the pleasant novelty has started to wear off. There were no Uefa-style time-keeping regulations here and games regularly kicked off more than three quarters of an hour late. Many was the time my team were huddling in the tunnel to keep out of the 42 degree heat as they waited for jumbo to trumpet the Indian national anthem for the third time.

As you can imagine, because I was an Obsessive Compulsive Disorder (OCD) bordering stickler for timekeeping, it was beginning to burst ma tits. My colleagues at Jamshedpur were understanding, but there was little they could do to hurry along the proceedings once they had started. My main concern was for my players, who were preparing the right way for the game in a warm-up and then standing idle for more than half an hour before the kick-off. At the final, again at the Kalinga stadium, I had arranged for two tents/gazebos to be erected so my players and coaching staff could sit in out of the sun, heat and rain when it came. The home team coaches approached me and said: "Mr Gordon, Mr Gordon, Mr Gordon [news had spread of my new moniker], there is a big storm coming." I said: "I know, but don't worry my players can sit out of the rain under the tents." But this time the storm wasn't just a biblical downpour... it was a mini cyclone! Before I knew it my squad went from sitting pretty, stretching and preparing for the game while watching the elephants, dancers and politicians go through their routines, to a cross between 'Bedknobs and Broomsticks' early 70s cartoon style football pitch and the Wizard of Oz. If you have ever seen that popular half live action, half animated Disney film, you'll be able to picture the scene as my gazebos, assorted shin-guards, strips, equipment bags and one or two players ended up doing 50mph cartwheels through the marching band. In my mind it also seemed like the dancers were whipped up in a spiral tornado 'Oz style' along with the elephants and the politician, who somehow continued undaunted with his speech, blabbering relentlessly into his microphone. It certainly blew the cobwebs away as the team were great and we won 1-0.

The extremes of weather in Asia really do astound you. In Scotland we moan about weeks and weeks of constant rain and grey, low cloud that eats away at your soul at times, but we resign ourselves to it and get on with things as they are manageable. When it rains in India during the monsoon season, it fucking rains - like a million brewers' horses pishing on you from the clouds. We arrived early for one away game in Lucknow, Uttar Pradesh the next state to Jharkhand, on Saturday, 13 February, 2015, to give us preparation time for a Sunday afternoon kick-off. We had a nice dinner at the five star hotel and then Lee and I spoke to the players about how we wanted them to play. I arrange for an 8am alarm call for myself, but at 7am there is an urgent banging on my door and our administration manager Krishna is having a canary. "Big problem Mr Gordon, big problem." Rubbing the sleep from my eyes, I'm immediately thinking that Krishna has been contacted by the police to let him know they have found out who stole his vote during the elections. In a semi-confused state I'm trying to climb into my Sheffield tracksuit, grab my passport and wallet, process whether they mistakenly think it is me and consider whether I could survive the jump from the window. But good old Krishna gets to the point and informs me through the door that there has been torrential rain through the night and the pitch is literally under two feet of water.

We get the players up and I go to inspect the pitch to see for myself. It is no exaggeration to say that the pitch was totally flooded with water that would reach to mid-shin. The only sport with a ball you could play on it was water polo. "That's it then," I say. "Let's get back down the road, the 'games aff' as they would say back home."

But, no, a decision is made to postpone the kick-off by three hours from 2pm to 5pm. I look at Krishna with a "who are they kidding?" kind of expression and shake my head in exasperation and frustration that they are even considering another inspection on this pitch anytime that month, let alone later that day. But I was rubbing my eyes in disbelief less than two hours later as the 35 degree blistering heat which followed the monsoon had evaporated most of the water from the pitch. Everyone is congratulating one another on their patience and the ground-staff for their local knowledge, and we set about preparing for the match. We even take our warm-up off the pitch to protect the playing surface as much as possible before we start, and then go back to the dressing room for a final team-talk. When we come back out, unbelievably, there's the obligatory herd of elephants, dancers and this time a wee quirk – 12 Land Rovers – entertaining the crowd with a carefully choreographed routine! My jaw nearly dislocated my knee as it hit the floor, as I watched them progress with their pre-match pageant regardless of the condition of the turf. Two hours previously they would have had to use hovercrafts and the dancers would have been synchronised swimmers. I'm sure the elephants would have had a whale of a time in the pool though. Believe it or not, we ended up winning the match 2-0 and a bonus was that the local politician didn't give a speech this time. No, this one decided to kick the game off fully kitted out in the home strip, to the delight of his cheering constituents, and then proceeded –

despite being about 40 years-old and 40 stones in weight – to play the first ten minutes of the match. I'd like to have seen Jack McConnell or Marion Fellows try that at Fir Park.

Next morning I was awoken in my hotel room at 7am by someone else banging at my door. The night before we had enjoyed a terrific celebratory meal with a few shandies to celebrate our win, and I can't believe for the second morning in a row I am roused early from my bed. Standing there is a fully-decorated bell-boy, resplendent in his finest robes and he hands me a bunch of red roses, whilst wishing me a "Happy Valentine's Day, sir". "Happy fuckin' Valentine's Day?… you must have the wrong room mate." He replies: "No sir, today is Valentine's Day and this gift is from the hotel manager." As I go to accept the flowers from him, fantasising that I might use them to beat him about the head like John Cleese famously did with his wee red car, I realise that as I glance down the hallway, every one of the 50-odd rooms are also receiving a bouquet delivery. I'm 6,000 miles from home, on my own and now in possession of the biggest bunch of flowers I've ever seen. All I could think of, while standing there confused and with a mild hangover, was how I could get these to Yvonne and take the credit. We were six hours ahead after all, so it would only be 1am in Motherwell. Eventually I managed to reason with myself that hiring a Tuk Tuk was not the answer, and went back to my scratcher.

On my trips back home from India, Yvonne and I would regularly make the most of our time together and head out for a meal several times during the days I was back in Motherwell. Ironically, one of our favourite places to visit was the Indian Villa restaurant in the town's Windmillhill Street. I noticed very quickly that the Indian cuisine we have here in Scotland has been developed for our tastes and the original dishes back in India are, in fact, quite different, but both are equally delicious from my point of view. A Rogan Josh for me and a Korma for Yvonne at the Indian Villa was always a treat and we loved to book a table either for just the two of us, or with friends. We got to know the owners - proud Scottish second generation Indians - quite well and once they found out I was commuting to Jamshedpur for work at that time, they wanted to know more. I was surprised when they told me that most of them had never even set foot in India and they would insist on plying Yvonne, me and our friends with complimentary drinks, to stay on late at our table to regale them with up-to-date tales and news from their ancestral homeland.

I just lapped up that sort of role as being a cultural town crier and giving my friends at the Indian Villa a monthly (at least) update of what was happening at the Tata Academy, letting them know whether I had managed to tempt Prime Minister Modi to visit their restaurant since I knew him so well, and telling them how much I enjoyed my latest trip to an iconic Indian landmark… and also how much was the going rate for a Tuk Tuk ride if I was driving! It's now been six years since I left my work with the Blades in India, but I am still a regular at the Indian Villa and my friends there are still keeping my glass topped up and urging me to recount the tales from that period of my life and it is honestly a pleasure to do so.

A very different kind of eye-opener was the TFA Trials. Every two years TFA scouts would tour the footballing hot spots of India from the north in The Punjab to the south in Orisa, and from Kolkata to Kerrella and every station in between. Such was the reputation of the TFA, teenage players would walk miles to Jamshedpur given the facilities and opportunities to be found there. Their aim was to join those scouted nationally for a chance to become a professional footballer. Once they had 'passed out' after two years of football development and general education, they would be able to look forward to a decent career, as they would be snapped up by India's big clubs.

My first problem was that many of the local Jamshedpur players were of a poorer quality to the rest of the country, and they weren't best pleased when they realised that nearly 500 players from across the country had been 'invited' for the seven-day elimination trials - honestly it was like X Factor with fitba boots. The pissed-off locals decided to have a sit-in protest outside our complex and around 2,000 of them rattled pots and pans at the gate, which they then proceeded to chain up, making it impossible for us to continue. I then do my impersonation of former UN Secretary General Kofi Annan, and I decide to allow 20 selected locals to join the trials. This seems to placate the protesters and it's game on.

Predictably, those who were chosen are all sons of prominent local businessmen or politicians and many had Tata Steel connections. In this town, as Tom Jones would say, "it's not unusual" for something as blatant as this to occur, given that 40,000 people worked in the local steel plant. None of the locals could kick doors at Halloween, but it was the only way I'd get the trials up and running, let alone completed on, as old Tom would also croon, the "green, green grass" of their home town.

My team and I were tasked with an unbelievable selection and filtering process. With much discussion, debate as well as the odd argument, given the subjective nature of football opinion, we eventually select a shortlist. After five days of games and exercises, we all agree on a group of 40 players which we would eventually trim to 24, upon further scrutiny. The criteria stipulated that all players would have to be under 16 years of age to qualify for the two-year contract, much sought after by India's hopefuls. TFA, to their credit, give me all the help possible and the final cross-check Tata insist upon is age clarification carried out at the local hospital, with all players subjected to dental as well as bone density measurements. Why, you ask? Well, birth registration is not the same in some parts of the world as it is in Europe. Just ask Craig Brown about the 1989 Under-16 World Cup final at Hampden, when Scotland lost to a Saudi Arabian team that many people say looked way older than 16, and you can understand our need for clarification. I remember Broon telling me that he was told by someone much later on that the average age of that team was around 23!

On top of the technical trials, we'd interviewed each player to ascertain their date of birth, place of birth and medical records. The standard, we all agreed, was excellent and we had the correct balance of position specific players to facilitate the new intake. All was looking good and the vice presidents from Tata commented that they'd never seen this level of organisation in 30 years. Cue a retreat to the bar for a few lagers, to allow the medical staff to carry out their tests. For a wee laugh, we all took a sweep to guess at the percentage of 'rogue' ages that would turn up. With the guesses all in, the consensus was that we felt we would only have to bin, at most, between 5-10 per cent of the intake for lying about their age. I was really excited to get in the next day to find out how many rascals had tried to pull the wool over our eyes, but more importantly to get the numbers down to 24, so we could announce the squad to the press and make plans for their inauguration.

The next morning, I say: "Hello doc, have you separated them?". "Yes," he says, "here they are", and he hands me one bundle of papers. Yip, you've guessed it, every one of them was over age. The nearest to 16 years of age, according to the tests, was a couple of lads at 18 and the average was 21. It was either back to the drawing board or back to the pub. Of course, the professionals that we were, we persevered until we eventually managed to get the numbers required from those who met the criteria.

In my travels by planes, trains and automobiles throughout India, I was lucky to see many sights and visit many cities you are taught about in geography class at school. I was privileged to experience a host of celebrations, which invariably involved noise, colour and fireworks. Kolkata was an unbelievable continuous cauldron of sights and smells, with an intensity of people that you could never imagine, and I lapped it all up.

One day I flew from Ranchi to Bagdogra and then took the biggest white-knuckle vehicle ride of my life – not counting a late night Tuk Tuk trip – to rival any Top Gear challenge. It involved a four-hour car journey up and over a mountain range dubbed 'The Scotland of the East' to Gantock and Sikkaam in a 4x4 jeep with a crazy driver, who I know took personal gratification at my gasps and screams when the wheels were teetering on the edge of some 800ft drop. I endured all of this terrifying experience to coach my team in a prestigious national tournament. We managed to get to the final – quite a feather in our cap – and due to our continued success here, it meant that I spent the longest continuous period in India at this time, about one month in all. If I'm honest, at the end I was hoping we'd just play the tournament again because I was shitting myself at the prospect of the return journey. I stayed in Gantock until we were defeated, which turned out to be in the final and one of only three games Wal and I lost in two years! The games were intense and you basically stayed until you were beaten, with training curtailed to tactical sessions and me filling my afternoons by shopping in the bazaars and cultured shopping centres, a far cry from the basic fare in Jamshedpur. I brought back two suitcases full of 'fake' items which the kids binned. How ungrateful! Although, to be fair, I gave Robbie an "ABIDAS" tracksuit and Jenna said the "GUCCCI" jumper had three sleeves. What I did enjoy was that the further north you ventured, the culture changed and the only time I enjoyed red meat in India was when I was there. Goalkeeping coach Gumpe Rime knew of a restaurant that did spare ribs and steak and honestly my lips are still smacking at the thought of that meal just now. The team had travelled by train – a 19-hour journey from east to west – which the players took in their stride. However, keeping everyone in clean strips was a problem given we played eight matches in total. So I wasn't too surprised when I walked from my boutique hotel to meet the players at their less grand accommodation and saw the match strips hanging out every window drying. If we were in Motherwell the team would be playing bollock-naked after the first game. From my hotel window, I could see the third highest mountain in the world, Kangchenjunga, from its base in Nepal. This gives you an idea how far north we were staying. Growing up in Glen Court, Motherwell, as a boy, all I could see from my bedroom window was the ashy bing.

Our collective luck ran out in the final when we lost 1-0 to the local team in front of 35,000 frenzied fans. But, from a personal point of view, my luck improved when I got a flight straight back to Delhi, avoiding the four-hour nail-biting return car journey and meaning the unhinged driver couldn't tell his pals about how he had the most petrified man in the world in the back of his jeep.

Whenever I was in Delhi I visited sights such as the famous Lotus Temple, as well as The Red Fort, former seat of Mogul power, the Qutub Minar minaret, Victory Tower and India Gate – which shares a similarity to the Arc de Triomphe – and a poignant memorial to more than 80,000 fallen Indian soldiers from WW1. If you add in Humayoun's Tomb, The Scottish Cemetery in Kolkata housing the graves of the Scottish settlers who arrived during the British Raj, as well as the world-renowned spiritual Ganges River, I managed to add a bit of personal cultural development to my football experiences.

But way above them all, and by far the greatest sight I have ever seen, was the Taj Mahal. During my time in India, I had been invited a few times to visit, but due to my ignorance, it wasn't top of my bucket list and I never took up the offers. That was until one day Gumpe Rime told me his family were over visiting him in Jamshedpur and they were all going to Agra for the day and I had to go along with them. It was so beautiful, tranquil and mesmerising. I was speechless… and for me that's saying something! I will be eternally grateful to Gumpe and his lovely family for insisting I go to see the most wonderful sight and, quite rightly, one of the seven wonders of the world. By contrast, Lee and I would also take a wee walk every lunchtime downtown to Jamshedpur's Bistapur bazaar. There, we would buy the latest replica western clothing styles and technology. We'd see "NIIKE" branded goods with two ticks and "ARMINI" shirts but, to be fair, we'd get some great bargains to take home, which always went down well with my family. Not! Our favourite fashion extravagance would be choosing cloth from the bazaar and taking it to a cracking wee tailors shop, where expert tradesmen would make a made-to-measure suit in two days for £20. This would become the ideal parting gift we would present to our visiting Sheffield United coaches as a reminder of their stay in Jamshedpur. Though thank fuck Ashey Foyle didn't choose to wear his on the way home or I might never have spotted him at Howrah Station!

Lee and I were also honoured to receive an invitation to attend the wedding of our physio, Shashi, who was renowned for treating every player on the pitch with a block of ice. This technique reminded me of the old Boy's Brigade football 'wet sponge and stamp your foot' remedy. A bang on the knee: wet sponge, stand up and stamp your foot. Elbow to the forehead, black eye and six-inch gash: wet sponge, stand up and stamp your foot. Never did us any harm, did it? When we arrived at Jamshedpur FC, Shashi only had a ramshackle collection of equipment and this department was one of the main areas that would benefit from the United expertise.

We received an impressive gold-leafed invitation declaring the marriage of our physio, or "Doctor" as it says on the invite, to his intended bride. When we get there I have to ask. "Doctor?", I say to our medical friend. "Yes," he proudly tells me with a handful of titled documents proclaiming his qualifications. Turns out Shashi was a bit of a medical equivalent to 'Rag Arse Rab', although definitely a much nicer guy. I understand he made a more exaggerated use of his "club physio" title to secure his arranged marriage, for which the bride's father would pay a higher dowry given his lofty title. Why did I not tell Yvonne's dad, John, that I was the manager of Barcelona!

The wedding lasted about one week and every night we'd be going to a different ceremony. I can honestly say it was another outstanding memory. I think Lee and I saw the bride before our physio even met her, given the cultural arrangements, which included street parties, the viewing of the bride, who sat in the living room window for a whole day, and numerous other noisy and colourful pageantry.

As part of the agreement with the Blades, there was an arrangement for TFA to send a team to Sheffield every two years in order for the players to be showcased and to form part of their personal development. The itinerary Lee and I put together was, if I say so myself, outstanding and left no stone unturned to achieve the best experience these young players could have. They flew the same route as Lee and I through

Dubai with Emirates and were picked up in a luxury coach, which would transport them to all of the sporting and cultural events that we'd planned. This would range from matches against several different United sides, including one at Bramall Lane, to visiting London and Manchester and taking in both Old Traffords (football and cricket).

The TFA squad stayed in The Copthorne Hotel adjacent to the stadium and ate every night in an executive box within Bramall Lane. Sheffield City Council afforded them a Civic Reception and a full three-week programme was set out encompassing matches, training, recovery sessions and days off to enhance sightseeing opportunities from Sheffield's ideal geographical location. The lads played a lot of matches, predominately against non-league clubs in the area, with TFA more than holding their own. The best performance came in a match against a strong Sheffield United reserve team at Bramall Lane. An opportunity to play against Sheffield FC, the world's oldest club, was exactly the romance that TFA craved and was also appreciated. This was made possible due to Lee's relationship with the club, where he was both player and manager, as well as the affinity they shared with The Blades.

As I was travelling back and forth from Motherwell - with the occasional detour to take the golf-loving Farzan (Tata vice president and chef de mission for the trip) to St Andrews to play a few rounds - my son, Robbie, would come along with me and train with the team. He was an academy player with Motherwell at the time and a decent player in his own right and was immediately accepted by the boys. Lee suggested we play him in one of our games based on his displays in training, despite the fact he was only 16 at the time. It has to be said, the matches against the Yorkshire non-league teams would sometimes get a bit towsy, as the locals thought we were a bunch of no-hopers out for a picnic. But when we'd hand them their arses, the tempo and the ante changed. So by the time we played this particular side, the word had spread that we weren't 'Rag Arse Rovers', and the opposition would field a strong team, which is what we wanted.

As the players had their names across their backs, which is customary now, Robbie wore the injured striker Arjun's No 10 shirt and the stadium announcer duly read that out. So the game started and Lee and I took our seats on the bench to hear a nervous home defender rally his side by shouting, "Let's get into these Pakistanis." Seconds later, as the vocal player cleared the ball, Robbie followed through leaving a little bit on him and whispered to his ruffled opponent "By the way, they're from India not Pakistan." "Fuck me, they've got Scottish Indians!" opines another opposition player and that set the tone for the rest of the game as the home side's back four collapsed and we took advantage. There's certainly a Braveheart in him and I was very proud of Robbie that day.

If I nearly ended up in my very own Carry On movie scenes with a Tuk Tuk in India, the next tale of my time as Sheffield United international manager nearly takes me into bizarre porn film territory. Jamshedpur FC and the TFA were bubbling along nicely when we got a call from the Chinese Taipei FA in Taiwan linked to Taipei University, who were interested in finding out more about the 'Sheffield United Way'. Since their league had been disbanded due to a scandal of some sort at that time, the Blades agreed it would not be a bad idea to send me to spend a week or so assessing, overlooking and advising on what they should put in place when the league started back. This had the backing of the Chinese Taipei FA and they had sent me footage of decent players who could be looked at.

I trusted Lee implicitly and was happy to leave him in charge to take a flight from Jamshedpur to Delhi and from there on to Shanghai, where I jumped on another plane to Taipei, the capital of Taiwan. I was greeted at the airport by some lovely officials from the Taipei University and an agent from England, who would also act as my translator and give me the lowdown on my schedule while there. As part of the agreement, there was also an additional caveat that I would do some talent identification and take a look at some young teenage players that United might want to take an option on if they fancied any of them. We were happy to do this, but even if we did like what we saw, visas and work permits would be very difficult to obtain.

It was another brilliant experience and with two nights to go I had identified one or two good young players whose families were very keen on helping their teenage sons make the grade in England, regardless of the expense or difficulty. The agent and the club liaison officials had obviously done their homework on me and they discovered through Facebook or LinkedIn that it would be my birthday the night before I left. Word must have filtered through to the eager parents, too, who were being very friendly and accommodating, and invitations to dinner and drinks on them were extended. It's not something I would normally do, but as it was my birthday and I was away from my family in Motherwell and not even able to go for a beer with Lee in Jamshedpur to celebrate, I thought, what the hell?

So it was that, along with two families – mums, dads, the teenage protégés and their siblings and a couple more extra guests – my agent friend and the club liaison officials, I found myself in an exclusive private dining and karaoke complex. The hospitality was excellent. Sushi, champagne, wine, beer and spirits are all flowing and everyone is taking a turn to sing a wee song – mine was The Gambler by Kenny Rogers and I face-timed Yvonne and the kids to let them hear me murder it as usual. The assembled party-goers are also taking loads of photos and selfies on their mobile phones to mark the occasion.

I'm having a great time and notice that a couple of scantily-clad young women, who have been keeping themselves at arms length a wee bit, are also taking their turn on the microphone to great applause from the families. Surprise, surprise, the birthday cake arrives and as I blow out the candles and thank everyone for their lovely hospitality and a great evening, the mother of one of the young players explains to me through my translator, that they have all chipped in to pay for two hookers as a birthday present for helping to make their sons football stars. You really couldn't make this up. I decide to make my excuses and get the fuck out of dodge – and think to myself, thank fuck I'm not wearing that bloody bright red Sheffield United tracksuit, which would stick out like a sore thumb in any photo taken that night that could be posted on social media. But just then the translator grabs me and says that if I do not accept the hosts' kind offer they will be offended. I try to explain – through her – that things like this are not part of my culture and what they are offering me is unacceptable. Not wanting to see the services of the well-mannered and polite 'working girls' go to waste and to avoid the assembled company taking offence that their kind gift was rejected, one of the boys' fathers steps up to the plate – with the approval of his own wife – and decides to take the ladies into an adjacent room kitted out for this exact purpose, to give them a good seeing to.

This seems to satisfy everyone, especially the lucky father, and a diplomatic incident was averted. Jings, the only thing I had ever accepted from a parent while coaching at Motherwell was a sherbet lemon or a sour ploom from a poke handed to me at the side of the pitch on a cold winter's day, and even that was frowned upon!

I had only just completed my second year of a three-year contract with Sheffield United when I left to become assistant manager to Mixu Paatelainen at Dundee United in October 2015. Around this time the Tata contract with Sheffield was nearing an end but, strangely, and right on cue, I get an invite to dinner with several vice presidents from the group, who cut to the chase straight away and make me an offer. They are very smart people and their reasoning matches their intellect, so they wonder why they should pay an organisation for outside intelligence, experience and expertise when they can replicate it by approaching individuals and obtain the knowledge at a cheaper rate. Why pay Sheffield United £X when they could hire Gordon Young for £Y? Nice try big stuff, but if you want to ditch SUFC, you will need to pay me £X rather than £Y. In any case, as much as I enjoyed it, I couldn't have stayed for another three-year contract living constantly in Jamshedpur. If you've seen one steelworks, you've seen them all.

The Dundee United move came out of the blue, even though I had built up a strong friendship with Mixu over the years, and once again I was not actively angling for a move, as I enjoyed my role as an international academy manager. Sheffield United were very gracious and allowed me to cancel the final year left on my contract to take up the position with the Terrors and I thanked them for their understanding. I still keep in contact with many people from the club and I'm so pleased they were recently back where they belong, in the English Premiership.

Before I left Jamshedpur FC and Tata Football Academy, their officials wanted me to give them some recommendations going forward. I could only think of one, Lee Walshaw, but as explained previously they were already looking at cutting ties with The Blades. I had no hesitation in recommending Lee for my role. In the end they decided to run down the time they had left with Sheffield and then got into bed with Athletico Madrid, who they are still affiliated with.

As was the case at Motherwell, as part of a handover I was asked to write up a realistic plan for the club, outlining the steps they would have to take to gain promotion to the Indian Super League (ISL), and then from there become champions and go on to dominate the Asian Champions League. As always, I did my research and produced a proposal detailing incremental development and advising on costings and what might be achievable in a 15-year timescale and it was presented to the Tata main board. Alas, collectively these guys are not blessed with great patience and they wanted it to happen in a two or three-year period. At time of publication it has been six years since I have left and they are still only a mid-table ISL club.

Even though they are people who ultimately wish for instant success, at least they are up front with it and do so with transparency and honesty and I have great respect for my Indian friends. As you read on you will find that I've experienced the other side of this and come across many more faceless, spineless people within clubs, who have unrealistic expectations which are fuelled with hidden agendas designed to be liked by fans. As I have always said, every day in this game is a school day. To put Tata's expectations into context, even the Japanese Football Association – bearing in mind the 'can do' outlook of this nation – are only 16 years into a 40-year plan to win the World Cup and they are reaping the benefit of small steps to glory.

But when I was in India in the heart of their steel industry, I began to understand the mindset of the Indian nation and its ambition and why, for example, Tata would buy the floundering Corus – formerly British steel – for £6.2 billion, way over the asking price, in a dramatic bidding war with Brazilian rivals CNS. It's because it is a source of national pride that they are now the third biggest steel-making country in the world behind only China and Japan. Ironically, maybe one day, written into Jamshedpur FC's history, might be the part played by a wee coach from a Scottish steel town, working for a club from an English steel town, that helped them become a footballing superpower too.

CHAPTER

Golden Aye... D'ye Ken The Sarge

*Mixu Paatelainen offers me the role as his assistant at
Dundee United - what an opportunity*

As mentioned before, coincidences crop up in football all the time and surprise, surprise, another one followed me as I took the next step in my coaching career. As Sheffield United international manager I had been based in India, not far from Kolkata in West Bengal. When it was known as Calcutta, it had taken over from Dundee as the epicentre of world jute production in the early 20th century. So, I was swapping jute-growing country for the place where they once imported the raw jute and used whale oil to machine spin it. The thing is I knew just as much about the great city of Dundee as I knew about jute... the square root of fuckall. Obviously I've researched and read up on the history and it turns out that it's a rough fibre extracted from a family of old world plants and can be spun, woven and manipulated to create the ideal sack, which is what, coincidentally, this move turned into for the man who ran my new club at that time, Stephen Thompson.

Regardless of how it ended, I was really excited about the move to Dundee United, one of Scotland's iconic clubs. I had spent many a happy Wednesday night watching them on TV in the 80s, thrilling us with their European adventures and knew about their large fanbase, and that they could once again become a real force. But the main thing that made me decide to leave the Blades' role, was the opportunity to work with Mixu Paatelainen. When the former Hibs, Dundee United, Aberdeen, St Johnstone, St Mirren, Bolton, Wolves, RC Strasbourg - jings, he's had more clubs than Captain Caveman - and Finland striker, was learning to take his early managerial steps with Hibs and Kilmarnock, I was at Motherwell and had met him a few times. An agent had also contacted me while I was Academy Manager at Fir Park to see if I would take a look at his son, Joel, who was doing well in a similar playing role as his father, banging in the goals for Cowdenbeath, the Blue Brazil. I was always one for taking a punt on inviting young players who were recommended to me. Clubs like Motherwell can't afford to miss out on hidden gems and, from time to time, some rough diamonds would pop up out of nowhere.

On the pitch there were a lot of similarities between Joel and his father. He was a good, strong and skilful centre-forward with a knack of getting himself in the right place at the right time. He was a player we might well have taken on, but for the fact he had a problem with one of his knees. Because of that, we did not offer him any terms. Indeed it would turn out that this problem would persist and trouble him throughout his career, mostly played out in his native Finland. However, he was a top young man with the intelligence to carve out a longer career for himself in sports therapy, whilst playing at a good level in Helsinki. But, as always, I tried to be as up front as possible and explained the situation to Joel and met Mixu personally, to give him an appraisal of his son and was frank about the reason we were not going to sign him, which he appreciated.

The next time I had dealings with him roles were reversed and it was Mixu who was giving me an appraisal of what he thought of my boy, Robbie. As Well academy manager I had built up a good relationship with the Ravenscraig Sports Centre – built on the site of the old steelworks – which had excellent football facilities, including an indoor Astro-turf 11-a-side pitch. It was one of only two in the West of Scotland – the other being at Toryglen, near Hampden – and I had a block booking for several days during the week and a Saturday as an option for our training needs, in case the weather had cancelled matches or put paid to us going through our paces outside at Dalziel Park. That meant that the Ravenscraig facility was in great demand and, when we weren't using the indoor pitch, they were inundated with requests from fellow professional clubs to beat the winter conditions. Dunfermline, Partick Thistle, Celtic, Kilmarnock and Hibs were just some of the clubs eager to make use of Ravenscraig if we weren't and we were happy to offer slots to all of them.

One particular day Mixu's Kilmarnock were scheduled for a slot back-to-back with our reservation, but we changed the schedule, freeing up the 60-minute booking. As we still technically had the first slot booked, I said to my teenage son, Robbie, that he was welcome to go up with his friends for a bounce game until Killie arrived at their allotted time and he nearly bit my hand off to take me up on the offer. Just like me, though, Mixu prides himself in being punctual and arrived early with his squad, around half an hour before their official time.

When he spies Robbie and his friends – of all shapes and sizes and wearing everything from a Take That T-Shirt to a Glasgow Warriors' rugby shirt – playing a bounce game, he thinks they are a bunch of wee chancers and tries to hunt them from the pitch.

"You have to go lads," says Mixu.

"This is our pitch for another half an-hour," replies Robbie, "I'll phone my dad and he'll tell you." And he presses speed dial on his phone.

"And what's your dad going to say…and who does he think he is anyway?"

Robbie has a quick chat with me and then hands the mobile to the Killie boss and I say: "His dad controls the block booking of the pitch and he says you've to get aff the fuckin' pitch, as you're not meant to be on for another half an hour!"

Mixu eventually realises who it is and collapses in laughter.

"Sorry, wee man," he says, "We'll let the lads play and I'll check out your boy while I'm at it."

After a successful season in Ayrshire where he guided Killie to a top-six finish in 2010/11, he was lured away to become manager of Finland, something he was understandably unable to resist after winning 70 caps for his homeland during his playing days. Then a chance meeting at an SFA Continual Professional Development (CPD) event in 2014 at Rugby Park allowed us to meet up with each other again. We took time out to have a coffee and found that we hit it off, personally and professionally, and became firm friends. We discovered our football outlooks and philosophies were very similar and we would regularly talk through our ideas on the golf course. We had such an appetite for what the future would hold and what we would do in our next appointments. You know immediately when you speak with football people if you can work with them and that was certainly the case when I met Mixu. Neither of us were desperate to jump at the first available gig that came up, and that allowed us to discuss scenarios which might arise and how we would tackle them.

We would play golf, analyse the current market and take in matches where we would look at players and systems of play. Anytime I meet people who have operated at a high level, I like to question their experiences and picking Mixu's brains about his International time with Finland was particularly fascinating. It was also interesting what he would do differently from his tenures at the domestic clubs he had previously managed in Scotland.

In September and October of 2015 several jobs became vacant in the Scottish top flight – Motherwell and Dundee United being two of them – and Mixu's name was being linked to them all. He called me and said he was going to speak with United and, if successful, would I be interested in becoming his assistant?

"It's a no-brainer, big man", I quickly replied.

As explained earlier, despite being happy at Sheffield, I felt the opportunity was a good one and I thought it was a great chance to put our much talked-about ideas and football philosophies into practice. Our preparation was such that we even had training schedules as well as formations and systems of play detailed in readiness for our next project. It was looking promising for my Finnish friend to be offered the job and he removed himself from the Motherwell short list to open the pathway for a United return, but nothing had been confirmed. I was home from India and we looked at the fixtures coming up just before the October international break to see if we could get our preparation for taking over at United underway, even before we signed on the dotted line. It was decided I would go and watch Dundee United play Partick Thistle at Firhill and Mixu would go and watch Hearts play as they were to be the Arabs' next opponents.

A good contact, Ian Maxwell, now chief executive at the Scottish FA, but then director of football at Thistle, was happy to organise two complimentary tickets for me, thinking I was on some form of scouting mission for the Blades. As I was home, I was always looking to catch up with as many of my mates as possible and was happy to take my friend, Craig Reid, along with me. Reidy had played a bit of football to a high level in his younger days and I would have been interested in his thoughts on the team Mixu and I would inherit. He also likes a laugh and we spent the journey into Firhill, as well as during the game, reminiscing about the characters we socialised with. We're driving along the motorway and the traffic starts to back up at Provanmill, so I dip the shoulder and spin off at the next exit to avoid the traffic and take a shortcut through the back streets to make the kick off. As we crawl through the leafy suburbs of Robroyston, twinned with Kabul, we laugh as an E class Mercedes draws up beside us. Craig comments that they better keep moving or they'll be sitting on bricks with their jewellery removed and ransom notes sent to their loved ones when I recognise the Dundee United chairman, Stephen Thompson, accompanied by three fellow directors.

Now, what to do? Should I chap their window and ask about the United pension scheme and give my sizes for the kitman to save time when I arrive? Or drive through the changing traffic lights and save my intro for another day, if it arises. We deliberate for two seconds, then I floor it to nick their parking space at Firhill. We get to the stadium and pick up our briefs, declining the opportunity for boardroom passes and settle for the obligatory pie and Bovril, a slight change from ice tea and peanuts I enjoyed at my last match in Kolkata. The game starts and I settle down to make notes and put together an analysis document to discuss with Mixu when midway through the second half, Craig turns to me and says: "You'll have your fucking work cut out for you with this mob, Youngy." How prophetic that statement would be for me.

Still awaiting confirmation during the international break, we had to carry on with our own plans and I was preparing to return to India and Mixu was getting ready to fly to Chile to work for Uefa at the Under-17 World Cup when we had to drop everything for 11th-hour discussions. Mixu was actually on the way to the airport when he diverted to Stephen Thompson's house for further talks. I was on my way to Aberdeen to watch Iceland's under-21s take on Scotland, as there were a couple of players on the radar of the Blades. Mixu was armed with the aforementioned technical and tactical training plans we had worked on as well as budgetary projections, which separated him from the other interested candidates. Hindsight is a wonderful thing, but, if we had known then how dysfunctional the club was at that point in time, and given how high his stock was, we would never have contemplated throwing all our energies and determination into a project virtually doomed from day one.

My Finnish friend had always waxed lyrical about how good a club they were and what a great time he had enjoyed there as a player. So, maybe, with some tangerine-coloured glasses on, we couldn't wait to attempt to help them escape relegation as a priority, implement our strategy and then restore this well supported club to the higher echelons of Scottish football. My agent asked me to take a holding position at the Westerwood Hotel, at Cumbernauld, while Mixu hammered out a plan with United. Three or four hours – and about 10 cups of coffee – later I get the call and our partnership gets the green light. But, on the downside, I need to make an awkward call to Sheffield United, who kindly agreed to release me from the final year of my contract. I then drive across country and meet up with Mixu in Edinburgh and next day he is unveiled as the new Dundee United manager. But, as my international clearance had not yet come in, my position as assistant could not be revealed at that time. But it was game on.

The Thompson family had invested time and money into the Arabs from season 2002/3 when Eddie Thompson bought a controlling share in the club from legendary manager Jim McLean. The north-east convenience store chain, Morning, Noon and Night, had been his baby and he worked similar hours to try to bring the glory days back to Tannadice. Eddie sadly died of prostate cancer in October, 2008, and to show how much respect he was held in, the East Stand at the stadium was named after him. Eddie was brought up a Motherwell fan before he switched allegiances when he moved to Tayside to make his fortune and a new life. I only learned this when I attended the Dundee United Ladies Dinner and was seated next to his widow, Cath, daughter Justine and celebrity fan Lorraine Kelly from Good Morning Britain… "Och well, not to worry."

They were all great company that day and Cath told me while chatting that Eddie watched the Well win the 1952 Scottish Cup at Hampden against Dundee and an old piece of memorabilia belonging to her husband is still proudly shown off at Fir Park. It turns out his old wooden rickety rattle is mounted in a display case in the boardroom.

"Fuck me," I thought. I had often wondered how the owner of that thing had ever managed to swing it around in a packed Hampden with more than 136,000 fans jammed in like sardines. This is the biggest attendance there has ever been for a game outside the Old Firm. Maybe seeing that many Dundonians in the one place buying into the idea they could possibly defeat the likes of Johnston, Kilmarnock and Shaw,

Cox, Paton, Redpath and Sloan, Humphries, Kelly, Watson and Aitkenhead planted seeds in Eddie's mind that they would buy anything from a convenience store! Upon Eddie's death he effectively left his son, Stephen, and his daughter, Justine, in charge of the club. But for whatever reason Justine sold her shares in 2013, leaving Stephen Thompson in full charge as chairman.

My impression of Stephen was that he talked a good game, but was a bit of a strange and insecure character, always trying to prove himself. Taking him at face value, he would always back what Mixu and I were doing at the club and he told the press on several occasions that we were there for the long haul, regardless whether we survived relegation or not. But this is football and maybe we should have been more conscious of the dreaded backing of the chairman when push comes to shove. Ironically, the Terrors have only returned to the Scottish Premier League in season 2020/21. Goodness knows how much money has been spent since we left on coaches, players and short-term fixes for them to regain their place in the top flight of Scottish football. If he had backed our overhaul plan, I am convinced we would have made an immediate return to the Premier League, given the depth we had planned for long-term reconstruction.

Stephen Thompson sold his own shares and parted from the club in 2018 as they faced yet another season in the Championship. Is this coincidental? Who knows? But it has reinforced my contention that we arrived at the club at a time when it was a shambles on and off the pitch.

The chairman had made it clear right from the very start that we would have to cut the wage bill and reduce the first-team squad we had inherited. United had started the season very poorly, hence the exit of the previous boss – Jackie McNamara – and we were expected to turn things around. But it was our firm contention, after assurances from Mr Thompson himself, that if we did go down at the end of the 2015/16 season, we would be given time to stamp our own mark on the team and have a go at bringing United straight back up. Our first task was to evaluate the 57 – yes, that's right – 57 first-team players we had on our books. We were lucky if we could field a team of players each week who actually played in their preferred positions, as we had five goalies; about 40 central midfielders and very few options up front or in defence.

In the previous couple of seasons the club had cashed in on the likes of Andrew Robertson, Nadir Ciftci, Gary Mackay-Steven, Stuart Armstrong and Ryan Gauld and, to be honest, had replaced them with quantity rather than quality. The players we had weren't bad people. Paul Paton and Chris Erskine were two talented and experienced players, but were suffering from long-term injuries and John Rankin, Billy McKay and Paul Dixon were left to be mentors to Premier League fledglings like Blair Spittal, Charlie Telfer, Mark Durnan and the likes. Scotty Fraser and Jamie Robson were kids

I liked and there were others like Simon Murray that given time and experience would make it. United had a very good youth system under Brian Grant and, if the worst came to the worst, I told Mixu we could build the new side around a promising batch of young players which we could mould into our style of play. Many of the inherited first-team players were not what we were looking for and we were instructed to see if they could be moved on. However, several were under very lucrative and lengthy contracts and the club was not prepared to pay them off. Thompson was hoping the ones who were not in our plans would get the message and find other clubs themselves.

Eh, hello! Ironically, neither Mixu nor myself had that contractual security that allowed some players to metaphorically put their slippers on and get their pipes out, as we had clauses in our contracts which meant that our roles could be terminated without the club paying out the longevity of the agreement. An error I won't make again.

But it wasn't just the playing squad that needed overhauling. The entire club was in need of a reboot from top to bottom. Shoddy and inefficient administration became a real issue for us. Mixu, especially, would get frustrated by the lack of professionalism in this area and it fell to me to once again put on my 'heidy tennis' shoes. I remember regularly double-checking various travel, pre-match meal, accommodation and scouting arrangements to make sure they were correct. I would also get the wrong teamsheets sent to me regularly, which was just another needless layer of admin I would have to concern myself with, taking attention away from coaching duties. On one occasion we requested tickets and car parking for the Hibs v Falkirk game at Easter Road, so we could go on a spying mission to watch the Hibees who would be our opponents in the Scottish Cup semi-final. The next morning the tickets are lying there waiting for us, the only problem was that they are for Inverness Caledonian Thistle v Hearts! We had problems with this sort of thing throughout our tenure, but the worst and most well-publicised one came during my stint as caretaker manager at the end of the season.

Despite me being assured of their clearance to play in a game against Inverness Caley, the club were fined £30,000 and docked three points after two young loan players Alistair Coote – who came on as a sub – and unused sub Jamie Robson, were deemed as ineligible. You just couldn't make this shit up. Never should a club the size and stature of Dundee United have been allowed to operate as poorly. That sort of thing rips your knitting as a coach and nobody on the outside had any idea of the internal mess that had been allowed to manifest itself.

At our St Andrew's training-ground base, Mixu and I worked tirelessly to try and get things right for matchdays. As you know, Mixu and I love our golf, but despite being based in the spiritual home of the game, we never once graced the local links while we were working together for United. Mixu wasn't keen on being seen in the public eye having a good time, while his team were languishing in the league and I agreed fully with this stance he took. It was only when my friend got his jotters in May, 2016, that we took in a round at the Old Course. We actually stayed in the Old Course Hotel and played the famous links course, whilst taking a few days to debrief on the previous nine months, scrutinising what we did and what we would have done differently.

Mixu's a very clever guy and a deep thinker of the game. He is continually analysing himself as well as the team and his attention to detail is second to none working in the professional game. Despite his fearsome exterior, he's a very generous guy and great company to be in socially, which I would go on to discover later in our journey and we are still very close friends today. It's funny, I'd be at a game and be sitting next to someone or they would pass by, who'd say: "How's big Mixu doing?" I'd say: "Yes, the big man's good." If it was someone he'd played against they'd say: "I remember he broke my nose." Another would quip: "He split my head and see these teeth or lack of them!" But then they'd all say: "He's a good guy."

Interestingly, he's spent more time in Scotland than Finland and he's very complimentary about the country and the game here, despite trying to convince me of the ludicrous suggestion that 'Flower of Scotland' took inspiration from 'The Winds of Finland'. Mixu on the touch-line was the most animated and at times, according to some opposition players and management, the most fearsome they came across. This was much more about his passion and desire to see the plans and attention to detail being carried out, rather than a desire to be confrontational. That said, I spent a great deal of time pacifying the fourth official who'd say: "Tell the big man to calm down." He was always full on and the detail he'd given in terms of instructions was always paramount in his head during games. One game at Rugby Park against Kilmarnock, I remember their winger, Tope Obadeyi, turning to catch a diagonal pass heading towards our dug-out when he came to a dead stop like a fast-running cartoon character curling up the road in a plume of smoke, as he'd seen Mixu standing ready to catch the ball. As a lot of us in the game are superstitious with certain items or actions depending on results, the big man was never sure whether to wear his club suit or tracksuit on the sidelines. On this particular occasion – a cold winter's day on Rugby Park's artificial pitch – he chose a heavy wool overcoat and he looked like an extra from Lock, Stock and Two Smoking Barrels, and the bold Tope froze on seeing this threatening looking colossus catch the ball in front of him.

Dundee derbies are terrific spectacles, unless you're involved with one of the protagonists who could be getting relegated! One, in particular, at Tannadice live on Sky Sports on a Sunday, was unbelievable in terms of excitement. There were goals as well as on and off-field flare-ups, pure TV gold. The problem at Tannadice is that due to segregation for big games, the Dundee fans were housed in the Main Stand above the dugout areas. The level of abuse that we took that day, especially towards Mixu, was as fierce as I'd ever experienced, with objects ranging from coins, cups and lighters – along with the obligatory big grogger spit balls – raining down on us. The crowd is raucous and Dundee go into a two-goal lead at half-time, but we come out fighting and level in the last minute to make it 2-2. The home bench erupts with emotion and Mixu probably receives the most warmth from the United fans since his return as boss.

Captured on camera, he famously gestures to the rival fans cupping both hands behind his ears in jubilation. Bearing in mind the abuse he has taken over 90 odd minutes, it was a heat-of-the-moment automatic action that has been used by many in the game. That's honestly the happiest I ever saw Mixu that season and I was so pleased for him. Like many times that season we thought it would be the springboard to turning us around, but we couldn't build on a decent result. Ironically, the next day I was sitting in Wishaw General Hospital with my dad who was getting a check-up. All around us in the waiting room, people were reading the match report and commenting on what had gone on the previous day in the world of Scottish football, without knowing that sitting there with a baseball cap on listening to their take on 'The Rumble in Dundee', was someone who was right in the middle of it. Only when the nurse called William Young, do a few recognise the other half of the Terrors' tag team.

Incidentally, in the other dug-out that derby day were Paul Hartley and Tam Ritchie, who are now my great colleagues at Cove Rangers. The record would show that Mixu was charged with inciting the crowd, but was later admonished due to an unbelievable amount of correspondence from Dundee fans, who said the treatment he received from their fellow supporters was disgraceful.

The controversial touchline roles would reverse later when we go to my spiritual home, Fir Park, for a game. This time it's me who needs a settler after a touch-line bust-up with the former Motherwell manager, Stephen Robinson. At that time he was assistant to Mark McGhee, my old gaffer, who was in his second spell at the club. Both teams were in the relegation dog-fight and every game was a nerve-jangler, with the stakes of demotion potentially having huge effects on both clubs' future operating levels.

Like so many times that season, we started terrifically well and take the lead through Henri Anier (ex-Motherwell player). But on the 46th minute and into disputed overtime before the break, the Well equalise. Robbo's excitement carries himself into our technical area, which I'm not really keen about. The half-time whistle eventually goes and the walk down the tunnel involves me issuing him with a request to 'get this settled', much to the amusement of Mark, Mixu and Davie Bowman who are looking at the two smallest guys in both camps letting their passions overflow. I'm particularly angry because it's the first time I've ever had to face Motherwell at a professional level (only other times were as a kid beating Fir Park Boys Club in the Scottish Cup with Netherdale and Fairholm respectively, the latter occasion scoring the winner).

We lose 2-1 again, and I can't let it go and at the post-match drink in Mark's office, you could cut the tension with a knife between Robbo and me as we growl at each other. But the 'grown-ups' (Mixu, Bow, Stuart Gardner and Mark) are pissing themselves laughing. To compound this, I still live only a 10-minute walk from Fir Park and therefore I have to stroll home like Mutley from Whacky Races, still growling and snarling.

Two weeks later I ask Stuart McCall (one of the assistants to national boss Gordon Strachan and his assistant, Mark McGhee) to see if he can organise me a ticket for a Scotland v Denmark match. I take my son, Robbie, with me and as I go to collect my complimentary brief from the Hampden office, I turn around to be greeted by Robbo, who's put in the same request to Mark McGhee. We lock eyes and just burst out laughing and kiss and make up. What a great job he'd go on to do at Motherwell when he took over as manager later on.

The problem with the United squad was none of the lads we were coaching had ever been in a relegation dogfight and they just couldn't string two wins together on the spin to take us out of the danger zone and build some momentum. During our time we had also been in the lead nine times and couldn't hold on to take the three points. If we had drawn all of them, we'd have been safe and, if we had won them all, we'd have finished in the top six. But we just didn't have a killer instinct.

We were lucky to inherit an excellent backroom staff, including Dave Bowman, Stuart Gardner (Screamer to his mates and someone who was a very strong champion of me getting the job after Mixu left) and kitman Ian 'Cat' McIntyre and had very good support from commercial manager Paul Reid and David Southern, who recently left the club as chief operating officer. Paul is a very funny guy and, as well as being very good at his 'day job,' he is one of the best turns on the after dinner circuit, with a talent for mimicking all the top sportsmen. David was also a very nice guy to work with and before United he was managing director at Hearts under Vladimir Romanov, which makes me think his book will better than this one. It was while working with people like this that I truly believed that we could right the listing SS Dundee United and sail on to success. But, in our first transfer window, we lost two of the few strong members of our squad when John Souttar moved to Hearts and Ryan McGowan signed a contract with the Chinese Super League Club Henan Jianye.

The January transfer window is a false market in many ways as there are very few players who are out of contract at that time and that means splashing out money.

A combination of John heading to Gorgie at the end of the month-long window, and the fact that any fee the club would get for him was already being earmarked to be frittered away on something else, meant that our hopes were pinned on the chances we were taking on a few new bargain signings, and that they would come good. But luck proved to be against us.

We trialled lots of players, only signed a few, but the ones we did certainly had pedigree.

Guy Demel – An experienced Ivory Coast international defender who had played with Arsenal, Borussia Dortmund, Marseille, Hamburg and West Ham United, but his best days were behind him. Guy was a giant of a man with a humility and personality to match. I really took to him, but, after a few weeks, I couldn't understand why he kept calling me 'Sarge'. It turns out during an informal cup of tea with Guy, Mixu and Bow had told him I was previously a Sergeant Major in the army after he commented to them about my steely demeanour and insistence on discipline at times, even saying I was scary! Mixu himself explains: "What sums Gordon up perfectly was a nickname we created for him at Dundee United – Sergeant. It is his mannerisms, it's the way he goes about things, he is a bloody Sergeant! It was so fitting and that was coming from the backroom staff. That sums him up. He is fantastic, he is very disciplined, but if you strip that away, he is fantastic with the players and understands them and is tremendous with them.

"When I am a manager, I don't have assistants, I have colleagues and Sarge was my colleague. Everybody knows the final say is with me as I am the manager, but we work together and put our heads together to find the best solutions to win football matches. Unfortunately at United, we were not that successful, I thought we improved, but it wasn't enough. But nevertheless he was the Sarge and that describes him so well in a positive way."

Fuck me, Guy was 6ft 4ins tall and built like the proverbial outside toilet and here's me, a wee 5ft 7ins lightweight and he was scared of me. This literally came to a funny head when he scored a fantastic bullet header, to open the scoring against Hearts (yet another game we were leading in) and promptly marched to the dug-out and gave me a salute prior to a bear hug, scary huh? On his departure from the club he signed his shirt with a message 'To Sarge, the best,' high praise indeed from a good player and my turn to be humble again.

Florent Sinama Pongolle – Another player I really took to. He was a forward who had played in the Champions League with Liverpool and been capped by France. He came in and looked good in training, but did his hamstring during the first half of his debut. What a great guy he was, too. He had a terrific attitude and professional habits, but, unfortunately, he wasn't able to get any more out of his body at that stage of his career. This is a player who along with Guy played at the very highest level and I don't know if any of the young boys tapped into their experience, but, if it was me, I'd have pestered the life out of them for tips and advice, something both would have offered unconditionally. We got them because of their age and condition, but the ability to source them should not be understated and is testimony to the contacts Mixu had. When we gave them free time to go home, these two would always come back with a delicacy or a gift for the other players and staff, which just highlights their class.

Eiji Kawashima - A Japanese goalkeeper who played in three World Cups and more than 90 times for his national team. We signed him from Standard Liege in Belgium and was one we really thought would make the difference. Eiji was similar to Guy and Flo in terms of professionalism and humility and was a true gent, with impeccable linguistic skills and manners. He was a terrific shot-stopper and, perhaps, his inexperience of our game with a continual bombardment of high balls, was his only weakness but, all in all, he was a tremendous acquisition. Paul Hartley would tell me later when we were working together, that the game plan for the New Year's Day Dundee derby, played in torrential rain, was to bombard the Japanese goalie with high balls, which resulted in him fumbling the winner. Clever boy that Hartley.

Riku Riski – A Finnish winger who we snapped up on loan from IFK Gothenburg. Mixu toyed and toyed about signing him with the Finnish connection before taking a punt on him. However, we were getting him at a good rate – which was important due to the constraints of our budget – and we brought him in. The Dundee Courier's headline said it all when we unveiled him 'Riski Signing For United' and they weren't far wrong. The lad made his debut against Celtic at Tannadice live on TV one Friday night and was like a deer caught in headlights. I remember Bow whispering to me: "I think he's shit himself."

In their pomp you couldn't put a price on these four collectively and the only reason they'd ever have been in Scotland would have been a stopover similar to Elvis at Prestwick Airport, let alone sign for Dundee United. If you chuck in Eddie Ofere, who came in for the last 13 games, a Nigerian international who did have previous experience in the SPL with Inverness, it gives you an idea how certain players become available and at what time in the season. Basically, and this is not rocket science, you need to get your squad assembled during pre-season when you have the chance to disseminate the budget with the targets and move for the types of players you see being most beneficial for the campaign ahead. Any manager going into a club mid-season is automatically at a disadvantage and any players out of contract at the same period, are up for grabs for a reason. Unfortunately, they weren't deemed suitable for the incumbent managers when they selected their options at the beginning of the season. Sometimes you can get lucky, but the situation we were in required major surgery and time, which was not a luxury we had.

We also took on a trialist from Juventus, who was recommended to us by an agent. Good life lesson here, there must be a reason why someone who has been on the books of the 'Old Lady' is being touted around the far reaches of European football by an agent. So it's the middle of winter and we are training at St Andrews and the lad sidles up to Cat the kit man, just before his first training session starts.

"You have gloves?"

"Here you go," says our efficient kitman.

"You have hat?" Yip replies Cat.

"You have snood?" Aye.

"You have tights?"

"For fuck sake, son, if you can play, I'll get the needle, thread and the sewing machine out to make you whatever the fuck you want, OK?"

After 30 minutes everyone knew he couldn't play and the Cat didn't give him any more gear. Later that day I organised a shooting drill and arranged for crosses to be clipped in for the big high-maintenance trialist striker to attack. One ball came in and our hopeful connected, only to send it 60 feet over the bar. Another player a good five seconds later quipped: "Fuck me, it's still rising!" Cat was brilliant to have around and as is the nature of kit men up and down the country, a crabbit bastard. They're so protective of 'their' kit and probably among the best people at a club, who always manage their budgets effectively. Agents were forever offering up players for us to try and similarly, as when I was at Motherwell, we were not in a position to look a gift horse in the mouth and were happy to have a look at them.

Gavin Gunning was one quality player who we had high hopes for at Tannadice. I worked with him at Motherwell under Stuart McCall and he did a great job for us and played in the 2011 Scottish Cup final against Celtic. He subsequently moved to the Arabs and had three good seasons before sealing a deal at the end of his contract to go to Birmingham City where he injured his posterior cruciate ligament on his debut, a League Cup match against Cambridge United, but never pulled on the blue strip again and was released at the end of the 2014/15 season.

After his rehabilitation, he went to Oldham Athletic on a short-term deal and then became available on a 'pay-as-you-play' arrangement for us. It has to be said, though, despite the fact he was a quality player, we came to realise that most of his injuries seemed to be more psychological than physical. During his time with us, which spanned 19 games, he was most famous for picking the ball up against Inverness Caledonian Thistle while the game was still going on. I remember Mixu looking at me in surprise and with a "what the fuck is he doing?" vibe. Getting to the bottom of it, he had wanted to come off the pitch and, before we could organise a substitute, the ball had come to him and he just picked it up and walked off. He then returned to the playing field and was treated for an injury before being hauled off. The referee was bewildered and so was everyone else inside Tannadice. We hurriedly subbed him off before he was sent off. But then he took it into his head to offer a sarcastic handclap to the home support, who didn't take kindly to that and he had to do the walk of shame and run the gauntlet of abuse to the corner dressing rooms at the stadium. We had to issue a statement saying that, while he remained a United player and could come back to training, he would not be considered for selection and could take an early summer holiday. He left the club very soon after. Gav was "high spirited" and all the boys at the clubs he played with would testify to that. But again he was not a bad lad. He'd sit in the jump seat next to the driver going to away games, that's if he wasn't walking up and down the aisle finger pinging the ears of anyone who was sleeping. After the win at Ross County when we were down to ten men and qualified for the semi-final, we jubilantly danced into the away changing room to find a 'steward' wearing a hi-vis jacket, hat and clipboard addressing the players as they came in. Yip it was Gav who had found the gear in a cupboard adjacent to the shower room. You need guys like that in squads, but preferably when you're winning and they're playing well.

Mixu and I gelled very quickly with our inherited backroom staff early on and one of the best times we had was the night before the aforementioned game up at Ross County's Victoria Park in the quarter-final of the Scottish Cup on Saturday, 5 March. We had arrived early to prepare the squad and we all decided to have a quiet glass of wine once the players had gone to bed. We were getting to know each other and the patter was flowing well. We made a point of making sure the entire backroom staff interacted in the right way in order to build camaraderie and a spirit that would rub off on the playing squad too, and it rarely involved a drinking session. We organised competitive games such as darts and everyone from the assistant kitman to Mixu the boss, joined in and it brought us all closer together. With personalities like Dave Bowman, Cat the Kitman and Mixu in attendance everyone was sure to have a good time and were able to relax in each other's company. That night they even bonded at my expense when my frozen shoulder (more later) saw me flounder in a game of round the clock with the arrows. I made more holes in a wall that night than the whole of Berlin did on 9 November 1989!

Next day spirits were high amongst the coaches, everyone was encouraging the players to the full and despite being 2-1 down and a man down, we ended up winning 3-2. During the match, Mark Durnan was sent off and Mixu and I had a tactical discussion on the sidelines and went to a 3-3-3 formation when most teams would go to a 4-4-1 set-up. This is something we discussed when playing golf all those months before and therefore we had no hesitation in implementing the call. There's nothing nicer when a bold move like that pays off in a match. The strategy was that, as we were losing, leaving a solitary man up front would encourage their full-backs to push on, overloading the midfield and, even if they didn't score, we would be pinned back in our half. So by keeping three up to play against their back four, we used our three defenders to let us build up against their two strikers, and our midfielders would have the hardest shift against their four opponents. Carol Vorderman on Countdown might have struggled to work this out, but we knew what we were doing. Mixu and I (and Paul and I are now the same) believed that you must practise these things in order to be successful. In Latvia, where we will travel later in the book, the players couldn't believe that I would even practice kick-offs so that everyone knew what was expected from them.

Striker Simon Murray is a lovely guy. But, as much as he was sharp in the box on the pitch, I don't think he would be upset if I said that when I was at United, he wasn't the sharpest tool in the box when he wasn't playing. Now, most clubs have a fining system and structure that keeps everyone on their toes. It usually sees players having to shell out a few quid if they forget or lose kit or are late for anything. The proceeds generally go towards the Christmas and end-of-season nights out as well as charity donations and children's hospital gifts. Well, we changed it slightly to incorporate a new bye-law that if anyone left kit in the changing room during tidy-up, it would be taken to the club's front office and the offending player would have to go and bid for it.

Young Simon, who was perfect for a dressing room with his personality and the fact that everyone else was in on a plan to stitch him up, he ended up having to put his hand in his pocket more than anyone else. He couldn't work out how during clean-up one of his flip flops would always end up at the front office. After the first or second time, anyone else might have just left it there, bought a new pair and kept them close by from then on. Simon ended up paying out £240 for a pair of £12 flip flops during the eight months I was there! He was one of these guys who did things without thinking about it and was a wee bit naïve when the patter and high jinks were in full swing. But I'm sure he has matured and cottoned on to things now as he has progressed in his career. He was an effective striker and scored a few goals, especially in my three games in charge at the end of the season. But it was hard at times to get tactics and systems of play into his head.

One Friday in January at Tannadice we were doing a bit of shape work as Simon and seasoned pro Billy McKay would be in the starting line-up for us the next day.

I was trying to get the strikers to make complementary runs. If one goes front post, the other spins and goes back post - and all the while to do it with pace and sharpness. Stopping the practice at one point in frustration, after a good half hour of explanation and attempts at perfecting it, I said: "Si, where are you going to run if Billy goes there?"

"I would just run with him." he says.

Exasperated and wishing to move on to something else, I said: "Just you do that then."

The next day we gub Killie 5-1 at home and Simon, despite not scoring, chased after every ball up front and set up a couple of goals. Sometimes you have just got to let an effective, enthusiastic player play.

Simon also holds the title of having the worst tattoo I have ever seen in my life. I was talking to him in a crowded dressing room one day at St Andrews as he was getting changed, and noticed a perfect rectangle badge on his side at the top of his backside. "Hawd the bus!" I exclaim, "Whit's that?" and like all good football team banter, immediately drew everyone's attention to it. There in perfect font as you would see on the side of a wall reads the name of an electrician firm with full address, telephone, e-mail and social media contact details. I'm not surprised when he tells everyone that he lost a wee wager with the owner of the Montrose company which sponsored him, and the forfeit was for him to get their advert tattooed on his ass. My marketing training told me this would be bloody ideal if you're looking for a sparky when doing the butterfly in the local leisure centre, or sipping sangria from a straw on the beach at Magaluf, but otherwise the firm's prime target audience would be missing out big time. That is unless he was going to do a Nicklas Bendtner, who pulled his shorts down after scoring for Denmark in the 2012 Euros to reveal a bookies' logo on his underpants. But even I couldn't see Simon bearing the side of his arse live on TV in a match against Ross County!

Technology is forever evolving in football and the use of GPS is now commonplace at most clubs where information on individuals can be key for their technical and tactical development. I am a big fan of it and evidence can be given to improve players, which is ultimately your job as a coach. Training sessions as well as matches are filmed and then cross referenced to the GPS stats, giving you complete access to all you need. One morning after training had finished, Mixu and I were debriefing the morning session when we received the 'player data load' for our perusal. Immediately I see an anomaly in the figures, with Simon having run nearly 3K more than anyone else. We wonder if he's managed to do some extra work on his own, but on viewing the video of the session we get the answer. I had worked with the strikers at the end, which was the norm, and discovered that the extra distance was created by Simon running to collect the balls which he had missed the target with and which had travelled a good 50 yards behind the goal we were finishing into. No wonder we were bottom of the league! It's normal to use a goal which has a huge net behind it, but, as the winter was so wet, we had to alternate the penalty box areas available and this particular day meant a vast grass expanse behind the featured goal.

Throughout my career I haven't been immune to becoming the butt of jokes and pranks myself and that's the way it should be – if you give it out you need to be able to take it. At St Andrews one day I was demonstrating a drill and I fell arse about tit over a hurdle, with everyone in tears of laughter at my You've Been Framed moment. I had been suffering with a frozen shoulder and trying to protect myself, I fell over like a drunk man and, in the strictness of dressing-room banter, they showed no mercy. So, in the showers, Mixu and Davie Bowman made sure my shower gel was always placed as high up on a shelf or window sill as possible so I was unable to reach up and get it.

As you can imagine even big nice guy Simon Murray was happy to get in on the act and I'd catch a glimpse of an electrician firm's logo being stretched out on a big arse, as my Lynx Africa was hoisted to the heavens.

Talking of baring your arse reminds me of a time I was staying at my digs in St Andrews. The club had kindly given me a small budget to stay for a couple of nights a week in the town – usually a Monday and Tuesday – while we trained. This saved me a bugger of a commute each morning and night back and forth to Motherwell, and trying to fight my way through traffic build-up from the construction of the new Forth Road Bridge at that time. I managed to set up a deal with the husband-and-wife owners of a cosy wee eight-bedroom hotel – courtesy of my financial advisor, Alastair Lafferty - always good to keep in with him with a mention – on the road that looks directly onto the 18th hole of the Old Course. It's probably been on the TV several times when Seve or Tiger have strolled up to victory in the British Open, with guests hanging out its windows cheering them on.

It was usually closed over the winter months, but they made a special dispensation for me as I would be a regular visitor and a low-maintenance guest at that. This was because I would regularly organise for Big Dave, the Dundee United chef, to make me a plate of food to take back from the training ground at the end of each day, so negating the hassle of them making me my dinner. I was the only person, apart from the young couple who lived in as housekeepers, rattling about in the hotel and it was the ideal spot for me throughout most of the winter. I had room No 3, an en-suite bathroom and had the downstairs lounge all to myself. This meant I would regularly have a stretch out on the sumptuous sofa, while watching Monday football on the satellite TV. It was great and meant I didn't have to travel up and down every day to Motherwell in the darkest and coldest months, which that year were particularly dark and cold.

After a day on the training ground my routine would include walking to my digs, running a hot bath and soaking there for at least an hour dissecting how the session had gone that day. One wet Tuesday evening in February, I've just eased myself into the bath, getting past that point where the heat allows you to get your arse down. I'm reliving a wee bit of shape training that has not gone to plan earlier in the day when the doorbell goes. As the housekeepers are away for a couple of weeks on their own holidays, I have a set of keys to let me in and out as well as having the run of the kitchen. But I'm intentionally ignoring the ding dong, which is disturbing my soak and Smooth Radio easing out hits from the 80s. But the bell keeps on ringing and ringing and I hear it even when I put a wash-towel over my head and submerge myself. Ding-dong. Ding-dong. Ding-dong. These guys are the worst-ever players of ring-bell run-away I have ever come across, I think. But it's obviously not going to stop, so I grab a towel and traipse down the stairs to chase whoever it is for ruining my nice, hot, relaxing bath. I open the door and there before me are 12 soaking wet Japanese tourists with one brandishing a piece of paper and one still with his finger jammed in the doorbell. DING DONG! Another chime for good measure as the lead visitor launches into a spiel – in just passable English – on how he and his friends have booked this very hotel for the night and they have the documentation to prove it. Standing there half naked in a towel, I'm fighting a losing battle trying to explain to my Japanese friends that the owners are themselves on holiday, guests are not expected till the tourist season starts and why the fuck, if that is the case, am I also standing there soaking wet in a hotel that is meant to be empty? I decide that the best thing I can do is invite them into the sitting room/bar out of the rain for further explanation. This for many of them, is the go-ahead to make themselves at home and they start organising tea and coffee from the table top tray, cups, saucers and kettle. With my towel slipping at an alarming rate, I put a hasty call into the owners who are having a great night on holiday in some hot far-off climes.

They assure me, in the middle of their beach party, there must be some misunderstanding. "You think?" I say, as I pass the phone on to the leader of the group and head back upstairs to get dried and changed. When I come back down it's bedlam with nobody any the wiser. Then I get an unbelievable lightbulb moment – we have a Japanese player on the books and not just any old player, the national team's No 1 legendary goalie and a jolly good chap who speaks perfect English – jackpot. A quick call to Eiji and both he and his wife appear at the hotel where they are surrounded by their adoring country folk demanding pictures and autographs. There we go, he'll sort it out and I can relax. And he did and they all stay the night! Not what I was expecting, but the least I can do is direct them to the cosy wee bar and help them drink as much as they can. I phone Yvonne and Mixu telling them about another night you couldn't make up, when I think, fuck, who's going to cook them breakfast? I'd like to embellish the story and say I knocked up an array of Scottish delicacies, but I dipped the shoulder and did an early dash in the morning, to avoid any further forays into the hospitality business. I relay my bath-tub interruption to Mixu, Bow and Screamer when I get to the training ground the next morning and they begin howling with laughter. As a result we've stumbled on a venue for the next staff night out. However, I can't stop wondering if any of my knowledgeable visitors might have brought their fitba boots with them and if they might fancy a wee trial… couldn't have been any worse than that belter from Juventus! Every time I think of him it reminds of that old joke when the Blackpool donkey meets the racehorse and in an attempt to impress him, shows him a photo of a zebra, and tells him that was him when he played in Turin!

I was always happy to see my mates from Motherwell and the Electric Bar and from time to time they would head up to Dundee to take in a game and have a couple of beers. One good pal, Mikey Stevens, called me to ask if he could bring along his nephew to take in a United home game. I'm happy to help and organise a couple of complementary tickets for him at home to Partick Thistle on Saturday, 12 December, as his nephew and brother-in-law were fans of the Jags. Mikey isn't as interested in football or its finer points as the rest of my mates and I just had a feeling in the back of my mind that it could easily all go the shape of a pear. After the game, which had a traditional 3pm Saturday afternoon kick-off, I'm wrapping up my post-match routine and duties and checking my phone messages – as we have a mobile phone cut-off point for the coaching staff and playing squad of two hours before a game on a matchday. Sure enough, there are the regular good-luck messages from before the match and the congratulations or, more often than not while in Dundee, commiseration messages from after the match. But, unexpectedly, there, timed at 3.20pm, is a message from Mikey asking me where it was he had to pick up the tickets! Despite the fact I was in communicado, what the fuck did he expect me to do if he did manage to get me on the phone halfway through the first half of the match, with me standing next to Mixu on the Tannadice sidelines, trying to save the club from relegation?

"Eh, Mixu, just need to run along the track, out to the front door and make sure my buddy and his nephew have got their comps. I might ask him how his big collie dug is getting on, too. Did I ever tell you about the time we kidnapped his dug from the Electric Bar and sent pics of it to Mikey with a ransom demand? I'll just make sure his nephew's got a hotdog and a Bovril, show them to their seats in the stand and be back in 10. OK?"

This is the guy who used to play the guitar and sing the classic Neil Diamond hit "Love on the rocks… is sore on your piles." and went with us to the world cup in Italy in 1990. He returned early with a broken collar bone from a drunken escapade, just in time to announce in the Electric Bar – whilst brandishing a much sought-after match brief for the Brazil crucial qualifier – "who wants a ticket for the game?" shouts Mikey, just seconds before the kick-off on the pub's big screen!

Saturday, 16 April, at Hampden saw us stroll out on the pitch to play Hibernian in the semi-final of the Scottish Cup. Mixu and I had come to the conclusion that this was make or break for us. Relegation was looking probable at that time, but was not a foregone conclusion. If we could reach the final of the cup, where we would meet either Rangers or Celtic, it could be a launching pad for us to take into a relegation survival drive or promotion campaign the following year. But, if ever the season was fated for failure, the final series of league games and the semi would reveal by just how much. Hibs had won their quarter-final replay up in Inverness, a game we both took in and shared a belief that we had a good chance of beating them, especially as their first-choice goalie, Mark Oxley, had picked up an injury and had to be subbed off. In the lead-up to the semi-final the Edinburgh club hunted for a replacement and settled on bringing in Conrad Logan, a journeyman keeper, who looked more than a little heavy. We identified him as a weakness and told our lads to shoot both low and early, given his supposed inability to get down, a worry I know their staff had due to some inside information, which has a tendency to leak out. The semi-final was his first senior game in 16 months, but that, and his extra tonnage, didn't stop him having the game of his life against us that day at Hampden. We had prepared very well for the match and the lads were up for it. They gave everything and but for Conrad – who kept out three one-on-ones against the normally deadly Billy Mckay and two net-bound piledrivers among his other notable saves during the full 90 minutes and extra time period – we would have won.

To put the seal on it, he managed to save two penalties in the shoot-out of a match, which had ended 0-0 only because of his performance. This probably summed up our luck, or rather lack of it, and sometimes in life I believe that what's meant to be, is meant to be regardless of what you try to influence. 'Tough Titty', as they say in some parts, but it's hard to take when you analyse the effort that goes into reversing fate. Logan endeared himself to the Hibs faithful and the club would go on to beat Rangers in the final and win the cup for the first time in 114 years.

If that wasn't bad enough, just over a fortnight later our relegation was sealed when we were beaten 2-1 live on Monday night TV against our Dundee rivals at Dens Park. We were 1-0 up (there's a surprise) in that game well into the second half, but ended up conceding a 90th minute goal to send us down. Dundee boss that day was once again Paul Hartley and his coach, Tam Ritchie, who I was delighted to team up with later at Falkirk and am currently working with at Cove Rangers. It really is a funny old game. They love recalling this derby game when we're reminiscing about our football adventures over a few beers, but, to be fair, they never gloat about it, much!

But there was nothing funny about being dealt the two hardest blows I have ever had in my coaching career. There certainly was absolutely fuck all funny about walking the 200 yards from Dens Park back down the street to Tannadice, walking a gauntlet of gloating Dee fans and Terrors' fans baying for our blood on the relegation of their team at the hands of their fiercest rivals. That 200 yards felt like 2,000 miles.

My admiration for Mixu was certainly enhanced, though, by the dignified way he handled this enforced 'walk of shame', showing the inner strength of character and class of the man. This is where Mr Thompson, the chairman, showed his lack of class and his real true colours by reneging on his vow that we would not be sacked if we were relegated. The next day we were still in charge, but I am heading to training at St Andrews when I get a call from Mixu to say he has to go straight to Dundee for a chat with the chairman. When he gets there a BBC film crew are already outside. I know the media could easily have put two and two together after our relegation, and I am just speculating here, but could it be that they have got wind of something being an-

'He is very equipped to be a manager himself'

Mixu Paateleinan summed up his relationship with Youngy: "Gordon Young is a top guy and I loved working with him. He is a very intelligent and thoughtful football coach who is very open minded and wants to learn, think about and try new things.

"We met before we worked together through Scottish FA seminars, at some matches and on other occasions. He also had my son in training with him at Motherwell for a while, so I learned he had a lot of good knowledge, was very open and was someone I could work with.

"I realised we would complement each other very well if we worked together because of his character. Gordon's character with the players and how he handles them is tremendous, and he is very well equipped to be a manager himself. He is fantastic to work with on the training field, too. I usually let my strength and conditioning or fitness coach take the warm-up. Then the next part of the session is very important and I would hand over to Youngy to prepare them, before I would take the main part of the training. Then, at the end, I would hand back over to Youngy who would take the positional part of the session on the pitch, which I also think is very important. That worked really well for us. The way he goes about his business and the way he teaches the players is excellent and it has been a privilege to work with him.

"Of course, we also got along as characters off the pitch as well. I found Gordon really good company and very witty. I have always loved the Scottish character and before we worked together, we played some rounds of golf a few times and Gordon was clever enough to let me win, as I am very competitive about everything.

"I am so happy to know Gordon, both personally and professionally, and am hopeful of working with him again in the future."

nounced before we even find out ourselves? If that was the case, it's a very poor way to treat a good servant to the club as a player and a coach, if you ask me. Later that morning I get a call from Mixu who tells me he has been sacked and he has been instructed by the chairman to tell me I'm in charge until the end of the season. I'm all for standing shoulder to shoulder with my Finnish friend and paying Simon Murray to get a new tattoo, saying 'Shove Yer Job Up Yer Arse, Mr Thompson' and sending him a picture of it. Better yet, maybe that pish Juventus triallist or, even better, a soaking wet Japanese tourist could call the chairman up and tell him that he can keep his job and can "go and boil his heid." Not sure how that would be translated into Italian or Japanese, but I was raging at the time.

Even harder was explaining to my family that the full contract wouldn't be paid out, as there was a tiny wee clause allowing us to be emptied with a severance period equalling exactly zero pounds sterling. But Mixu convinced me to hang in there and take the job.

It was another real hard body blow to take, especially as when Mixu had taken the job his stock was really high in the managerial world, and I had walked away from a secure position at Sheffield United, so convinced we were that we could resurrect a sleeping giant and we both thought it was a terrific project. Mixu is a terrific man with strong principles on how he thought the game should be played and his pre match information was concise and clear with the practices mirroring the game plan. Our partnership was both enjoyable and diligent with total commitment as a given. I hoped we would work together again and, as time would tell, we would and who knows where the future will be. As they say "it's where the ball takes you", literally.

So, for the fourth time in my career, I am caretaker manager of a Scottish Premier League side, but this time I don't have a table full of Young family experts, armed with condiments and Brussels sprouts, to give me some words of wisdom. No, I get my very own turkey in the shape of Stephen Thompson piling into the dressing room when I am talking and giving the dejected squad his version of a pep talk for the last three games of the season. He tells them all I will be taking charge – which they knew already – and that when the season finally ends there will be a review of those with contracts and those whose deals have run out, or will not be having them renewed. I'm inheriting a squad that were already feeling very sorry for themselves and this was exactly the inspired leadership and man-management expertise we all needed at that time. Thanks a bunch. Especially when I was starting to convince myself that if I could get them playing in the last three games, I might have an outside shout for the job full-time. Working alongside Thompson would be a hurdle, I knew, but that would be something I would have to clatter into, if this scenario came to pass. As much as I had been in partnership with Mixu, I was happy to take his lead and help implement his vision for the club as he was manager. Now that I was in charge, I had a few ideas of my own to implement due to the cards that we had been dealt.

I gathered all the players together for a chat. I arranged for all the foreign lads to be released early and head home and try to tie up contracts for themselves for the following season, which they were all grateful for. I also announced that I would be playing players who were out of contract, as a couple of our final games were live on TV and they would be putting themselves in the shop window to secure a deal at another club, if they turned on the style. Finally, I told five young players at the club that I would be giving them their debuts in the last three games and this was their chance to shine and make a name for themselves. I hoped these measures would create a hunger and sharpness on the pitch for the games to come. Training in the days that were left of the season would be more light-hearted as the pressure was off now that we had officially been relegated. I also wanted to encourage more freedom of expression and reduce the tactical element we had employed while trying to beat the drop.

Here's how my three games in charge panned out:

Inverness Caledonian Thistle away – won 3-2

First game up and true to my word, I picked the strongest team I had available to me with the boys going out of contract all playing. This seemingly caused TV pundit Chris Sutton to criticise me as he believed I should be sending out a team of kids. Really? Well I can't remember him having too good a management record. Anyway, I had a responsibility to the players who, as I had intimated to them, would be able to show-case themselves and receive a win bonus as well as their appearance money. I was also hoping that a good victory would help restore some credibility to the club, some pride for fans who travelled up and watched on TV, show the other teams in the league we were not going to be pushovers at a time of the season where a place up or down means financial rewards, and lastly give myself some kudos in Scottish football. After the game, which we won 3-2, I went in to see big Yogi Hughes and Chipper (Brian Rice) his assistant, who were always hospitable at any time I locked horns with them over the years regardless of win, lose or draw, and enjoyed a cup of tea with them dissecting the current events of the hour. When we were about to leave around 10pm – given the evening kick-off – I asked for a couple of cases of beer, which I wanted to reward the players with on the road home, which can either be the best or worst journey depending on the result.

Knowing we wouldn't get to Dundee until after midnight (1.30am for those who stayed in the West of Scotland) I decided against bringing the players in the next day for a recovery session. Instead I arranged a compromise through captain Sean Dillon that all the players would send a picture of themselves in a local gym, performing the prescribed regeneration session, whilst holding a copy of the daily paper – highlighting the date – before 11am. To a man, all clips were sent in before 10am. This is an example of how man-management can have an effect on players, as I knew the extra hour in bed and absence of a commute to undergo a recovery session, would sit better with both themselves and their families.

Partick Thistle at home - drew 3-3

To keep the momentum going, I kept the fun, but competitive, element in training and picked another side which I thought could deliver three points. This game at Tannadice wasn't live on TV, so I rotated to give some players more recovery time, before the final match against Kilmarnock. I gave some youngsters their debuts, notably Harry Souter and Matty Smith. Despite going 3-1 down, the players showed tremendous character to come back and draw 3-3. Probably the highlight of the match apart from the young players' debuts was making John Rankin captain and taking him off five minutes before the end, to allow him a standing ovation for his service to the club in what was his last match.

The response and backing I received from United fans was humbling, as was the respect I received from the Scottish press, which was something I will never forget. Many were strongly suggesting that I should be the next manager and, if not, at least seriously considered, which seemed to be echoed by the staff, players still under contract and sections of the Terrors' fans. Unfortunately for me, this was never considered by the owner. The last meeting we had was at the training ground in St Andrews, the day before my last match in charge against Kilmarnock, and was probably the most cordial we ever shared. He admitted to me that a new manager had been agreed and he would be bringing in his own staff. Perfectly understandable as this is the norm. Taking the chairman at his word, my understanding was that he wanted me to stay in some capacity. I suppose my efforts for the club were vindicated when he doubled an improved severance pay from three months to six!

Kilmarnock away - won 4-2

To finish the season we'd go to Rugby Park and play a team who had to win to avoid a relegation play-off against Falkirk (coincidentally a team I would work for in the months to come). Again I sprinkled the team with out of contract players to highlight their capability and availability, along with young kids who deserved a debut. We were outstanding in that game shown live on Sky TV. Harry Souttar scored and would secure a lucrative transfer to Stoke City on the back of his performance, Kilmarnock would have to face the play-off match due to the 4-2 defeat and, played in blazing sunshine, life in football is good when you are winning. The Killie backroom team of Lee Clark and Lee McCulloch (a Motherwell lad, Jig and I go back a long way and completed our Uefa Pro License together) were excellent and in the post match pleasantries, a tentative offer was made from them for me to join them for the following season, but their budget was tight and despite Lee's desire for me to go, a deal couldn't be struck.

The last three games of season 2015/16 may have been dead rubbers as far as the survival of the club in the Premier League was concerned, but we regained some pride, went unbeaten winning two away games and drawing at home against Partick. We had played well and I had introduced some new young blood into the first team, which is always a good sign for the future. I thought I might have had a good shout for the job full-time, but I wasn't even given an interview for the role. The work Mixu and I put in while at Dundee United was unbelievable and we deserved better, but I was too long in the tooth to believe that it gives you a god-given right to succeed. I've seen high-profile names in the game come into jobs and wing it and con their way through things and come out smelling of roses, that's just football... but you don't have to like it. You put the experience in your tank and move on to the next challenge.

Two things I remember vividly after the final game of the season against Kilmarnock. The first is that I am standing giving a post-match interview on camera in the tight tunnel at Rugby Park when out of the corner of my eye I see Stephen Thompson and we can't help but end up facing each other. He sticks out his hand, with his head scanning the floor for worms, for a handshake and goes to ask something, but only manages to get the word "What..." out of his mouth. Quick as a flash with a cheeky smile on my face, I grab his hand, shake it and I finish his statement for him by sarcastically saying "What a great day to get the sack!"

The second thing I remember afterwards from that game is Stephen Craigan, former Motherwell and Northern Ireland captain, saying in his TV punditry after the match words to the effect of: "People won't forget how well Gordon Young has done with this Dundee United team over the last three games of the season. It won't go unnoticed."

For the next six months it felt like it did.

CHAPTER 11

Bantam Of Solace

A period of unemployment took its toll, but boxing training helped me fight off depression

My family took me out for a meal after my last game with Dundee United, and even though we were not celebrating, I really enjoyed myself. I felt Mixu and I had done as much as we could with the hand we were dealt – inheriting a massive squad who had suffered a really poor start to the season, only being given one transfer window in which to wheel and deal, and just 32 games to transform an entire club from top to bottom – and I personally thought two wins and a draw as caretaker boss was a decent return for the club, even though we were relegated by that time. Stephen Craigan's positive comments about me after the game against Kilmarnock were ringing in my ears and I thought I could enjoy a few weeks at home with Yvonne and the kids, catching up with my mates, getting round to fixing that garage door and tidying up the garden, before the firm offers would come in.

Soon I accepted an offer to go across to the USA for a summer coaching stint in California, which I had done regularly in the previous five or six years due to a relationship I had built up with David Robertson and his club, Davis Legacy. I would go out and work with Robbo's club as their technical advisor and deliver at international coaching symposiums with the Norcal Premier League governing body. I was also fortunate to work alongside some top-class international coaches such as Frans Hoek – Louis Van Gaal's right-hand man – and Ronato Ferreira from Benfica, as well as many more from all corners of the globe.

David is a Newarthill boy who worked for Motherwell FC's community department, as well as being a PE teacher and semi-professional goalkeeper, playing for some prominent clubs in that format. Whilst summer coaching in the Davis area, he met his wife, Sarah, and has been settled there with a beautiful family for ten years, carving out a very successful career as a technical director working for Davis Legacy as well as Norcal. Robbo is well respected and is a great example of personal development and I am proud of what he has achieved, some 6,000 miles from Newarthill, a 'small fishing hamlet' to the east of Motherwell. He is truly living the dream and is a credit to his parents, Len and Margaret, who I pop in to see from time to time. They, too, are bursting with pride at how he has developed. He has gone from being a house guest of host families when he was a student coach, to a much respected football operator living in a beautiful detached villa in the leafy suburb of Davis, a close-knit affluent university city where most people cycle around enjoying life. My relationship with Robbo, his family, his mates and professional colleagues is as strong as my circle in Scotland, which is a testament to our friendship.

In those previous summer clinics, Robbo would organise everything depending on who was with me. Sometimes I was alone, which meant more golf, and sometimes Yvonne and Robbie accompanied me. I would present in the classroom and on the field up and down the Bay area, culminating with the International Symposium, which was unbelievably well organised and also incredibly well attended. After one of these sessions, which was hosted at the University of San Francisco and which was very well attended, Robbo and I were in the car complimenting each other on how well it went as we were driving towards the city for a well earned shandy. At that point I looked in the mirror to see Alcatraz, with the Golden Gate Bridge to the East. We were indeed on the famous Lombard Street, where a tram with tourists was gliding up alongside us. We just looked at each other, smugly sighed and smiled. It was like George Best getting asked by the hotel porter "where did it all go wrong?". My working environs couldn't get much better than this.

Once the 'work' was over I'd always build in a vacation, which would be traded off reciprocally against my duties. We would enjoy some tremendous locations such as Lake Tahoe, The Nappa Valley, San Diego, Malibu, Los Angeles, Santa Barbara and our favourite city by the Bay, San Francisco. Robbo would make sure I was suitably recompensed. He arranged many great golfing experiences, as well as social events involving his family and friends who, as a result, became my friends. The hospitality I was afforded, as well as the mutual respect, was again so humbling and the desire to learn from most of the coaches was very rewarding.

On one occasion, Yvonne and Robbie were with me and once I finished the symposium, we travelled down the Pacific highway to Los Angeles. There, we met up with my daughter Jenna, who was in Orange County enjoying a summer coaching camp. Yvonne and I are fiercely proud of both our kids, with travel being just one example of their ability to flourish away from ML1. At this point Jenna was 19 years of age and she had travelled to California to work the summers with UK Soccer after I helped her fast-track her levels 1 and 2 coaching qualifications. She would later take a party from her school to Malawi to assist in the building of water wells and developing schools, while sponsoring children she met on her adventures. Throw in another travel excursion back packing through Asia and you get the feel for an outstanding young woman, who I believe has found her perfect vocation as a Guidance teacher. I believe she'll end up becoming the "heedie" somewhere as she's so talented and driven.

Around this time, Robbie had just returned from representing Scotland at the International Children's games held in Seoul, South Korea, where they won the football tournament. Later on he'd travel on his own to trial for UC Davis Aggies who are the soccer team representing the University of California and play in the NCAA Division 1 Football Championship Subdivision. This culminated in a contract offer which was the largest given to an international placement in terms of scholarship contribution. However, he would decline it, firstly in favour of Fort Lewis College in Colorado, then Lander University in South Carolina, where he enjoyed a successful career and was selected to play at regional level for their 'All American' team. He was also part of a side that won the league two years in succession, rating them at No 6 in the entire USA at one point. Later on when I moved to California for a full-time coaching job (chapter to come), Robbie would fly from Colorado to visit me and I would beam with pride as we drove over the Golden Gate Bridge. I remember face-timing Yvonne as we cruised around San Francisco with the sunroof open and the music on, soaking up the rays. I loved hanging out with him and introducing him as my son.

How cool is that? My wee family from South Muirhouse driving about South California, having it large. Jenna was a massive hit over there and built up her own network, which she still keeps in contact with, and it was great to see her being able to travel to the USA as a 19-year-old, whilst completing her teaching degree. What an incredible family to have travelled so far and wide meeting people and being successful into the bargain. I laughed when Jenna bought me an A4 map of the world where you scratch off the silver foil covering any country you've been to. After a few minutes I had to stop to get the vacuum cleaner out when I found myself up to my arse in silver foil, with all the places we've all had the privilege to visit scratched off.

But the hospitality shown to us in Davis was reciprocal, as we even managed to organise a trip to Scotland for one of David Robertson's elite girls teams and this was a resounding success, with both football and cultural exposure for the girls and their families. They were based centrally and were able to travel to major tourist attractions, even going south into England to visit Old Trafford and beyond. I arranged for them to play against the best girls' football programmes in Scotland, mainly Rangers, Celtic and the most successful in the country, Glasgow City. The yanks whipped them all and Robbo recalls that the seconded Scottish bus driver was regularly to be seen careering up and down the touchline at games and 'encouraging his girls', who he was chaperoning and had grown attached to. I'll never forget them giving him a farewell present on their departure, he was so emotional he nearly bought a round. The girls enjoyed the tournament – which they won hands down – and visited Edinburgh, Loch Lomond, St Andrews and Glasgow. They were based at a Strathclyde Park hotel, where they could enjoy all the leisure pursuits nearby and the theme park adjacent. Good memories of our great country indeed. Robbo and I even arranged for golf for the dads who had accompanied the girls, culminating in our own version of the 'Ryder Cup' at the magnificent Gleneagles course, which hosted the real event. The funniest moment from that trip occurred when I said to Robbo to bring himself and some of the guys to my house for a barbeque on their return from a trip to Edinburgh. Sure enough, they brought the full 57-seater bus, complete with driver who couldn't manoeuvre in my cul-de-sac and my back garden ended up looking like Howrah Junction.

While my most recent wee summer stint in the USA provided it's own valuable time to reflect and refresh from my Dundee United experience, I ultimately had to come back, but not before a wee opportunity presented itself in Toronto. Football is truly global and in theory there are opportunities everywhere. Armed with a Uefa Pro-Licence and my experience, I thought I would be in a good position to offer expert advice and consultation. I had toyed with becoming a full-time coach educator, travelling all over the world presenting coaching symposiums and training the coaches, but had never taken the plunge. I had a discussion with Kevin McGreskin, another highly qualified Scottish coach who had been part of Jackie McNamara's backroom team at Partick Thistle and a regular presenter at coaching licences for the home nation FAs. He had also recently been the national technical director of the Bahamas Football Association. At that point Kevin was the technical director at Burlington Soccer Club just outside Toronto and he invited me to deliver a coach education week there. I enjoyed another wonderful experience and was grateful for his hospitality, so much so that we continue to keep in regular contact. I genuinely considered going down that route of coach educator at that moment, but it quickly passed and I focused once more on trying to get back into the game.

Everyone I spoke to after I parted company with United, both inside the game and out, wished me well and assured me I wouldn't be out of work for long. All I had to do was keep the phone close and wait for the call. Lee Clark, who at that time was the gaffer down at Kilmarnock, got in touch and offered me a role coaching their Under-20s side. I was flattered but I didn't think that was the right fit for me at that time. Soon the garden was the best in the street and Chelsea were on the blower, but a slot on the suburban section of the RHS Flower Show was not what I had in mind.

The first month off was OK, but then the days and weeks began merging into one another, and after painting the house from top to bottom, I began to notice I was taking longer and longer to get out of my bed in the morning. Then, a wee chink of light. Through my agent, Scott Fisher, I got an opportunity to interview for the head of coaching job at Burnley FC, who had just won their place back in the English Premier League. They were putting the finishing touches to their new training ground, a magnificent facility which I could see myself operating in. I later learned that initially I was the left-field candidate, and really only got an interview due to Fish's relationship with Dave Baldwin, CEO at the club. I apparently blew them away with the first presentation, which wasn't a surprise given I had embraced the Elite Player Performance Plan (EPPP) club operating model set out by the English FA, whilst rolling out 'the Sheffield United way', before I went to Dundee United, so I was right up to speed. The next process was analysis and session planning, which again was not a problem given my experience. Then it was announced that the successful candidate would be chosen from a shortlist of two, whittled down from more than 150 applications. The final process would be a practical training session with the Under-23 Burnley squad, followed by a debriefing interview and the best and last man standing would win. No problem, Marquis of Queensbury rules and everything above board, right? Fuck no, this is professional football.

I found out that the guy who was leading the process was previously at Bradford City at the same time as Stuart McCall. So I called Stuart to get some background. "Hi mate, do you remember Jon Pepper?", I asked. "Sure," says Stuart, "he thought I was responsible for him getting emptied from the club." "Were you?" I asked, but knew the answer already having worked with Stuart and could vouch for his honesty and credibility. "No," he said. The problem was Jon might not have shared that view, and Stuart was one of my references. Surely this guy wouldn't hold it against me, right? But why not judge for yourselves. I was geared up and looking forward to the last two challenges. It was also a chance to coach Robbie Leitch again who was in the Under-23 squad, having transferred from Motherwell where I signed him as a schoolboy, and he would be in the session I was going to deliver. There was also a gentleman by the name of Dick Bate in the mix. He had been hired as a consultant by Burnley, to advise on all football matters given his exceptional experience in the game globally. But in particular Burnley hired him as he was a previous technical director of the English FA no less, making him a kind of Craig Brown equivalent in terms of knowledge and integrity. In addition, he had presented on my Uefa Pro-Licence course and was very well received by me and my peers.

So, I go down the night before and book into a Travelodge, where I run over the session I'm going to deliver the next day. I rock up the next morning very composed and totally clear on the theme I have been assigned, and decide on a practice which I had performed many times with first team and youth players – "defending from the front" and high press in particular. Michael Duffy had recently retired after a very successful playing career and was the incumbent coach of the talented Under-23 squad. When I finished my session, he whispers "outstanding mate, can't wait to work with you". Yes, I too felt it was a competent performance. As I walked back from the salubrious pitch on a beautiful autumn day, I was passed by a very military looking bloke resplendent with English FA tracksuit top, his top tucked very neatly into his shorts and his full length socks pulled up to his knees, whilst brandishing a clipboard. I admit I did have a wee chuckle to myself little knowing, but somehow suspecting, this was 'the competition'. He looked like Brian Glover from the film Kes, but I swooped away to get changed before the debriefing finale.

I chat to the club chef, a physio and a lovely lady who was the staff member all clubs have... elderly and friendly who I knew would be a players' favourite and might hand them a wee sweet treat when no one was looking. The debrief was short, gratuities were exchanged and then I was told an announcement would be made over the weekend, where loose ends would be tied up. On my drive home I phone Fish, my mate Stan and Yvonne. "We'll wait and see, but I couldn't do any more," I tell them.

I cut the call short, as another came through from Robbie Leitch. "Hi Youngy, nice to see you earlier and just to give you a heads up, Jon and Dick pulled six players in after both the sessions and asked them for feedback." I ask what the verdict was. "You pissed it and the boys are all looking forward to you coming in and so is the gaffer. Michael Duffy asked me about you and I gave him the thumbs up." That's encouraging, I think, and wait for the call. This took seven days to come and when it did, it was from a mobile, while Jon Pepper, the caller, was out walking his dog. Professional, right? Fuck no, this is professional football. "We couldn't split you both, Gordon, but unfortunately..." And before he could go on, I press end call. Jon promptly phones back and says "Sorry it's a bad signal." But before he can utter another word I say: "No it's not, I hung up on you."

The last thing I need is a poor man's Jim Bowen telling me 'here's what you could've won'. I'm pissed off and resign myself to being the victim of a 'job for the boys' decision, when I get a call from a withheld number. "Hi Gordon, it's Dick Bate here and can we keep this confidential? I am disgusted at the decision not to hire you. I am a consultant and the final decision, quite rightly, is made by the department head." I agreed before he humbly and genuinely continued: "If there are any jobs you are interested in I will act as a reference and also if anyone is on for my advice, I will recommend you without a doubt or reservation." I've been blessed to have come across some top blokes and Dick – who passed away in April, 2018 – showed his class by making the call, which he had no need to.

Next up for the custard pie experience was St Andrews, not the home of golf where I had spent a shitty winter, but a club on the sunshine island of Malta. Again through Fish, I was invited out to Valletta to have a formal interview with the president, who had strong links to the Scottish game. He had used Scottish coaches in the past, most notably ex-Rangers captain Ally Dawson, as well as an exchange venture linked to a modern apprenticeship programme with Cumbernauld College, coordinated by ex-Celtic and Scotland legend David Hay. Before we flew out, Fish intimated to them a salary figure which would be acceptable to me and this was given an unofficial thumbs up, with the caveat that the owner would confirm everything when we sat down. I get the tour of St Julian's Bay, where I would be based, and have a look at what office I could use, as well as the accommodation that was on offer.

This is all cordial and I take my laptop into the meeting to highlight my philosophy for the project and what I expect from the club in terms of support and infrastructure. I wanted to bring in an assistant – my former Blades buddy Lee Walshaw – with all other personnel remaining until I was settled and happy with their contribution. Bringing an assistant in during the early stages wasn't possible, but something that could be added once we were into our stride and hitting the targets, which I set. All straight forward, right? Fuck no, this is professional football. The owner, a French eccentric who wouldn't know a ball if it hit him in le visage, pushed the contract over to Fish and myself and the salary was only a quarter of the agreed amount. "Why don't you go and have a think about it and we can meet again in the morning?", Monsieur Clouseau announced and even suggested we have dinner and drinks. "Why don't you go and pelt yourself with balls of your own shite," I think to myself. "I think he might come round a bit," says Fish. "He'd need to fall off the Eiffel Tower and land on his wallet," I reply, and the following morning's session was a waste of everyone's time. Fish asks: "Are you going with the initial number or not?". The answer that comes back is a long-winded "non". So we say thanks and goodbye and head to the bar... "and the tab's on you for wasting our time!".

These were the only 'real' opportunities I had in six months since moving on from Tannadice and it was the longest period of unemployment I had experienced since I had left school… and it was beginning to affect me big time. I think it may well have affected me more because of how close I was to a couple of new positions, only for the rug to be swept from under me, through no fault of my own.

Before I go on, I want to take a moment to say that I was always aware of how well off I was, relatively speaking. I had a great, supportive wife, family and friends and my physical health was good. I knew there were many, many people worse off than me, going through tougher times in their lives, but depression does not discriminate. I hope this description of what I was going through at this time does not come over as wallowing in a 'poor, poor me' self-indulgent episode, looking for people to feel sorry for me. But I was starting to feel really down for the first time in my life. And for the joker in the pack, the life and soul of the party, the guy with the cheeky-chappy personality, that was hard to take to say the least.

I had known coaches and players going into a spiral of depression when they had been sacked or let go and had sympathised with them and tried to help. I always text or phone people I know when I hear they've been emptied, but I never thought it would happen to me until it did. Depression was something that happened to someone else, especially not a Lanarkshire lad of my generation. In many places you were perceived as weak if you were seen to show any natural emotion other than anger, and maybe a touch of disgust every now and then if a tear was ever shed.

Wee things were irritating me. I would find myself in the company of my fantastic group of mates and for some reason beginning to dislike people and events, just because they were happy and I wasn't. That made me feel even worse. I was being nippy with people and biting the heads off people I loved, and I was finding that I preferred my own company, which helped to exacerbate my downward spiral. Quite frankly, looking back at how I was in those dark days, I could understand if people would rather have hammered nails into their own balls than spend time with me. What made it worse was that my peers in football were empathising and trying to help and it just irritated me even more.

"You're too good to be out of the game, Youngy…"

"You'll be fine, Gordon, decent coaches are always much sought after…"

"Ever thought of stand-up comedy wee man, you'd be brilliant on stage…"

Aye right…Who makes the clown laugh? Everyone meant well, but they were in jobs and not in my position and these were easy things to say. The reality was that the longer I was out the game, the more demoralising it became and it was so hard not to feed on the bitterness and feel sorry for myself. Questions started to enter my head about whether I was good enough. I had never played at the very highest level and I was doubting myself massively, putting pressure on everything I was doing and becoming really anxious. I was just hoping I would get a call offering me a job and I would come out the other end. But it never came and I realised I had to do something quick.

I eventually ended up in my doctor's surgery and had a good heart-to-heart with my family GP, Dr Barr. He was a very easy man to talk to, and being a Motherwell fan, he was really understanding about depression. It was good to speak with someone totally independent from my life and get their perspective on things. It was confirmed, as I suspected, that I was well on the way to suffering from full-blown depression. He discussed the many options, which ranged from therapy groups to prescriptive drugs designed to restore your mental and chemical balance. I said I would check out the offers and online workshops he directed me towards, as well as a dosage of anti-depressants and away I toddled to the chemist to pick up the pills. As I waited in line for my prescription, I began thinking of what was happening to me and how it was affecting my life and those around me. The chat with the doc had helped, but I was unsure if I wanted to take medication.

In the pharmacy I watched people with various conditions as they collected their medicines and repeat prescriptions. I saw a guy I vaguely knew, come in and wait for his daily methadone and I nodded to him as he headed off after swallowing his dose. "He was a decent player in his time," I thought to myself as my name was called and I collected my package. I drove the short distance home, glancing every now and then at the paper poke with my name written all over it, sitting on the passenger seat beside me. When I got home I went straight to the kitchen and made myself a coffee and sat down and stared at my would-be chemical saviours. I then drained my mug and scaled the kitchen unit, to put the coffee jar back in the cupboard and the unopened anti-depressants on the top shelf. And they are still there to this day, more than five years later unopened… a reminder and an inspiration to myself.

Yes, I could have easily taken them and they would have helped re-balance the serotonin in my head and set me back on the path to the old me. But I felt like I had gotten myself into this state, primarily by feeling sorry for myself, and it was up to me to get myself out of it. Now, I know that these pills are essential in many cases to help people who are depressed and I'm not belittling anyone who takes them to assist in their recovery. But I felt the visit to my GP surgery had acted as a kind of half-time team talk and my tactics would have to change if I were to produce a result.

A chance meeting with an old mate and keen boxer Tommy 'The Sheriff' Murphy, engaged us into a conversation about training and not pulling any punches. See what I did there? "You're a bit out of shape wee man," The Sheriff observed. "Get yer arse up to the Impact Gym in Holytown and I'll put you through your paces… or the living room windae, if you don't turn up!"

Football had brought us together when I was 17 and farmed out to junior side Thorniewood United. Tommy, then 27, was a no-nonsense experienced midfielder who used to run me to training and games in his car. He would take me home after games, stopping off at his house where Anne-Marie, his wife, would give me dinner despite having two wee boys, Stephen and Paul, to look after. We instantly became great mates and have been ever since. My designated report time was 7.30am and Tommy would batter me for a 90-minute session that would raise my adrenalin and my spirits, but by 2pm in the afternoon, I would be back under a dark cloud. Very quickly Tommy recognised that I was not my usual self and he knew how to help me. I used to laugh sarcastically to myself every time I gloved up at the gym and looked up at the inspirational quote on the wall from boxing legend Mike Tyson: 'Everyone has a plan until they get hit.' That fucking summed me up to a tee at that point, but hitting the bag and punishing myself with boxing training really helped me. Tommy was one of the few people who was not irritating me at that time and my stress and dark thoughts drained away from me in the gym.

The Sheriff is a naturally motivational man as well as an absolute head case, who constantly told me I was a winner – which was very important for me at that time. It gave me the focus I needed and a reason to get out of bed in the morning. I also went to the gym's circuit sessions at night and trained with real gems, who didn't give a fuck who you were or what you did. You were there to train and if you don't like it you could go fuck yourself. So I upped my visits, till I was there virtually seven days a week, and the anti-depressants remained unopened in the kitchen cupboard.

Iain King, a well-respected football journalist and a keen boxing fan came out to the gym to do a piece for the Daily Record and when the snapper came in, I've never seen so many confident people disappear so quickly… camera shy allegedly! Incidently, Kingy was another top bloke who would do me and a few others who were 'between jobs' at that time, a real turn. He recommended Ian Murray, James Fowler, Stevie Campbell, Peter Nicholas, Bobby Mimms, Paul Simpson, Joe McBride and I to a Nike-sponsored soccer camp run by Joe McLaughlin. This was based at Nottingham University and we had an absolute blast for a month, where we coached players released by clubs and showcased them in trial matches. I struck up a great relationship with them all and in particular Ian 'Nid' Murray, who I still keep in regular contact with.

This was probably the only time in the six months of unemployment when I actually enjoyed myself, as I was with good football people and training twice a day. We discovered a small members' bar on the campus and after a productive day's coaching followed by some personal fitness, we would retire to the bar and have an absolute hoot to ourselves, as we integrated with the 'interesting' locals who didn't have a clue who we were. The banter and patter was 'unplayable' and we were all at ease within our comfort zone, where the reminiscing and storytelling were of the highest order. This helped to revitalise us all. It was great to get in every morning to a 'football environment', discuss the day's coaching content, which was long but much needed, by a group of guys who were all 'between jobs'.

Shortly afterwards most would find new roles. Peter Nicholas is an absolute legend, but he wants to watch my counter-attack drill more closely, and Paul Simpson would get back into the English FA set-up headed by Gareth Southgate – tell him I owe him a half lager, Simmo! Joe McBride would get hired by the SFA in the performance school programme and Stevie Campbell would land a role as assistant manager at Brechin City.

Nid and I hit it off immediately and our travels down on a Sunday and return journey on the Friday night became legendary. He's now the manager of Airdrieonians FC – in the same league as Cove Rangers – and we kept in touch, despite our travels in the wake of the Nike gig, taking him to Norway and me to the USA. Even now we'll speak on a Saturday morning and then on a Saturday night, win, lose or draw to give a post mortem on our games and analyse each other's matches. This despite us being in competition in the same league, which I understand is quite unusual in the modern game. He's another top bloke that "gets it" as far as I am concerned.

Kingy had brought us all together like the cast of the football 'Dirty Dozen' and after a successful career in journalism, he himself has since followed his own football coaching dream to Canada, where he is now technical director at a club in Nova Scotia.

The Sheriff got me physically and mentally fit and I learned an awful lot about myself from him, and an awful lot more about how to help people who may be struggling, to get the best out of themselves. This is something I have eagerly incorporated into my professional and personal life and have made it a top priority in any new role I have taken on since. Having been through a period of depression, I realise how it creeps up on you. It's a domino effect that leads you to get worse and worse and before you know it, you are not able to get out your dark place without some help. Maybe it crept up on me because people around me assumed I was always happy-go-lucky Youngy, always up for a laugh and a joke and a cheery quip. Maybe they thought depression would be the last thing that would affect me. Well, they were wrong.

That's why now more than ever, I make sure I engage with everyone under my charge, never ignoring anyone, always greeting them personally in the morning when they come in to training and trying to get to know them more as individual human beings. I'm hoping that this knowledge, as well as being personally fulfilling for me as a sociable person who truly wants to get to know them, will help me identify players who might be struggling emotionally or mentally and in need of some early assistance. For example, a couple of the players I have worked with since have had children who are autistic, and getting to know their domestic situation allowed me to easily give them time off when they needed it to attend to any challenges they may have at home.

Things are changing in the macho world of football and most coaches and managers are encouraging it to be a 'no brainer' – no pun intended – for players, coaches and staff to let us know about any issues with their mental and emotional health, just as easily as they would report to the physio with a sprain or strain. As it stands right now, Scottish Football is currently taking the affect of mental health within the game much more seriously. Some excellent work is being carried out through the SPFL Trust and the Chris Mitchell Foundation and more than 310 people throughout Scottish football have qualified as mental health first aiders. Currently, just about every SPFL club has taken part on sending staff on the two-day course, with proposed plans being discussed to make the scheme mandatory for every football club in Scotland from the start of the 2021-22 season. The Scottish FA has also recently launched its first ever Mental Health Action Plan, as they aim to end the stigma around the issue in football and create an environment for people to talk openly about their mental health in the game. Their new plan was launched in October, 2020 as part of the Scottish FA Equality Framework; Football Unites, which aims to make Scottish football representative and reflective of the demographic of Scotland at all levels. That's all good news and coming from someone who has been there, a good step in the right direction. But everyone needs to play a part, especially the coaches and managers. At my peak in the gym Tommy said I was a ten-stone man punching like someone who was 16 stones in weight, as I took out all my frustrations on those poor boxing bags. Jings, it's amazing the faces you imagine are on those things when you are in full flight punching away, and I'm sure you could easily piece together from what you have read so far, who would appear regularly. I would still readily admit that I am no battler and couldnae beat sleep. However, this was undoubtedly a challenging time in my life. My livelihood was taken away from me through these long months from summer 2016 until February, 2017. Without the help of Tommy, Yvonne, my family and my understanding mates, who all stuck by me when I was nippy, dopey, angry, grumpy and all the other seven dwarves joined together at the same time, I don't know where I would be today.

One of my mates – enter again Mikey Stevens – chapped my door late one night and assured me that he would make sure I would not want financially, should my period of unemployment continue. 'The Mex' as he was known due to a full moustache, shakes my hand and whispers in my ear: "I've more money than a horse can shit, so you know where I am wee man." And then he jumps on his motorbike like Michael Elphick from Boon, disappearing into the South Motherwell horizon. I was so grateful to him to make the offer, and while I was not on the breadline at that point, it couldn't go on like that forever. It was a great relief to know that my mortgage would be covered if I was not earning in the near future. The thing is he meant it.

When I think back to that time I am humbled at the love of my family and the generosity, loyalty and affection my mates have for me and I for them. So I would like to apologise to them here in print if I ever upset or offended any of them with my actions during this time. However, still to this day, I feel a sense of injustice about the time I spent out of football. I felt I had done well as a coach, but the phrase that is always churned out is that this is a results-driven business. Well, bollocks to that. Not everyone can win the league, so maybe a result should be judged on key performance indicators like other industries. Coaches might reduce the age of a squad, they might increase the value of players, up the attendances at games, or create a pathway to the first team from the academy. Brentford FC have a model where they concentrate on performance individually and collectively, as well as against their competitors, rather than results and have a matrix where as long as they are progressing in the chosen areas, then results will eventually follow. Many clubs use 'Moneyball' type programmes for recruitment, but not many go the whole way like Brentford in charting their goals.

These are all successful KPIs, but we live and die on results and, if you don't win in Scotland, you are considered a dud. I feel we should offer more longevity to the plans of positive-minded coaches. Paul Hartley and I seem to be currently doing that with Cove Rangers and fingers crossed we'll be given the time to bring them to a conclusion.

As 2016 came to a close, I was grateful to French Academy side Edusport, developed by Chris Ewing, for offering me some coaching opportunities. Chris remembered the assistance I gave him when he was starting up his business and asked me to come up and deliver some training sessions, so at least I was back out on a pitch and coaching once again. Then, out of the blue, came a call from Barry Smith, the new boss of League One side East Fife, who asked me to become his assistant. I knew there wasn't a lot of money on offer, but at that stage it was about keeping my sanity and getting back on the pitch. I accepted the offer. I keep saying this coach is a top guy and that one is a top bloke, but the majority of people I have been fortunate enough to have worked with have been exactly that. Baz and I were on the Pro-Licence together and it's in that two-year education period that you pick each other's brains and get to know each other's footballing thought processes. And he was another great bloke who helped me out when I needed it.

But despite my troubles during this period, I somehow knew I would eventually be OK. Despite the dark lows, a voice inside still told me I would have the mental strength to pull the boots on, set out the cones and markers, talk tactics and motivation with players and start again. More than anyone I have Tommy Murphy to thank for helping to turn up the volume on that voice. To this day, if I ever get complacent about who I am, how I am feeling, how I am behaving and where I am going, I just open the kitchen cupboard, glance up at the happy pills and get back down to the gym. Everyone I know is also delighted that I still maintain a good number of boxing sessions every week to keep me smiling and on my toes. Though my default position, just to be sure, is that I am a short-arse and I am not able to grab the box of pills even if I get up on my tippy toes!

CHAPTER

Odd Job In East Fife

A lifeline from Barry Smith at Bayview helped to
get my coaching career back on the rails

Barry Smith and I had studied together for our Uefa Pro-Licence and shared a respect for one another during that two-year spell. In early December, 2016 he had landed the East Fife job and called me to see if I would like to join him as his assistant. Barry had taken over from player/manager and former Scotland and Everton full-back Gary Naysmith, who had gone to Queen of the South as full-time manager after guiding the Fifers to promotion to League One the season before. When Barry called, I obviously put him on hold immediately and consulted my personal management team, who were trying desperately to shoehorn all my football commitments into my busy schedule!

Other than having more space than Han Solo in my schedule, the main thing that swayed me was a nervous looking glance up to my top kitchen cupboard. It was another no-brainer. Even though there was barely any money on offer – a small stipend and some travel expenses – I jumped at the opportunity and will be eternally grateful to Barry for thinking of me. I would be back coaching in the professional game, albeit part-time, two nights a week at the Oriam National Performance Centre for Sport in Scotland at Heriot-Watt University in Edinburgh (where the Fifers train) – putting me in the shop window and giving myself a better chance of finding a full-time post.

The other thing that gave me a real buzz about the role was something simple, primeval almost, in-built within every single person who plays, coaches, or watches football: the build-up to a match on a Saturday. I was genuinely excited that I would be looking forward to having that feeling again, one that has given me so much joy from the first time I was ever involved in a match. Time to break out the lucky Y-fronts that hadn't been washed for months - or years, come to think of it - and embrace all my rituals and superstitions that go along with preparation for a Saturday game. Preparing my bag the night before and going over the game plan are always right up there for me, as is always being early for the pre-match meet-up.

Yah fuckin' dancer! Never had the mention of East Fife put so much exhilaration and delight into one person, since Eric Morecambe had uttered the East Fife 4 Forfar 5 line. A score which only came true as a football result just over a year after I left in July, 2018, when the Loons beat the Fifers 5-4 on penalties in a League Cup tie.

I know I have said this a lot about the people I have met and worked with during my football coaching career, but Barry is another great lad who I have been lucky enough to work with. We enjoyed a successful three-month spell together in Methil. Baz would say that our personalities were different and so we gelled immediately. But I'll tell you, he has a great sense of humour and knows his way around a tactics board.

However, it was over as soon as it began, due to me receiving an offer from the USA, where I would swap Bayview for a View of The Bay, near San Francisco. This was the clever strapline by Iain King, the chief sports editor of the Daily Record, who as mentioned earlier came out to the Impact Boxing gym to do a piece on me before I crossed the pond. As a big boxing fan, Kingy promptly joined in the session with Tommy and myself whilst gathering information for the article and coordinated the photographers during our work out.

Barry would move on from East Fife too after a successful stint. We both had an agreement from the chairman that we could leave if we landed a full-time offer and so Barry went to rivals Raith Rovers and a return to full-time football. He might have regretted that one, though. That's for Barry to tell, but we keep in close contact and it's the lowest I'd known him due to the surreal events he experienced in Kirkcaldy.

So what about my brief spell in Methil? Well, I was quickly accepted by the lads at East Fife and there was quality in the squad with some incredibly dedicated professionals on the books, some of whom had played at a higher level. In our time at East Fife, Barry and I formed a formidable partnership and were undefeated in 13 games, we went close to securing a League One play-off spot and reached the last 16 of the Scottish Cup after beating Livingston at the Tony Macaroni Arena (or Almondvale to give it its proper, well-known name - I know clubs need to make a buck any way they can and sell naming rights for everything these days but I just can't get used to calling Scottish football grounds by any other names than their traditional one). That wasn't bad for the newly promoted team!

First things first, I had to put in the work and help Barry to improve the Fifers and it was matters close to home which I had to deal with first. My next door neighbour would be the one and only signing I would bring to the club. Nicky Paterson had just returned from a stint playing football in the US and he was literally the boy next door to me. His mum and dad are still there after 25 years and as a family you couldn't get any better to share your wheelie bins with. His brother Jonny has also distinguished himself on the fitba field, having captained the Scottish Cerebral Palsy football team and has represented Great Britain at two Paralympics. I mentioned to Barry that Nicky could do us a turn and after a few training sessions, we offered him a contract. He repaid us by going on to score the winner in that Scottish Cup game against Livingston, to earn us a quarter-final money spinner with St Mirren.

It was the Sunday morning after that game – when we phoned each other for a de-brief – that I told Barry of my Stateside offer and I felt I had just pissed on his parade after that great win. But true to who the guy is, he said he was delighted that I had received a better offer. The chairman was unaware of my situation and phoned Barry that night to offer some extra budget to bring in a player or two, thanks to the money from the cup run. Barry never mentioned to him about my new role and phoned me to say he would give me the extra money at the expense of new players, if it helped me to stay. Another humbling thing to be directed towards me from someone in the game and it shows you the mark of the man, despite him knowing the offer I had to go to the States.

A positive progressive experience was what I had at Bayview. They are quite simply lovely, honest hard-working people and a credit to the whole of Scottish football. They didn't meddle with what Barry and I were trying to do and they supported us in every, and any, way they could. There are always exceptions to the rule, but it is fair to say from my time in the professional game, that the smaller the club, the better the person you find there. People who will go out of their way to perform any little task that is needed around the club and who are not afraid to get their hands dirty in the process. These are the determined employees who are fans as well and, more often than not, work hard more for their love of the club than for payment. At these clubs it's the owner or chairman you'll see with brush in hand, sweeping up after a game. These are the stalwarts who are taking a photo for the match-day programme one minute, then painting the pie stall the next. They might act as receptionist in the morning and then be plunging a septic tank in the afternoon. They will then gladly make a pot of soup and sandwiches for the railway enthusiasts who rent out the boardroom on a Tuesday evening, and then have to plunge the septic tank once again on the Wednesday morning, as they come face to face with a familiar looking set of half digested soup and sandwiches! Hats off to them all.

Worryingly, my eyes were opened on several occasions as to how in some Scottish football heartlands, we have not moved on with the latest developments in sports nutrition and eating correctly. But this was down purely to kindness, rather than any kind of naivety. I had always promoted fruit and pasta before and after training and games, but to my amusement and slight horror, I was shocked to see that after every training session the players were presented with a box of 36 Dunkin' Donuts to gorge themselves on, from a lovely well-meaning kitman who thought it was a wee treat, bless him. "There you are lads… get stuck in, the chairman can sweep up the sprinkles later!" It didn't fit within the realms of professionalism that Barry and I had been used to, but it was a genuine act of kindness and players love a wee sweet treat. Professionalism is what we instilled in the squad, and in the club, in the short period that we were there, and our results proved that. But that's not to say that the coaching and backroom staff discouraged in any way the after-match spread that was laid on for us at Bayview, with all the quality fayre on offer from local butchers and bakers who were also sponsors of the club! Yvonne was raging that I did not take her out for a Saturday night meal very often in those three months, as I was always so fed at East Fife.

We had some good players too. Jason Kerr, St Johnstone's cup double-winning captain who now plays for Wigan, was on loan. We had Kevin Smith, a former Hearts and Leeds United player, and Kyle Wilkie, who was voted PFA player of the year as East Fife won League Two the year before. My favourite was Scott Robinson, who moved on to play for Livingston in the SPL and is now starring at Kilmarnock. He had come through the Hearts academy system and I felt he was capable of playing at a higher level which he is proving now. So we knew we had the makings of a good side.

The players became more focused and we encouraged them to pay more attention to detail in the game-plans we created for them and insisted on intensity and sharpness during our training sessions, which continued into our games. They embraced our high intensity and focused professionalism and began to play with a swagger, taking 14 points from a possible 18 at one stage of our tenure. I was quoted in Kingy's Daily Record article just before leaving as saying: "I got so much support and respect from the players and the run the club are on is down to them. East Fife will always hold a place in my heart now." And I totally stand by that.

We were looking really slick and had raised the game to a new level. This was brought home to me during one home match. I had set out my usual warm-up, which had gone well. Part of it included a match situation section, which involves separating the strikers and defenders into groups to practice various game scenarios. As usual, the groundsman was out tending to the turf and making sure it was as good as it could be before kick-off. But out of the corner of my eye while I am conducting the warm-up, I see him leaning on his pitchfork like a character from a Two Ronnies sketch, and clapping at what we're doing. As I conclude the warm-up drill and swing close to him to pick-up some cones, the laid back Fifer exclaims: "Listen son, that's the best warm-up I have ever seen in my life!". Jings, people from the Kingdom are easily entertained, but I respond quickly. "And that's the biggest divot I've ever seen in my life, so why don't you get your finger oot and your fork spiking to put it back in, so we can put what we've learned here in the warm-up into practice for the win." As I walked away to collect some more cones in the near vicinity, I wondered whether the fork might be spiking straight through my sternum from the rear, but it failed to materialise. "Must be making a positive impression with the locals," I thought, as they don't suffer fools gladly. Delighted that I wouldn't need emergency first aid after this wee altercation, it wasn't long before that very subject had to be lanced.

In the middle of our purple patch, Barry and I were on our Sunday morning de-brief when five minutes into our call, Barry says the club chairman was on the other line. We called a halt to our chat so Barry could find out what he wanted. Another five minutes go by and my phone rings, it's Barry and there's good news and bad news. The good news is the chairman is absolutely delighted with how we are doing; the bad news is that East Fife, despite having arguably the highest qualified dug-out in Scottish football, with two coaches possessing Uefa Pro-Licences, doesn't have anyone with an updated First Aid badge to put a sling on. It turns out that we might not be allowed to play if we don't get someone qualified in first aid on the bench. Apparently we need to tick that necessary box as soon as we can.

A fucking first aid certificate? We've got more badges than Blue Peter between us so surely we can find someone who can put an eye patch and a splint on a wee teddy bear. Apart from basic outdated first aid courses associated with my early SFA badges, which were a necessity, the nearest I had ever been to CPR or mouth-to-mouth resuscitation was when our family budgie was lying prostrate on the floor of its cage, with my dad using an eye dropper to give it a nip of whisky to revive it. Teenage me was puckering my mouth and practising lip muscle exercises and thinking how I'm going to pinch open its jaws to give it mouth-to-beak relief, before my dad got the old Grouse out the drinks cabinet! Happily, the blended liquor did the trick and our family pet perked up, started singing The Old Rugged Cross and challenged my dad to a fight, before attempting a triple back somersault from its trapeze perch... without a net. Anyway, cue the invitation for the Dunkin' Donut kitman to step up and become the first aider at the club!

Just before the US offer was confirmed in early January/February, 2017, Mixu called to update me on an opportunity we were considering. He had been through two interviews and was virtually a shoe-in for the Port Vale job down in England. He was also impressing the chairman and was confident about the positive feedback he was receiving. Yes I'll go with you, I told him, but what was the chairman like? Norman Smurthwaite was the man in charge and he was suitably blown away by Mixu's presentation and, more importantly, his vision of how the club could be run with objectives and strategy. He liked the thought of Mixu coming in as something of a coup. The man he would be replacing, Portuguese coach Bruno Ribeiro – the club's first ever overseas manager – hadn't lived up to expectations. Ribeiro's assistant, Michael Brown, was the other candidate for the job, but as the club were in a relegation fight under his watch, we should have been favourites. Mixu's detailed planning must have been manna from heaven for him, you'd have thought? Fuck no, this is professional football remember.

Mixu was invited down on 2 January, 2017 for the next few games and gladly outlined how things would operate under our stewardship. He even travelled away to Oldham Athletic, such was the relationship he was building with the club, and after each match and meeting he'd call me to update me on the situation, which was seemingly very positive. Lee Erwin, a former Motherwell Academy graduate striker who had won a move to Leeds United and was then on loan at Oldham, called me after that match and said "I hear Mixu and you are going in to Port Vale". Players get in 'the know', very quickly. But Smurthwaite for some reason – I do have a good understanding of why, but can't substantiate it – swithered on making a final decision and by now I had received strong interest from the promising job lead in America.

So I was weighing it all up in my mind. Even if Mixu is offered the Port Vale job, how hard would it be for me to choose between a rainy Stoke-on-Trent in February or sun-kissed California? As I was travelling through to training in Edinburgh one night with Nicky Paterson, I confided in him and asked what he thought. "It's a no brainer for me," said Nicky, who had spent some time in Nevada, the neighbouring US state to where I had been offered a job. I agreed with him. But, for the record, if the Port Vale chairman had plumped for us, then I'd have gone to England with Mixu.

In the end, the Vale chairman plumped for Michael Brown and they were relegated on the last day of the season. So California dreamin' just became a reality for me. But just as I'm getting my shit together, as they say in the land of the brave, I get a couple of interesting calls. Firstly, Celtic's Raymond Farrelly gets in touch to invite me into Parkhead for a discussion about a short-term deal to represent them in China, with the prospect of something longer once the secondment is completed. As much as I liked their international model, which was similar to Sheffield United's but much larger given Celtic's global fan base, I felt it wasn't what I was looking for. I was flattered but declined because I felt it would have been taking me out of the mainstream game once again.

I relay this offer to my mate, Stan, as he's a well-respected scout at Rangers. He suggests I make a call to the blue half of the Old Firm, as they were in the process of starting up an international department playing catch-up to their city rivals. I duly do so and a meeting is arranged at Ibrox with managing director Stewart Robertson. I'd worked with Stewart at Motherwell and knew the club's academy manager and so there was a knowledge of each other's abilities. Rangers had fallen behind their rivals in a few areas but were interested in what could be achieved globally in terms of reciprocal ventures and income streams, based on their global following. How this had never been tapped into previously was a puzzle to me, considering how Celtic had proactively and successfully gone about capitalising on their unique market place internationally. By this time, I had received my US visa as well as my provisional flight tickets. I did realise it was a good opportunity and one that might keep me at home nearer my family. I also felt Rangers and their brand could easily replicate the 'United Way' model and had development promise. I know what we did with the Blades crest and I am sure with the 'Aye Ready' version, I could have taken a tried and tested business model to a completely different level, especially due to the exposure that is available throughout the world in countries with huge ex-pat communities, as well as club allegiances that Rangers FC would open up. But I wasn't sure the project could sway me at the expense of California and, in any case, unsurprisingly, I got a call to say that Rangers didn't have the money to roll out the plan I had outlined to them. They did say, however, that there might be a way to combine a project to coach the girls team, integrate the community department and initiate the international project. 'Scattergun' and 'unfocused' were the thoughts that immediately sprung to my mind, and the passport got dusted down in preparation for Youngymania breaking America.

Dr No Way Man

*Impact Soccer in the USA wants me to transform their
youth coaching set-up... I can do that*

had already reached out to David Robertson, my good mate in the US, to spread the word that I might be open to a coaching position Stateside, and he promptly let it be known that I was available for hire. After returning to Scotland from an extended summer coaching stint in 2016, and slipping back into my depressive cycle, I didn't want to sound desperate, but it was getting close. Barry had come to my rescue with the East Fife assistant role, but there was little to no money in it at all, and no matter how much I was enjoying it at Methil, I knew I would have to take the next full-time coaching job that was offered to me. Leave it to Robbo to come up trumps for me. He was contacted by a few interested parties, who I engaged with, but it was Gavin Glinton who impressed me most in early January, 2017, with an interesting offer. Gavin was a former LA Galaxy and San Hose Earthquakes striker as well as a Turks and Caicos international, who at that time was technical director/director of coaching at Impact Soccer in California. Gavin had been present at several seminars and football coaching events I had presented at and liked what he saw. Once he knew I was keen on coaching in the US, he went to his board of directors with an innovative proposal. He suggested that he should take a step down to become boys director of coaching – which would involve a reduction in salary – and that Impact Soccer should hire me to take over his role, so that he could learn from me! Once again another humbling experience to be a part of. A diamond of a guy, is the least I can say about Gavin and we would go on to strike up an excellent working relationship and friendship.

Impact Soccer are a club/organisation associated with the Northern California

(NorCal) Premier League based in Brentwood, near San Francisco. They operate a fee-based system where parents pay for their children to be taught how to play soccer. When I took on the role of director of coaching, the organisation had 36 coaches and 700 players, stretching to 2,000 when you incorporate the non-travelling summer players (or recreational league players as they're known) all from 10-year-olds to adults. But they did not have a first-team franchise playing at that point in the professional league. In many areas of the US, fitba, or soccer as we all know they refer to it as, is a wee bit arse aboot face… as we would say. They have clubs and organisations with excellent facilities and a competent youth structure progressing onto high school and college teams, but many don't have their players progressing to their own professional teams as they hit a glass ceiling, upon which the collegiate programmes are the Holy Grail for the best players (put a call in to one Mr Robbie Young, Uncle Sam!)

I was to use my experience from working at Motherwell especially – as we know a professional club who decided to redevelop their Academy structure to make it work better for the development of players for the first team – to lay the groundwork for change at Impact Soccer, by signing a three-year deal. In the States there are several very good organisations – Impact and Davis Legacy being two – who pay a lot of money for coaches to develop their young players without them having a professional club for them to progress to. That's not to say the players won't end up moving to become professionals, but they have no direct club first team to aim for. Part of my remit, apart from enhancing and modifying Impact Soccer Club and their coaching set-up, was to work out a feasibility study for merging two local organisations into the one professional Impact SC first-team franchise. It was an opportunity too good to turn down. Good money was on offer and an added bonus was that my son, Robbie, was, at the same time, settling into life on a football scholarship at Fort Lewis College in Colorado, a 90-minute flight away, and I also had several good friends living and working in-country at the time.

On 4 February, 2017, I boarded a flight at Glasgow Airport to Heathrow and then connected to another bound for San Francisco. I get chatting with a couple of Scots guys on their way to the States on business. One of them recognises me from my Motherwell days and before I know it, I am invited to a plush and exclusive Superbowl party at a big hotel these guys are attending when we arrive in Frisco on 5 February – even though the game between the New England Patriots and the Atlanta Falcons is in Texas! Jings, what is it with me and massive sporting events interfering with my football career? Nearly missed a flight home from Kolkatta due to the crowds thronging to Sachin Tendulkar's second last farewell Test at Eden Gardens Cricket Ground, and now I am landing to take up an important new coaching role on the day of the biggest razzamatazed-up sporting event the US puts on every year. As I am due to be picked up at the airport by Gavin Glinton and Lance Welker, the Impact Soccer girls coaching director, it's obvious what the answer has to be. Walking through the arrivals gate at San Francisco Airport, I catch sight of Gavin and Lance and choose my words carefully in order to make the best first impression I possibly can.

"Right lads, we're going to an all-expenses paid Superbowl Party!"

I thought to myself that, if they had known, the local press at the conference to announce my arrival at Impact, would have been delighted that a 'Scottish Coach Embraces US Culture Immediately!' Gavin, Lance and I had bonded very closely before we had even started working with each other and this was something we'd develop over my tenure in the East Bay. We worked hard and we enjoyed the fringe benefits of living near the Bay, and San Francisco really was a wonderful place to hang out in.

The first three weeks of my tenure saw me put up in a hotel in downtown Brentwood till my permanent accommodation was sorted out and what a three weeks it was. That February affectionately became known as the wettest period in Californian history I was told, and people I was getting to know were eyeing me suspiciously as the Scotsman who had brought the rain with him. I, in turn, thought I was coming to the Sunshine State, when instead it was like a holiday in Oban... or Stoke-on-Trent, which is where I could have been. What the fuck was going on? My room was on the first floor of the hotel and every morning, without a word of a lie, I was woken up by the hotel swimming pool overflowing with a tidal wave of rainwater.

As I was waiting on my own flat becoming available, I was making friends with the hotel staff. I am genuinely interested in people and have a friendly nature, so I would happily chat away to the Hispanic chamber-maids and the reception staff. If I was out for long periods or staying at a friend's home, I would regularly say to them to help themselves to any food I had in my room fridge, as I knew they would not be on great wages. I really enjoyed their pleasant company and when I left, I made sure I bought them all some wine and chocolates, as they had really looked after me and made me feel at home in my time staying at the hotel. They knew I was heading to an apartment that I still had to furnish and kit out and on my last day in the room, to my astonishment, a note was left on my bed with a key.

"Hola Mr Gordon," it read, "This is the key to the clean linen room, there are lots of very nice towels and bed sheets in there. Adios amigo!"

Jings, my eyes were welling up as I helped myself to some useful items. In fact, I think I had to use a crisp new towel to wipe the tears away. Hope lack of fresh linen wasn't the reason why this hotel chain, with a base in downtown Brentwood, has since gone out of business?

Initially, to get my feet under the table, I operated in an observing role, assessing the structure of the organisation and watching the coaching sessions taking place, as well as familiarising myself with the facilities and playing areas. I discovered that we have access to a 12 playing field local council-owned facility with an office adjacent to a warehouse. This warehouse caught my eye and kicked off a plan that had already proven skill-improving mileage and success in my previous roles. So, without any further ado, I organise my first coaches' meeting for my 36 subordinates. As always, I have something already prepared, which I have used several times before and am ready to deliver an engaging piece, covering standards and behaviour I expect and also the objectives I will be setting the coaching staff.

In my hand, I have a list of all the attendees at the Impact Soccer HQ that night and, sure enough, they all arrive on time and are keen and enthusiastic to impress. My own first impressions of them, in a nod to comedian Kevin Bridges, are that they all seem to be typically nice US Chad Hogganesque type characters. Without exception before they take their seats, they all come up to me and say "Hi coach!" and very pleasantly tell me about their day. For some reason, I've never taken to "coach" and as directed in any of my travels I've requested people, no matter their position, to call me Gordon. From there on, the more I get to know someone I would find "Youngy" comfortable, especially if they had dialogue with contacts from my past.

Anytime I hear 'coach', I think of Nicholas Colasanto in his acting role from the hit US comedy Cheers. As his character was thick as shit, I would associate that trait with any dick I met who dined out on being called 'Coach'. Then in comes one guy, and I will never forget this, in full US Army desert fatigues, boots – complete with medals – and salutes me. I'm having flashbacks to Robin Williams in Good Morning Vietnam and fuck knows what he's having flashbacks to.

"Good evening coach sir!"

"Ehh…good evening, please take a seat."

"Sir, yes sir!"

Straight away I realise I'm going to be dealing with a pretty intense 'John Rambo' character here, and am already trying to work out what my options are if I have to bin him and he decides to show me his Magnum.44. He sits in his chair bolt upright and for the entire presentation I can't get him out of my peripheral sight line. The fact that I'm using a laser pen to highlight bullet points in my presentation gives me the fear if I turn around too quickly and he sees the red dot coming towards his forehead, we could all be taking evasive action. It seems though that in the US it is entirely normal for reservists – and this guy is an army chaplain – to rock up anywhere in their uniforms at any time and place. He thought this would make a suitable impression on me as head coach and it did. Out of everyone, he caused me the most frustration and amusement in my time at Impact Soccer.

One of my checks was to observe matchday performances of both players and staff in order to facilitate a comprehensive CPD programme, borne out from quarterly appraisals, which in their own right were entertaining to say the least. I attended 'the Chaplain's match one day and Gav was with me sitting in the bleachers with a coffee enjoying a game involving the under-15 side he was in charge of. From time to time, I'd covertly send instructions to the incumbent coach from my aerial viewpoint to assist, and at no time ever to be insulting or demeaning. I was there to help.

The following chain of events happened and Gav and I still piss ourselves laughing thinking about it to this very day. I notice that the Impact team are defending too deep – they were on their own 18-yard box most of the time – and I suggest to Gav that we inform the coach to squeeze up a bit, which he duly does. The Chaplain, who was a ranter and raver, then screams at his back four to get higher up the field and promptly demands they hold their line some 20 yards inside their opponents' half. We've now gone from one box to the other! The oppositions' three strikers are now 20 yards onside behind our defence inside their own half, and Gav and I look at each other speechless.

Other howlers involving the Chaplain include him ordering his players to set up a 'double wall' at an indirect free-kick with eight players – two rows of four. And I kid you not I also saw a game he coached with two different sized goalposts! He looked even more like Brian Glover from the film Kez than my rival for the Burnley job did, but he was much more likeable. When he organised 'scrimmages' (a US term for a practice match), he would join in and smash into players – girls and boys – but they'd pick themselves up and easily pass around him. He was organised, but clueless, despite telling me he had more licences than the BBC.

Another 'loonball' coach on our books, was a maverick who once played with Lance (girls head coach) back in the day. We hired him to coach a few of our girls' teams, as this was apparently his skill-set. His life was more than a little complicated and a bit chaotic – poor guy. Really Gordon? You're in America after all. This reminded me of a conversation I had had with my uncle John, a few weeks before I was leaving for the States when we had sadly attended the funeral of my young cousin.

"I hear you're going to America?" He casually said aside to me over a sausage roll, "It's a fuckin' open-air asylum!"

I wouldn't go that far, but i'd definitely recommend more fitba therapy.

Well, this guy seemed to be completely unhinged, but eventually turned out to be harmless. Kurt Cox was his name and he was funny, but his opening-line introduction to a group of girls flagged a warning to me and I made sure he was aware of his role and how to conduct himself in future.

"Hi, call me Coach Kurt." Then he chortled like Sid James and continued: "As my surname's inappropriate."

He used to sleep in the office and would insist that Gavin locked him in at night. Feedback I had from others in the organisation, labelled him everything from goofy, strange and different to "Get him the fuck away from me." But, overall, the first meeting went well and from there it was decided to introduce weekly coaches' meetings. These turned out to be some of the best times I had with Impact Soccer. They would start at 9pm on a Thursday night and the first hour would be a debrief of what had been happening the previous week. Then I would let the coaches know what was topical and what the current coaching trends were and how they could be expected to implement them into their sessions. Educating the coaches I am in charge of is very important to me and I was keen to help them develop their skills as much as possible. I would give them assignments aligned to Uefa licences in order to widen and broaden their knowledge. Most embraced it, especially Gavin, who would lap this up. But I'd tend to work with him one to one, as he was so much more advanced than the rest. Then from 10pm we would order in pizza, have a beer or two and play round-robin head tennis matches – sometimes till midnight or 1am – to help build camaraderie. These evenings were fantastic and really created an excellent relaxed environment for all the coaching staff and we all became closer as a unit. I would crack jokes during the presentations and slip in some Scottish humour or football banter, but it was mainly way over their heads. Though Gav, who had been a professional player and travelled around in the game, would "get it".

One day I was standing on one leg outside the office at an ATM machine and one of my colleagues said, "Hey what are you doing coach?" and I said, "I'm checking my balance."…Whoosh…tumbleweed. But I was left like a comedian dying a death onstage on several more occasions. Another time I was in my office when I was informed of a visit from a father wishing to see me about his son, Arnie.

"Send him in!" I said, and in walked the pensive parent.

"Take a seat, Mr Matthews, how can I help you?" I enquire.

"It's about Arnie, I would like to know why he is currently in the B Team?" He asks.

"Easy," I say, "It's because we don't have a C Team!"

I was honestly trying to break the ice a wee bit and start the conversation going on an engaging note, and then have a more in-depth discussion about his son's recent assessments. But before I knew it he had risen from the chair.

"Great, coach, thanks for the feedback, I'll get him to work on that."

And then he was gone as quickly as he had arrived and I really knew my patter was shite!

I'd also show them clips from European games, mostly English Premiership when explaining themed topics in relation to their coaching education. One day I showed a clip from the Old Firm match when Hugh Dallas got struck by a coin and a guy fell out the top tier of the Main Stand. They couldn't believe the passion we had at games like this. And on another occasion we watched a live Scottish international qualifier where they saw a Coach Gordon, who was a wee tad more animated. Despite their humour bypass and lack of football nous, they were a very generous community-driven group, as were most of the people I came across and, in times of need or crisis, they would rally to the cause. I witnessed this first hand when the club organised a collection of supplies, clothing, food and money to address the horrendous forest fires, which swept across the Nappa Valley and subsequent counties that year. This raised communities to the ground and clubs we regularly played against were destroyed. The warmth and compassion that the club showed and all others in the NorCal organisation, was incredible with aid trucks being mustered and fire crews being assisted. The fires are a blight on a wonderful state and are a direct result of the heat, which it is famed for, and climate change. I witnessed the devastating aftermath later when I was travelling to matches or golfing and saw one side of a highway completely burned out. It was very distressing.

They were a good group, but I really had to raise the bar in terms of coaching qualifications, and laid out what would be an acceptable level for each individual coach to attain in the way of coaching badges. This would help some of the coaches immensely as there were a few who had zero coaching qualifications. I held one-to-one meetings with them all for evaluation purposes and worked out a CPD programme for them to attain and a timescale for them to do it in. If they did not match this they could find themselves without a job. So I had to balance being fun and fair, but firm at the same time, and most bought into that view. What you have to remember is that in the US, soccer is a very upper middle-class sport and parents are paying big bucks to have the pleasure of getting their children the best coaching. I can tell you that each and every one of the coaches on my team were all paid more than the coaches I worked with at Sheffield United and Motherwell – £40,000-£60,000 per year – despite the fact that virtually all of them were nowhere near the standards of coaches in the UK.

During my one-to-ones, proof of coaching badges went from the sublime to the ridiculous. They were coming in with certificates of all kinds printed out from a home computer and one guy even came in with a series of cotton patches – that you would receive in the Scouts – sewn onto one of his football tops. I wanted to give all of them a chance, but I knew that many would struggle. I had to embark upon an observation operation to see each and every one of them in action during their coaching sessions, to really assess what I was dealing with and find out who could be helped and who would be helpless. This is, in my opinion, a real downside of football in the States. As there is loads of money swirling about, some coaches have found themselves in cushy, well-paid roles and have just settled in and hunkered down without being encouraged to develop and improve their skill-set beyond their comfort zone. I had inherited a broad range of coaches varying from those who wanted help to improve, and those who were going to try anything to resist having to do some hard graft to improve themselves. Gavin loved this new approach and was right behind me, as were the board. I had come in with no axe to grind and no biases towards any of the coaching staff and had the remit and permission to make the changes necessary to improve the whole coaching set-up of Impact Soccer.

A typical American coach would wear a baseball cap, sun glasses and flashy boots. They would have a bag of balls, all of various different sizes and colours, pinnies (bibs) and a set of pop-up goals that you'd play long shootie with your granny in her hallway with. I was horrified at what I saw from dudes who'd say to me: "Yeah coach, I've been doing this for 25 years."

"You've been doing something for 25 years," I'd reply, "but it's definitely not fucking fitba coaching."

Some would pitch up late with the aforementioned 'tools of their trade' slung over their back and perform some of the most ridiculous time-filling dross I've ever seen. This would consist of getting the best player to juggle the ball and get the rest of the group to count how many they could manage. "No way man, are you fucking shitting me!" I was even starting to swear US style. I realised that one of the first things I had to do was use my Motherwell Academy experience to get the right coaches to coach the right age-groups. We realised early on at Fir Park that it was not ideal for coaches to start with an under six age-group and for them to progress with them as they advanced in age. That's acceptable in amateur youth football as usually the coaches have a child in the team and that is the reason why they become volunteer coaches. Even if they didn't have a child in the team, they naturally formed close friendships with the parents and families of the players they coach. This is especially the case when they are travelling to tournaments and festivals for weeks at a time, and they begin to form close social bonds. Unconsciously, this can easily lead to coaches veering towards favouritism, preferential treatment and impaired judgement on certain players. So we put an end to that.

This is where I formed my 'Spark Plug' theory where it's important to get the correct distance between player, coach and parent. Too close is unhealthy and too far, there's no connection. It really is so important to get the correct skill set aligned to the appropriate age group. I had no favouritism to any coaches at Impact Soccer, except obviously to the ones that wanted to learn or improve. So to a few I became a dose of salts that left the taste of reality in their mouths.

All the while Gavin and I were talking and he was picking my brains about what could be achieved at Impact Soccer and his thirst for knowledge on tactics and systems of play, was unquenchable. I did my best to provide him with answers to all his questions and more. I knew at some point he would be taking over the role I was currently inhabiting and I encouraged him to complete his coaching education, whilst grooming him for his future pathway. All the coaches became even more desperate to impress me. At the 11-a-side stage every age-group had a first and second team. One coach of the under-13s B team turned up in a shirt and tie at one game, in 35 degree heat, under the misapprehension that how he looked would somehow have some positive affect on my views on him. And, as I sat there watching him sweat and wilt away as his team floundered, I was positive that he wasn't what we were looking for.

I watched another coach lose his rag at a decent young keeper, who had a bit of a nightmare one game, which culminated in him being lobbed on the goalline from 35 yards. I asked the coach post match, why he did not go and offer some encouragement to the goalie during the game or even afterwards, to try and keep his head up. But he just couldn't grasp that, in those situations, it was the coach's job to salvage confidence and help the young player move on to the next game and rebuild their playing esteem. I had a few coaches who may have had an answer for everything, but good solutions to very little. But there were more who had a lot of potential.

Lance Welker was an immediate convert to the methodology and he made sure the girls' programme carried out the curriculum with great commitment and vigour. Lance and I used to play golf when we could and he showed his true colours one night when we ended up in an unsavoury spat with a few local arseholes who were racially abusing Gavin – who despite the provocation handled himself calmly and with class. It was the bold Lance, no bigger than me, who made sure the vociferous rednecks backed down and suitably pinned his much bigger opponent against a wall. Must have been the boxing training that he did with Gav, Gav's brother Duane – one of the most laid-back guys I've met with a lovely personality and another who bought into the CPD model of personal improvement – and myself at the Punch and Crunch boxing gym in downtown Brentwood, run by an ex-marine by the name of Mike. Mike was as hard as Tarzan's feet and the type of guy who you'd imagine would shit on his own hands and clap. The Sheriff and him would have made a formidable tag team.

Gary LaFleur was a guy with big presence. He was a former player himself and had a heart as big as his frame. When I got there, he was quite a bit overweight, but by the time I had left he had shed something like 90 pounds and his lifestyle changes continue to keep him looking slim. It's easy to let yourself go, having punished your body with strict training regimes most of your formative years when young and then subsequently playing professional sport. That's why I stress to my colleagues wherever I am, to keep fit as the job can consume you. I have seen it with my own eyes and from personal experience. It is not healthy to survive on coffee to keep you alert and red wine to put you to sleep, albeit for a few hours before you wake up with systems of play in your head and decisions on who to play.

"You were effing and blinding during the night," Yvonne would tell me some mornings, and, on more than one occasion apparently, I have sat bolt upright and shouted some garbled tirade during the night. "I don't care if you're offering me a million quid a year to take the Barcelona job, I'm staying with Motherwell!" is what I like to think would have made me sit bolt upright in the middle of the night, but, more probably, it was: "Fuckin' caretaker boss again!"

Gary was the recreational director and he was a really terrific guy with a great ability to use guided discovery with his teams. I'd watch his sessions and he'd quote terms I'd previously used verbatim in his delivery, then engage his players with questions as to what and why we were doing a specific routine. He was a lovely man, who along with a few others from Impact, has promised he'll come to see me in Scotland. This was due to our tight relationship, as well as me banging on that in Scotland we invented everything and had the best scenery in the world. They need to give me notice when they come, though, so that I can tart the place up a bit. I think there's a group of local kids who have used my garage door as a goal during the time I have been away, as that needs fixed again, and the garden looks like the new set of I'm a Celebrity Get Me Out of Here, but I'll get onto it. I was becoming close friends with all these guys and gals and being Scottish, I couldn't help but always find nicknames for those I was hanging out with in my spare time. Gary soon became Gash, forcing a lovely lady called Gary-Anne to become Gash-Anne (to be fair she never knew of this). We were in our local sports bar one night when, as was the norm, someone would hear my accent during our congenial bar chat and asked the usual questions: "Where are you from? What part of Germany is that?" Or "My great grandfather is Scottish, did you know him?" When suddenly, upon hearing someone in our company hail Gary in his nom de plume, a voice booms out from a large frame, in a dialect I know well "I'm the Gash and I'm from Scoatland" in his best jock accent. Cue a happy reunion with a fellow Scottish traveller, someone I didnae know, but do now.

Obviously the whole raison d'etre for transforming the coaching structure and raising standards was to ultimately improve the technical ability of the players at Impact Soccer. Athleticism is something that is built into many American kids, due to the seasonality of sports. Many soccer players may also play baseball or basketball at different times of the year and they tend to keep very fit. But it was the basic skills that I wanted to hone and once again a skill centre area – similar to the one I initiated in the away stand at Fir Park – was on my mind. Cue the building adjacent to our HQ office that I had my eye on from day one, and immediately set to work. This time, though, rather than use the services of a petty criminal looking for a second chance, on day release from a local prison (flashback to Fir Park), we had Steve Purvey the husband of a board member and the best damn handyman this side of the Delta. He listened to my ideas and set about creating the best environment possible for the kids to use and practise in. He would recycle anything I needed, to provide equipment for me and create the ideal training environment. He even installed cameras, so we could playback footage and advise on better technique. He was a terrific guy with a lovely family and his wife, Lyndsey, was also of great assistance. The Purveys, along with the other board members, were so helpful in accommodating my stay there. There's always a thorn in the crown, however, and at Impact it was the president, a member of the: "I've been doing this for 25 years" gang and a crutch for the under performers who it seemed to me he'd use to form a shield. Gavin was forever butting heads with him as he'd endured his perceived anti-progressive attitude long before I arrived. Our first meeting was legendary. We had been on the pitch all day some 24 hours after me touching down in Brentwood and attending the annual 'try-outs,' when El Presidente strolled on the pitch with a bin bag. He proceeded to hand me out my club attire, which was like the contents of a lost-and-found box. Out the corner of my eye, I can see Gavin buckled up in laughter as the brazen president ceremoniously hands me my 'new' gear and he's looking for me to doff my cap. The ironic thing was he was decked out top to to in brand new Adidas apparel. This made my mind up to go out to open tender with other suppliers.

I recommended that we all move to Admiral, who had reinvented themselves again in the USA, after their early dominance in the UK some years previously. In the 1970s and early 80s, Admiral pioneered the introduction of the replica shirt market to coincide with colour TV coverage of the matches. Leeds were the first to wear Admiral- branded kit in 1973-74 and the English FA soon signed a deal with them, coincidentally just as Don Revie – a big supporter of the manufacturer – became national manager. Motherwell, Aberdeen and Dundee were among the first Scottish clubs to wear Admiral strips and they are synonymous with my memories of growing up playing and watching football at that time. Manufacturers made an absolute fortune out of the soccer model in America given the pay-to-play status, which generates thousands of dollars worth of income. But I got to know Admiral's managing director in the States, a lovely guy called Paul Hamburger, who would ensure that a club our size would get more value for our dollar and a good service, which proved to be true. I was happy to help them grow their brand as I liked the quality as well as the range – and I was a wee bit sentimental for them, as one of the first Motherwell strips I got for Christmas as a kid, had the big claret Admiral sign on the righthand side of the chest.

Admiral were impressed enough with the Impact deal – kitting out all our teams – and offered me a brand ambassador role. This I accepted as long as there was no financial benefit to me personally, but they knew I would happily wear the branded kit in media and match situations. Many of my family and mates are still running about with Admiral kit on to their training or golf.

To illustrate the naivety and unrealistic thought processes of some of the parents, who think that because they have money, they can send their little angels onto soccer stardom in the States and beyond, one particular tale sticks in my mind. Jennifer Charvet, secretary of Impact, the glue that held the club together, came up to me one day and told me that I had a meeting with the parents of 17-year-old Luke.

"What's it about?" I ask.

"Not sure," says Jennifer.

The parents arrive and I meet and greet them in my office and listen to what they have to say with incredulity.

They inform me that Luke will not be coming back to play with the under-18s next season because he is going to the UK to join Liverpool FC. Apparently, they liked the uniforms the Anfield side play in and they are just going to flit their family from California to the Wirral and enrol their son under the tutelage of Mr J Klopp. I helpfully suggested that I would kindly call Jurgen and inform the club that Luke is a size medium, likes bananas on toast for breakfast and would be able to make training four times a week! They walked out crestfallen after I had explained the ins and outs of being scouted for a top-tier professional team and the little matter of any player signing for Liverpool being fucking exceptional. Luke, although a decent player, had none of these things going for him. "Try giving Dundee United a wee call," I suggested as they closed the door.

I was really getting my head down and working hard for Impact Soccer, but I was still actively keeping in touch with my contacts in the UK about potential opportunities, while, at the same time, not having to worry about applying for any old vacancy that came up. I still stand by the adage that you've got a better chance of getting a job if you're currently in one, honestly I'm such a visionary. Anyway and removed from my ability to spout gems of wisdom, Barnet FC, who were then in League Two offered me their academy director's job, but it was nowhere near worth it financially. They wanted me to stay in London for £28,000 a year, a fee which was even upped three times by a smashing lad who was the technical director. There was no accommodation, car or relocation package, but they did offer me a free gym pass! What was I going to do? Sleep on the rowing machine and eat the dumb bells? Needless to say, I wasn't tempted. You see, that's the thing with football clubs, they know that people want to be involved and especially ex-players who are coming to the end of their careers. Players see it as an 'in' no matter what the role is and some clubs take advantage, as they feel, incorrectly, that everyone has made a fortune from playing the game and they can offer low wages to keep them involved in an industry where they've known nothing else.

Working in the US provided me with an excellent standard of living and a very healthy work-life balance. Yvonne was able to come across regularly and I was able to meet up with Robbie, who could pop down from Colorado to visit his old man and tap a few dollars from me at the same time. It also gave me the chance to socialise with my mate, David Robertson, and his family. I was also able to regularly meet up with a good family friend and cousin of one of Yvonne's best mates, Jim Walker. I was at school with Jim, but he had moved over to Frisco with his husband, Mark, who landed a job in Silicon Valley. David, Jim and I had brilliant days out playing golf or going to Golden Gate Fields for the Dollar Day horse racing. The golf with Robbo and another good mate and coach, Justin Sealander or 'Bombo', was terrific and I managed to tick off many of the West Coast's best courses, all thanks to their hospitality, and I will always be grateful to them for that.

Bombo could pass as Scottish as he's off his head, but, as a coach, he had the kids eating out of his hand. He would invite us for dinner, spend the whole day cooking, then take us wine tasting the next day. He did this whilst stopping every five minutes as we drove through the Nappa Valley, so that he could pull out his binoculars and give us the rundown on whatever species of bird he saw flying overhead. He'd also do this with Robbo and I while golfing, which gave us a wee chance to kick his ball into the rough while he was waxing lyrically about a great lesser spotted barn owl or some other inhabitant of the area. I took Bombo to the Electric Bar when he was over with Robbo's team and after I came back from the toilet one time, I found find him sitting in the middle of a group of veteran Motherwell football casuals holding court and singing tunes of glory. In America you'd call him entertaining, over here you'd call him a fucking head case.

We played golf at the Olympic Course SF, Bodago Bay – where scenes from the film The Birds were filmed – Chardonnay, which was absolutely beautiful situated amidst the grape vines of the Nappa Valley, but the ultimate in my eyes was Pebble Beach.

Dollar Day racing was another great release. As it says on the tin, everything was a dollar - entry, beer, mimosas, hot dogs. I used to do that thing upon entry that we used to ask the assistant in the Candy Box sweetie shop in Motherwell, when we were wee boys: "How much are your penny caramels missus?" On Dollar Day it gave me a chuckle to see a yank stare back at me blankly when I would ask "How much is it to get in?" The only thing left to do your heid and your wallet in, were the ponies themselves. Each event attracted some 35,000 Bay area socialites in their Sunday best and the atmosphere was outstanding. I must say it rivalled an all-day shot in the Electric Bar before a taxi over to the Saints and Sinners meeting at Hamilton Racecourse - minus the kebab on the way home.

Jim Walker had been a grade one referee in Scotland. He had run the lines on several top professional league games and had refereed more than a few in the Junior leagues, so as well as being a school mate, I had come across him during my football career in an official capacity, too. The first time I met up with Jim in the States it was his 53rd birthday. He immediately reminded me that the last time we had been in each other's social company back home, I had loosened the top off a salt bottle in the chippie at

Motherwell Cross, and he had unwittingly engulfed his full poke of chips with the stuff.

"Fuck sake, Jim, we were 14 years old, get over it!"

You can take the boy out of Motherwell, but you'll never take Motherwell out the boy. In fact, if anything, I might have become even more of a Motherwell joker, while travelling around the world. Jim – also a fellow Motherwell fan – was great company and an invaluable conduit and friend in my time in California. As his other half Mark would travel a bit due to his high profile job, Jim would come up to Brentwood to stay, watch training and games, giving us plenty of days to reminisce about the Well and people we knew communally. More often than not, I'd either go down to meet Jim on a Saturday night after my game and stay over for Dollar Day on the Sunday.

Season 2017/18 in Scotland saw Motherwell have another good season under new Northern Irish boss Stephen Robinson, my old sparring partner. They reached the two domestic cup finals that season and, as much as I wanted to, my calendar of games was too prohibitive to fly 6,000 miles to see my team play, so it was not an option at that time. But, as you would expect, Jim and I met up to find a bar to watch both the games. The first was the League Cup final on Sunday, 26 November, 2017. This was a 3pm kick-off at Hampden, but for us that meant a 7am start. Not only that, but, as you would also expect from two guys fae Motherwell, we had to meet up a couple of hours before the game started to get into the cup final mood with a couple of Don Revies.

I had travelled down to Frisco on the Saturday night and at 4am on the Sunday morning we were up, eating rolls and square sausage and ready to go in our claret-and-amber Well strips. Jim had scouted an Irish bar, which also doubled as an unofficial Celtic Supporters' Club, and we headed there as we were positive they would be showing the game. In it we found three third generation Scottish Celtic supporters and a dog, and we all sat and watched the match together. The game was rotten from a Motherwell point of view and Celtic ran out 2-0 winners. We emerged into a soaking wet San Francisco morning just after 9am and agreed it had been a damp squib, so we trudged home, nipping into a couple of other bars to drown our sorrows on the way.

Motherwell made it to the Scottish Cup final the same season, once again with Celtic as the opposition, and once again Jim and I made plans to meet up again to go and watch the game. This time, Jim had done even more research and once again at 5am and again sporting our prize Motherwell tops and scarves, we headed up to San Jose Celtic Supporters' Club – to a place where we could be guaranteed to find the game being shown with a great atmosphere. This time the place was packed wall to wall with Celtic supporters and when we walked in wearing our Motherwell tops, the iconic scene from American Werewolf in London, where the US characters enter an English country pub to total silence, started playing out in my mind. All eyes turned to us and I did the only thing I could do in that 'Custer's-last-stand' situation. I looked around for the biggest Celtic supporter I could spot in my immediate vicinity, strolled confidently up to him, looked up into his eyes – a full foot above me – and said in as loud a voice as I could muster:

"Right bawheid, get the drinks in!"

My gamble paid off and the ice-cutter worked to uproarious laughter. We had an absolutely brilliant day along with the Celtic fans. And even though we were once again beaten 2-0, the atmosphere and back-and-forth friendly patter and hospitality was tremendous. Before that point, many of these Celtic fans never knew Mother-well had their own songs. But once we got started we traded songs for songs, as de-spite their ignorance of Well history, most of this mob were born in Scotland, so they knew the 'Hampden roar'. These were all hardcore lads, but, when you show your balls, you're accepted no matter where you are in the world. These guys would get up every Saturday morning at 6.00am to watch the games live and created their supporters' club complete with memorabilia, in the lounge of a diner in San Jose.

Motherwell, unfortunately, never really laid a glove on Celtic that day and the Hoops fans were in full voice, belting out their full repertoire of songs. The drunker I got the more outrageous I became, singing the famous Well songs and Jim was a nervous wreck given the odds against us. Being a keen punter, he knew that 50 to 2 was a long shot, though everybody would like a 25/1 winner and that's how the Bhoys saw it. Every time they'd start a song I'd interrupt it until they gave up. Jim was shaking as the Celtic fans kept plying us with drink to shut me up. When we left much later that night, having been in there since 7am, they wouldn't let us pay, at least I think that's the correct version!

I had also formed close friendships with several of my American 'cousins' who worked in and around Impact Soccer and where I lived in Brentwood. I have mentioned guys like Robbo and Bombo as well as Brian Bugsch, who was a great lover of Scottish links golf courses due to the time he studied in Glasgow and where his youngest daughter was born. A tee-totaller, Brian became the designated driver on many occasions when we were all out. My social circle also included great guys like Paulo Bonomo, Benja-min Ziemer and Shawn Blakeman who were the founders and owners of the NorCal Premier League. In all my years in terms of visiting California, but also during my time living there, I have never experienced such generosity and compassion. They wouldn't mean much to my mates back home, but they meant such a lot to me in my time over there to help me get settled in.

A Monday night was when the North California Soccer (NorCal) clinics were held and this was where player development programme selective coaching took place. PDP was designed to select promising players and showcase them for college. Training and games were organised and one of my duties was to go and watch a selected game in an evaluation role and to help develop the PDP, as well as influence coach education. One day I drove to watch a Sacramento Republic match and asked Robbo, Bombo and a few ex-pats if they would like to join me on the trip. They were only too happy to oblige, as they would be able to take advantage of the VIP hospitality on offer as my guests. I was not imbibing as I had an appointment to speak with the president of the Sacramento club about a few football-related matters – so even Brian could enjoy the trip as a passenger for once. But all the others in my party decided to get heavily involved in the free 'swally', as you do.

Trouble was I couldn't find them in the stadium afterwards and it was only by chance that when I returned to my vehicle in the car park, I heard Bob Marley blasting out of a customised monster truck also still parked there, where all my mates were having a party with some fans. They were all having a 'Wailers' of a time and it didn't take much for them to persuade me to drive us all into Sacramento, park up and book a hotel and hit the town… and what a wonderful night it turned out to be.

Another friend and coincidently an ex-employee at the SFA, Michael Sharp was then a director of a club in Nappa. If his teams were playing in the East Bay, he'd come up and stay with me on the Thursday, take in my coaches' meeting, and then we'd play golf next day.

"Nobody is doing this stuff, Youngy," he'd say to me, which I would reply: "I know, but what have they been doing for the last 25 years?"

Sharpy is another example, like Robbo, of someone who has emigrated and done fantastically well for himself and his family. Both know how to 'play the game' combining the needs and wants of the area with the covert infrastructure they know to work. Incidentally, both were school teachers back home and have the grounded Scottish nature to know what is chicken salad and what is chicken shit. The thing about both Robbo and Sharpy is that they know how to integrate, blend in and use their organisational skills to outshine rogues. This is essential in a part of the world where bullshit camouflages ability and gullible non-football people get suckered into parting with their dosh in a pay-to-play format. They also know where to get access to Scottish fare like steak pie, haggis, Tunnock's Tea Cakes and Irn Bru. Robbo would fix up the best golf courses to play and during the round Sharpy would phone a Scottish butcher he knew, who would send someone with our orders to collect at the 19th hole.

Michael Renwick, Mixu's assistant at his first club, Cowdenbeath, was another good lad to catch up with in America. Talk about a small world. He and I became good friends as he worked near San Jose. Mikey was a former Hibs player and is friends with both Ian Murray and Paul Hartley, so anytime he's over in Scotland these days we get a catch-up, with beers of course. The thing about working in America, which slowly becomes normal, is the astronomical distances you travel without realising it to play games, do some scouting or to network in relation to football. Gone were the days of scouting a game in Scotland and afterwards calling a Redline Taxi to take me from Firhill back to Fir Park – £20 plus tip! Incidentally, the best tip I ever had was "Never, ever, put camp fires out with your face."

Across the pond, you might have to drive for three hours to find the slip road for the freeway! It was easier for this wee guy from Motherwell to get a train or catch a flight and then book a room at the local Hilton Hotel through my hand phone app. It really is a different world out there. Robbo had adapted very well and lived his life on his phone. He could order a Chapman's (famous Lanarkshire butchers) steak pie with link sausage in it, and get it delivered to California from Wishaw Cross before I could get my Nokia antenna up to make a call.

At the same time as I was enjoying life in Brentwood with Impact Soccer, I made sure to keep up with my mates back home. I called them as and when I could for a catch-up. I have done this wherever I have been and it really does you good psychologically and it kept me abreast with what was happening in Scotland. One day Mikey Stevens, who we have mentioned two or three times before in previous chapters, calls me and informs me he is coming over for a visit. Affectionately known to us all in the Electric Bar as 'The Mex', he was a little bit older, very intelligent, retired, divorced, held some 'traditional old school' views on things, was independently wealthy and loved a bevy with his mates. I was going to say he played the guitar, but let's leave that one alone for now. His heart is in the right place most of the time, though sometimes you might think he was operating in a parallel universe to what is going on around him. And, ironically, he is at the moment recovering from some heart problems, which he suffered at the height of the pandemic lockdown, so let's hope it beats back into the right place again very soon.

So, before leaving for the US, he calls and furnishes me with his flight times and I arrange to pick him up at San Francisco airport. As always with anyone who visits, I am there early to make sure I meet him on time at International arrivals. At the airport, I am able to see the carousel area and the arriving passengers from Mikey's BA flight from Heathrow gathering to pick up their luggage. But there's no sign of The Mex, a moniker which he even refers to himself as. Despite being at retirement age, he's a big, well-built man and with his facial hair, you could see him and, more often than not, hear him coming from a mile off, but there is not even a hint of him. I'm actually pissing myself thinking about the poor bastard who's had him sitting next to them for the last nine hours, and hope and pray it was radio DJ Ted Stryker. After a while the passengers thin out from baggage reclaim and move towards passport control. It's not long before there is no one from Mikey's flight left in the area. There's not a trace of him anywhere, save for a large top-of-the-range suitcase doing a lap of honour on the carousel. I just know it's his, but I'm stumped as to where its owner has got to. Not even Mikey could get launched off a jumbo jet at 35,000 feet, could he? A scenario was forming that maybe he had got pished and launched into one of his top ten favourite arguments with a stewardess such as – according to him Christmas Day and New Year's Day are always in two separate years, never, ever in the same one. He would argue that till his 'tache turned blue. Or the theory that you can't fire a bullet at 10,000 feet while on a plane. Fuck no, someone might have tried to test that theory out in-flight, just so they could enjoy their dinner. Maybe he had already been kicked off the plane by Homeland Security and was at that moment getting water-boarded in the airport holding cells?

I tried calling him… no answer. Where the hell could he be? After a while a security guard starts to take a big interest in the lone piece of luggage circling the carousel and I catch the eye of a sniffer dog and handler on their way to investigate.

If I'm not careful here Mikey's bag is going to be blown to bits in a controlled explosion and fuck knows what they are going to make of a half pound of Chapman's square sausage and a round of black pudding vacuum packed for my consumption, which I know Mikey would have brought over for me, oozing out of his spare socks.

Sure enough I watch the security guards pick Mikey's bag off the carousel and take it away… and the sniffer dog's got a hard on from the smell of sausages. Where the fuck is he? It shouldn't be this hard to pick someone up from the airport.

Was this Mikey finally getting me back from the time at the World Cup in Italy 1990? Back then I played a part in shaving his moustache into a small mouser and slicking his jet black hair into a side shed, just before we took his drunken hulk to the hospital to get his dislocated shoulder fixed. A funny wee prank we all thought until the medics refused to treat him at first, as they were offended by his uncanny resemblance to a monstrous German dictator.

Thinking fast I speak to a security guard this side of the arrivals area and explain the situation. I call Mikey again and he is still not answering. The security guard takes me through to the carousel area and we start scouring the area, toilets, seating sections… when we notice a little outside terrace.

Sure enough, sitting outside, with not a care in the world, is the oblivious Mex… soaking up the Californian rays.

"What took you so long, wee man!" growled Mikey when he saw me.

Thank goodness he was OK. But before we can take the Bay Area Rapid Transit (BART) system train back to Brentwood, we need to go and negotiate the release of his bag, which the bomb squad were just about to wire up for detonation. I had deliberately opted to travel down on the BART in order to show Mikey how it works, so he could use it at his leisure during his week staying with me. Brentwood is the end of the line

'I watched him get more out of people by reaching everyone in the room'

Gavin Glinton, former LA Galaxy and San Jose Earthquakes striker as well as a Turks and Caicos international, who was technical director/director of coaching at Impact Soccer in California, said: "I met Gordon after one of the NorCal Symposiums where he was a guest speaker. A little over a year later, I did everything in my power to give him my job, so that I could study and work under him. To this day, I'm still not sure what persuaded him to join our club...maybe it was for the stories he is telling now!

"I was unsure about how this experience and background would connect with Impact Soccer, a small youth club in California, but Gordon's work ethic, humility and leadership had me on board immediately. He taught me what it means to work as a professional coach/director, no matter what environment you find yourself in.

"Gordon set short, mid and long-term plans to improve every aspect of the club. Long hours every day dedicated to improving the way we train, play, work and live. Attention to detail and pride in simple things like keeping the office clean. His ability and constant reminders to 'keep the powder dry' and 'keep cool' when tempers were hot, were very helpful. In addition to what he brought in terms of football knowledge and experience, I was able to watch him get more out of people with his ability to reach everyone in the room. A quality that I now realise is rare amongst leaders, even more so, having to achieve this in different communities and cultures.

"If I had to guess – and I probably shouldn't – I would say it comes from Gordon's genuine interest in helping people and a humility that forces himself to continually improve. I can honestly say now in my current job, that two days don't go by where I'm not grateful for having worked with and learned from Gordon due to some situation or another. He was also fantastic for discussions on life, bullshit or just to hit the punch bags with. As slippery as they come and a fantastic friend!"

and it only takes 40 minutes to get into the heart of San Francisco, and from there it was a short hop to the airport.

There's a BART every 15 minutes or so and honestly, it is so easy that there was no way anyone could go wrong on it. Oh aye they could! "Brilliant wee man, I've Googled a place just off Embarcadero which makes guitars and I'm going to get myself one." Oh no, you're not I think to myself.

I get him back to my flat and he settles in. As luck would have it Jim is not working that week! A private joke as I had been ribbing him that he had never worked in his four years there, as Mark had a super duper job in Silicon Valley. Thankfully it's arranged for the Mex to meet Jim the next day for a catch up – both know each other from back home too – and that allows me to get back to work.

So first thing in the morning I take him down to the BART station at Brentwood and stick him on a train to central San Francisco to meet Jim. I tell Mikey what station to get off at, tell him what time I'll meet him back at Brentwood Station and tell him to also make sure that he keeps his phone on at all times, and to answer the fucking thing when I call. Honestly, I was beginning to feel like I was his carer after spending less than 24 hours with the man.

Jim meets Mikey no problem… and that's the only thing that went right for the rest of the day. "I'm going to buy a guitar." Mikey tells Jim when they meet up and I change my mind and wish he had, as I'd have smashed it over his head some 14 hours later.

They catch-up with each other quickly and decide to go for a complete yahoo bender throughout the city, a proper all-dayer. Try as they might they can't locate the famous guitar emporium, but apparently they had no trouble finding every bar from the Golden Gate Bridge to Alcatraz. To Jim's credit he manages to get our visitor onto the BART just after 7pm.

Busy as I am at Impact Soccer, I make sure that I'm there to meet Mikey at Brentwood at 8pm. The train arrives and once again the curse of the travel port strikes me, as there is no Mikey Stevens to be seen alighting from the train.

"Lumpin fuck." I think… he's doing it to me again!

I call him, no answer. I watch the trains come and go and by 9pm, no Mikey. And by 10pm no Mikey! I call Jim and he is steaming drunk, but he assures me he managed to pour Mikey onto the train at the allotted time, before he himself staggered home.

I'm now beginning to worry, that he's jumped off the BART at the wrong stop and is wandering around the Bay Area somewhere, like a human version of the San Andreas Fault, ready to erupt and crack at any time. By 11pm, there's still no Mikey.

I manage to get the Brentwood Station staff to check for the Mex on their CCTV system to see if I have missed him, but he is nowhere to be seen. Anyone would have noticed a drunken Scotsman like him who had, I think just to spite me, recently shaved off his very noticeable bushy moustache, cartwheel off the train, but no dice.

Back to my apartment I go, thinking by some miracle he is collapsed in a heap at the entrance to the gated community where I live, but he's not there. I realise that would be wishful thinking as he has only been there the once and has never walked back from the station before sober, let alone out of his face.

By 12 midnight, I'm in pieces and watching the news looking out for stories of tragic deaths. I call his sister back home in Scotland and break the news to her that I've lost her brother. I clutch at straws till 2.30am – wondering if I should call the cops to scramble a helicopter with a searchlight to comb the area – when I hear a paramedic ambulance pull up outside my apartment, and hear words to the effect of… "That'll do us here chief!"

I rush outside and see the Mex stumble from the vehicle carrying an Indian takeaway meal in his hand and wearing a big stupid grin on his face.

Turns out Mikey had indeed made it back to Brentwood, but had fallen asleep and had travelled up and down the BART line from Brentwood to the airport all night, without waking up. So he was pushing out the big ZZZZZZZs and didn't even hear his phone ringing, if it even had any charge left on it, which it didn't.

Luckily, the time he did wake up he fell out at Brentwood Station. But he still managed to find an Indian restaurant open for food. He never even thought that the priority might be to give me a bell to tell me he was OK. He then tried to get a taxi, but couldn't remember the address of my flat, even if he could have hailed one.

A paramedic ambulance driver was the first transport Mikey came across and he managed to persuade the driver to take him to the area where he thought I lived, and trust to luck. On the way he recognised something to get him to my flat. Fortune smiled on him, but I certainly wasn't smiling.

Honest to fuck, I was effectively babysitting the former head of Motorola's East Kilbride factory…and for a £10 booster and louder ring tone on his phone, this full pantomime could have been avoided.

Before I left for work the next day, I toyed with the idea of preparing post-it notes for Mikey to stick on his person while sitting on the train, just in case he nodded off again, saying 'Wake this Man up at Brentwood!'

But you could never stay mad at Mikey for long and a couple of days later Jim and I took the Mex to see one of the finest cultural extravaganza's the US has to offer… The San Francisco Gay Pride Carnival. We bought him a whistle and a rainbow flag and I thought if he still had his well-groomed moustache, he would have fitted in perfectly with many of the guys on the floats. We all had a brilliant day tooting and waving and making loads of new friends. Just shows you that traditional old school views can easily go out the window, when you are having a good time.

I like to think I made a good and positive impact at Impact – don't worry I made sure Mikey got nowhere near the place – again continuing with my All Blacks inspired philosophy of trying to the leave the role I was in at that time, in a better position than when I found it. Some of the anecdotal feedback I received would appear to back that up, especially from those I still keep in touch with and one person is the former secretary of the organisation Jennifer Charvet. One of her sons worked for me as a trainee coach and her other one was an outstanding college runner.

After a few months working at Impact, she said that when I left, she would retire. She could have had a job at Impact for as long as she wanted, but she told me that after I moved on, she could not think of anyone else who could fill my boots and make the working environment as enjoyable.

True to her word after I left, both Jennifer and her husband Francisco, a native of Costa Rica, took early retirement, bought a camper van and began to tour the USA. She packed in her role and went out on the trail. Last known correspondence was Tampa, Florida, so I'm expecting them to appear at ML1 any time soon.

I've never been short of people looking out for me during my life and career and out in the States was no exception.

David 'Digger Bill is a Motherwell lad who served his apprenticeship at AB's (Anderson Boyes), where my dad had worked and emigrated to Los Angeles nearly 30 years before. He'd married a girl called Dianne who was at school with Jim and I, small world eh? And was a cousin of Yvonne's best pal Alison.

Confused? Doesn't matter, he's another top character – I'm beginning to realise that every time I use the word character I mean head case, but in a good way – who enhanced my stay in California despite him being in LA and me in SF.

He was a clever cookie who designed rides for Disney at their theme parks and is now a successful businessman in his own right. First time I met him was about 15 years before, when I was with my mates golfing in Florida. As he kept in touch with a few of them on a regular basis, especially 'Bodie' and 'Les', who both share support like him for a small team in Glasgow who apparently like to think that they 'are the people!'

One day Digger and I go into a Starbucks and when the girl asks our name for the side of the cup, Digger immediately says "Tadger".

We duly wait at the end of the line for her colleague to shout: "Cappuccino for Tadger!"… Silence.

"Are there any Tadgers in here?"

"Aye!" Digger says to me

"It's fuckin' full of them." Before heading up to the hatch to collect and pay for our coffees.

I was only a month into my stay in Brentwood when he called me saying that he was coming up to Oakland on business and that he would book a hotel near me for a catch up. I was still staying in a hotel at that time, but had the keys to my apartment which I take him to look at. A week later when I'm in the office, Jen shouts there's a delivery for me from DHL and I think it will be the new football kit and tell her to sign for it.

She comes through later saying that she had not opened the delivery, suggesting that it wasn't the shape of a box full of coaching apparel. So I go through to see a large flat box, which when opened contained a 52 inch state-of-the-art TV. There's no packing note or information and it's only when we investigate the sender via DHL, which wasn't easy, I discover it's from Digger's address in LA.

Immediately I call him and express my sincerest thanks and he announces: "You've fuck all in your apartment, Tadger, so I thought you'd need it." That generosity wouldn't end there as he'd send me allsorts from golf clubs to a half pallet of Heinz Baked Beans – 360 tins! It got to the stage where the staff would get excited whenever I received a delivery from Thousand Oaks in LA, as they would no doubt be onto a share.

Dianne did make me laugh as she said there were two Mr Bills, a David when he was in Thousand Oaks and a Digger when he was with me. Digger was far funnier.

We were driving one day and looking for a car park space when this guy cut him up and 'stole' the spot. The bold Digger then saw a perfect opportunity to equalise as he had a pint of milk and the other guy had an open window. In my experience the smell of spilled milk inside a car in 30 degree heat, takes a while to go away.

"You can keep the fucking space Tadger."

An action, which takes a hell of a lot of balls in the US, given the prevalence of firearms.

Digger really is a top bloke who would drive up with Dianne and his adoring son Robbie, whenever Yvonne was visiting and we would have some wonderful times in San Francisco. One of the best was when Yvonne and her cousin Alison came over with her husband Johnny and we also hooked up with Jim and Mark for the weekend. It seemed Motherwell had moved to San Francisco for those two days and with that line up we could have been sitting in the Electric Bar, regardless of the fact we were actually wine tasting in the Nappa Valley. It's not where you are, but who you are with.

A year to the day that I started at Impact Soccer, I was off again on another adventure and forging another partnership with a former well-known heavyweight of the Scottish game. Another fantastic guy, who I would form a management team with and become very impressed with, step forward Hamilton born (everyone has a cross to bear), Paul Hartley.

CHAPTER 14

ThunderBairns

*Swapping Calfornia in the States for the one in Forth Valley
with an offer from Paul Hartley at Falkirk*

'm loving life in the States. The weather is superb at a balmy 30 degrees, I'm earning good money, playing golf several times a week, socialising with brilliant people, holidaying with my family regularly and doing well at Impact Soccer, to the extent that I've been headhunted by Fresno FC – another great opportunity and challenge. So, what do I do? I jump at the chance to come back to Scotland for a third less money and the prospect of visiting Glebe Park, Brechin, on a pishing wet and freezing Saturday in February. I would be filling a role as assistant to Paul Hartley at Falkirk. The post had been vacated by respected veteran Jimmy Nicholl, who had agreed to become Graeme Murty's second in command at Rangers following his final game with the Bairns at Dunfermline on 2 January, 2018. Coincidentally, Jimmy and the Gers would be jetting off to the States around the time I had decided I was heading home. Taking advantage of the winter shutdown, they played in the Florida Cup in the Orlando sun against two famous Brazilian sides – Atletico Mineiro and Corinthians – before Jimmy and his new side would head back for a midweek game against Aberdeen at Ibrox, and then a seat in the Dingwall dugoot to watch his side play Ross County on a freezing, pishing wet Sunday at the end of January!

As happens so often, it all came about so quickly. I was home for Christmas and

New Year 2017/18 and upon my return to the USA, I was ready to take up the reins as assistant head coach of Fresno FC and my return flight to California was booked for 15 January. This time on Christmas Day, the Young family couldnae give a burnt Brussels sprout about the first-team line-up I would field for Fresno, and there was no danger of the dining room table being cleared to work out the tactics I should use – though they were employing some emotional blackmail tactics to get me to pin down some dates when they could come over and visit.

I'd stayed home longer as it was Robbie's 21st birthday and at his party – where else but the Electric Bar – I got a call from Fresno confirming my appointment, which was to be announced upon my return to America. Unbeknownst to me, around the exact same time, Craig Brown had been asked by Scottish Championship club Falkirk to vet a shortlist of four or five possible replacements for Jimmy Nicholl, who would be able to provide positive assistance to manager Paul Hartley. They had a look through the high-calibre candidates and then asked Paul whether they had considered yours truly. Paul – who I had helped previously by loaning him Motherwell Academy players when he was Alloa Athletic boss – was intrigued by the recommendation from Broon and trusted him implicitly. He asked if I would be available and Craig intimated that I would. Coincidentally, as I was sitting in a plane on the tarmac at Heathrow Airport, a text from Archie Knox about another role which might be available popped into my phone just as I was preparing to switch it off for the flight – and at the exact same time I was trying to call Broon to discuss the Falkirk opportunity. Jings, it never rains fitba opportunities, it pours!

When I eventually got through to Broon (he probably had to put Sir Alex or Arsene on hold) I only managed 30 seconds to get half of the gist of what was on offer, before the call came abruptly to a halt. "Stewardess, can I ask the pilot to put the brakes on for five minutes or so?" The tantalising lure of getting back into mainstream Scottish football at Falkirk, a good traditional club with a bright and talented young Scottish manager in the shape of Paul Hartley, really appealed to me. But I never got any real details and had to switch my phone off to prevent a sky marshal and two or three air stewards and stewardesses bearing down on me to ram a pistol and assorted implements down my throat.

You can imagine that flight. I barely slept wondering what it was all about and there was a further boot in the plums when I landed 11 hours later, and it was 4am in Scotland. To be fair, Craig would probably have taken a call from me at that time in the morning - maybe not Archie though, who I would have been able to hear in California roaring like a bear from Scotland, even without a phone. Eventually I get to speak with Craig and then also to Paul to get the lie of the land about what was on offer. It sounded like it would be a great fit for me. For the next ten days I play things close to my chest. I don't even tell Yvonne, to avoid building up her hopes that I am coming home for good rather than for a holiday only for it all to fall through, as had happened a few times previously. By the same token, because nothing had been agreed, I'm still tidying up my move from Impact to Fresno FC and proceeding as if it is going ahead. They get to the point of taking my sizes and ordering all my training kit and arranging my accommodation. On Friday, 26 January, 2018, I'm sitting in on an online conference call with the chairman of Fresno FC and he tells me they are going to announce me as assistant head coach on Monday, 29 January. Falkirk tell me they are going to announce me as assistant manager on the morning of Tuesday, 30 January.

Fuck's sake, looks like I'm going to end my time in the States with another headline - 'Young Swaps California USA for California… in Falkirk!?!' - but this time without a superbowl party. Cue a few awkward phone calls to the nice people at Fresno. Keen to entice me to stay, they offer me even more money! It is America after all. If in doubt, offer more dollars. If truth be told, I didn't feel as if the role at Fresno was right for me given that I was to be assistant to Adam Smith, a nice lad and the son of an agent I got on well with. The club were a newly formed franchise headed up by Frank Yallop, a British-Canadian ex-pat who was the same age as me. He played 389 games for Ipswich Town, scoring a goal in a 2-1 victory over Manchester United at Portman Road in the English Premiership in 1993. He amassed more than 50 caps for Canada and also enjoyed a great coaching career with a few notable MLS clubs, including San Jose Earthquakes, LA Galaxy and Chicago Fire. He was the general manager, Adam would be the head coach and I would be his assistant, but I would run the training as well as, in Frank's own words, "mentor" Adam. It all sounded OK but not OK, if you know what I mean? Still, it would have been my introduction to the United Soccer League (USL), the second tier to Major League Soccer (MLS), and there was an agreement that they wouldn't stand in my way to a better offer further down the line.

I would have gone with the Fresno offer and I could have made it work. But then another twist arrives which convinced me more than anything that California in Forth Valley would be better than the Silicon Valley option as my next destination. I get a call to say that Fresno would be partnering up with an MLS club – Vancouver Whitecaps – which is quite normal, as some clubs enter their second teams in the USL or loan seven or eight players to an affiliate franchise, with the USL team securing first options on the players if they don't cut it in the big league. The entire American sports franchises are built this way, whether it be baseball, football, hockey or basketball. The problem was that part of the deal was to send Robert Earnshaw to join the coaching staff, at the insistence of the partnership agreement. He was a highly successful player in his own right, winning 59 caps for Wales and playing for Cardiff City, West Bromwich Albion, Norwich, Derby and Nottingham Forest, and he also had a loan spell at Greenock Morton.

I do the math (jings, I still surprise myself with some annoying Americanisms):

Adam is a rookie, Frank is a successful coach but is now GM, Rob has been coaching kids and by all accounts, from what I hear, is allegedly being sent to Fresno in a more 'out of sight, out of mind' arrangement by the Whitecaps hierarchy. Compounding all of that is the fact that the Fresno ground and pitch is a converted baseball stadium – playing across part of their dirt bases – and the franchise agreement is only for two years. My uncle John's parting comments of "it's an open air asylum", are steering me even more towards the Bairns. This turns out to be a good decision as, sure enough, later on Fresno implode and the franchise gets wound up after the two years has expired. The last I heard they were looking at relocating to Monterey, next door to Pebble Beach Golf Course… if they want me for a summer job I might consider it!

Now I've got three calls to make. On Sunday, 28 January, I call Yvonne to tell her I'm on my way home to my loving family for good, to a job paying only a third as much as I was currently on in California. She is delighted… I think… and so is the garage door. Next I call my mum and dad and immediately burst into tears (of laughter) as I can finally tell my dad that every night when he Skyped me – yes every night at 5pm UK time for the previous 12 months – all I ever saw was the red suitcase on the top of his bookcase, despite me telling him to adjust the camera. He was 84 and I rarely missed a call. That's one of the big differences with us and the yanks. Football is ingrained in us. My mum could tell me the Albion Rovers score or give me a transfer news round-up for the whole of Scotland if I asked her, which Gavin Glinton loved whenever he was in my company when they called. The average soccer dude in California didn't know whether to pump the ball or stuff it. The last call is to Gav and I arranged to meet up with him, Lance, Gash and Jennifer. They are gutted and try to suggest all kinds of ways in which they could create a job-share scenario in an attempt to keep me State-side. Once they knew I had made up my mind, they organised a flight home on the Thursday for me and I wrapped up my enjoyable time with them with genuine regret. Memories of them all made me smile as I started to study Falkirk's forthcoming match schedule.

The move meant I'd be back in the hurly burly of Scottish mainstream football, at a great traditional Scottish club with a really decent home support and excellent potential. I was also excited about working with Paul and another Scottish football great, Alex Smith, who was the club's director of football. At that point I never knew Tam Ritchie would be there too. He was the fitness coach who'd been with Paul since he began his management journey and the pair had forged a friendship from their days at Hearts, where Tam worked for a decade. The phrase 'hand in glove' springs to mind as a description of their relationship and it was easy to see how we'd work in harmony, both on and off the pitch at Falkirk. This has continued to our current Cove Rangers collaboration where we've become even closer.

Before you know it, I get all my affairs in order in Brentwood and I'm on a flight home to Scotland. Next stop is the Falkirk Stadium dugout for the home game against Livingston on Saturday 3 February and I feel right at home back in a proper football environment, despite getting pumped 3-1. When I walked in to meet Paul I immediately knew we'd hit it off. I had landed late on the Friday night and had gone to the match on Saturday in time for the pre-match meal, and at half-time he invited me to offer my comments on the first half despite not knowing the team. He'd prepared them, but was still humble enough to get my thoughts and let me air them to the group. That's class. I couldn't wait to get back in on the Monday morning, but as I got up to leave the house at 7.30am, I had to clear three feet of snow from my drive. Fuck me, five days earlier I had played golf with Robbo in a lovely 80 degree heat in Wild Horse, Yolo County, California. My bones and my toes were questioning my decision, as I chattered and skidded all the way up a one-lane M73.

You never know how things will turn out when you work with someone new, but this was meant to be and the relationship that developed between Paul and I would end up a long-term one, as we're totally comfortable with each other on and off the park. You meet a girl at the dancing who looks gorgeous. As you're both in a happy place, you move in with each other then, after a short while, the two of you find out you both want to choke each other and this happens a lot when people work together too. But not with Paul. He is a straight-down-the-middle guy and players know where he stands all the time. His only downside is that he's from Hamilton! He knows the game inside out and he's a winner. You don't get that combination too often… Hamilton and winner. We complement each other well and our working relationship is so comfortable, which comes from his desire to do things the right way. He doesn't take short cuts, he respects my thoughts on the game, he has trust in me and this makes our collective decision making the best it can be. He is very knowledgeable about the game and his ideas are fresh, which is a big help when you're planning strategies on systems of play.

The main task at that time was to keep Falkirk in the Championship and mount a challenge for promotion to the Scottish Premier League the following season. We went on a great run from February to May and ended up finishing eighth in the league. Paul had inherited a tired squad with a limited budget (that's how you get these salubrious gigs) and if the league had started in January, Falkirk – the form team – would have won it given the run we went on. I know what you are thinking here - "If pigs could fly…" or "If you can keep your head when all about you are losing theirs and blaming it on you, you'll be Scotland manager my son!"

Another thing to emerge from my return to Europe was a part-time offer from Mixu – then head coach of Latvia – to come and work as his assistant during the international breaks. This was another great opportunity for me to develop my skills and Paul realised the added benefits this could have for Falkirk's players, with me bringing back new coaching tactics and styles of play to give more experience to our squad. So I was given permission to head to the Baltics every international break, which would roughly work out at six double-headers per season, lasting nine or ten days and incorporating Euros, Nations League and World Cup fixtures. But more on that later.

Next up after defeat by Livingston was a Scottish Cup fifth-round tie away to Cove Rangers, my current club, where that old coincidence thingymajig once again came into play. We travelled up north on the Friday night and Craig Brown came to the hotel we were staying at, to see how his recommendation was coming along and we had a chat for a couple of hours. Paul and I love his company and all the old stories circulated again, with us always knowing the punchline, but folding up none the less at the content, the people involved and the master who was delivering them.

It was there that Craig reiterated the compliment of saying that one of the mistakes he made when he left Motherwell for Aberdeen, was not insisting on taking me with him and Archie. I've used the word humbling quite a lot in this book, but for a man of such stature in European football to say that, meant so much to me. The boy Hartley's no fool and as we were becoming closer, he told me that he'd also done his own checking up on me and received a glowing recommendation from Derek McInnes, the then Aberdeen manager, about my abilities. That's the thing about this game, everyone knows who can and who can't and believe me there's a few "can'ts" out there!

Cove's new stadium was in the process of being built, so they had to play the game at Inverurie Loco Works' Harlaw Park ground and we ran out eventual 3-1 victors. Cut to the present day where Paul Hartley, Tam Ritchie (fitness coach) and I are the management team at Cove with a spanking new 2,600-seat stadium and a contract until at least 2025. More on that later too.

The thing that sticks out most in both Paul's and my own memory from the cup game, was that when he was doing his post-match press conference, his comments were drowned out by the clattering of metal studs on the concrete floor. This was courtesy of the Cove bootboy (man) Doadie, a lovely guy who we would team up with later. If you search online for this footage you'll see Paul laughing in amusement.

In the next round we were drawn against Rangers at Ibrox, totally justifying my decision to return from the USA. I was back in the big time.

As mentioned previously, there are proper football people at Falkirk FC, none more so than the very well respected Alex Smith, a veteran who had managed St Mirren, Aberdeen, Dundee United, Ross County and Falkirk in his time. What he might not have managed so well – understandable for a then 77-year-old – is screening the calls to his mobile phone. In his role as director of football at Falkirk, Alex was responsible for overseeing the development of the reserve team squads and mentoring the younger coaches. Whenever there was a game at home, Paul and I would be there to cast our eye over the up and coming youngsters and we would sit in the stand just behind the dugouts. One day we had just taken our seats at the same time as Alex takes his in the dugout, when a mobile phone starts ringing. Alex, recognising the ringtone, immediately reaches inside his club jacket and answers. All you hear echoing round a deserted Falkirk Stadium is Alex's booming voice: "For fuck's sake, how many times do I have to tell you son… I don't want to apply for a PPI claim!" He hangs up and the true pro that he is, cracks on as if nothing has happened, leaving Paul and I hee-hawing and laughing in the stand.

One player at Falkirk – who shall remain nameless – certainly wiped the smiles off our faces. He sums up a sort of 'sense of entitlement' emanating from a few unrealistic players these days. He came in to see both Paul and I in our office to ask why he was not in the first team. "I think I'm worth a start," he says. But we explain to him that we don't think he has done enough to earn one. "Aye, but I came away up with you and the squad to Aberdeen for the cup game against Cove," replies our employee. Paul and I look at each other and just about in unison, say: "But that's your job, son!"

The backroom staff were mainly a great bunch, especially physio Ross Grady, who bears more than a passing resemblance to Nicola Sturgeon and, like Nicola, was very competent at handling a medical emergency. He was a real hard working guy and he's now moved on to Hearts. Bobby Wilson was another lovely old lad who was absorbed into the backroom staff due to his affiliation with the club and Alex Smith in particular. He is similar to people at lots of teams in the UK who contribute to the harmony of the club and do a multitude of wee jobs to support the backroom staff. I took a shine to him especially as he was diagnosed with Parkinson's disease (like my dad) and his role at the club enhanced his confidence and benefited everyone.

The problem was that Bobby would arrive in the mornings and set up the drills/exercises that the coach had planned, by laying out cones and markers, something he'd been doing with the previous managers. However, both Paul and I like to set up ourselves to give us an idea of distance, as well as last-minute adjustments we'd recognise due to our experience over the years. That meant we'd start to arrive earlier, so as not to upset Bobby and pass off the miraculous set-up as if the fairies had laid them out. The norm was that we'd be in the stadium about 8am prior to training starting at 10.30am, but we'd find ourselves coming in earlier and earlier to get set up before Bobby came in. I kid you not, it got to the stage where Paul was sitting in the car park at 6.45am waiting for the stadium manager to open up. To be fair, he's always in earlier than anyone else and Tam says he was like that as a player too. A man after my own heart, following the mantra that time keeping is top of the things that require zero talent.

My first opinion of the board of directors, led by chairperson Margaret Lang, were that they were very nice people who were desperate for their club to do well. General manager Craig Robertson, executive director and director of commercial operations Kieran Koszary (now at Queen's Park) and another football legend in these parts, Alex Totten, were all smashing people to work with. And with a backroom staff of this calibre, I really felt the club had a chance to do something special. They had been starved of success and with such a tremendous fan base – probably about the tenth biggest in Scotland – expectations were high year on year.

We finished the season strongly and ended up a creditable eighth in a strong league, after a poor start to the campaign. Our sights were set on the following season and both Paul and I were excited at what we could achieve. The fans of this famous old club also had high expectations and were confident we would take the Championship by storm in 2018/19, and return to the SPL.

During the summer of 2018, the board decided to take a bold step of changing the way they attracted players to the club. They adopted the Brentford FC recruitment model – which had proved successful for them – and hired a player recruitment manager who was based down south. The club was without a notable youth system as the academy had been scrapped, much to my amazement as the central belt has a track record for producing good players. I'm on record as saying that no matter what the circumstances are, a club should never fold their youth system. They should keep it no matter what and beg, steal or borrow to keep it alive. As well as the much needed pipeline to the first team, it should be a matter of pride for fans and they will always support it.

The recruitment manager's job was to source decent young English-based players who had not made the progression to the first team from the academies of big clubs. In theory, clubs with a decent budget would benefit from this and could attract some of the best players jettisoned from the bigger clubs. We bought into this, as it would save us some money and give the hungry young potential starlets the opportunity for game time and put themselves in the shop window for a bigger move – again providing us with a valuable income stream.

But Falkirk would only be able to offer them £500-600 per week. This meant that the standard of player we could attract would not be the best and it was ultimately doomed to failure. Don't get me wrong, there were one or two good players from the likes of Watford, Leicester and Chelsea who agreed to come to us. But having never played first-team football before, hairy arsed, experienced Scottish pros in an unforgiving Scottish Championship would have them for dinner as soon as they came up against them.

After our pre-season, we realised that unless the young kids hit the ground running, it could be a steep learning curve. Around 16 players were signed that summer from down south through this model, with loanees or freed youngsters selected with the intention of showcasing them and polishing them up for further progression. This model needs time and the fact that it was scrapped once we left highlights the lack of depth the plan had. Even the bigger clubs who use this system cannot guarantee overnight success, as the recruitment process needs longevity. We could see the players would struggle. And with the fans' expectations so high – a record amount of season tickets were sold that pre-season – we knew before the season had even started, that failure to win consistently and early would quickly bring the inevitable calls for a change of management.

But we pressed on and booked The Vale sports complex down in Cardiff for a ten-day pre-season training camp. Home to the Welsh Rugby Union and training centre for Cardiff City, The Vale had magnificent facilities and we hoped it might galvanise the new young squad under our charge. But we kind of knew when we were putting them through their paces and playing some practice matches, that it was going to be hard. The quality of training was exceptional, but the proof in the pudding is transferring it to games.

The weekend before we headed down to Wales, we had a full-on wardrobe malfunction, which could very nearly have left our first-team squad looking like a pub team on the pristine Vale turf. It stemmed from a difficult situation that arose involving our kit-man. He wasn't a bad lad, but was someone who couldn't give us the commitment we were looking for. He was already a wee bit tender that our Vale trip landed slap bang at the same time as his brother's wedding celebrations, and one thing led to another and we parted company.

I like to think I am a big enough man to admit when I have made an error of judgement, and this was one such occasion. My approach of using reverse psychology and attempting 'good cop bad cop' style humour during the discussion did not go as planned and the kit man handed in his rifle. I thought it might bring him round to our way of thinking, but sadly it did not. I misread the situation and trying to be funny gave him the perfect out ball.

This led to a situation on the Friday before heading to The Vale on the Monday, whereby Paul, Tam Ritchie, Vicky Logan our administration manager, Derek Jackson the goalkeeping coach, and I had a full season's worth of training kit and equipment for all our players to sort out. The chances of it being ready for the Monday were slim to non-existent and I had teed it up nicely for us to be left in the lurch. The top priority was the gear they would need for the ten-day trip to Cardiff. As anyone will tell you, the amount of kit involved on a match-day is ten times what was needed back in the day. When you're going away on a pre-season tour abroad, you'll negotiate equipment to be provided by the facility – such as poles, mannequins, cones, etc - but if you're on UK soil, you tend to take all that with you, as well as your own training balls for consistency. In addition, as you will probably be doing double sessions, the requirement for extra kit is essential and the provision for all weathers needs to be taken into consideration. You also need to form a good relationship and understanding with the laundry staff and facilities staff on site and most of these will understand the need for a quick turnaround for sports teams. But you also need extra kit as new players may join during the camp and as you are away from home, there is also the need for leisure training gear to wear during recovery and relaxation time.

This is something they certainly don't teach you on the Uefa Pro-Licence course and it took all five of us a full ten hours to turn it around. I already knew what a great, important job kit men and women carry out at professional football clubs, but I certainly have an even greater respect for them after that shift. The fish suppers that Paul sent out for after our exertions never tasted so good and were demolished instantly.

Only a few clubs in Scotland have an abundance of staff, with most employees doubling up roles, and for me the real pros are the ones who dig in when the chips are down, literally. I'd never known anything else, having served my apprenticeship at Motherwell, and when I went to Sheffield United I couldn't believe the amount of staff that were utilised performing the roles that we did at Motherwell with a fifth of the numbers. At Falkirk, for example, it was not uncommon for Tam and I to collect the breakfast supplies from Tesco for the players, who would only see the end product of a fully-stocked dining room, complete with fruit, carbs, cereal and anything else that was required. It never occurred to us to get a loyalty card, the points on which could have bought us another player as well as topping up our severance pay, which was on its way.

Mitch, the recruitment manager based down south, covered the matches and did his best to provide us with the talent needed to compete in the Scottish Championship, but to reiterate, the budget required was not at a level commensurate with the expectations of winning the league. In reality, many of the players we signed should have been playing in a development squad. This would have sat below a strong first team and players would have migrated incrementally to the top team, rather than all chucked in to learn to swim in a sea full of sharks. We really needed players with the calibre of Andy Nelson and Alex Jakubiak, who we had on loan the previous season.

There were some good kids there who had enjoyed great experience at academies down south. But the downside to academies is that sometimes they're too nice. Players go into clubs at six or seven years old and get lifted and laid for ten years, before being sent out into the real world. Here, their comfort zone is well and truly left behind as they say goodbye to the cosy bubble made up of equal game time and regular 'well done son' praise, where results don't matter and coaches smother them.

One of the young players who springs to mind at Falkirk was Dennon Lewis. He was an instantly likeable lad who had come out of the Watford academy. But, without being unkind to Dennon, he'll be better remembered for his stint on the reality TV show Love Island. Subsequently, I would take him on trial to FK Liepaja later on and at one point I was considering a contract for him, but ultimately we weren't a match! Ruben Sammut was another young player I really liked. He was on loan from Chelsea and it would have needed a few more like him to bring the required success, but the budget was not elastic enough given the amount of players we had to bring in. When we realised their weaknesses we signed Paul Paton, who I had worked with at Dundee United. A few more like him might have at least quickly steadied the ship.

Despite all of this, our pre-season preparation had gone relatively well and after a narrow defeat against Aberdeen, Derek McInnes was asking about one or two of our players. We finished the League Cup section second to St Johnstone and thought that the addition of three more players would stiffen us up a wee bit and allow us to play. Our fears for our inexperienced squad were borne out, though, as the season started. We lost the first three games on the spin. It was certainly not what we, the fans and the board had hoped for.

Chairperson Margaret Lang suggested that Paul and I meet her at the Dakota Hotel just off the M8 near Mossend, Lanarkshire, to draw up a shortlist of three or four experienced pros that could help us stabilise in the league. However, unknown to us, around the same time, the rest of the board were panicking a wee bit and discussing Paul's removal as manager. I've got total respect for Margaret as both she and Craig Robertson were genuinely looking at ways they could help us, but how can you respect the other board members who were plotting behind both her and Paul's back? Some had allegiances to former players and were also influenced by the negativity brewing amongst fans on social media, so they were looking for ways that would assure self-preservation.

It's also worth noting the vitriol of a section of the home support, where the personal abuse directed at Paul on match-days was so disgusting that his partner Lisa and their lovely three-year-old daughter, Olivia, stopped attending the latter matches. In this day and age of calling out discrimination and abuse, I don't know why football managers and coaches should have to endure the personal verbal abuse that they do by sections of support at games. I am also especially enraged by cowardly keyboard warriors, who would get jailed if they ever carried out their verbal attacks in public.

On 27 August, the club announced that Paul had left by mutual consent - and guess who was left in charge of the first team in a caretaker role? By this time I must have had more caretaker roles than the whole cartoon series of Scooby Doo! I was having flashbacks to what happened at Dundee United and felt it was absolutely disgraceful

– knowing how hard Paul had worked at Falkirk – that they could get rid of him after just three games of the new season. It was, in my opinion, an absolute disgrace and unprecedented to terminate a manager at this juncture of the season.

There were 33 games remaining and very quickly the recruitment model was binned in line with an appointment of a new manager. In my opinion, Falkirk changing managers this early in the season – we were not even out of August – set a danger-ous precedent for many other clubs to do likewise, especially if they were on a dodgy run. Indeed, in the opening stages of 2018/19, there was a domino effect and a record amount of clubs changed managers in the first quarter of the season that year.

Paul's departure also left me with a dilemma. There was only one more game – Ross County away on Saturday 1 September – before the international break, when I would be away for ten days with Mixu and Latvia. As boss, Paul had been encouraging me to take this on, but now as caretaker boss, it put both my jobs in jeopardy. If I stayed with Falkirk throughout the international break, the Latvia gig would be up the swanny, but I could still get binned when a new manager was recruited by the club. If I headed to link up with Mixu, my full-time role at Falkirk would definitely be terminated. I told Falkirk I would stay the week and head off to Latvia after the Ross County match, but they needed a decision on whether I wanted to stay in that role until they appointed a new boss. To be honest, I felt that I was holding a gun to their head as I wasn't prepared to lose both jobs. But it was taken out of my hands as Ray McKinnon – who succeeded me as manager of Dundee United – was announced as the new Falkirk manager the night before the County match and it was agreed that I, too, should move on.

As usual, I tried to leave the way I came in and I wished the club well – still do – and they honoured their outstanding financial commitments to me. I must admit, now an-ytime I am going through a tough wee spell at a club, I half expect to see Ray hanging about outside! It's probably a bit similar to how factory workers must have felt if they ever saw STV's business reporter Alan Saunby doing a piece to camera outside their main gate.

Falkirk beat Ross County, the eventual league champions, but they were still relegat-ed to Division 1, despite a complete overhaul of the squad and 33 games to recover. Nice job, board members. I never want the clubs who I have worked with to be unsuc-cessful, as there is a bit of personal pride attached to your time with clubs and what it means to the fans, despite a small minority being horrible. In fact, in early 2020, I remember watching the results of the clubs I had been involved with and FK Liepaja (more later) were due to play in the second round of the Europa League, Motherwell were sitting third in the Scottish Premiership, Sheffield United were top six in the Eng-lish Premiership, Dundee United were clear in the Championship, Falkirk were lead-ing Division 1, East Fife were in the play-off positions and, more importantly, Cove Rangers were 13 points clear in their inaugural season in SPFL 2. It's an easy game this!

It was satisfying to see them all doing well and it's also nice to return either in a coaching or scouting capacity. All of these clubs I can honestly say have received me with warmth, and I can always say I gave my all and never-short changed them. That's why I really get pissed off with the most overused description of a manager's frailty: "It's a results-driven business." Oh really! Well, for what it's worth, here's my take on that grossly unfair gauge of a manager's tenure...

In Scotland, with 42 teams, it's not that unusual for a team to win the treble in the top flight, so that's three trophies gone. Three teams win their respective leagues beneath the SPL, so that's another three trophies gone. For argument's sake, say no club got promoted through the play-offs, then does that mean 38 teams, and in particular the coaches, are hopeless and should be sacked? Bring in 38 new managers and replenish all the players and, hey presto, we're doing the same thing next year again. Away and howl at the moon. No one compliments or praises things that are tangible results for all clubs. As I said before, what if you reduce the average age of the squad? What if you increase the home attendances? What if you increase the player value? What if you promote academy players? What if you just play an attractive style that entertains the fans? What if… What if… What if you can keep your head when all about you are losing theirs and blaming it on you? You'll be Scotland manager my son!

Not a chance. If players underperform, sack the manager. If players are sold to keep the club afloat, sack the manager. If wee Boaby who has a laptop and wouldn't know a ball if it hit him in his warped little head, posts a comment on social media… yes you've got it, sack the fucking manager!

Some clubs in Europe now have different operating KPIs given to head coaches, which involve the progression of the club with all departments judged simultaneously. The coach's job is to compare the performances of the team against their capability, and even games lost are not considered as failure as long as the performance is improved, in relation to the targets set. That seems fairer to me. Give a head coach three transfer windows and clear objectives to meet before deciding their fate. I can honestly understand it when fans are unhappy and they are entitled to a grumble or two – I'm a fan myself – but try explaining that to the online keyboard warriors after his or her team loses a couple of games.

Maybe these are the folk who were unfortunately bullied at school and now want to be the bully troll, maybe their wife or husband hogs the TV remote. These are the very same fans who when they meet you ask: "Any chance you can get me so and so's shirt?", before going home and assassinating you on their laptop with a club sticker on the front.

With punditry now equipped with NASA style analytical tools, everyone is a fucking expert. Can you imagine going into the work premises of @Jizzmastersuperdooperfan – he's the guy who has the club duvet cover, wallpaper and kids named after a former player from the 80s who's now skint and driving a taxi – and saying to his boss "sack that prick" for giving me gloss instead of satin paint. That's the third time he's done it and remember please don't tell him it was me who said it! Anyway, I had other fish to fry in the Baltics and this would challenge me on so many other levels, as well as giving me some real success and a real eye-opening experience.

CHAPTER 15

On Mixu's International Service

*Mixu invites me to combine my Falkirk job with a
part-time role with the Latvian national side*

Despite being thousands of miles apart – me in the USA and Mixu in Thailand coaching Ubon UMT United – we kept in touch regularly. He knew that I had taken up a new role at Falkirk and was pleased that I had settled in well with Paul. The club had stayed up at the end of the 2017/2018 season and we were looking forward to the start of the next season. Around this time Mixu was also looking for something closer to home and secured the job of manager of the Latvian national side in May of 2018 and, immediately after, asked me if I would like to become his assistant. It was an excellent opportunity for me to test myself as a coach at international level, so I approached Paul for his thoughts and hopefully his approval. If he had any doubts at all, I'd have made my apologies and thanked Mixu for the offer, as Falkirk was the bread-and-butter gig. No need to worry on that front as both Paul and the club were great and encouraged me to take on the role, which would mean me heading off with Latvia during the regular international 8-10 day breaks. The feeling was this would allow me to enhance my coaching skills, bring new training techniques back to Falkirk and double up as an excellent scouting opportunity, to see if I could identify any up-and-coming Latvian players, who would be a good fit for Falkirk.

Believe me, there were as Latvia had, as they still do, a good crop of young players coming through who regularly get snapped up at a tender age by predators from larger countries, in both central and Eastern Europe. Young Latvian players are now plying their trade in Russia, France, Holland, Czech Republic, Poland, Kazakhstan and Switzerland. Later on I'd recommend a central defender to Rangers and Sheffield United, but his trial got postponed due to an injury. He's subsequently been transferred to

Gdansk in Poland, but I thought he was a typical Scottish-style centre-half. So I was off to coach in the Baltics. But before I made it to my first national version of the Finnish/Scottish dream team at a two-week camp in late May early June for a friendly against Azerbaijan and the little matter of the Baltic Cup – a historic bi-annual tournament similar to the old home nations we used to compete for in the UK – I had to tie up some loose ends in California.

As always, before departing my role in the US, I made sure that, despite me leaving, I would exit on as good a set of terms as I possibly could. This led to me happily agreeing to go back in the summer of 2018 for a short series of training sessions and clinics, as usual organised by my good friend, Robbo. He'd tell me more people would sign up for my sessions than any of the other clinicians, which would always help my self-esteem. Clever boy that Robbo. They either couldn't get enough of my skills, or they wanted to see if I would bring Mikey Stevens along with me to see what the one-man wrecking ball could possibly get up to, while I was busy coaching. Just my luck that my Stateside trip was the week before I would have to link up with Mixu in Riga. It was tight, but it was doable.

I finished my coaching stint without incident and with a customary few games of great golf thrown in (not my actual play being great, but the courses we'd play). I then took a flight from San Francisco to Amsterdam and from there to the Latvian capital of Riga. This would be a bit of trek, even for Michael Palin. But, in all my travelling, I somehow never saw the physical, as well as mental, challenge it could entail as an ordeal, but rather as an adventure. I could write another book dedicated to international calamities. Like the time I left the Under-20 World Cup in Turkey, which was part of my Uefa Pro-Licence assignment. In order to catch a flight to Philadelphia from Glasgow, I had to organise an early departure from the main party, but got stuck in Istanbul for eight hours. This left me meeting Robbie and Yvonne on the tarmac at Glasgow Airport where I changed the contents of my suitcase before giving it to my father-in-law, John, through the immigration gates, and then boarding our flight to Philadelphia, where we got caught up in a lightning storm. "All in your stride wee man," I'd say to myself, mining the rich seam of resilience from the south Motherwell school of 'and whit? Is that yer best shot?'

This time all I had to do was manage the jet-lag and plan the forthcoming Latvian sessions. It would be my first experience of a 10-day international training camp, in preparation for the upcoming Baltic Cup tournament with Lithuania and Estonia, plus the friendly. When I arrive at lunchtime at Riga Airport, I am picked up and whisked away to the Jurmala Hotel and Spa – HQ for the national side – on the beautiful Bay of Riga on the Baltic Sea coast. I am feeling fine at this point, but am wondering when the jet-lag is going to kick in. When I arrive, Mixu makes me feel very welcome indeed and introduces me to all the staff. The players are at this point resting in their rooms after a morning training session and preparing themselves for an afternoon and an evening stint on the pitch.

It is amazing the subtle differences you see all over the world in how culture affects the way sport is taught and coached. In India it was the way they seemed to over-work the players in high temperatures and the deference that was expected towards the coaches. In Latvia, Mixu and I also had to review a few practices, which we felt were inhibiting the relationship between players and backroom staff, perhaps a legacy from the ex-soviet era of rank and file. One of those was a literal curtain separating the staff and players in the dining rooms. This was quickly removed when we were there, as we felt it suppressed the relationship between the two and we wanted to build a together-ness about the squad.

By mid-afternoon on my first day as an international-team coach, the curtains are nearly closing on my eyes and I am jet-lagged out of my tits. As I am preparing to leave for my stint on the training ground, I have knocked back six double espressos. Mixu is concerned that I may not be functioning at my full capacity and asks if I am sure I want to take part. But I am keen to set a good example and step up to make my mark on my first day, especially as it was working with the strikers, which I really enjoy. After all, they're the ones who get the glory and functional work with them in terms of timing runs and creating angles, as well as refining their technical prowess, can make the difference between winning and losing.

My big Finnish buddy had briefed me that Latvia were very solid defensively, but that they lacked a cutting edge up front. As I am by nature an attack-minded coach, we decide I should work on a strikers' movement session. At 5pm on the training pitch, I am introduced to the players – a really good bunch of lads – and I have about 60 minutes to wait until my training stint. But by this time I have gone nearly a day with-out sleep and my eyes are drooping big time. Mixu jolts me out of my drowsiness and says that I am up and I set up my planned drill complete with defensive mannequin dummies, for our strikers to compete with. To be honest, I was in a bit of a daze and I can't remember too many details, but I think it went very well and I made a good impression on Latvia's best strikers. Though they couldn't understand why I was instructing a red, metal, human shape that he should be pushing into his marker to gain a yard before making a sharp angled run to the near post. I think, in the end, the dummies won 3-1!

The Baltic Cup – which began in 1928, but had a hiatus from 1940-90 due to being part of the Soviet Union – is Lithuania, Latvia and Estonia's version of our now defunct Home Internationals, and since 2008 had been held every second year. So as you can imagine it is quite a big deal in that part of the world. Our first game in the 2018 tournament was against Estonia on 2 June in Riga, two days after they had beaten

Lithuania 2-0. This gave me the chance to meet up with some old friends from my Motherwell days – Henrik Ojama (who had scored against Lithuania) and Henri Arnier – who had established themselves as mainstays of the Estonian national side. They were both good, attacking forward players, who coincidentally had benefited from my use of mannequin dummies while at Fir Park and it was good to catch up with them. It would remain to be seen whether the Latvian strikers and the rest of the squad – who I had really hit it off with – would also grasp the nettle and take on board my words of advice. So, when Jans Ikaunieks took a short corner and worked an opportunity for himself, just as we had practised, and struck the back of the net in the 70th minute, I saw it dawn on the Latvian players, who rushed over and pointed to me on the bench, that this wee Scottish coach knew what he was talking about. Our eventual 1-0 win set us up to go into the final game against Lithuania in Vilnius, needing only a draw to secure the cup.

I have always loved Mixu's attention to detail as a coach and manager and his planning going into a team meeting is outstanding. The one we had the night before the Lithuania game was no different and the players were left under no illusions what was expected of them on the field the following day. As always, as part of his presentation, Mixu was showing the squad some footage of the opposition playing in recent matches – which included, ironically, a match against Scotland in 2016 – to show them their system of play. The whole squad is assembled in the hotel meeting room and listening intently to what Mixu is highlighting on screen when Scotland score and Mixu pauses the film. "YYYeesssssss! Yah fuckin' beauty!" I roar from the back of the room and run around the startled squad bare-chested and swinging my training top around my head.

"C'mon Scotland!!!"

They are all looking at me incredulously witnessing a Tartan Army veteran of the 1990 World Cup in Italy show them how to really celebrate a goal scored by your national side. Mixu instantly gets where I'm going with this and starts laughing his head off, which encourages everyone in the room to join in. It was the first real icebreaker and it showed players previously treated in a supressed fashion that these two guys were personable and would encourage them to communicate their thoughts and feelings. After that the bond between players and coaching team really became much stronger, trusting and determined and they relaxed in our company and were able to focus much more on the instructions we were giving them. The next day, June 5, we flew to Vilnius and went out and drew 1-1 with Lithuania and won the Baltic Cup once more for Latvia.

After the game and as per an agreement I had with Mixu, I was looking forward to jetting off to link up with Yvonne in Portugal for a long overdue holiday. It meant that I would be excused a trip to play a friendly against Azerbaijan four days later. I had an early flight at 5.00am the next day, but because of the cup success and the bond we were forging with the squad, Mixu didn't need to do much persuading to encourage me to enjoy the impromptu celebrations about to start at the hotel we were staying in. Mixu himself takes up the story here. "We are both wine lovers, so I had bought some good wine for my room to either celebrate or to sink our sorrows. We won, so we had the right to celebrate and we did so by drinking the lot. Then we moved on to the mini-bar and cleaned that out too. Then we ordered more from room-service and drank all that too. Before we knew it, it was about 4am and Gordon, who hadn't slept a wink and was still in the same gear he had on during the game, said goodbye and went to his room and collected his luggage and headed off to the airport." Suffice to say, I only make it to the airport in Vilnius for my short one hour and ten-minute flight to Frankfurt – where I am to connect to another flight to Faro – with the skin of my teeth, wearing the same clothes I was partying in with the big man, namely my red Latvian international tracksuit complete with Baltic Cup medal round my neck. It's a rush to get through customs, but I make my flight and the sleep monster grabs me just as I click myself into the seat and I start pushing out the ZZZZZZs. In what seems like the blink of a sleepy eye, I awake as the passengers are disembarking at Frankfurt and realise I am not wearing any training shoes. Dishevelled, shoeless and attempting frantically to get my bearings, while trying to explain to the kind, enquiring Lithuanian lady sitting next to me and the helpful German air stewardess who think, due to the national badge on my kit, I am Latvian, that I am, in fact, Scottish and trying to get to Portugal - and where the hell are my trainers?

"No shoes, no shoes," says my fellow passenger pointing at my tootsies.

"Sir did you leave them in the airport?" asks the stewardess.

Bingo. In my rush to get through customs and catch my flight, I had checked in my main suitcase and made a beeline to the security checks. I had placed my carry-on bag wallet, watch, spare change and my Adidas Sambas in a tray and we all breeze through the metal detector and scan. But for some inexplicable hangover-induced reason, I had forgotten, in my haste, to put my trainers back on before scooting off to my gate, which was calling last orders for boarders. "What a fud!" I thought to myself as I gingerly walked down the plane's metal stairs, taking care not to slice the soles of my feet wide open on the steps. I hurriedly made my 'walk of shame' on my stocking feet, through a smirking passport security check, double-take glances from half of Central Europe and into the departure lounge. With all my other footwear already zipping through to my next flight, all I could do was hastily dip into the first shop I could find and buy a pair of flip-flops for the onward journey to Faro, where a knowing shake of the head awaited me from Yvonne who met me at arrivals. Mixu added: "I was in stitches later on the next night when Gordon called me from Portugal, saying he had left his shoes at the airport security in Vilnius and ran onto the plane in just his socks. It was hilarious."

My involvement in international football with Latvia – winning the Baltic Cup and competing in the Euro Nations League – gave me some wonderful opportunities with memorable and enjoyable experiences to go along with it. After leaving Falkirk I remember travelling with the squad to Tiblisi in early September 2018 for a game against Georgia in front of 65,000 fans. The intensity of their support was unbelievable and I remember our bus having to get a police escort to the stadium where huge policemen used their batons to smash the wing mirrors of cars, who were making it a tight squeeze for our driver. We came away with a creditable 1-0 defeat - to a last-minute penalty - and our lads were not intimidated by the imposing atmosphere, even though I could swear I saw some cops parading a washing line of Mercedes, BMW and Audi wing mirrors trackside and tapping their batons off them in time with the chanting crowd.

There was our trip to Kazakhstan, where a combination of lateral thinking and innovative sports science aimed to keep us on Latvian time, despite the five-hour time difference. Fuck knows what time that made it on my watch that day, travelling from Scotland. This saw us training at midnight in the national stadium, eating our dinner at 2.30am and breakfast at noon! But there must have been something to it as we held them to a 1-1 draw on the astro-turf pitch, which just a few short months later would see Scotland come a cropper 3-0. Mixu even passed on a wee dossier to the Scottish FA about Kazakhstan's team and the sports science programme that worked for us, but who knows if they acted on it.

My Latvian adventure also highlighted the close coach and assistant relationship we had and the freedom to agree and disagree with each other on just about everything, if it was for the right reasons. Again Mixu elaborated on just this point: "I don't want to work with yes men. I want people with strong opinions on the game beside me who can offer a different view on things and I liked that about Gordon. I wanted someone who would say 'Mixu have you thought about this or what about this?' I am strong on what I think, but I also wanted someone with their own brain beside me, and then I decide whether we go with it or not. I found Gordon totally complemented me and gave me so much more on my management team."

During the game in Astana – the capital is now called Nur-Sultan – we played indoors at their 40,00 capacity stadium as it was -35 degrees outside and the coldest place I've ever been. I suggested an extra midfielder to secure the draw rather than a striker. Mixu looked at me curiously as we are both positive-thinking coaches, and we were playing well at that time. But even against his own instincts, he decided to go with my suggestion. At the end of the match, the appreciation of the man for this tactical switch and a deserved away draw will live long with me. I had to remind him of a pact we made from a previous tangerine experience, "let's not lose."

Another experience that will live long with me was a visit to Andorra, who are without doubt THE most frustrating team I have ever had to face as a coach. To put it a good old-fashioned Scottish way, they certainly 'pish with the cock they've got'. They have actually enjoyed a relatively long list of "not getting beat" performances and they really test you with time-wasting, diving, feigning injury and breaking up play at any opportunity. The first game in Riga was only six minutes old when their right -back rolled around the pitch slapping the turf, as if he had been hit with Gareth Southgate's bar bill from Lucerne. Fuck me, I said to the fourth official who, along with the ref and linesmen, were from Northern Ireland, if we start adding on time from now, we'll be here for a week and Falkirk's got a game away to St. Mirren on Saturday. The game ended 0-0 and it was the lowest defensive block I've ever seen. This wasn't parking the bus, this was Asda car park at the click and collect bay on a bank holiday.

This meant that the second game in the beautiful principality was towsy from the start. They had a man booked in the second minute and we ended up having a man sent off before half an hour was on the clock. We should still have beaten them, but they held out for another scoreless draw, again adopting a defence similar to John Wayne and his mates at the Alamo. The bad blood was simmering as we trudged off up the longest tunnel I have ever seen, at the Estadi Nacional in Andorra la Vella. I could see it coming and, as the players walked shoulder to shoulder towards the dressing rooms, with our aggrieved striker looking to vent his anger at the Andorran defender who he felt got him sent off. It boiled over and a full-scale 'rammy' broke out, with Mixu and me right in the middle of it. The players were a tight unit and to see their coach defend their honour and leading from the front, afforded him a standing ovation when he returned from his press-conference performance. He always defended the players, verbally and then physically, if necessary.

All I could think off while ducking and diving and throwing a couple of arsehole winders, was 'thank fuck' for a wee bout of depression and prescribed boxing training treatment from the Sheriff. He used to say to me: "Look wee man you're not going to win the golden gloves, so what's the point with a six-shot combination. If you don't put him down with two punches, run like fuck!" Sound advice as the peaceful, neutral, independent principality of Andorra, sandwiched between France and Spain in the Pyrenees Mountains, fought against Latvia, who were aided by a Finnish and Scottish tag team. Mixu is a colossus and he backed his team to the hilt that night and showed he was as passionate and dedicated as his tactical knowledge.

I had flown with the squad to Girona from Riga, but on the way home, as it was the end of the international break, it was easier for me and six players – including the Latvian captain Andris Vanins who was playing his 99th match – to head to Barcelona and back to their clubs from there, rather than return to their home country.

I say goodbye to Mixu and we all jumped into a chauffeur-driven people carrier and set off on the three-hour journey down to Barcelona. After a wee while, the captain takes on the responsibility of asking whether we can stop off for some "Coca Cola" – his words. I'm thinking that the mentality of these athletes is great and that they want to try to get some sugar back into the body to replace what they lost during the game. I even suggest that they could have a couple of beers if they wanted, and gesture to them with thumbs-up to show them how happy I am that they have accepted me. "No thank you coach, just Coca Cola," says the captain.

So, I instruct the driver to stop at the next service station. We all pile off and after a few minutes we are back at the vehicle and the players have two litres of Coca Cola each. They have also bought me a bottle of red wine as a thank you for stopping, which I am touched by. As we head back onto the motorway to Barcelona, I twist off my Coke Zero bottle cap and think to myself what a great example they would be to several Scottish footballing names. But then I catch a glimpse in the rear-view mirror of something that makes me want to spray my mouthful of sugar free all over the driver just in front of me. It's then I realise that the Scottish names in question would be Johnnie Walker, Whyte & McKay and Arthur Bell as each and every one of them produces a bottle of duty free whisky from their bags that they must have bought on the flight to Girona.

The Coca Cola was just a mixer.

"Enjoy your wine coach," they said, as I turned around and they all raised a dram and coke to me to say cheers!

I loved the international experience and in particular the content of the double-headers, which became the norm. Liaising with Mixu over player selection and planning the content of the camps was very enjoyable and another 'school day', as I'm particularly interested in 'periodisation'. Definition: the systematic planning of athletic or physical training, aiming to reach the best possible performance in the most important competition of the year. It involves progressive cycling of various aspects of a training program during a specific period, which is something I ask about first at whatever club I visit and whichever coach I speak with.

I believe this is critical to success and the balance between workload, analysis, team meetings, as well as sports science and medical awareness and is essential to the big picture at a football club or international team. Planning the camps is key to the harmony and success of the time you are allotted working with someone else's players, and I can say, unreservedly, Mixu got this spot on at Latvia, drawing on his prior four years of experience with Finland. The players immediately bought into our organisation and attention to detail as Mixu showed his man-management style, by treating the players holistically and allowing the exact amount of freedom given the time you were away with them. He would scout the opposition months in advance and build up a dossier on their systems and players, as well as plan the working schedule in relation to our fixtures. Anyone thinking that this was an eight-day jolly could not be further from the truth as the workload was full on, with many moving parts associated with the training and playing schedule.

To give you an idea, we'd meet up normally on a Sunday, but some players may be playing that day so would arrive later. We would work out who played at the weekend and decide how much training load each player could do. A full medical would also take place for all players and staff involving blood, urine and scans to determine everyone's general health and well-being. As you can imagine, the quality of food was of the highest standard and at every sitting a selection of supplements was provided to make sure everyone's system was operating at its optimum level.

Mixu and I would engage with the support staff and, by their own admission, create an environment of relaxed, but professional operations which they had never experienced up to that point. I, in particular, struck up a close bond with the doctor and head physio, who were both northern European 'look-a-likes' to myself, tall, blonde and handsome! Our trio were referred to as 'the brothers' and would greet each other with 'morning brother', followed by a big embrace, which became a source of hilarity for the players and staff. The doc and I would go for a swim in the bay of Riga each morning at 7.00am and jog back for breakfast. The days were full on and people don't realise the amount of preparation that goes into the planning of the meetings and training sessions. This is also true of day-to-day football clubs, where outsiders still think you roll in at half-past 10 in the morning for a wee game of football, then slope off at noon to play golf, go to the bookies or go for a pint.

Mixu would work with our analyst, Ilya, to clip the footage for our daily meetings and illustrate either the demands for training that particular day, or setting the game plan for the forthcoming matches. Players also need to have some 'free time' or the body will capitulate, and the mind for that matter, and I found two ways to help. Exercise would always be my default and I'd encourage Mixu to come swimming with me in the hotel pool and also do a 'fat-burner' workout in the gym. He is one of the most competitive people I've ever met and the swim, designed for relaxation, would turn into a 25-yard freestyle race between us and anybody else we could rope in, complete with national anthems and podium placings. I'm sure you can picture the man mountain pounding up the inside lane, elbowing anybody who came near him, and a small tsunami engulfing the poolside rest area adjacent.

Mixu said: "I might be over 50 now, but I am as competitive as I was when I was 18 years old. I want to beat everyone at everything and be the winner. Even though every day you get older, Gordon and I are fighting a losing battle to keep ourselves fit. We would both use the pool and swim a number of lengths or go to the gym together. Unfortunately I can't run because of my knees and ankles due to my playing career, so I need to find alternatives and swimming is something I've done quite a lot of. It came about that younger members of the backroom staff heard that we were swimming and they said we were just basking in the water. Well, Gordon and I said bring it on, let's have a look at you guys in the pool. Gordon organised quarter-finals, semi-finals and the final and, luckily, I ended up winning.

"That evening meal, Gordon and I walked into the meal with our chins up, chests out and heads held high as if we had won the World Cup."

Mixu also coaxed me into going for a nap in the afternoons, which I started to do and still enjoy today. I used to think, "fuck that sleeping malarkey, if I'm sleeping I'm missing something that's going on." Now I love a wee nap to recharge the batteries. Mixu had worked with a 'sleep doctor' in Finland to search for those small margins, which can make the difference between success and failure. He explained to me the cycles we dip in and out of when we hit the hay. That is just a small example of how intelligent he is and the attention to detail he'd go into.

Once we had the player load agreed we would plan the camp into specific elements for the fixtures involved, with detailed sessions on attacking/defending with and without the ball, patterns of play and the very important set-pieces. For example a typical camp would cover the following:-

Arrival on Sunday with medical and welcome meeting outlining the days ahead. Players love to be 'in the know'. Then kit issue, which would be both practical and plentiful. I'm still wearing most of the surplus some three years later, so is my son, Robbie, and anyone else I know who is the same size as me.

Monday – depending on who can train – we'd work on a general theme designed to incorporate the style of play for the first game, with the players who played club football on the Sunday going with the medical team for a recovery session. Prior to the session we'd have a pre-team meeting and then a short team meeting highlighting the day's itinerary. Lunch would follow and then, after our swim battle and a short nap, another team meeting would analyse our next opponents. This would take place before going back out for a short tactical session, working on the points highlighted about our challengers. After this it would be back to the hotel for evening dinner, then a staff meeting to debrief and discuss the day's events and fine-tune the schedule for the next day.

Tuesday/Wednesday, would be the same set up logistically, with emphasis one day on defending and the next day on attacking.

Thursday would be game day and we'd do a light session in the morning at the national stadium, covering all the points made previously and go over set plays, which are potential game winners, making sure everyone knows their responsibilities.

The day after the game could either be a recovery session for the starters, or a visit to a cryotherapy chamber, with the non-starters doing a high-intensity work-out to replicate the numbers covered by the players during the game the previous night. I particularly enjoyed these sessions as Mixu would trust me to deliver them, with the attitude and work-rate of the players exceptional. We would replicate these five days for the next game coming up, taking into account the various travel arrangements, sometimes involving long hauls. But we made sure every time we travelled it was always by charter flight, giving us comfort, flexibility and optimum planning options.

Mixu left Latvia soon after the Andorra game and that meant my time as an international assistant manager had come to an end, too. But it was definitely worth it, as it put me in the shop window for clubs in the Latvian league and led to me taking on my first solo role as a boss at FK Liepaja.

CHAPTER

Live And Let Liepaja

*My first time as boss leads to European qualification,
but also a rollercoaster ride in Liepaja*

Now ladies and Gentlemen, strap yourselves in, there could be turbulence ahead. As you might expect my first contact with FK Liepaja (FKL) came about while I was involved with the Latvian national side. In early June, 2018, at a Latvian training camp, while I was still assistant at Falkirk, I was approached by the sporting director of FKL asking if I might be open to joining them. It seems they were concerned that their Argentinian management team did not have the Uefa qualifications needed and they were looking to bring in someone who did. I dismissed the unofficial approach out of hand, as I was still convinced Falkirk was the place to be working alongside Paul Hartley. In late August, after settling up with the Bairns, I was out in Riga for another nine-day international camp for games against Georgia (away) and Andorra (home) and had just finished a welcome lunch with all the players and staff. Shortly afterwards I was in the foyer of our hotel when the same persistent sporting director popped up once again and asked if I had any other thoughts about joining them. As they say, when one door closes another one opens and the timing was absolutely perfect for me. I agree to meet club president Māris Verpakovskis, a former Latvian international with a serious European pedigree. He was a decent lad and a proper football guy due to his standing in the game, having played in Spain and Russia at the highest level. After lunch I have two options literally on the table. Maris, having worked under Gary Johnson, the English former Latvian national team manager, liked the idea of a British coach coming in. This was not the norm in the region, with predominantly Russian and similar regional managers employed. The other ex-national player I came across, when he was manager of FK Jelgava, was Marians Pahars the former Southampton forward who I really liked. In fact, I liked Jelgava's hospitality anytime we played there and I had already met a few of their board members on international duty due to their representation on the international committee. Both Marians and Maris were similar in terms of the number of international caps they had and having both played at top clubs in top leagues across Europe. Therefore I understood their frustration at the Latvian league and their FA when they compared them to the respective countries they had plied their trade in. So, should I take a short-term deal and see how it goes, or plump for a long-term contract – both would also allow me to continue my role with Mixu and the Latvian national team. The short-term deal was on offer from August to December, bearing in mind in the Baltics that takes clubs to the end of the season, and I thought that would be a good introduction to see if the fit was right.

I shook hands on condition that our collaboration had to be kept confidential due to the pending international fixture in Tbilisi involving players from all of the top clubs in Latvia. After flying back from Georgia with the national team, I would take up my new post as head coach of FKL. On that flight back I even managed to gain the upper-hand on my new club's next opponents Riga FS (RFS) – one of the capital's dominant clubs. It just so happened that the Latvian national side's goalkeeping coach Aleksandrs Kolinko was also the assistant manager at RFS who at that time were the second top side in the Latvian Higher League or Virslīga.

We were to play them next, but my big goalkeeping mucker, who at that point 35,000 feet up in the air as we travelled back from Tbilisi, was totally unaware of my new role – which had not yet been officially announced. I sat down next to him on the flight and he was openly swatting up on his team's tactics, style of play, line-up and full game-plan for the forthcoming match against, yip, you've guessed it, FKL. "What you up to Aleks?" I asked and there then followed a lengthy detailed and in-depth discussion – with laptop presentation explanation – of the strengths and weaknesses of my new team and his team. Unwittingly, he gave me chapter and verse on everything I would need to know in order to set my new team up against his. I was even debating, internally, whether I should ask for his bank details and the secret ingredient to his Pelēkie zirņi ar speķi (Latvian national dish).

Without cracking a light, I got up to return to my own seat for landing and wished him all the best for the game to come. Mixu was pissing himself laughing and commented: "You've got some balls, wee man. He's a madman." Then he paused and followed up with: "What am I saying, you're a madman as well!" Mixu would be invaluable in the short term as his duties entailed him keeping check on the local players, and, based in Riga, he'd do a match report for me – always without compromise to his position and always totally professional. Can you imagine the face on my big 6ft 5ins, brick-shithouse built friend when I met him in the tunnel a couple of days later, as we were leading our teams out for the big game. Remember, this is the ex-Crystal Palace goalkeeper who could really take care of himself in the penalty box – what the fuck was I thinking about? We beat them 1-0 and I made a mental note not to end up alone in the same sauna on international break with him again, even though he eventually saw the funny side. I had done my research on Latvian football when I joined Mixu to help out in their national set-up, but even I wasn't that familiar with the team from Liepaja, who had been re-formed in only 2014 after financial troubles. They boasted a long history dating back to Russian occupation and, like many eastern-bloc teams, were derived from works of national industry. The Liepaja team was aligned to the steel-works, which was the main employer in the city. Does this sound familiar?

A so-called 'phoenix club', they had risen from the ashes of the Liepājas Metalurgs club, who had gone into bankruptcy the year before. FKL, therefore, incorporated their players, youth infrastructure, ground – the picturesque seaside Daugava Stadium – and even their place in the Virslīga. A good starting point for this new club and they finished fifth in the league in their first season. They'd kept themselves in the top half of the league ever since and won the Latvian Cup the year before I took over. But, when I grasped the reins, they were struggling and sitting third bottom of the ten-team league. But it's amazing what a 1-0 win against one of the league powerhouses – albeit with a little bit of insider knowledge – does to team spirit and morale and it certainly got me off to a flying start. The team already boasted three or four players from the international squad and that really helped. They also found it immensely amusing that the national goalie coach had spilled the beans so easily to me on the plane back from Georgia. So that all filtered through to their fellow club team-mates and helped break the ice immediately - and in the Baltics that literally can be a hard thing to do. However, we would go on an unbelievable run from that moment on and finish fourth, qualifying for the Europa League, which I rate as one of my best achievements in professional football

Liepaja, a southern coastal town, was beautiful, sitting on a 10km white, sandy beach. It is particularly lovely in the summer and welcomes thousands of seasonal tourists, but it is cold in the winter. However, it had always been important for the country in times gone by due to the fact that it boasted a harbour that rarely, if ever, froze solid in the winter. A declining steel town – there's that irony creeping in again – it once had a population of more than 100,000 people, but, due to the demise of industry, it had shrunk to just under 70,000. The city is known throughout Latvia as the 'city where the wind is born' due to what seems to be a permanent sea breeze. This had led to a massive wind farm being built nearby.

The Daugava Stadium is sandwiched between a smashing park, which hosts an excellent summer music festival and the beach. My apartment was a 2km walk away and I used to stroll along the lilywhite sands every morning and drop in to a quaint beach-side café for my first coffee of the day before heading in to work. It's a hard life. One day, I am waiting on my coffee with Richard Othen, my new strength and conditioning coach, when I get a tap on the shoulder. "Gordon Young! What are you doing here?" No one had spoken to me in three months outwith the club. It was the Edinburgh-born Keith Shannon, the British Ambassador to Latvia, and a massive Hibee, who had recognised yours truly from my time at Motherwell and Dundee United along with Mixu – who, remember, is a Hibs legend. He was in Liepaja for a special gala dinner to celebrate 100 years of British and Latvian collaboration – minus the 50 years or so of Soviet Russian rule, of course – and ended up inviting me and Richard along. It never ceases to amaze me where a career in football can end up taking you. Richard and I were treated like royalty as we quaffed our champers and canapes whilst adorning the red carpet. Before we left, he asked me: "Are you really from Motherwell?" Yes, I replied. "Has Francie McCabe got a house yet?"

On their departure, the Argentinian management team had left their Chilean strength and fitness coach Ricky, short for Ricardo Madariago Ascencio, marking time seeing out his contract until the end of the season. But he quickly became my best mate in Liepaja. We made a pact on a Wednesday night after training that I would treat him to sushi, he would bring some nice Chilean wine and I would help him improve his English at his request. I'm not that fluent myself, so he'd have to go with the North Lanarkshire style. But he was so driven to learn English, so that he could have a chance to work in America. He would regularly push a letter through my apartment door on a Wednesday morning, with phrases which I had to translate and talk him through later in the day. I thought the best way to help him would be to familiarise himself with football-related sentences littered with the vernacular – well, that's how the kick-ball game works. This manifested itself with a little bedevilment from myself when the morning pleasantries were dished out at the club. Ricky who was disregarded somewhat as he was part of the old regime, would be blanked by the owner who would breeze past him and gush a "Good morning Gordon" to me in a thick Russian drawl. This amused my Chilean friend and he'd regularly acknowledge the owner with a "How are you doing big arsehole?" To cover my tracks a wee bit, I also encouraged Ricky to welcome me with "Hello Gordon. Up yours gaffer!" Ricky was a great guy and I still keep in touch with him. I remember the win bonuses that we amassed through the remaining games of the season meant so much to him as his basic pay wasn't enormous. When we won and he received his bonus, he would get me to drive him to the nearest large city, the Lithuanian seaport of Klaipeda, an hour from Liepaja, so he could buy presents for his kids and family back home. He would log in a wee notebook who we beat and what he had bought with his bonus – it was all so humbling and I was happy that I had helped the team win to enable him to do that.

On a memorable Sunday morning after a recovery session, I asked him what he was going to do for the rest of the day, to which he replied sincerely: "My friend, today I go to my home and do the fuck all!" His English is coming on fine, I purred to myself. In particular, he would tease the owner's young adult son, as you do when you're on the road out, and I would double up laughing as his accent was now a cross between Antonio Banderos and Rab C Nesbitt. One day I'm in my office and I hear a conversation from the adjacent room. "Do you want coffee, Ricky?" A voice says. "Si, does the bear sheet in the woods?" came the reply. But my ultimate favourite was any time he got chastised by the Latvians, his reply was: "Go and take the flying fuck to yourself!" This, I think, may help him in many situations globally in the future! We would order sushi, drink Chilean wine and he'd practise the funniest one-liners. I would then video his efforts before sending them back to my mates, who have adopted him as a legend, due mainly to his rendition of 'Since I was Young', a favourite Motherwell fan chant. Everytime I hear Despacito by Luis Fonsi, it reminds me of him as he'd translate the lyrics for me and we'd sing in full voice together every time we won, which was, well, almost every week!

When he finally left at the end of the season, he turned to me and said: "Thank you my friend, Gordon, you are the dug's baws!" By that time he'd saved enough money to visit Italy and Spain before he returned to Chile and we had great fun plotting his route, which was a book in itself. The film Trains, Planes and Automobiles springs to mind to describe his travels, as he left luggage all over southern Europe and, if he retrieved it all, I'd be surprised - and happy. I gave him all of my kit, which he wanted to give to his sons and father, and, sure enough, on his return to Santiago, he face-timed me with all his family cloned in Adidas rig-out adorned with a GY monogram. What a boy.

I have waking nightmares of him working back home in South America and greeting English-speaking players or coaches in his best Motherwell accent. "Ola yah wee fanny, that big striker is pish and he wouldnae get a baw in Sports Direct!" Ricky, you truly were a godsend for me at that time and we had an "El balon, dos cervesas. Por favoramigo."

I had to remember it was a different culture I was embracing in Eastern Europe. The club owner – a successful Russian businessman – was initially very nice, though as much as he supported the club, he did not really know too much about football. In fact, he knew very little about football and an example of this was his hiring of the previous under-qualified Argentinian coaching team. A clear example of homework not being done as a Uefa Pro-Licence is required to manage in any top tier in Europe. He was the unofficial 'King of Liepaja', but it was the influence of his son, who fancied himself as a wannabe Roman Abramovich, that would eventually put a spanner in the works. At the start and when we were doing well, the owner would smother me with kindness. I became scared to say if I liked anything as I would end up with copious amounts of it on my desk the next day. It also seemed that my club car changed every other month too.

Early on, I was invited to a Russian spa with the owner, where for three hours I was beaten over the head and body with birch leaves and branches, thrown out in the snow bollock naked, and fed herbal tea until my bladder was about to burst out of my body and go and join the Greenham Common peace camp. This was a treat, I was told. Fuck me, I was winning every game and he said that every time we won he'd pay for this glorious service. "Fuck that," I said, "Every time we lose I'll come." Now there was an incentive not to lose. During a relaxing break in the steam between all this activity, he asked me if I liked honey. Yes, I said, adding: "Putting a spoonful in my tea in the morning is a nice wee treat." The next day a whacking great pot of the best honey appears on my desk. I could have put a spoonful of it in my tea in the morning every day for the next 350 years, and would still have had enough to paint my bathroom with! So, there it sat behind my desk until one day, one of the younger coaches brings his father in to introduce him to me. I shake his hand, but his English is not very good and his son is doing his best to translate. "My father asks, how it is going with the team?" says the young coach. "The team is playing well and results are good." I reply, to a blank stare.

I see that does not register and look around the office for something to substitute as a trophy, so I can pretend we are winning and spy the huge Champions League of honey pots. At this point I hadn't opened the five-litre tub, which must have taken millions of bees to make. But some dirty bastard had been at it – I think I must have invited anyone with a sweet tooth to take some when they wanted, to try show the owner it was being appreciated – and the lid hadn't been replaced properly. I clumsily reach for it and fumble the lid as I hoist it above my head, pretending to be Tom Boyd lifting the Scottish Cup for Motherwell in 1991, and four or five pounds of honey overflows and cascades down over my head and face. I'm like Pooh Bear gone rogue. Turns out that the culprit who had not screwed the lid on tight enough was the young coach standing in front of me with his 'old man', and, out of embarrassment and guilt, he hurriedly owns up to me, while at the same time explaining to his dad that this was not some bizarre Scottish football ritual. Though to be honest, I would've even given that a fucking go when I was at Dundee United, if I thought it would have done any good. His old man sat there with his jaw on the floor thinking who is this mentalist as I walked into the shower with all my clothes on to wash off the sticky honey. A similar thing happened with caviar. Again I must have mentioned to my generous boss that I would happily give the much-sought after exclusive and expensive eastern European delicacy a wee try, and, sure enough, 24 jars of the stuff appear on my desk the next day. I tell Yvonne and she Googles it and finds out this particular brand is retailing at 500 euros a jar! I end up spreading it on my toast in the morning like it's John West tuna and washing it down with a cup of honey-laced tea. I was quick to share it with Ricky too and I found it amusing that he had 500 euros worth of his boss's caviar on his sandwiches, as he walked into work telling the owner that he was a "horse's arse"

During a cold Lanarkshire winter I would regularly hear my mates quip: "It's so cold out there that when I came indoors, I went into the fridge for a heat!" And that's certainly what it was like during the winter in Latvia. It must be the only area on the planet where you start the season playing and training in minus 25 degree blizzards, perhaps play a full round of games (nine of the 36) on Astro-turf facilities and then play the other 27 matches of the season outside on grass in 30 degree heat. I remember one training session when all I could see was eyes peering at me, as everyone had every square centimetre of skin covered up against the cold. Our kit manufacturer, Adidas, even provided us with insulated items to combat the extreme conditions, but players trained as normal and I've got nothing but admiration for them as it didn't affect their commitment or quality. If you had £1 for every time someone back home uttered the immortal words "it's Baltic out there" in reference to the cold, I'd be pretty well off. But to actually experience the Baltic wind-chill cold, puts standing at a Scottish game with a Bovril in hand into perspective.

Something the club must have been inspired to do by East Fife was the customary presentation of sweet confectionary every time you win. But this time Methil doughnuts weren't the order of the day, but the biggest cake you have ever seen. At about two feet high and three feet wide, I could have used it as a duvet, and, as we were clocking up the wins regularly, my office was beginning to resemble Greggs in Glasgow's George Square hosting the Great British Bake Off. They are very proud of their pastries in this part of the world and the cakes were something else in Latvia, with decorations to commemorate everything and anything. It would also be customary for players to bring them in for birthdays and anniversaries. Another delicacy was soup and a throwback to the days when you used anything in the field or on the beast to create a hearty meal. It was customary for me to adopt the old Dundee United trick of getting the chef to plate me my evening meal for take away.

I was putting all these wee quirks down to the culture of the country and it certainly wasn't worrying me. But, in hindsight, maybe the way our bonuses for winning the league were paid should have made me more wary. Every time we won, everybody in the club was paid 500 euros as a bonus – that's everyone from administrators, to kitmen and the first-team squad, 36 people in total. With three games to go, we need-ed only four points in the final three games to finish fourth and secure the final Uefa League qualifying round place. I suggested a one-off bonus for all concerned of 2000 euros if we qualified, and nothing if we failed. My colleagues were more than hap-py with the prospect of claiming an extra 500 euros than they would have done had we snared three victories, so they hastily agreed. As we were playing so well at that point, we took nine points from the next three matches to finish fourth, secure a well-deserved European spot and the enhanced bonus as agreed. Again, if we had amassed the same points total during the first half of the season as we had for the second half of the campaign, we'd have pissed the league. As it was my idea for the bonus scheme, the delighted owner walks into my office the following Friday with a brown paper McDonald's takeaway bag, sits it on my desk and walks away without saying a word. Inside is not a McChicken Sandwich meal with salsa dip that I think I had mentioned I had liked to him on several occasions, but 100,000 euros in cash, which I don't think had anything to do with the popular Monopoly game card associated with the fast-food chain.

I realise it's the bonus money and happily arrange for it to be shared out among the staff and players. But I have to admit I wasn't 'luvin' it' the way things were panning out on the administrative side of the club. Once everyone had been paid, there was 28,000 left and he asked me if I needed it for anything. No, I said and it was handed back. How I wish I had shoved it in my drawer for a few months further down the line. There was still one game to play and my focus switched back to concentrating on the football. Our opponents were Riga FS again. I would be locking horns with my big pal from the Latvian national set-up, who had given me the 'full washing' on how they would play months before. So, I am sure he was looking to get some payback on me and FKL on this occasion. The fact that they needed one point to secure their own Champions League qualifier spot made the tie even tastier. It was effectively a dead rubber for our players, who had to all intents and purposes, done their work for the season. Added to that, they had no bonus incentive to play for apart from pride, and a belief which I was keen to instil in them right from the start of my tenure that they should go out and try to win every game. We absolutely hammered them 1-0! Prompting one of their strikers to ask our centre-half: "Why are you trying so hard? What bonus are you on?" To which my player replied: "No bonus today. We are doing this for coach Gordon!" That's what he told me anyway and I had no reason to dis-believe him. But, as I had helped guide him to an extra-sized bonus and a shot at the Europa League, he could easily have been blowing smoke up my ass. One thing's for sure our captain Deniss Ivanovs – who had been capped 60 times for Latvia, had played in the Czech Republic, Russia and for Ajax - OK Ajax in South Africa – but a good level nonetheless, said to me one morning, as I was preparing for the session ahead:

"Every day you come in here to FKL, you make the place better." I took that as a major compliment and liked to think it referred to the training schedules, our style of play, the aesthetics of the changing room, the positive relaxed and fun atmosphere created, and not my services to local dentists dealing with sweet tooth FKL employees sneaking into my office for cake and honey!

From September to the end of the season in early December, we played 18 games – won 14, drew two and lost two. Not bad going and we were playing some good football. I got to know the strengths and weaknesses of the team and deduced that, if we scored first, we would win the match, as, of the 14 wins, eight of them were 1-0. Game plan settled, go out press like mad men, score first, then sit back and watch them defend with so much ease. I could have stuck the kettle on and had a wee cup of tea and, of course, some honey. So, from a purely football perspective at least, my self-imposed probation period had gone well. I was enjoying managing and coaching and before I headed back home for a six-week Christmas break, and a well-earned rest before pre-season training would begin at the end of January to prepare for the start of a full new season in March, 2019, I signed a two-year contract.

The logistics were ideal with weekly flights going from both Edinburgh and Glasgow to Riga, as well as the Lithuanian city of Palanga, a 40-minute drive from Liepaja down the Baltic coast. This meant the trip going back and forward for myself, as well as for visitors would be in essence a penalty kick compared to travelling to California. For the record, Mikey never got to visit me in Latvia, which is a real shame for the Latvians, but a diplomatic incident averted is a good thing. Having Mixu in Riga at the start was also great as I'd go up on my days off for a game of golf and stay over at his. Afterwards, we'd go out for a meal and a beer. Another upshot of the geographical position was that I could arrange to visit clubs in the near vicinity by way of a good friend and agent based in Poland. He organised trips to Sparta in Prague, as well as to Polish Premier League teams, where I could quiz their staff on new practices and operations as well as broadening my experiences in coaching terms.

Jan Lokaj is his name and I'd initially met him when in Scotland and I wanted to use him for the pre-season camps in Turkey. However, a Russian agent got the gig instead, against my wishes, but not against my coaching assistant's, which seemed strange to me at the time, but now, on reflection, it does not. I'd also go to Belarus and Serbia on scouting missions where I could see potential targets at close quarters rather than rely on unscrupulous agents with fourth and fifth-rate players, looking for a payday from naïve owners, who only saw a list of their previous clubs, forgetting to check how long it was that they had played with them. I'm sure, if I sent certain agents in a video of Wullie Pettigrew, they would have managed to get him a deal even though he's in his late 60s. But I planned the season as I would normally and had no reason to believe I would not be staying the full length of my contract. I also had a list of visitors lined up to come out and see our set-up, Paul Hartley, Stan, Barry Smith, Tam Ritchie and Fish – my agent. I even had Sky Sports primed for a visit to see the wee Scottish coach who was doing alright in the Baltics.

I started to liaise specifically with trusted agents and was in the process of tying up a collaborative arrangement with clubs in England and the USA to circulate players to everyone's benefit. I was in the process of signing Ryan Moon, a South African international, and I had an agreement with Victor Otto, the sporting director at Leeds United about young players coming to FKL on loan. The latter connection would afford me a couple of days at Elland Road with Marcelo Bielsa, taking in the training and his day-to-day activities. I also spoke extensively with my good friend at Sheffield United, Carl Shieber, about a similar agreement with the Blades and even offered international players going the other way. I've kept a strong bond with Carl and others at SUFC, which has allowed me to call, visit and keep abreast of things with potential for reciprocal arrangements. But it was also a pleasure and an unbelievable gesture by Victor to invite me down to watch Leeds United, Bielsa and all, for a few days. Without letting the cat out of the bag, Bielsa's English is better than Ricky's. Around that time the owner of FKL was insisting I should commit long term to the club and bring my wife over, whilst providing accommodation at any of the many properties he owned in the city. "Why do you want to go anywhere else?" He'd say, "Stay 10 years." Aye, no bother, big stuff I thought, but, to be fair, when things are going well it's easy to slip into a false sense of security.

I was assured by the owner that I would be allowed to build my own team, with my own players, and my own coaching staff, and I was looking forward to it. He even suggested I should choose two squads, one for the domestic campaign and the other for the Europa League sortie. However, when I was away over Christmas, my understanding was that my erstwhile Latvian assistant who had been helping me since I started in September, had begun colluding with the owner's son behind my back and starting to bring in their own players. While I was back in Scotland, my friends at the club called to fill me in on what was going on. It seemed that rogue football agents had the ear of the owner's lad, who now had a working title of recruitment director, and were helping to scout and offer him players from 'Bellshill to the Bahamas' and everywhere in between. At that time, however, I did not see any real problem and assumed that no one would be signed without my say-so and I would be able to take back control and assert my autonomy over football affairs. Alas, when I did return in January with all my new hopes and plans, I found the guts of half a new team who I didn't know from Adam. The owner's son and my assistant assured me they were looking after my interests and that of the team. But they had even taken it upon themselves to cancel the contracts of some of the players I had wanted to keep, and the ones they had brought in were of lesser quality and did not fit into my plans. This would be the first of many alarm bells that would start to ring as my first full season in charge began to go the shape of a pear. The club then agreed to loan out four players, surplus to my requirements, to a fellow Latvian league side, who I'm told were coached at that time by a former coach of FKL. At the daily meeting, I then enquire how much the other club's contribution to their wages would be – a standard aspect of a loan agreement with any other club around the world. What I am told astonished me. But, as my relationship with the owner was still strong at that point, I get him to stop the loan agreement immediately and bring the players back. My understanding is that the players were eventually paid off, with no censure to anyone involved in organising the deal.

I should not have been surprised, as I had wondered about another odd example of players disappearing off the payroll. There were three Nigerian players who did not feature in the first team who came a cropper at the club. It was not their fault that after they had been signed – months before I had arrived - they turned out not to be what we and me, in particular, were looking for – but they were entitled to come to Latvia to make a living at the game and contracts should be honoured regardless. But the manner to which they were treated was terrible. It was known that they all ate in an Asian restaurant regularly together. The story allegedly goes, so I am told, that the local cops may have been tipped off that three 'illegal' immigrants were there one night. Before we knew it, the three lads were deported and no longer employees of the club. None had featured for me and I felt that might explain their disappearance aligned to their non-contribution.

These unsavoury instances were beginning to play on my mind, but I pressed on with our pre-season plans and hoped that my strong relationship with the owner would triumph over the naivety – putting it mildly – of others in the club. A four-week training camp based at Antalia in Turkey in a five-star hotel and sporting complex could be just what the doctor ordered and I put my thoughts into football coaching. I had been there with Motherwell and knew it to be a first-class set-up which the players would love. One of these players would be a new signing organised by my new recruitment director – who is beginning to get right on my nerves. He gleefully announces that a Colombian player by the name of Escobar, would be joining us in Turkey and that he was going to be the best player in the Latvian league. He had graced the MSL In America and had played for Dynamo Kiev, who had purchased him back in the day for a good few quid. He had the video to back it up, and the data stacked up, but the problem was it was back in the day. That's like me sending a profile picture of Brad Pitt to a dating agency and the unlucky lady disappointed when she meets me. I took a look at him and, at 14 stones, he might have been a good player a few years previously, but had definitely, like his more infamous Colombian namesake, seen better days. I note with a wry smile in the news on the day we leave on the flight from Riga to Turkey, that Latvia makes the biggest drug bust in its history. I shit you not, although it was coincidental, you couldn't make this up. The camp itself went well and Richard Othen made sure the players were in excellent physical condition, banning lots of things he felt, correctly, were not conducive to the body compositions I was after, in order for them to perform consistently for the season ahead. This led to an amusing conversation between Richard and my 'not-so trusted' assistant, who insisted the players only played well when they drank a specific type of energy drink. However, Richard pointed out this was a concoction of every banned stimulant you could imagine. This stuff wouldn't help you develop wings like another more reputable one, but could help you grow a second set of bollocks under your armpits. We trained really well and held our own in pre season friendlies against the likes of Dinamo Tbilisi from Georgia, Olimpik Donetsk from Ukraine and Shakhter Karagandy from Kazakhstan as well as the Belarussian champions, Dinamo Minsk.

Around this time my great friend from my stint at Sheffield United, Lee Walshaw, was looking for a new challenge and enquired whether there might be any good opportunities available at FKL. To be honest, I would have taken him on as my assistant in a shot, but the politics that were developing meant that my then current No 2 was in with the bricks and had the ear of the owner and his son. However, I was able to offer Lee a role as youth academy development manager to help with the progress of the decent crop of young Latvians emerging from FKL – along with a wee sprinkling of foreign youngsters they had on their books. He would also be a good ally to have on my side. I told Lee to have a good long think about it and discuss it with his lovely wife, Joanne. Although I couldn't have foretold what would ultimately happen, I didn't want him to close his ties with his boyhood club, SUFC, and to this day I regret offering him the role. If I could rewind that offer, I would. However, his new role was required by the club and approved by the owner and, after a few weeks, he commented how good a guy Lee was. That came as no surprise to me and I thought everything was rosy, especially as Lee would carry out my plans regarding the development of the young players and their integration to the first team. This was part of my long-term strategy I was putting in place to recruit the best young Latvian players and gradually reduce the need for foreign players unless they were of better quality. This plan would also have created sellable assets for the club and created a pipeline which I had enjoyed previous success with at more renowned clubs than FKL. By this time my wee sweary friend, Ricky, had gone home and I was also looking to bring in a strength and conditioning/ fitness coach to replace him. Tam Ritchie, who had been with me at Falkirk, was my first choice. I spoke with Paul – who always had Tam in his corner at clubs, but both were not attached to any club at this point – to ask if it was OK to approach Tam and he said: "No problem." I outlined the knowledge I had and what my plan was to Tam. But the homework and research he did on the club and the Latvian league must have been better than mine and he claims to this day that turning down the role was the hardest, but best, decision he ever made... and I don't disagree with him. Whilst we were in Turkey I get a call from Lee to say he's still not into his apartment and he gets the feeling things are not as cordial as they should be. I had insisted Lee would run the coaching for the development squad, but it seems he was being undermined by an ex-player employed by the club. I tell him not to worry as I would clear it up when I returned. Then my own undermining assistant informs me that Lee doesn't have the qualifications to manage the academy and development squad. These requirements were never highlighted to me and, if I had known this, I could have let Lee down gently, whilst encouraging him to get the formality of the license required and hired him at a later date. Remember these are the guys who had brought in my predecessor from Argentina, without any badges. I also learned that my hypocritical assistant, at various points before I arrived at the club, would allegedly sit on the bench with an earpiece in, listening to instructions from a Latvian with an A licence to satisfy the governing body of their credentials.

Lee is devastated and both Richard and I cannot pacify him, understandably so. His treatment is scandalous and I phoned Joanne to prepare her, but already she is worried about Lee and how this could end so quickly and unjustifiably. Lee had left a secure job at Sheffield and I still hurt at this, although he acknowledges that it was his decision to come with me. Looking back, this was the start of my real deterioration in my relationship with the club from top to bottom, with the exception of the players and selected backroom staff. Lee had really bought into my two-year plan and was the perfect person to assist me, given his personality and expertise in the role. I had been given the green light to put this into operation, naively thinking the assistant was on side, but he became the cancer that would eat away at my association with the club.

Another example of the unsympathetic behaviour presented itself when we had signed a Georgian striker. He was a lovely lad who had played at a good level and had international caps, but was physically completely done. He had been signed in the same manner as the rest, tarted up by an agent, this time through a connection to my assistant. He was promised good money, subsequently bringing his wife and daughter over to stay with him, but he couldn't train or play two days in a row. You could see he had been decent, but, once the legs go, well the legs go. He knew this and I tried to work with him in terms of rehabilitation in an attempt to use his experience. After all he had been a proven goal scorer. This could be helpful, I thought, get some younger players to do his running and leave him in the box to score the goals. However, it never got a chance to materialise as he was forced to cancel his contract, take a small settlement and disappear. Before he left, he called me to warn me to watch my back, naming certain individuals as not to be trusted. Matte, you were spot on mate. When Tam declined the offer to come and join me, as mentioned previously, I managed to recruit a former Liverpool strength and conditioning expert Richard Othen, and, like Lee, I regret him coming on board as he would end up leaving not long after with me, albeit with his six-month severance pay, which is something Lee never got. Richard had left a job in England and really made an effort to bring a professionalism to the role and, like Lee and myself, had planned visits for the year ahead for his family and friends. I had seen the good times in Liepaja, probably because I was being successful, but I regret that Lee and Richard never got that opportunity. When it's good over there, it's very good, but when it's not going well… To put it into context they hired four head coaches after me in the last six months of the season, which highlights the basket case it was becoming.

Alarm bells are sounding louder and louder in my head about what was going on. I certainly don't believe that the irregular things I was finding myself on the periphery of were exclusive to FKL, it all just seemed to be normal football culture in certain quarters. Everything came down to money. At the end of the first season I was there and with two or three teams still in contention for Europa league spots, incentives were the talk of the steamie. One club owner even offered to pay our win bonus if we drew with another club. "Let me get this correct," I said. "How does he know we are only on a win bonus and nothing for a draw?" Forget that, we always go all out to win was my reaction and it went to the back of my mind as I focussed on securing another three points. Needless to say, I said absolutely nothing to our players about this before the game, which did legitimately end all square as it turned out.

The ball was leaking air big time, but it ended up totally and utterly burst for me when we were beaten 2-1 by one of our rivals just a couple of months into the new season. Things had been coming to a head with myself on the one hand and my assistant and the owner's son on the other. The assistant was the real problem and the players knew this. This is the same guy who would ask me to send him on scouting trips to Spain or Tenerife in November on the owner's dollar and include tickets for his wife, which I never did. But, strangely, he didn't fancy going to Kazakhstan to watch a player I made up just to test him. Let me think, five days in Tenerife at 30 degrees or seven days in Astana at -40. I rest my case, your honour. I knew I had the majority of the playing squad on my side, as they had let me know how much distrust they had for my No 2. But there were a few players they had brought in which I assume were in their camp. The demeanour of the owner towards me had definitely changed. I had pinpointed a couple of British based players to bring in and these requests were rejected, whereas those identified by the owner's son and my assistant were approved. Even more concerning was that I was told that one of the players brought in had also been involved in a previous match-fixing incident. On top of that the owner insisted that his son sit in the dugout at the expense of our physio, due to strict numbers allowed in the technical area, and this was seriously pissing me off. Richard had told me that the son would sit and collude with the assistant, while I was coaching the team on the sidelines in the technical area. I feared I was in danger of becoming embroiled in an intolerable situation and an innocent pawn in their distasteful game. But I could also take a stand and leave.

The Saturday game against our opponents sealed the deal for me. We were winning 1-0 at half-time. In the dressing room my assistant is insisting that our striker is injured and should be taken off and replaced by one of the new players brought in by him and the owner's son. I speak to the physio who came down from his seat in the stand and he says the player is fine to carry on. So, I override the advice and he goes out for the second half and lasts until about 15 minutes to go, when he is starting to tire. I reluctantly realise he needs to come off and agree to put on the new Latvian player. We end up losing the game 2-1 and it becomes the first occasion in my time at FKL that we lose a game from a winning position. After the final whistle in the changing rooms, I break a habit of a coaching lifetime and show my emotion and anger at the player who came on, who, with his unprofessional slack play, is culpable for the two goals we lost. In the aftermath of this game I realise my time with FK Liepaja is over.

On the Sunday, Richard and I take a 45-minute drive down to Palanga, just over the border in Lithuania. In normal circumstances, it's a day out with a mate to a nice place on the coast. But, at this point, it's an opportunity for me to be up front and explain the situation to a friend and colleague that I was done with FK Liepaja and how this would impact upon him, especially as I was the person who had brought him in. He was brilliant about what was going on and already knew that he would have to go too. In fact, he believed my assistant and the owner's son were already conniving to remove him from his position. On the Monday morning the owner agrees to meet me and I give him an ultimatum that, unless my assistant is removed from his role and his son plays no part in team affairs, I will be leaving the club with 18 months to go on my contract. I even offered to see the season out, partly to be involved in the Europa League run and terminate the remaining one year of the contract with a reduced settlement, but this was rejected. Not a surprise. As you can imagine, he wasn't very keen on that and we agree to make a settlement on my departure and work out what I was owed in severance pay. I also make my concerns known to him for my own coaching team. Richard had cleverly insisted on a clause in his contract before he signed that gave him some protection, but he still had massive balls to make sure he received everything he was due. Unfortunately, Lee was not so lucky. To this day, he is still fighting through the English FA and Fifa for settlement of the six months' pay due on his contract.

How the end of my time in Liepaja unfolded was a worrying example of how volatile and unprofessional some countries are in the way they treat qualified coaches and sportsmen and women. It was agreed they would pay me £40,000 in compensation to buy out my contract, and to pay £20,000 into my bank account and give me £20,000 in cash. I wasn't comfortable with that at all and called my agent for his thoughts. Like me, he doesn't like the arrangement, but we collectively think it would just be better to take the deal immediately, get out of Dodge, and contact the UK Inland Revenue on my return to sort out any tax implications. I inform the owner it is a goer and he arrives in my office with forty 500 euro notes and accompanied by two associates. I put the money securely in my back pocket and sign the release agreement. By the time I pack my things, say a couple of hasty goodbyes and reach the main door of the stadium to leave for the last time, the 20,000 euros has mysteriously disappeared from my sky rocket, without my knowledge. I immediately contact the local police, who say: "It's a shame that you have lost it, but these things happen." My next call is to the local UK consulate. Maybe Keith Shannon and his mates can be of assistance. They are infinitely more sympathetic, but, as I have no actual proof that it has been stolen from my person in the stadium, as opposed to losing it, they say I am on to plums getting any chance of an investigation from the local authorities. Since returning home, I have subsequently reported the incident to the Latvian FA and they said they would investigate, but they came back to me with the same indifference as everyone else. I even spoke with a good friend who is in a senior position within Uefa and his reply was "prove it." A calm, but honest, response to a situation which was not uncommon.

When I had sorted out my affairs and packed my bags at the apartment, it suddenly struck me when driving to the airport that I was still using the FKL company car. Could I sell it, fill it with diesel instead of unleaded, or at the very least leave some honey in the coffee cup holder? Also on that drive I received a call from the club tailors, who tell me that my-made-to-measure Hugo Boss £5,000 suit, ironically with club badge, my full name and the word 'Forever' embossed in the lining (Aye right), is ready for me to pick up. Could I sell it, iron a double seam into the trousers, or at the very least leave some honey in the inside breast pocket? The car and the suit combined could fetch around £20,000 I was thinking, but I knew I was bigger than that and I was determined to take the moral high ground and leave with the same dignity that I arrived with, despite the unsavoury treatment I had been subjected to and witnessed. Richard was keen to drive the car home on a farewell road trip and I had a fleeting thought to torch it, but, in the end we parked it in Bay 64 at Riga International Airport. I was extremely glad I was getting out of that situation and my only regret was that I would not get to lead the team into a Europa League qualification campaign. It had been an experience I will never forget and the way that it ended is not one that I ever want repeated, as it overshadowed some really good memories from my first role as a club manager. It is my understanding, and borne out of information given to me, that the club had been saved by the owner, who had bought it so that his son could have a toy that interested him. It seemed that my rogue assistant had a strong hold over the boy, making him untouchable and poisonous towards anyone, player or coach, who could see him for what he was, pathetic. Now, to be fair as I think I am, I witnessed that same excuse for an assistant save a woman's life. We were walking out of the stadium one day after training and, at the end of the avenue, we saw a woman drop to the ground and writhe in a puddle in distress. She had swallowed her tongue and he retrieved it before placing her in the recovery position whilst we called an ambulance – so he wasn't all bad. The owner was also not a bad person. He enjoyed immense wealth and owned half of the city, but wasn't interested in football. He simply craved the love of his boy, who, in his defence, was also not a bad kid. While I was there, the lad took receipt of a new Lamborghini limited edition car, which was bright orange, with the only problem - he hadn't passed his driving test. He was a clever lad who could have copied his very intelligent and delightful sister to study at university in the UK. But instead he had this notion of running a football club with the help of his 'mentor', my assistant, who didn't have a pot to piss in, but big hands to reach out for a payday. He was like the Pied Piper and had an unhealthy hold over him despite the 20-year age gap. The owner was not stupid and knew how to make a buck, therefore he and I enjoyed a good understanding about budgets and financial plans, which we both agreed couldn't balance. Hence the reason and need for his philanthropy in order to give us a disposable income. The problem was his English was not good and the interpreter we used was none other than our good friend, my assistant. This meant the information could get distorted at any given opportunity and latterly became consistently inconsistent with the truth. He would make the bullets for the owner to fire and this would include stopping certain players' wages, designed to elicit a reaction by me. Players not getting paid was not uncommon in that region, and in one team meeting where I was expressing my displeasure about it, a player who I hadn't signed, stood up and said he thought it was correct to suspend the wages. What chance have you got? "I'll suspend you from the ceiling," I thought, as he was one of the players I didn't trust.

It's horrible when things go sour and especially when you see an opportunity to create something tangible with people you take at face value. I truly believe we could have created a strong club based on infrastructure and sound operating principles, if I didn't have the political internal issues to contend with. Perhaps the owner wouldn't have invested in the club if it wasn't for his son, but I know he was a clever businessman who, from having no interest in football, actually started making suggestions on who to play where, at the end of my time there. Time once again to go and change my ring tone...
"This used to be a funhouse..."

Before I move on I have to say that, as mentioned previously, I've been very fortunate to take advantage of my travels to see places and meet some wonderfully interesting people, which was also the case in Liepaja. It is the home to the national tennis centre and its facility was adjacent to our stadium. This enabled me to sit and watch the young upcoming stars practice whilst I sat in the autumn sun. I would really enjoy taking a wee afternoon break, stroll down the beach, grab a cappuccino at my favourite café, before settling on a bench to watch the tennis for half an hour, before heading backto my office. Latvia had two players in the ladies top ten at that time and I met Jelena Ostapenko, when we did a promotional video for the city, along with and by far and away Liepaja's most famous sporting export – Kristaps Porzingis – who plays basketball for the Dallas Mavericks, having been bought from the New York Knicks. Basketball is huge in the Baltic States and ice hockey is second, with football in third. Kristaps was a football fan and would stream the FK Liepaja games live in Dallas, as well as popping in to the stadium when he came back home. He was a top bloke and with his accumulated wealth has created a foundation in his home city with many basketball courts built as a legacy, as well as scholarship opportunities for young budding basketball players. If they find my 20,000 euros, which I "lost", they can use it to help these youngsters, as my thank you for the good times I experienced – which I have to admit that there were – in Latvia.

However, my football journey was about to lead me to another very exciting opportunity alongside Paul Hartley and Tam Ritchie once again, this time at Cove Rangers.

The Living Highlights

*Joy at being reunited with Paul Hartley for a five-year
Scottish Premier League plan at Cove Rangers*

Sometimes when people find themselves in serious situations they inexplicably burst into uncontrollable laughter. This was one of those times. Richard – on his way home from Latvia at the same time – and I both sat at Riga Airport and tried to rationalise the previous few weeks, but could only come to the conclusion that you couldn't make this shit up. When you have reached the point of no return, it is best to get out as quickly as you can. But both of us had asked friends and family to come to Liepaja to visit us, so at the airport we were constantly making calls to explain the situation and cancel trips. I called Yvonne and let her know I was on my way home and called Paul Hartley, who was gearing up to come over and visit me at Easter time, 2019.

No one could believe how quickly things had soured, come to a head and ended at FKL. But I admit that I must have made an impression on the clubs and places I visited while on pre-season tour with FK Liepaja as in the following weeks after my return home, agents were regularly on the phone to me to sound me out about various international club roles. However, I was in no hurry to jump into anything and as 'once bitten, twice shy', I was determined to do my full research and more into any future opportunity. This situation of uncertainty was also in complete contrast to the Dundee United exit and I felt more relaxed about what would come next.

Before I left Liepaja, I had brokered a deal to take a goalkeeper from Parma in Italy to the club through a Finnish agent, and received an offer from him to consider managing KPV in Finland. They were rooted to the bottom of Finland's top league at the midway point of the season. But it was a five-hour drive from Helsinki and in a remote part of the country, where Bear Grylls would have thought twice about visiting. I felt this would have been a nigh on impossible job as the club were perennial yoyos, gaining promotion and then being relegated between the top two divisions. They were in a slump and had an owner wishing to sell up and a depleted squad which would be hard to strengthen, meaning a return to the second tier was imminent. But the agent felt that if I was successful, coaches were invariably apt to get an offer from one of the bigger clubs, but Mixu knowing the league in the country of his birthplace agreed the club were doomed and I declined the offer. Time would confirm the inevitable as they were relegated five months later.

Another call I received was from a member of the Latvian FA who had been involved with clubs from all over the 'old Russia', enquiring if I fancied managing a club side in Belarus. It seemed that North Eastern European football had a bit of a hard-on for my style of coaching. Mindful of my recent experience, I really did my homework. From the outside looking in, it seemed like a state-controlled league and I really would have been out of my depth in terms of communication. Another issue would have been a severe lack of friendly faces to call on when I was looking for a bit of social rest and relaxation, a game of golf or a beer, to discuss the challenges of management. I wasn't feeling it at all and, anyway, I was not desperate to take the first thing that came along, despite the sobering memory of what happened after finishing up at Tannadice.

Opportunities then seemed to go from the bizarre to the ridiculous, as another reputable agent who I was dealing with previously regarding the transit of players from Africa to Europe, gave me a call. He wondered if I would be interested in the chance to join Zambian Premier League club Nkana FC, who are based in the city of Kitwe, as head coach and with the incentive of a great financial package. Apparently they have won more titles than anyone else, but hadn't done so for the last seven or eight years and played to crowds of 20,000. But, regardless of the fact that Zambia is one of the more stable African countries, the place where I would be situated was very close to the border with the Democratic Republic of Congo, in an area that UK Government advice suggests you should only travel to in the company of Kate Adie and a platoon of UN Peacekeepers. I checked what position Kate played, realised she might have lost a yard or two of pace and decided someone else could write a chapter of their book about their experiences coaching Nkana FC. After all I specialise in a different kind of shooting drills.

I knocked all these offers on the head and settled back into a routine with a few weeks at home over Easter and caught up with friends and relatives. I also met up regularly with Paul, who was also without a club, talking about football and possible next moves.

He was telling me the worrying news that his partner Lisa's father – John Sheran, manager of Cove Rangers – had suffered a heart attack. It looked very doubtful he would be able to lead his dominant Highland League-winning side into the League Two play-offs final after their victory over Lowland League winners East Kilbride FC in the semi. I had met John with Paul when we were on holiday in Portugal a couple of years earlier and we played golf over there, which coincidentally was a few months after Falkirk had played Cove in the Scottish Cup. Due to his link with John, and with his blessing, Cove – based in the Cove Bay suburb area in the south east of Aberdeen – approached Paul to see if he would come in and help out during the preparation for the final against Berwick Rangers, in John's absence.

Paul was not in a full-time position at the time and was happy to assist, helping with training and tactical input, as the club romped to a famous 7-0 aggregate victory over the only English-based club in the Scottish League. Berwick have an eternal place in the record books after their historic 1-0 first round Scottish Cup victory over Glasgow Rangers in 1967. But much as they delight in the glory of beating their illustrious namesakes, it was another Rangers team, which emphatically scudded them home and away, to take their place in the Scottish professional leagues for the first time.

In speaking with Paul around that time, he was extremely complimentary about Cove. "It's a smashing club, Youngy and one that has big ambitions." I remember him telling me.

In view of John's health (he's since made a full recovery) and his continued reha-bilitation, discussions had to be conducted surrounding the best way for the club to progress, especially with them stepping up to the Scottish professional ranks. It was felt by all parties that a different approach to the management structure would have to be made. However, at the same time, and quite properly and correctly, they wanted to tip the hat to the management team and coaches who had helped them progress so much and to three successive Highland League titles, prior to their play-off win. Every-body at the club wanted to do the right thing by John and his team and he was made Director of Football and a club director, with Paul coming in as manager to implement a five-year plan to drive the club towards the Scottish Premier League. How about that for big ambitions? The possibility of rising from Highland League to SPL in less time it took to build the Scottish Parliament and guaranteed with less own goals scored!

Once again Paul offered me the chance to become his assistant and I honestly didn't need to think too hard about my answer. I hadn't met the chairman, but I had con-fidence and trust in the information that Paul was filtering back to me. So, without hesitation, the deal was sealed on a verbal agreement between us, and planning could start on our next assignment. Next call would be to Paul's stalwart fitness coach, Tam Ritchie, and, boom, we had lift-off. Anyone who knows us will testify that we don't do anything by half-measures, and immediately we set about the task of creating the environment that every successful club needs from bottom to top.

We meet everyone at Cove and relay our plans, which are realistic but very demanding. We make it clear that, if you're the kind of person who wants to drift along aimlessly, then you will find out pretty quickly you're not what Paul Hartley, Gordon Young and Tam Ritchie are looking for. It's not a pissing competition, but I believe the slack arses always get found out and they generally hand in their rifle when they realise you've rumbled them. My dad brought me up with the mantra of 'if a job's worth doing, it's worth doing well' and that's how Paul and I see it.

I must admit that I got a great feeling about the place when I arrived to meet the chairman, Keith Moorhouse, and found his vision for the club as a breath of fresh air. It really was an upbeat and positive situation coming into Cove as they had a good squad of players who were used to winning matches and leagues. This is a far cry from when you come into a club to replace a sacked boss, players low on confidence, more often than not in the middle of the season and when the team's languishing near the foot of the table.

Paul and I were very excited about what was on offer at Cove and were impressed by the chairman's ambition to take them to the next level, and rival the tradition of Aberdeen being a one-club city. We would be dealing directly with the chairman, the club did not have any debt, had just moved into their new 2,600 capacity Balmoral Stadium, costing £4 million, and were looking forward to taking our place in Scottish League Division Two.

I was completely sold on every aspect of my new role, but just before I officially signed on the dotted line I received a phone call. A team on the beautiful Mediterranean island of Gozo – just off the coast of Malta – wanted to make me the highest-paid head coach in their history to resurrect a club that became defunct in 2011.

"We want to offer you 250 euros a week," said the enthusiastic club representative… err, and free ferry travel between Gozo and Malta."

"It's a tempting offer, but I've lost more down the back of ma couch watching the telly." I replied.

"OK, we'll throw in all your meals for free!"

Really, I'm built like a skeleton with a durex pulled over it and I would've needed to eat the equivalent of what the British Lions squad has for breakfast, lunch and dinner each day, to see me break even. This description of the conversation is a bit tongue in cheek, as I've never been driven by money and I really was grateful. I suppose that's the kind of offer I'd love in 10 or 15 years' time when I'm about to go into semi-retirement, so, if any club has a hot climate, golf course and can throw in the free meals, I'm your man. I thank them for their kind offer and officially sign on as assistant manager at Cove on July 3, 2019, just a week before the start of the season.

At a friendly against Inverurie Locos that night, we see straight away that we have a squad of good players, but will need to strategically add to it, to make us competitive in League Two. The chairman buys into our holistic view that we are in control of the

'Gordon is one of the best coaches I've ever worked with'

Cove manager Paul Hartley has been fulsome in his praise of his assistant. He said: "Gordon is one of the best coaches I have ever worked with and I have worked with some of the best. We are both the same type of character and think about our football 24/7. On the days we don't see each other at training or at games, we can call each other about 10 times in order to talk through some aspect of the team, club or football in general...and, in all the time I have known him, I can't remember us having a cross word with each other. I had some dealings with Gordon when he was Academy Director at Motherwell and I was looking to bring some good young players into Alloa, but didn't really know him that well. It was only when I became Falkirk manager that I really got to know him, on the recommendation of Craig Brown and Archie Knox. I had been looking to bring in an assistant manager and had a couple of candidates in mind, but Craig and Archie could not praise him highly enough in terms of on-the-pitch coaching and suggested speaking to him. I got him on the phone when he was in America and, within a very short time, asked him if he wanted to work with me at Falkirk.

"He really knows his stuff, is very knowledgeable about the game, I really enjoy working with him and his relationship with the players in the dressing room is excellent. I tend to keep myself a bit distant from that, but he is my link to what is going on with the players.

"We share the same thought processes – I think part of this is because we had similar upbringings – he in Motherwell me in Hamilton – and a similar sense of humour, his one-liners are brilliant and we enjoy nights out and social events together, too. Gordon is straight to the point and is very well respected throughout the whole of Cove Rangers FC. As soon as I got here I wanted to bring him in."

day-to-day running of the club. This combined with a brand new stadium, enhanced facilities and professional backroom staff, will all help us to improve the all-round ability of the squad. Tam Ritchie – who has been at Paul's side throughout his entire managerial career – really did take their fitness to another level, which helped immensely during the season.

At an early squad meeting, we deliver a presentation to the players outlining what we expected from them throughout the season, the demands that we would be making of them and the support they would receive from us. To a man they gave us everything

and their commitment to training was immense, especially considering the geographical location just south of Aberdeen, and the fact we would be traveling large distances
to away games. To enhance the DNA of the new Balmoral Stadium we insisted on
every training session taking place on our 4G pitch, which we correctly hoped would
encourage the unity and camaraderie of the players going forward and allow us to implement our coaching philosophy. We also discovered that, commercially, the club was
very well run and all our hospitality boxes were sold before the season started. Due to
the club's recent success, we were reaping the benefits of attracting new fans, especially
when Aberdeen FC were playing away from home.

Contrary to the myth that we were offering thousands of pounds to players to come
and play for us, I can tell you it was absolute nonsense. We operated on roughly the
same budget as we had in the Highland League. The Cove model and strategy was
the exact opposite of the Gretna boom-or-bust model. It was one of stability, incremental progression and development. But we did use our contacts with teams such
as Motherwell, Dundee United, St Johnstone and Aberdeen to snap up some gems in
the loan market such as Matty Smith (Dundee United), Chris Antoniazzi (Aberdeen),
John Robertson (St. Johnstone) and Josh Mulligan (Dundee). But the one who really
showcased his talents in our environment was Declan Glass, who was outstanding
and earned himself a new deal at Dundee United as a result of his performances with
us. Later on we'd speak with Chris McCart at Celtic who offered Ryan Mullen, Motherwell's assistant manager Keith Lasley would help us get Jamie Semple, and Dundee
United's Brian Grant helped us to sign Ross Graham on loan. I think all of these people
trusted our management of their players and the monitoring of their progress.

All those who came to us in that regard, contributed well to our season, rather than
just arriving to get game time under their belt. I believe another key to getting these
players was down to our style of play and the exposure the loan players would get in
terms of coaching, with a view to invaluable match experience. On the point of style of
play, during the early part of the season, I always took trackside notes about every team
we were up against. I had a specific focus on identifying the players who I felt could
come and compete for a place in the Cove Rangers team.

We made sure we were professional in everything we did at training. I'm a "fail to-
plan, plan to fail" guy and Paul and I have everything organised well in advance, complete with back-up plans to cover any scenarios. We enhanced the facilities at Balmoral Stadium to banish the possibility of complacency creeping in and upgraded travel
arrangements, pre-match meals and provided the latest approved supplements for the
players. The chairman backed us to the hilt and this was proven by the signing that
rocked the Scottish lower leagues in the January transfer window, with the capture, on
an undisclosed fee, of free-scoring striker Rory McAllister from Peterhead. This was
quite a coup for Cove and signalled our intentions, as we were able to land a lad who

had regularly turned down opportunities to go to much larger clubs down south, and who had in eight and a half seasons netted 193 times in a Peterhead shirt.

All the pieces seemed to be slotting into place, but our target was still to stay in the league and build from there. But it would become apparent after the first quarter of the season, that we were going to have a right go at winning it. Our first home game saw us destroy Edinburgh City – one of the pre-season favourites for the title – 5-0. We then embarked on a remarkable run, winning 14 league matches in a row and ended up as the only team in Europe to win all our home games in the full season, albeit one cut short by the Covid 19 pandemic. We were top of the league from day one until the season came to an abrupt halt in March 2020 (and we'd stay top of League Division One from the first day of the 2020/21 season until Saturday, 5 December, 2020, after losing 2-1 at home to Montrose), and the nucleus of the squad was the one we inherited and which had done so well in the Highland League. What an achievement by those lads.

I'm not saying that the adjustment to my part-time role as assistant to Paul at Cove and all the travelling from Motherwell to Aberdeen which that entails, has been easy, as I had been full-time in my roles for the previous 20 years. The main thing I got frustrated at was the shortened amount of time I had to spend with the players. It really is a testimony to their quality and football intelligence, which allows us to deliver all our information to them and for them to take it in – normally over five sessions – into only two. We explained early on to both players and support staff the importance of time management and from the moment we start each session, every second is precious. They also know that I'm not driving a 300-mile round trip to tickle their balls. But it has been worth the five-hour round trip three times a week when you believe in something so strongly and get such a positive feeling for the club you are working for.

A wee nugget from my Uefa Pro-Licence kept inspiring me while driving on the road north on a Tuesday and Thursday afternoon and Saturday morning, and it was expressed by Scotland rugby legend and current national team manager Gregor Townsend when he said: "Use your traveling time wisely." He explained that living in Edinburgh and working in Glasgow at that time for the Warriors club side, meant that he'd leave all his phone calls for the commute. This allowed him to devote his time to the club uninterrupted, while he could do all his calling in transit, clever boys those egg-chasers. So, with the wonders of hands-free phone technology, I have used my two-and-a-half hour stints in the car as a mobile command unit, where Paul and I commune with each other on tactics, training and the future. I also speak to players, agents, friends and family and keep on top of all my personal business, from paying bills to finally hiring someone to fix the fucking garage door properly! I have even used the journey home on a Tuesday and Thursday evening after training to talk through various chapters of this book with my writing partner, an arsehole of a man who has just been charged with being drunk in charge of a pen. That's for all the snide digs at me he's subtly included in the previous 16 chapters or so, in the guise of self-deprecation.

Paul and I drove up together on that first day on Wednesday, 3 July, and within a short time he had decided to move up permanently, which made a lot of sense as his partner, Lisa, is also from the area and had been commuting to her work – ironically with Aberdeen FC. If I had been full-time, it might have been an option for me as well, as it is important for the management team to be nearby for consistency, planning, pre-planning etc and the plan is for the transition to take place as part of the club's incremental plan. Soon after I had put pen to paper, Craig Brown had called me and offered to give me the use of his flat that he acquired after taking the Aberdeen job. What another lovely gesture from the man I respect so much. But I suspect he might have wanted me to also clean his windows and dust his cornices. Tam Ritchie and I continue to commute from the Central belt to Cove three times a week, and at the time of writing there is currently a people carrier making the journey picking up seven players on the way (taking heed of lockdown restriction regulations, of course).

I'd meet Tam at Dundee where we'd have a coffee, then travel together to Aberdeen, which in itself makes the journey much easier with great company and the opportunity to discuss the forthcoming session or debrief the previous one. It also gives the players time to slaughter me in private. We would even eat while travelling. My wife, Yvonne, would make the sandwich wraps and Tam's wife, Jill, would make the soup, not just for us, but for the players who were with us. I think that's the reason we attract players as the two of them are excellent cooks. This was time management par excellence. It is down to an absolute tee now where Lisa and Yvonne can't believe how I can possibly spend four hours at training talking with Paul and then continue talking with him on the phone for a further two hours, while travelling down the road. The reality is if we'd spent 10 hours talking we'd still have something else to plan in order to keep improving the club and ourselves.

Paul is also a very kind guy especially towards his family and the players benefit from his generosity regularly. The staff definitely do as he keeps us stocked with hospitality to manage our commute. This is not always the case with some I've worked with who are so tight they'd wake up during the night to see if they've lost any sleep. I worked with one guy who found a pair of crutches and went away to break his leg!

This came into sharp focus during the summer of 2020 when we still had lockdown restrictions and when most folk were working from home, I was working from the car. It is testament to our working relationship that we can work that way and cover so much ground. Ultimately, Paul is the man in charge, but the respect we have for one another is such that I can talk him through a training drill on the way up to training and by the time I get there, he has laid out the cones to the exact millimetre. Usually in football, it's the other way around. On times of reflection in my mobile office over the past few months, I have realised that since I became caretaker manager at Dundee United, I have hardly lost a game with the clubs I have been at. Paul has also deservedly racked up the plaudits, winning three manager-of-the-month awards during the league campaign, and would, undoubtedly, have been a shoe-in for manager of the year for Division Two, if the season had been played out to a finish and accolades had been handed out. He deserved that and I'm saddened at that not happening as he's been outstanding at setting the bar for the country's newest club.

It has been so rewarding and satisfying seeing how we brought our previous experiences to enhance the club and improve the professionalism of the whole organisation. This has included regularly scouting the opposition clubs, using video analysis, partnering up with a local gym in Aberdeen for special fitness sessions, improving on the players' nutrition and finding a brilliant travel sponsor and upgrading the team transport. Now we have the former Arsenal team coach to take us to away games. I know this for certain, because scratched onto the window next to where I sit is 'Arsene was here, yah bas!' Once again using our time-management to the best advantage – every small margin helps – it's kitted out with a kitchen, which allows us to feed our squad their pre-match meal enroute. This saves us from having to book a hotel and undergo the palaver of parking up and decanting everyone for their lunch. The result is that we eat at the optimum time before each game and can quickly progress to our pre-match build-up, complete with any meetings and briefings before we arrive at the away stadium.

By the time we played our last league match on Saturday, 10 March, 2020, we were really firing on all cylinders and crushed Stirling Albion at Forthbank 7-1. Another two wins from there would have sealed the league for us mathematically speaking, as we would have been so far ahead of our rivals by Easter, they'd have required snookers. But the resulting lockdown due to the Coronavirus, brought everything to a shuddering halt. However, everyone at the club recognised how necessary the lockdown was to prevent even more tragic loss of life from the virus and that it had to be implemented. We were eventually awarded the League Division Two Championship title. But when we started back training in the summer of 2020, I sensed a real disappointment around the club that players and supporters felt that they were cruelly robbed of their 15 minutes in the sun, winning a professional league at their first time of asking. Not only that, but they could have savoured it while playing good football, scoring goals by the barrel-load, and winning regularly by wide margins due to our dynamic style of play. The performance of the players was outstanding. It was a real shame that they did not get the opportunity to lap up the limelight, and deservedly take the acclaim from the fans, as well as the entire Scottish footballing public, who took the club to their hearts. I am confident that we became the score that everyone looked for after their own club to find out how the plucky Highlanders were doing. Most weeks the answer was "Braw!"

That first season was littered with club firsts, and this has continued in League Division One. These things are very exciting for a new club to the professional ranks and can be taken for granted when you're at long-established clubs. But I would say it spurs everyone at the club on to want more of the same. Memorable firsts have included the first time a Cove game was broadcast live on TV - against Connah's Quay Nomads away in the Challenge Cup. Then taking on Hibs at home in the Scottish League Cup again, a game that was live with Sky TV. Winning our first match in the SPFL was another belter, followed by our first-ever match at Hampden Park against Queen's Park, manager-of-the-month awards for Paul and the luxury of purchasing high-profile players such as Rory McAllister. Then we had a great result beating Championship club Alloa Athletic in the Scottish Cup and we were in the draw for an even bigger third-round tie. This landed a mouthwatering game against our mighty Glasgow namesakes. The list of firsts went on and on and everyone at the club still gets filled with immense pride every time we create another one.

It was then that we were all affected by a 'second' that no one wanted, a second season suspension due to Covid following on from the dramatic postponement of everything, back in March, 2020. By 12 January, 2021, while sitting second in League One, the Covid pandemic claimed another innocent victim in 2021. A second wave throughout the country and across the world led to the lower leagues, including Scottish Leagues One and Two and the women's Leagues One and Two and everything below that being suspended. This also meant that the Scottish Cup - and our tie at Ibrox - was also suspended. But with the roll-out of the Covid 19 vaccines and the spring approaching, there were small green shoots of hope that society and football could return to some sense of normality.

In early January, 2021, before the postponement, I personally clocked up a first in my own coaching career, which was very far from being normal, while I and my family were self-isolating due to Covid precautions. By the wonders of modern technology, for the game against Peterhead in the league at home I was watching the game beamed live through my computer into my home and relaying any advice I thought pertinent to Paul on the touchline. Problem was a delay on the line meant that this advice or instruction for a player was only pinging into Paul more than a few seconds after the instant it needed to be relayed. So, for instance, the play would rage on to us attacking with menace when Paul would get a message from me to tell him our full-backs should get wider to receive a ball from our keeper.

This could be a touch embarrassing, though, if you are reading the riot act at a player on screen for not passing and the message gets through only when he has beaten four men and smashed the ball into the top corner! Definitely a few gremlins need ironed out on that score, but fingers crossed we'll never need to use this option again.

Due to our success, before the first lockdown in March, 2020, everyone from 'groundhoppers' to celebrities such as golfer Paul Lawrie, Craig Brown and Aberdeen and Scotland legends Joe Harper and Jim Leighton, all wanted to visit the Balmoral Stadium to say they had been there. We were constantly praised and lauded for our attacking style, and that, as I mentioned earlier, is all down to the attitude and ability of the players. Never ones to miss a trick to inspire, we have already used our sense of injustice at the lack of celebrations and the desire to create even more firsts in the dressing room, to make our players hungry for even more success and to push on and try to replicate their first season in the Scottish professional ranks. By the end of January, every league below the Championship was put on hold for nearly two months before resuming with a reduced fixture list. This was only our second season in the Scottish Professional Football League (SPFL) and we were still on course for our third promotion in as many seasons. The ban on playing was only lifted on Tuesday, March 2, but that meant we had to play 18 games by Friday, 23 April – a total of 52 days. The intensity of that reminded me of being a young teenager playing with the school on a Saturday morning, the Boy's Brigade on a Saturday afternoon and then the boy's club on the Sunday, and then going out for a kick-about on the Sunday night with yer mates. Obviously, despite many misgivings, it was the only game in town, so we had to suck it all up and just get on with things without any moaning or complaints, at least in public. But things like this seriously hinder part-time clubs, especially those more than 150 miles from Glasgow. The games programme was relentless, wearisome and severely affected Cove's ability to perform on every match-day or night. At one point, we played four games in eight days and that morphed into six games in 11 days!

I really have to laugh when Manchester United and others moan about playing four games in 11 days with about 300 in a first-team squad and a medical team the size of Iceland's national health service. Oh, and enough staff to apply ice and fill cold baths for recovery of all their players, their families and everyone they have ever met, as well as the vast budget to employ bespoke air harvesters to carefully pluck frozen oxygen molecules from the air at the top of Mount Everest with chopsticks for use in each player's specially developed cryotherapy regeneration chamber that they sleep in at night.

I am convinced if we had continued to play Saturday to Saturday – with the odd mid-week game – we would have won the league. Instead we stuttered to a play-off place, with knackered and fatigued players, working full-time in day jobs and several carrying niggling injuries throughout. We had a nucleus of nine regular starters who we were playing all the time, while following all the protocols, which we were, of course, completely happy to observe. This meant that the people carrier mini-bus I was in charge of, to ferry the central Scotland-based players and staff to Cove for games and training, had to be shelved in favour of solitary car journeys. This took a lot of the joy and camaraderie away from the squad. We were unable to take showers after training – which more often than not we couldn't do anyway due to the game schedule and these turned into recovery and regeneration sessions – returning home on a two-hour journey in an uncomfortable state. Generally, we were unable to train at all, organise regular analysis sessions or rotate our squad in any normal sense of the word.

As we were playing football and had our own group bubbles and testing regimes, that had a knock-on effect on many players who had full-time jobs to make ends meet, and they had to be even harder on themselves to comply with Covid restrictions and keep themselves, their families and the fellow members of the playing squad safe. Everyone at Cove, from the chairman right down to the kitman, did an exceptional job in this regard and we never had a Covid case in the time after we restarted the season and all employees played by the rules. But it was natural that we would lose a bit of cheerfulness around the place. Like so many clubs, it was mentally draining for the staff, mentally draining for the players and when you add all this into the mix on the issues that have been raised about mental health and wellbeing in a previous chapter, it didn't bode well.

In the midst of the league campaign, we had to also contend with the small matter of the third round of the Scottish Cup against Rangers at Ibrox. Normally, a game like this would be manna from heaven for a small club like Cove and, if fans were allowed at the game, we could have expected to earn around £300,000 for the club. Now scheduled for a Sunday night 6pm kick-off, we managed to pocket around only a tenth of that. This coupled with the loss of two of our mainstay players during the game – Harry Milne and Jamie Masson who were very important to us for the league run-in – we were left feeling that it wasn't quite the exciting showcase for us that it should have been. Personally, though, I did manage to catch up with Gary McAllister, my fellow childhood 'Keepie-Uppie Champion' and Motherwell legend, and then assistant manager to Steven Gerrard at Rangers. Sadly, we didn't have time for a head to head to see who really was the best!

Despite this, it was a great experience for us all and so many people were very complimentary of our play and the fact that we 'had a go' at the eventual Scottish Premier League Champions. We lost 4-0 on the night, but we contained our illustrious namesakes and played well, something which many SPL sides were unable to do any better that season. Several of our players – returning north to their homes – did not manage to get to their beds until about 1am the next morning. They then had to get up for their work on the Monday morning, work again on the Tuesday and travel back down to Glasgow that evening for a game we had against Clyde. We drew this 1-1, but earlier in the season there was a good chance this would have been a victory. Full-time clubs have the luxury of scheduled recovery sessions, which part-time players do not, and I have so much respect for part-timers' dedication and commitment to the game. My respect for our own medical department – a physiotherapist, an assistant physio, a sports therapist and a club doctor – also knows no bounds as they were absolutely superb in helping our lads recover and regenerate in any way possible, given the constraints heaped upon them. They were honestly fighting a losing battle, but, remarkably, against all odds, they managed to get tremendous results in helping our players take the field.

They were in just about every night at the club seeing players – bearing in mind they also had their own jobs – as they helped them to recover from knocks, sprains and fatigue. Looking back at what transpired, dozens and dozens of Scottish lower league players were pushed to the limit, physically, emotionally and psychologically over those last three months of season 2020/21 and I really wondered whether it was all worth it. Football clubs and their senior staff all sign up to a commitment to promote the best welfare of our players and our staff, but, to me, during those days, how we were going about our business was the complete opposite of supporting their best interests and welfare. Everyone was always on tenterhooks regarding the pandemic, overloading the players with training, helping them to recover, wondering when the next game would be pencilled in and it seemed we were just lurching towards the end of season, struggling to find 11 fit players to line up for kick-off. That point in the season was as intense as it possibly could be, without the humour, joy and patter that normally surrounds the game, to give us a pressure release valve. It was the strangest atmosphere I have ever experienced in football and I hope never to experience it again.

It was hard going to say the least. In normal circumstances, due to our position challenging for the league, each game we played would have been in front of bumper crowds, relatively speaking for our position. Certainly, Balmoral Stadium would have seen sell-outs for our home games and that, in itself, would have given our players a big lift. One thing I will say, though, is that completing the season was a testament to how well our club is run financially. As much as we have been affected by the pandemic like everyone else, our structure means we are in a strong position to look at another promotion-chasing campaign in 2021/22.

In the end, it all caught up with us and we finished third behind winners Partick Thistle – who, with a late surge, won the title and automatic promotion – and Airdrieonians, who we would meet in the two-legged Championship play-off semi-final. We drew 1-1 at home in the first game on Sunday, 9 May – with Rory McAllister hitting the bar late on, which could have given us a precious advantage. Then, in the return match in Airdrie the following Wednesday, our top-scorer Mitch Megginson – and subsequent League One player of the year for the season – was forced off early with an injury after putting us in the lead. Airdrie equalised and then Rory McAllister popped up again in the second minute of injury time to give us the lead. A match against Morton for a place in the Championship was beckoning when we failed to defend a hopeful high ball into our box and Airdrie levelled again in the 94th minute, to take the game into extra time. The momentum swung behind the

Lanarkshire men – managed by my good mate Ian 'Nid Murray' – and they managed to score the only goal of the added half-hour to secure their tilt at the Championship, which ultimately proved unsuccessful.

Realistically, for Cove to make the play-offs for the Championship in only our second season in SPFL was beyond our wildest dreams. But I will leave you with my essential football statistical analysis – reinforced by my Uefa Pro Licence – on these two games played by our exhausted and drained players: We had combined possession of 63.5 per cent, had a total of 41 attempts at goal over the two games and Airdrie had a total of only five and one of them was an OG! If it was a boxing match, the referee would have stopped it, but, as we all know, if your aunty had baws she'd be yer uncle. Though maybe that popular Scottish phrase needs to be revised in today's enlightened and progressive society and perhaps should be – if your auntie had baws she'd still technically be entitled to call herself your auntie, if she so wished.

It disnae matter, I am getting distracted, despite being the better side, we were out of the play-offs and well done to Airdrie.

For the record, I have personally found the second Covid wave and lockdown the hardest to cope with, and I know many of my colleagues and our players have felt the same. But as I write this more than 40 million people in the UK (3 million in Scotland), have already been vaccinated, hope is springing eternal, everyone is yearning for some sense of normality returning and we are beginning to think about planning for season 2021/22.

As the words of Burns' poem 'A Bottle and Friend' etched in ink on my back say:

Then catch the moments as they fly,
And use them as ye ought, man:
Believe me, happiness is shy,
And comes not aye when sought, man.

Happiness is fleeting and you need to recognise and embrace these precious moments when they come. I like to think I have done that and savoured every one that I have shared with you. Some may say, especially an electrician in Montrose and my mate Peter, that it's not a patch on other tattoos, but it's mine and I'm constantly inspired by the thoughtful and philosophical musings of a literary genius, flaws and all.

Over the last 20 years I have met some wonderful people, been to some incredible places and had an absolute ball along the way, from Cambuslang to Kazakhstan, and all the pitches in between. I can't wait to help Cove create their own football poetry on the pitch in the seasons to come. Will we successfully complete our five-year plan?

Only a bottle or two, time, me and my blootered mate with a pen and a notepad will tell. What I do know for certain is that 'A Steelman's a man for A' That!' and the name's Young, Gordon Young… Uefa Pro-Licence to Skill.